# Chesapeake Bay Buyboats

# Chesapeake Bay Buyboats

## Larry S. Chowning

Tidewater Publishers
Centreville, Maryland

Photographs not otherwise credited are by the author.

Library of Congress Cataloging-in-Publication Data

Chowning, Larry S., 1949-
  Chesapeake Bay buyboats / Larry S. Chowning.— 1st ed.
     p. cm.
Includes bibliographical references (p.   ) and index.
  ISBN 0-87033-553-7 (Hardcover)
  1. Buyboats—Chesapeake Bay (Md. and Va.)—History. I. Title.
VM371.C49 2003
623.8'23—dc22
                          2003017882

Manufactured in the United States of America
First edition

*To Dr. A. L. Van Name, Jr., William C. Hight,*
*H. S. Chowning, Jr.,*
*and the late Carroll C. Chowning*

# CONTENTS

# PREFACE

To be honest, I'm surprised that a comprehensive book on Chesapeake Bay buyboats has not been written before now. Other writers and I began to think about and discuss such a project in the early 1980s.

I was busy working on other things, like *Harvesting the Chesapeake—Tools and Traditions* and *Chesapeake Legacy*. During the decade of the 1990s I felt that someone, somewhere, was already working on a book on Bay buyboats.

But as more books on skipjacks and schooners were published, I continued to be puzzled about why Chesapeake Bay buyboats were being overlooked. Probably, it was partly because of the romance people have with sail. Perhaps deck boats were simply not far enough into our past to be considered historical. It was obvious that Maryland's skipjack fleet, the last commercial sail-powered fishing fleet in North America, captured most of the headlines around the Chesapeake, taking attention away from the Bay buyboats. I contributed to that myself in my writing.

Over my two years of research and working on the book, I think I discovered at least part of the reason why I was the one to finally write the book. The history of Bay buyboats is not buried in the archives of museums—if it were, it would have made my job or someone else's easier. The history of these boats is still in the hearts and minds of the people who remember them, particularly those who worked the boats. These men and women range in age from their fifties through their nineties, and they have shared good clear memories of the boats and the times.

My home base on the Bay made a book on Chesapeake buyboats a natural fit for me. The boats were found all over the Bay but there was more work for deck boats in Virginia and on the lower Bay, where I was born and raised, than in Maryland.

The boats were used to haul freight and watermelons and to plant and buy oysters all over the Bay, but in Virginia they could be used for two purposes that were not allowed in Maryland—motor-powered dredges were permitted on private oyster grounds, and in the winter they could be used to dredge crabs. The boats worked extensively in these fisheries and, more importantly, the captains and crews of these boats could work year-round.

From March to June, James River provided work, as buyboats bought seed from tongers and distributed seed oysters to private and public oyster grounds up and down the Chesapeake. Nowhere else on the Bay was seed so plentiful as it was on the James, and hundreds of buyboats congregated in that area each year to handle the seed business.

From June to September, the Baltimore and Washington, D.C., watermelon trade carried many of the boats through the summer and into the fall and winter oyster harvest. Those that did not run watermelons bought fish and crabs during the warm weather months. Many worked in Virginia's wintertime crab-dredge fishery. There was year-round work, plenty of it, and plenty of boats to do it.

The boats were not limited to ownership by the large oyster, crab, and fish companies. The boats were affordable and there was enough work available so that an ambitious, self-motivated waterman could step up from working a pair of shaft tongs from a small deadrise workboat to owning a 60-foot buyboat and buying and selling oysters, crabs, and fish. Many did just that.

Gradually, freight became less and less a part of the work of Bay deck boats. Oystering, fishing, and crabbing became the main purpose of the boats, and much of this work was centered on the lower Bay because of Maryland's restrictions.

My home at Urbanna, Virginia, is on the once oyster-rich Rappahannock River, a main thoroughfare used by Virginia deck boats. When I was a boy growing up in Urbanna, four or five deck boats loaded down with seed oysters were as commonplace on Urbanna Creek in March as ospreys building their nests. My great-uncle used to mark the start of spring by the arrival of the birds and the boats.

If that weren't enough, Deltaville, Virginia, was seventeen miles down the road; the Northern Neck was just across the river; and Mathews and Gloucester Counties adjoined my home county of Middlesex. All were areas where deck boats were built in large numbers, and all were close to me. Living near the heart of the place where these boats were constructed and used made it easier for me to study and research the people involved with the boats. Since oral history has always been the core of my work, I could not have been in a better location.

This is not meant to minimize the role that Maryland boatbuilders played in the history of Chesapeake Bay buyboats. Theirs was an extremely important role, particularly in the years of conversion from sail to power. Nowhere on the Bay were more sail-powered log and planked bugeyes built than in Maryland waters. The hulls of these boats were extremely adaptable for conversion from sail to power. Literally hundreds of bugeyes were converted to deck boats, and Maryland boatbuilders also built a great number of traditional style Bay buyboats.

I realized early on that these boats were used as much for commercial fishing as for their "buyboat" function. For nearly twenty years as a field editor for *National Fisherman*, the nation's leading seafood trade publication, my photo files and my knowledge of the fisheries have grown.

I recognized that more than any other boat style in the history of the Chesapeake, the Bay buyboat is the most versatile. The boats ran muskrat pelts and barrels of salted eels from isolated wharfs, hogs and watermelons from farmers' piers, and passengers and freight across rivers with no bridges. They were used to buy fish, crabs, oysters, and clams; and also to harvest fish, crabs, and oysters from the Bay as well as clams and fish from the Atlantic Ocean.

There was never a question in my mind that there was a need for a book like this. I just had to be convinced that I was the man to do the job. Two events persuaded me to do this project. The first occurred during a trip to Chestertown, Maryland, to watch the launch of *Sultana*, a reproduction schooner, in March 2001. While I was there, David Cantera, owner of the buyboat *Muriel Eileen*, graciously gave me a tour of the boat that just a few years before I had been aboard to do some hook-and-line fishing. She was based in Virginia at the time.

At the end of David's tour of *Muriel Eileen*, I commented that much had been written about Bay buyboats. His response was, "Yeah, and you've done most of it," referring to my work with *National Fisherman*.

The final event that made up my mind to do the book came on Sunday morning, May 6, 2001. Jack Dozier of Deltaville called my home and informed me that the deck boat *Seven Brothers* was aground off Stingray Point, and he encouraged me to come down and take some photos because she was dying. I told him I had to teach a Sunday school class for my wife first, but I would come down after that.

He said, "You better hurry because the seas are going to beat her to pieces."

I arrived at 11:30 A.M. at Stingray Point and I could see the bow of *Seven Brothers* out of the water about a mile and a half offshore. I didn't have a camera lens that would reach her, so I went home and called Jack, who arranged for a boat to take me out that afternoon.

When we reached the sunken hull of *Seven Brothers* and I looked closely at her decks awash, I felt this was the defining moment for me. As I drove home I thought to myself that if I was ever going to do a book on Bay buyboats, now was the time.

The next morning I got a call from Jack to let me know that heavy seas had destroyed the hull of *Seven Brothers* and most of her had washed ashore.

Of all the books I have researched and written, I never had so much help from others as I did on this one. William C. "Bill" Hight has contributed greatly to this project with his knowledge, photos, and books related to the subject. He has gone far beyond being a helpful friend; he has located and called captains and mates and literally driven me to their homes. His passion and love for the boats has kept me inspired. He spent hours and hours searching for boats and working on the list of deck boat builders. This project would not be nearly as complete had it not been for him.

Jonesey Payne has helped me with other books, but he too took a special interest in this one. As a young man, he worked aboard *P. E. Pruitt* and other boats. His firsthand knowledge was always just a phone call away. He combed the oyster houses on the Potomac, Rappahannock, and York Rivers looking for old photos and information. His finds have greatly enhanced the book.

John and Vera England, John Collamore, Joe Conboy, and Ray Rodgers contributed greatly with drawings; they loaned me books and read over copy.

In February 2002, I went to Roanoke to interview Dr. A. L. Van Name, Jr., for the *Southside Sentinel*. Dr. Van Name was our family physician in Urbanna until he retired in the 1980s and moved to Roanoke to live with his son, Billy. Over the years, he had always encouraged me to write about the Bay. As I was getting ready to leave his home, he called Billy and together they gave me a small box packed full with negatives of boats and boats and more boats—photographs that he had taken since the 1920s. He said to me, "When I was out on the water, I was looking for sailboats mostly, but there are a few buyboats in there. You take them. These are yours." Bay maritime writers have used photos from Dr. Van Name's collection for years, and I've used a few in this book.

On the way back to the Hotel Roanoke where I was staying, I nearly cried because I knew what those negatives must have meant to him—a lifetime of passion and joy. To give them up marked the end of an era in his own life. Thank you, Doc!

I would like to acknowledge my father, Henry Shepherd Chowning, Jr., and also my father's cousin, the late Carroll C. Chowning, Jr. Both worked at Southside Marine in Urbanna as boys, when Bay freighters and buyboats were commonplace. They both loved the boats, and they instilled that same feeling in me.

My wife Dee, my children Damon, Peyton, and Hannah, and my granddaughter Michaela have paid the highest price of all for this project. I thank them all for their understanding and for giving me the time to finish it.

Finally, I thank all those I have interviewed or called for information—and there have been many. All have helped to document an important era in the maritime history of the Chesapeake Bay.

I only hope I have done justice to the topic.

# Chesapeake Bay
# Buyboats

*The term buyboat is familiar to most people who have spent time around the Chesapeake, but the word suggests only one of the many jobs that have been done by these versatile craft. Whether called a deck boat, freight boat, Bay boat, packet boat, mast boat, or runner, the same silhouette will come to mind.*

# INTRODUCTION:
# THE VERSATILE BUYBOAT

The era of Chesapeake Bay motor-powered buyboats started at the turn of the twentieth century when gas and diesel engines powerful enough to push a boat the size of a Bay buyboat became affordable and available for the general public. Though most people recognize the term buyboat, it is somewhat misleading because buying and selling seafood was only a small part of the overall use of these vessels.

In Virginia many were called deck boats, comparing them with the same size hulls used in the pound-net fishery that were not decked over but were open boats.

During the early years, the boats that hauled freight were referred to as freight boats, Bay freighters, and packet boats. If a boat was owned by a seafood dealer and was used to collect oysters, crabs, and fish from watermen, the boats were referred to as run boats or runners.

Toward the end of the commercial fishing era of these boats, many Chesapeake Bay crab dredgers called the boats mast boats because of the forward mast.

Though different names may be used, all refer to the same style of boat. They range in size from 40 feet to 100 feet. Some have frame-built hulls, some are log built, and most are deadrise or "box-built" boats. The distinguishing characteristics of a Chesapeake Bay buyboat and whatever else it is called is that a mast-and-boom configuration is forward of the hold, the pilothouse or house is aft of the hold, and the hull is decked over.

This book tells the story of how the boats were built and used throughout the Chesapeake Bay region. Only a few boats still work in the commercial fisheries on the Bay. One or two dredge crabs, a few are used from time to time to plant and haul seed oysters, and some work in the Atlantic Ocean in the hard clam fishery, but for the most part, as commercial workboats, the boats are at the very end of their era.

*In the 1980s and 1990s, when I interviewed several early twentieth century boatbuilders such as Hugh Norris, Lee Deagle, Lewis Wright, Alton Smith, and others, I did not understand the full significance of the fact that these men's lives spanned the history of powered Chesapeake Bay deck boats. They saw the switch from sail to power and at some point in their careers each had built, converted, or repaired many of these boats.*

*I certainly had not realized how quickly buyboats would become part of the Chesapeake's maritime past. If I had, I would have asked a lot more questions.*

# 1: BUYBOAT BUILDERS

The old saying about the three best things for a successful business—location, location, location—could easily pertain to Chesapeake Bay buyboat builders.

It was evident from *Merchant Vessels of the United States*—the books that list all registered U.S. commercial vessels—that most Virginia deck boats were built or converted at western shore boatyards near the ends of the peninsulas that were situated between the major rivers of the Bay. Since the oyster and fishing industries were centered on the James, York, Rappahannock, and Potomac Rivers, a man building boats on one of those peninsulas would certainly be in a prime location.

In the early years of boatbuilding most Bay fishing and oystering communities had one builder in the neighborhood whose main customers were the fishermen in that community. By the time deck boats and diesel- and gasoline-fueled engines came along, however, the Chesapeake Bay fisheries were regional in scope, and good boatbuilders attracted customers from other areas of the Bay.

Gilbert White worked out of his backyard at Foxwells, Virginia, near Windmill Point in Lancaster County's Northern Neck, the peninsula located between the Potomac and the Rappahannock Rivers. As early as 1902, White was building deck boats. In the early years

of his career, Herman Krentz built boats at Kayan, Virginia, in Northumberland County at the mouth of the Little Wicomico River. He later moved to Harryhogan, Virginia, still on the Northern Neck peninsula. The Rice family also built deck boats near Reedville and Fairport on the Neck.

Among those building boats near Deltaville, Virginia, in Middlesex County at the end of the long narrow peninsula between the Rappahannock and Piankatank Rivers were brothers John, Tom, and Ladd Wright; Lin Price and his son Milford; and others. John Wright built his first deck boat in 1904 when Deltaville was still known as Sandy Bottom. Many consider Lin and Milford Price to be the most prolific builders on the Bay.

L. R. "Lennie" Smith and his son Alton first built deck boats at Pepper Creek on Mobjack Bay in Mathews County, but later moved to Horn Harbor which is right on the Chesapeake. Harry Steve Smith also built in the Horn Harbor area, and father and son Alf and Ned Hudgins built in the Laban area, where there was a pocket of builders who turned out buyboats. Many had worked for Lennie Smith and Alf Hudgins and then started building in their own backyards.

Moving further south, James "Big Jim" Smith built boats in his backyard at Guinea Neck on Perrin River in Gloucester County; he taught his four sons—

Little Jim, Sidney, Jack, and Frank—how to build boats. They all built or repaired deck boats from time to time. J. S. Jenkins also built deck boats in that area.

Between the York and James Rivers, on the next peninsula south, Poquoson boatbuilders were not known for building deadrise deck boats, but for decades the area was a center of log canoe building in Virginia. Several log deck boat style boats were built there specifically for motorized power. J. G. Wornom and Clyde Smith specialized in building log boats.

There were also log boat builders in the Dare area of York County on that same peninsula. John and Kirby Smith of Smith Marine Railway and builder Alexander Gaines built several log buyboats. Smith's railway was started in 1842 and seven generations of Smiths have built and hauled boats there. The boatyard initially hauled boats with a horse-powered windlass, then switched to a Fairbanks-Morse gasoline engine, and eventually to a 10-horsepower electric motor with a 300:1 reduction that's still used today.

Down near the mouths of the James and Nansemond Rivers is Crittenden, Virginia, on Chuckatuck Creek. There Captain Lepron "Lip" Johnson built some of the largest deck boats on the Bay for the large oyster companies out of Hampton and Norfolk, Virginia. He was one of the few Bay builders who did longitudinal planked-bottom, frame-built deck boats. On more than one occasion, while interviewing longtime deck boat captains around the Bay, Captain Lip's boats were referred to as those "North Carolina boats." Many of the frame-built deck boats on the Chesapeake were in fact built at Crittenden.

Deck boats were also built on the Eastern Shore of Virginia. The *Merchant Vessels of the United States* shows that several deck boats were built at Hunting Creek and Deep Creek, Virginia, which are both located north of Onancock, Virginia.

Although many referred to buyboats as "down the Bay boats" because so many came from Virginia, there were also many built throughout Maryland's Eastern Shore. Irving F. and Walter B. Cannon built classic Maryland-style draketail deck boats at Fishing Creek on Hooper Island. Jabez Tyler built at Cambridge, Noah T. Evans at Ewell on Smith Island, William A. Noble at Oriole near Deal Island, and Wilfred Tyer at Honga on Hooper Island.

Lorne Tull, Oscar Howard, James E. Daugherty, Charles Dana, and yards such as Christie's Railway and Forbush's Railway built, repaired, and converted sail to power deck boats in the Crisfield area. Percy H. Linton and E. James Tull built deck boats at Pocomoke City, and C. Lyman Ewell built the Maryland-style log deck boat with a log hull and planked sides at Elliott on Fishing Bay near the mouth of the Nanticoke River. Maryland Eastern Shore builders built some of the most unique and distinctive Bay deck boats. There were also builders at Tilghman, Fairbank, Neavitt, St. Michaels, Salisbury, and as far north as Rock Hall.

While Maryland's western shore was not as active in deck boat building, boats were built at Havre de Grace, Benedict, Solomons, Compton, Ironsides, and Broomes Island.

Many builders operated railways and had bustling repair businesses along with their boatbuilding business. Those with railways launched the finished boat from the railway first with man-powered windlasses, then horse-powered, then steam-powered engines, and later gasoline-powered "one lunger" engines. Particularly in the early years, some—like Gilbert White, Lennie Smith, Alf Hudgins, and John Wright—built deck boats very close to the creek bank. They would wait for high tide, gather men from the neighborhood to help, and use long poles greased with beef or mutton tallow and wax to roll and shove the finished boat down the ways.

This chapter does not cover every buyboat builder on the Chesapeake Bay. Its purpose is to provide some understanding of the history and origin of the boats through some of the key men who were involved in the building as well as the conversion and repair of Chesapeake Bay buyboats.

## GILBERT WHITE

*Gilbert White was a pioneer in building Cheapeake Bay buyboats. As early as 1902, White was building buyboats at Mobjack in Mathews County, Virginia. He later moved to Lancaster County on Virginia's Northern Neck and established himself as one of the premiere deck boat builders in that area.*

*The interview with the Biddlecomb family was conducted during a nasty snowstorm on the night of February 27, 2003, at the home of Maria Biddlecomb Rodgers in Reedville, Virginia, on Cockrell Creek.*

Gilbert White built boats at Foxwells, Virginia, on a narrow peninsula between Antipoison Creek and Little Bay on the north and the Rappahannock River to the south. Windmill Point is just a mile or so down the road on the Chesapeake Bay.

Around the turn of the twentieth century, the Foxwells area was extremely remote by land but was fairly accessible by water as boats went right by there going up or down the Bay.

Gilbert was born in Mathews County, Virginia, in 1869 and he moved to Lancaster County near the start of the twentieth century. He and his family lived in a two-story house just yards from the water's edge. He built unique "elliptical" (spoon-shaped) chunk-stern, cross-planked-bottom deadrise boats in his backyard under a giant oak tree, with no electricity and no modern tools. Those who knew him say he never owned a foot adz, but built mostly with a hatchet and a "wood pile" axe.

Lillian Ruperti Hughes, a niece of White, remembers his gentle ways. When she and other relatives would visit, he would always stop work to play with the children.

She recalls him taking a butt plane and shaving thin strips of curled wood off a plank for the little girls to put in their hair, and he made small boats for the boys to float along the shoreline.

Others remember him for his boats. Brothers Walter and Alfred Biddlecomb had Gilbert White build several boats for them. He built *Dudley* and *Fred* for Walter and *Mary Trew* for Alfred. Another brother, Ralph Biddlecomb, also owned a Gilbert White boat named *Mabel,* which had been originally built for someone else. White built different styles of workboats but *Dudley* was a classic Cheseapeake deck boat style that Walter used in the deepwater pound-net fishery. Most of White's deck boats were used in the pound-net fishery and because of this the boats usually had lower sides and flatter bottoms than boats built to buy and haul oysters. The lower sides made it easier to haul the catch from the nets up over the sides, and the flatter bottom allowed boats to work in shallower waters.

Named after Walter's oldest son, *Dudley* is still owned by the family and is being used as a charter fishing boat in the Bay. White built the 64-foot pound-net boat in 1938, and Walter's children have fond memories of visiting the boatyard while *Dudley* and other boats were being built.

## The Biddlecomb Family

Four of Walter's children—Fred, Maria, Winifred, and Dudley—talked about the boats and the man who built them.

Gilbert White takes a break beside a shed at this home at Foxwells, Virginia. Courtesy Ella Jo Henderson.

"I knew the man," says Dudley. "I was just a little boy when *Dudley* was built but I remember him building *Fred.* We still have her sitting up on the hill. I also remember going down there when Uncle Alfred had *Mary Trew* built." *Fred* and *Mary Trew* are not deck boats but classic Bay deadrise workboats. The family still owns both of these boats.

"Mr. White had a small railway and he built under a big oak tree. He started all his boats, even the big ones, bottom up and that's why he got such a good fit on the bottom planking.

"*Lawson* (now *Mundy Point*) was bigger than *Dudley,* and Daddy wanted Mr. White to model *Dudley* after *Mundy Point.* I don't know that he built any bigger than *Lawson.*" (Built in 1929, *Lawson* is 67 feet long.)

"I made several trips down there when *Fred* was being built," says Dudley. "Mr. White was getting some

Gilbert White and his wife are pictured here at his yard in Foxwells, Virginia. Note the start of the spoon-shaped chunk stern and the cross-planked bottom on the boat in the foreground. The U.S. Coast Guard referred to White's sterns as being elliptical in shape. Courtesy Ella Jo Henderson.

age on him then. The way he put sheer on a boat was with a string, and he would put tension on the string until he got it about right, then he would back off and sight something at a distance on that string and make marks on the ribs that were sticking up. That's the way he got the sheer.

"*Fred* always had a little more sheer on one side than the other. I don't know whether the string dried out while he was working or whether he went in the house to eat his lunch and there was a shower of rain and maybe it shrunk up or stretched.

"My Daddy knew Mr. White well, and he told Daddy that he started out building log canoes. Mr. White had a dry type of humor and was sort of a comedian. He said his first experiment with boatbuilding

was a log boat, and she was so lopsided you only had to paddle her on one side.

"Captain John Robins said he remembered one of the first plank boats that Mr. White built," says Dudley. "It must have been around 1900 and he was building right there along the road. He started building this boat and everyone that came by gave him advice on how to build it. When the boat was about halfway finished, he stopped and went on the other side of the road and started building another boat. When people stopped by to give advice, he said, 'no, wrong boat, that's everybody's boat over there; this is my boat.'

"His oldest son told me he was from Mathews County and he probably learned to build boats from there." Mathews County has been a center of boatbuilding since Colonial days and Mathews builders were very active in building fishing boats when Gilbert White was a young man.

One of his better-known boats was *Jennie Dare*. White built her in 1926. Her registered length when built was 54.3 feet. The builder and his son Captain Gilbert White, Jr., cut *Jennie Dare* in two and added approximately 12 feet to her in the summer of 1937.

"His son told me about the time they cut *Jennie Dare* in two," says Fred. "Gilbert, Jr., said he stood in the fish hold and his father was on deck and they used a crosscut saw to saw the hatch coaming, then sawed across the deck and down the side. They repeated this on the other side, removed a couple of planks from the bottom and sawed the keelson and keel in two. Then they sawed the railway cradle in half, moved the cradle [halves] 12 feet apart, built a new section in the cradle and then built the new section in *Jennie Dare*. They did all this with nothing but hand tools."

## Remembering the Builder

Maria and Winifred remember visiting the yard when *Dudley* was being constructed. "It was our Sunday outing," says Maria. "The whole time the boat was being built that was what we did on Sundays. It was a long trip and it was the wintertime and usually very cold. Once we got down there, it was very pretty and his house was right on the water. It seemed a long way from Reedville and we thought we were on the other side of the world.

*Dudley* is about finished in 1938. Here she is underneath a giant oak tree in Gilbert White's yard. Courtesy Ella Jo Henderson.

"We would go inside the kitchen and Mrs. White had a little baby there, a grandchild. He was by the woodstove in a cradle and we admired the baby. It was hot in that kitchen and I guess we had our winter coats on. She would give us something to drink and cookies to eat. Mr. White had an old dog around there that was always splashing in the water.

"I heard them talk about the August storm of 1933. They were right down on the water and a real high tide would come up in the yard. During the August storm they had a skiff tied to the porch in case they had to leave," says Winifred. "It was close to the water. I can see where a real high tide would come up to their door.

"I think Mr. White started *Dudley* in late summer of 1937 and finished her the next spring in 1938. Daddy got the boat that spring," says Maria.

"I think you are right," says Dudley. "When he got her from Mr. White, Daddy already had herring traps out that spring and they had work to do on *Dudley* before he could use her. She had to be painted, rigged, and her engine installed. Daddy pulled the engine out of another boat to go in her and they had her ready to draw stakes out of the bottom at the end of that fish season. He had a stake-drawing rig especially made for *Dudley*.

"I don't think Mr. White ever had electricity down there. I know he didn't when *Dudley* was built in 1938 because there was none down there when *Fred* was built in 1946. I think *Fred* was one of his last boats he built.

"Mr. White was an old-time builder, I'll tell you that. He would go out into the woods and find a tree just right for a knee [frame] and cut it right there. Daddy said he never saw a foot adz on the place and that most chopping was done with a hatchet or a wood pile axe. It was very sharp and keen but it was just a common axe.

"From time to time, he had some help because another man was supposed to build the pilothouse on *Dudley*, but he was busy on another job so Mr. White ended up doing it. I think he hired men to finish a boat so he could start another one, but he didn't have any regular employees.

"On all the boats, my father and uncles supplied the lumber and they paid Mr. White for his labor," says Dudley. "At the start of the job, Mr. White figured the labor for the job for *Dudley* to cost $550, but the deck beams on *Dudley* were sawed out at Humphrey's Railway in Weems. So, when Daddy went to pay the balance, Mr. White turned around and said, 'you gave me too much' and gave him $20 back.

Gilbert White built *Jennie Dare* in 1926. After being lengthened in 1937, she measured 66 feet and was used in the Bay's deepwater pound-net fishery by Northern Neck fisherman Odell Fitchett. Courtesy William Fitchett.

"Daddy asked him, 'What is this for?'

"Mr. White said he figured the cost of cutting the deck beams in the original cost and it would have taken right much labor to cut those beams by hand.

"Instead, he cut a pattern and took the beams to Humphrey's and had them cut out on a band saw," says Dudley. "Daddy tried to give him the $20 back but he wouldn't take it. So Daddy went to the house, went inside, and put the $20 on the table and told Mrs. White this was for her.

"My Daddy and uncles accumulated all the materials for the boat," says Dudley. "The sides were made from long-leaf yellow pine and it came from Baltimore. The bottom and deck was spruce pine from

The Biddlecomb family has owned *Dudley* since Gilbert White built her in 1938. Fred M. Biddlecomb uses the 60-foot deck boat to carry fishing parties in the Chesapeake charter boat fleet.

*Facing page:* Two of Gilbert White's boats are side by side on Cockrell Creek. White built *Mundy Point* in 1928 and *Elva C.* in 1922. Courtesy David and Sheila Carr.

*Elva C.,* owned by Reedville Fisherman's Museum, is carrying members out to view the Turkey Shoot Regatta (skipjack races) on the Rappahannock River, October 18, 2001. Gilbert White built her in 1922 in his backyard. Courtesy Tom Chillemi.

somewhere over in Lancaster County. He bought it from Archie Beane, who had a portable sawmill.

"The story goes that when Mr. White finished *Dudley* and she was ready to be brought up the Bay, my Uncle Ralph and a mate that we called Cocky went around to get her. Cocky had one eye that looked straight ahead and the other eye went off in another direction. Well, Uncle Ralph was in a purse boat by himself towing *Dudley* and Cocky was on board *Dudley.* Cocky had a tendency to fall asleep, and when they got the boat home he was sound asleep in a chair by the galley door. He probably slept all the way up the Bay," laughed Dudley.

Another time, Dudley remembers, Cocky caught a nap at the wheel when they were going from an inshore trap to an offshore trap in *Dudley.* "He woke up and he was at a trap so he slowed *Dudley* right down. The whole crew watched old Cocky and they knew he had caught a nap at the wheel. They didn't say a word because all they wanted to do was torment and tease him. It turned out to be Captain Marvin Swift's trap and not ours."

Maria says that her father and crew always had to watch out for Cocky because he had only one good eye. "They always teased Cocky but we all liked him," says Maria. "The crew would do things around our house when they weren't working on *Dudley.* Cocky was the one who once a year went down into our well and cleaned it out. Somebody would be up top pumping the whole time to get the water level down. Cocky was in the well drinking the water because it was so cool and nice. When he came up, the men showed him a rotten, dead frog that supposedly came from the well and told him they hoped he hadn't drunk any of that water. Poor Cocky went over behind a hedge and got sick.

"Daddy worked pound nets in spring and summer in *Dudley,* dredged oysters in winter with *Fred* or *Mary Trew,* and he hauled bricks in *Dudley* too," says Dudley. "I remember going to a brick kiln and watching bricks being loaded onto *Dudley.* We hauled bricks in the hold, and he shored the decks up with trap stakes and hauled some bricks on deck. He hauled brick to St. Mary's City, Maryland, on the Potomac River.

For sixty-five years, *Dudley* has stayed in the Biddlecomb family, one of just a few deck boats on the Chesapeake that has remained in the same family its entire working life.

"We've never known a time in our lives when we didn't know Gilbert White," says Maria. "He built our boats. He built them well and you don't ever forget that."

## WILLIAM E. WRIGHT

*Throughout his life, William E. Wright of Syringa, Virginia, has been associated with Bay deck boats. He built deck boats, converted schooners and bugeyes into motor-powered buyboats, and worked aboard his father's boats when he was young.*

*His father, G. L. "Captain Ladd" Wright of Deltaville, was one of the early pioneers in building staved, cross-planked-bottom deadrise workboats in the Chesapeake. Just as the Poquoson area had become known for building log canoes, Deltaville builders became known for this style of building. Some referred to the cross-planked-bottom boats as "box" boats.*

*Captain Ladd built his first deck boat in 1916— C. E. Wright, which later became Lorie Robins. Interestingly, C. E. Wright was frame-built with longitudinal planking, and one of the few like it ever built in Deltaville.*

*William was yard foreman at Deagle and Son Marine Railway on Fishing Bay from 1935 until he retired in 1975. This interview was conducted in February 2002.*

### Boatbuilding Heritage

William's grandfather William Wright moved to Deltaville from Accomack County on Virginia's Eastern Shore around 1880 and married a Deltaville girl, Betty Hunley. They had five sons—Thomas "Tom" Walter, John Emerson, George Landon "Ladd," Tollie Franklin, and Charles, who died as an infant. The three oldest brothers went into the boatbuilding business.

"My two uncles, John and Tom, and my daddy, Ladd, all worked together in the beginning. They built boats at my Uncle John's house on Jackson Creek in Deltaville. One of their first boats was *M. B. Wright*. She was built in 1905 and named for Uncle John's wife, Mable Blanche. Uncle John used the boat to haul lumber and freight for many years before he sold her and settled down to building boats full time. In 1927, they built *Iva W.*, which is one of the famous buyboats or at least one everybody knows about today, but they built a lot before her. One of their early ones was *Miss Holland* and she was 65 feet long. They built hundreds of boats of all different sizes. The deck boats though were the largest boats that they built.

John Wright built some of the finest Chesapeake Bay buyboats at his backyard boatyard on Jackson Creek in Deltaville, Virginia. When he got old he built flat-bottom and deadrise skiffs. Courtesy Bob Walker.

"Their trademark was a sharp deadrise in the bow and staved cross-planked bottoms," he says. "I was told that Ike Thomas (an early Deltaville builder) taught them how to build boats."

The late Randolph Norton wrote in his book *Old Days on the Chesapeake Bay and Deltaville Virginia* that a Yankee named Ike Thomas, referred to as Ikey Thomas by some, moved from New York to Deltaville's Lovers Lane (a winding road on a peninsula wedged between two branches of Jackson Creek) around 1900.

Norton wrote, "As a boy walking to school, I stopped to watch Mr. Thomas lovingly fashion by hand each piece of the boat as if it were fine furniture." Thomas was building planked yawl boats for

Captain John Wright built many different types of boats at his yard including buyboats. This photo from the 1930s shows that Wright's yard was a busy place. Courtesy Bob Walker.

schooners. It is believed that Thomas taught the Wrights how to build boats. The Wrights' yard was on Jackson Creek and they built all kinds of boats.

"In those early years there were plenty of good men around to help build boats, [and] good wood from a local forest; and in 1931 electricity came to Deltaville," says William. "That really helped the boat-building business." Prior to 1931 every piece of wood had to be cut by hand unless the yard had steam-powered planers and band saws. Most backyard builders, however, did not have steam engines. Most of their work was done by hand with a foot adz, hand drills, and an ax. Electricity enabled boatbuilders to build boats faster. This also gave Deltaville builders an edge in the business, as some isolated areas in Virginia's tidewater region did not get electricity until the early 1950s. It should be noted that some Bay yards did have steam engines to power planers and band saws. As early as the 1890s, Reedville, Virginia, boatbuilder Isaac Bailey was using a steam-engine powered Josiah Ross planer and band saw. Samuel Butler and Joseph Davis bought the yard in 1906 and continued to use the steam-powered tools until electricity came to Reedville. The yard is still in operation today as Reedville Marine Railway, and the same planer and band saw are still in use today, powered by electricity.

The other advantage Deltaville builders had was an abundance of good wood and a sawmill about eight miles down the road that cut excellent boat lumber. "Old man Bernard Wood had the best boat lumber around," says William. "But, if we needed a special piece that was long and straight that we could not find at the mill for a boom or mast or something, we would go into the Dragon [Run] and pick out a tree that was just right. I've done that myself and I had someone cut it for me."

The Dragon Run, about fifteen miles from Deltaville, makes up the headwaters of the Piankatank River. It is an isolated swampy area that is very difficult to access. Over the years and to this day the remote Dragon has discouraged lumbermen from cutting virgin timber there. When an unusually large piece of lumber was needed for a mast or boom, the boatwrights would select a large tree from the Dragon. A tree cutter would cut the one tree down and a team of oxen or mules or horses would "snake" (meaning pull) the tree out of the woods to a location where it could be loaded onto a barge for water travel or, in later times, onto a truck.

Bernard L. Wood's sawmill in Lot, Virginia, which would later become Hartfield, played a key role in the boatbuilding industry in the Deltaville area. Wood started the business about 1905 around the same time

Built by brothers John Wright and T. W. "Tom" Wright in 1926, *Olive Virginia* is seen here crab dredging in the Chesapeake Bay in the 1970s. She was one of just a few deck boats on the Bay that had portholes in her sides to let light into the forepeak. Courtesy Carlos Smith.

the Wrights and others started building boats. By 1915, the mill was one of the largest in the area, providing boat lumber to a thriving boatbuilding trade. Wood's was one of only a few mills capable of sawing lumber that was over 40 feet long. Bernard died in 1941 but his sons ran the operation until 1972. When the mill closed, Deltaville boatbuilders had to look elsewhere for good boat lumber.

Throughout the Bay area, wherever boatbuilding took place, a good mill could usually be found close by. In the case of Cockrell's Marine Railway in Northumberland County and Smith Marine Railway in York County, a sawmill and planing mill were located on the yard and builders could saw and plane lumber to meet their needs.

Many men who worked for and learned from the Wrights eventually went off on their own to build boats in their backyards. Soon, just about every backyard in town had some type of boat under construction. Deltaville became a center for building wooden deadrise, cross-planked-bottom boats.

"My uncles and Daddy were building deck boats fairly early because my Daddy built *C. E. Wright* in 1916," says William. "He built it for himself and named it for my sister, Countess Elizabeth Wright, who was born in 1915.

"Daddy worked *C. E. Wright* a while and then sold her about 1919. He had a 25-horsepower Palmer engine in her and she had a steadying sail on her. I was born in 1918 and when I got big enough he stopped working with Uncle John and Tom and went on his own. That's when I started working with him. We built boats together and followed the water too.

"Uncle John started out working the water but later he mostly built boats. Dad and Tollie liked to follow the water more than John and Tom," says William. "Dad would work the water and build boats, but all Tollie wanted to do was follow the water."

## Years at Deagle's

"I started at Deagle's in 1935, the year Lee Deagle bought the yard at a public auction," says William. "I was there for the first boat and worked on every one until I retired in 1975. We did it all there from rebuilding schooners and bugeyes, to converting sailboats to powerboats, to building boats.

"Lord knows we cut a many a boat in two to make it bigger," he says. "We'd cut the boat in two and separate her by pulling the railway apart. The railway was bolted together at certain places and we'd separate the railway by taking the bolts out at a splice. We put

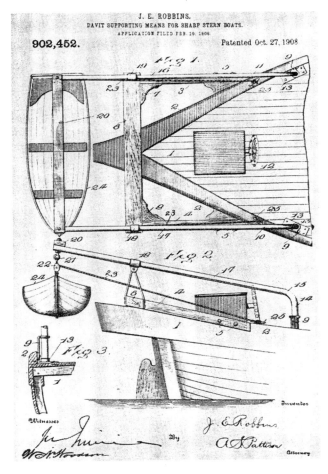

J. E. ROBBINS.
DAVIT SUPPORTING MEANS FOR SHARP STERN BOATS.
APPLICATION FILED FEB. 10, 1906.

902,452.

Patented Oct. 27, 1908.

These drawings from the United States Patent Office show how the patent stern worked on a V-stern bugeye. Note the ducktail stern in the drawing. Courtesy U.S. Patent Office.

the boat where we wanted it on the railway, cut the boat in two, took the bolts out and separated them, and pulled [the front half] ahead.

"We worked on so many boats that I can't remember them all," says William. "I remember *A. Booth* because Daddy and I worked on her. That was 1938 and she was a big schooner. We built a scaffold around her and rebuilt her on the ice. It was a cold winter, and we had to cut a hole in the ice but that didn't stop us.

"It wasn't hard to convert them. We would cut the masts off; take the house off to make room for the engine room; and from the deck up was where the pilothouse was built over the engine. The only thing we had to do to the bottom was bore a shaft log. Then we put a small mast back in. We could convert one in about a month from a sailboat to a powerboat.

"We converted *Sarah Conway, Ida B. Conway, Betty I. Conway,* and *Flora Kirwan*," he says. "We rebuilt a lot of sailboats too. We rebuilt *Harriett C. Whitehead*. She was the largest two-masted schooner on the Bay. That was in 1935.

"We put a lot of round sterns on schooners and patent sterns on bugeyes to give them more deck space," says William. "We put a round stern on the schooner *Lula Phillips*. We put patent sterns on two or three bugeyes but I can't remember their names. By that time, the patent had run out and we never paid any royalties.

"I put a lot of round sterns on deck boats," he says. "I put the round stern on *Nellie Crockett*. We would use Virginia spruce for planking. We had to cut back in the boat about 20 feet; take it all off, and then built from there back. We would stagger the planks so it would all blend in together. *Nellie Crockett's* got a pretty stern. The boys liked the round stern because it gave them more deck space and it is pretty.

"I built one draketail workboat for an Eastern Shore waterman when I was at Deagle's, but I didn't like it," he says. "There were quite a few draketail deck boats, and we worked on them from time to time.

"When I first went to Deagle's in 1935 Lin Price came over, and Lee Deagle and I both apprenticed under him for ship construction. Lee was the mechanic and there was none better anywhere, but Lin Price was the boatbuilder and he was one of the best.

"In 1951 we rebuilt *C. E. Wright* at Deagle's Railway and Dad helped," he says. "She was renamed *Lorie Robins* and was owned by John Willett, an Eastern Shore fisherman. I enjoyed working on her with Dad because he was proud of her and enjoyed telling people that he built her himself in 1916. As I think back now, [the days] working on her with Dad were some of the best days for me at the yard."

William Emanuel Wright died on November 29, 2002, at the age of eighty-three.

## ALTON SMITH

*"When Alton Smith come down to the creek to work on a boat with a rotten piece of wood in her, he'd come down with a little box with a foot adz and saw and whatever else he needed. He didn't sit there and look at it and think about it. He flew right into it because he knew what he was doing. He didn't hem and haw. You wouldn't believe what he could do, but of course he*

*grew up with it from a little boy," said Morris Snow, in a 2002 interview.*

When I interviewed Alton Smith and Edward Diggs for *National Fisherman* in 1991, I had no idea the significance of such an interview. Alton was one of the last old-time deck boat builders. His life just about spanned the entire era of Chesapeake Bay buyboats. Also, he and his father Lennie were among the premiere deck boat builders in the Chesapeake. Mathews County, Virginia, was a strong area for pound-net fishing, and open and decked-over deadrise boats were in great demand for that fishery. Lennie and Alton built many deck boats, first on Pepper Creek and later at Port Haywood, Virginia.

When Alton died in 1997, his daughter Mildred Stillman had "Master Boatbuilder" engraved on his gravestone. Alton was a legend in his time, and to serious students of Bay boatbuilding heritage, he will always be a legend.

The April 1951 issue of *Atlantic Fisherman* magazine carried a full-page ad for Pettit paints. The ad read, "Pettit preserves, protects, and beautifies," and several sturdy, wooden fishing vessels were pictured as examples of what the paint could do for a boat.

The top photo was of a boat named *Sea Pal,* a 78-foot Chesapeake Bay deck boat that was being used as a dragger in the Atlantic Ocean by Captain H. Milton Forrest of Seaford, Virginia. What the ad didn't say about this vessel was that Alton Smith of Susan, Virginia, built her.

In 1991 Alton was eighty-five years old and had been retired from boatbuilding since 1967. At the time of this interview his longtime associate Edward Diggs was still running Smith's old boat shop at Horn Harbor Marina in Port Haywood.

Alton was born in 1906 and at the age of fourteen in 1920, he went to work for his father, L. R. "Lennie" Smith at his yard on Pepper Creek.

"My mother died in childbirth when I was very young and that took care of what schooling I would have gotten," says Alton. In the early twentieth century, there was no mandatory requirement for children to attend school. In most families, the mother determined the amount of schooling a child received by deciding when the youngster would go to work. Most of the time, the job would be either working aboard an oyster boat, as a culling boy on a log canoe,

Edward Diggs, *left,* and the late Alton Smith at Horn Harbor Railway near Port Haywood, Virginia, in 1991.

This faded photo is of Lennie Smith's boatyard on Pepper Creek in Mathews County, Virginia, at the turn of the twentieth century. Courtesy Mildred Stillman.

or pulling fodder in a cornfield. In Alton's case, he had his father's boatyard to go to.

"I got my own toolbox when I was sixteen years old and learned to build boats from watching and

Lennie Smith was a striking young man and one of the most productive buyboat builders on the Bay. Courtesy Mildred Stillman.

This truckload of cedar lumber was delivered to Smith's yard in the 1940s. Courtesy Mildred Stillman.

listening," he says. "I worked ten hours a day, six days a week, and got practically nothing for it."

His father Lennie had learned the trade from his father, Peter W. Smith, who built and repaired boats and ran freight to Baltimore and elsewhere in a 53-foot bugeye named *White Wing*, which was registered at 52.9 feet by 14.3 feet by 3.6 feet. Peter Smith built *White Wing* in 1896 at New Point, Virginia. He had learned the boatbuilding trade from his father, who had been a noted Poquoson, Virginia, log canoe builder.

Over the next twenty years or so, the Smiths built and repaired boats at Pepper Creek. "We didn't build log canoes, but Lordy, we repaired many a one. The

biggest log boat [bugeye] we ever repaired was *David Goldstrom*. She had thirteen logs in her and was 63 feet long. She belonged to Alfred Pruitt of Tangier Island."

Alton says times were hard for his family. "There wasn't much money during those times. They were Depression days," he says. "We were lucky we had the fish and crabs from the Chesapeake Bay, because there weren't jobs [available] on land. If you didn't farm or you didn't work the water, you had to work somewhere, and there was a very large local work force to draw from at our boatyard. People didn't drive to the city—as they do today—looking for work, because things were worse off there than in the country.

"Today, there are very few people around that know how to repair and build wooden boats. But in those days, there were lots of good craftsmen and I was very lucky to have had many good people working for me over the years."

## No Electricity

When Alton started building boats, there was no electricity for the shop. "The two main tools were broad ax and adz," he says. "Things were rough, but we didn't know any different. We didn't get electricity here [at Port Haywood] until the early 1950s. Before that, it was all by hand. Most of the boats I built were with hand tools."

In the early years, lumber came from nearby forests or was shipped on schooners from Baltimore. "We bought all our pine undressed. We dressed all our own lumber until around 1960. We had a planing mill right on the place, but it got so we had to start buying fir and other types of wood because the housing business took all our good boatbuilding lumber."

The Smiths bought land at Port Haywood in 1939. Alton's daughter Mildred said that Lennie did not want to leave Pepper Creek, but Alton knew if he was going to stay in the boatbuilding business he had to get to deeper water.

"We needed more [deeper] water because we were getting orders for some big trawlers, and there wasn't enough water in Pepper Creek to launch the big boats," says Alton.

"We built a lot of boats, but I never kept count of just how many," he says. "When we moved from Pepper Creek, we had a gang of men working for us, but one by one they began to die and there wasn't anyone to replace them. Also, we built a lot of boats in the

Moored here at a Tangier Island dock in the 1980s, *L. R. Smith* was named after boatbuilder Lennie Smith who built her in 1926. When Lennie asked Captain Henry Armstead what he wanted to name her, Armstead supposedly replied, "I don't give a damn what you name her!" So Smith named the 56-foot deck boat after himself.

1920s, '30s and '40s for the pound-net fishery, and that fishery began to go bad."

As times got harder for boatbuilders, Alton diversified and built a marina to go along with the boatyard. "Young people just weren't interested in building boats because there wasn't any money in it and there wasn't the demand that there had been," he says. "The truth of it was carpenter's work and boat work paid some of the poorest pay around. They could do anything else and get better pay.

"It's better now. When I retired in 1967, we were only getting 35 cents per foot to haul a boat and now [1991] they get $2.25 per foot plus the cost of labor," he says. "We did the labor for whatever it cost to haul. Way back, we didn't get but $3 or $4 to haul, scrape, and copper a boat.

"I've built many a 36- to 38-foot deadrise workboat for $1,600, but now they get $40,000. I'm not sure I came along at the right time.

"I'll tell ya another difference," he says. "The boats that I built all had marine engines in them. Now you can't buy a true marine engine that I know of.

They're all converted truck or car engines. The best ones in my time were Palmer and Lathrop."

Alton and Lennie also built V-stern deck boats. These were used mostly in the pound-net fishery and when they were bought for other uses, the V-stern was usually replaced with a round stern. The sterns on deck boats included Hooper Island draketails, V-sterns, square sterns, patent sterns, classic schooner sterns, and round sterns, according to Alton.

At a 1990 workboat parade in Norfolk, Virginia, the captain of *Ellen Marie*, a 60-foot deck boat, received a prize for having the oldest boat at the event. Alton and his father Lennie built the boat in 1926 at Pepper Creek. "Boy, I must be getting old when my boats are winning prizes for being the oldest around," Alton says with a laugh.

Alton had made models of each boat that he built. "I'd make models and take the lines off the models for the big boat," he says. When he finished with the model, Alton says he would burn them in his woodstove in the shop. "I've been told I should have kept those models because they would now be worth

The Smiths built *Ellen Marie* in 1925 for Henry Owens. Here she is underway going out to fish pound nets. Courtesy Thomas E. Owens.

Alton Smith's wife stands on the dock in front of the deck boat *Mary*. Over the years, Mrs. Smith photographed many of the boats built by Alton and his father at the railway. Courtesy Mildred Stillman.

more than the boats I built," he says with a laugh. His daughter has three of the models he made of boats he built for himself.

Alton's boatbuilding records show that he also made hand drawings of boats he was building. It was not a formal plan but a guide he used in building a specific boat.

As an example of boatbuilding costs in the 1920s, the Smiths' records show that Lennie and Alton built a 55-foot V-stern deck boat named *Elizabeth D.* in 1926 for Stanley Pritchett of New Point, Virginia, for $725. The installation of the engine was an additional $50. The Smiths were paid $200 on September 27, 1926, for the first installment; $300 more on December 22, 1926; and $300 for the final installment on February 12, 1927. There was $25 worth of oil, fittings, and other things that brought the total price to $800.

## EDWARD DIGGS

*Edward Diggs of Redart, Virginia, has retired from the boatbuilding business but still builds a skiff or two in his backyard boat shop. Edward is considered by many to be one of the finest boatwrights in the Bay region and over his career has built, repaired, and enlarged several Chesapeake Bay deck boats, including adding new sterns.*

Lennie Smith and his son Alton built *Linda Carol,* originally named *Croaker,* in 1931, to be used in the Bay's pound-net fishery. Here she is in the 1990s being used in the winter crab-dredge fishery.

*When this interview was conducted in 1991 between Edward and Alton Smith, Edward was still building and repairing boats at Alton's old yard at Port Haywood. One of the last deck boats Alton Smith built was* York Spit *in 1949, and Edward did much of the work.*

In 1946, Edward Diggs came to Smith asking for a job. He had been building boats with his father (who had learned from his uncle) in Peary, Virginia.

"I'm going to tell you the truth now," says Alton. "I don't know anyone who can build a boat as good as Edward Diggs and boy, I've known a lot of boatbuilders in my time. He does the best work on every project, whether it's caulking a boat or building a hull.

"I've worked on boats most all my life," says Edward. "I was blowing sawdust off my father's mark when I was as tall as a saw bench, and when I was sixteen, I was building boats full time.

"After the war [World War II], people coming home had more money and they wanted little skiffs built for messing around the water. Outboard motors were just coming out and people could afford to buy

them. Dad and I must have built a million little flat-bottom skiffs.

"We were also building 42-foot deadrise workboats in the yard for watermen, and I learned most of what I know from my father," says Diggs.

The Diggses built their boats by "rack of eye." They rarely had any boat plans to work from. "I can only recall one time going by plans to build a boat and that was a design by boat designer Harry Bulifant. We built a charter boat for a man in Norfolk, Virginia. All the rest are built the way it was passed down to us."

After Edward started working for Alton Smith, several buyboats were built at the shop. *York Spit* was built in 1949 for J. H. Miles, Jr. Alton's hand-written boatbuilding records state that *York Spit* was "48 feet long by 13 feet wide with a deck, pilothouse, trunk, cabin, forward hatch, two bulkheads, forepeak finished with lockers, waist 16 inches high, engine and engine bed, shaft and bearings installed, rudder, tiller, shoe, and steering wheel. Built of fir and Virginia pine for a sum of $8,000. Finished October 22, 1949. Left the yard October 27, 1949."

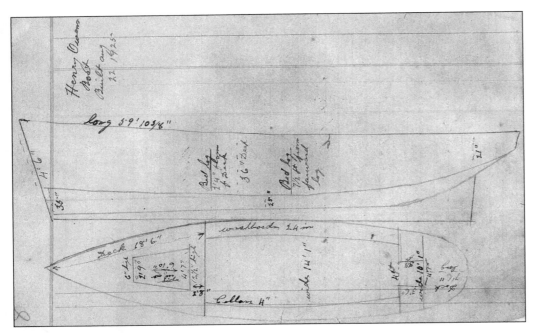

This drawing of *Ellen Marie* from Alton and Lennie Smith's boatbuilding records shows that *Ellen Marie* was built as an open trap boat. She was later decked over and made into a traditional Bay deck boat. She is still alive and owned by Paul Vrooman of Mathews County, Virginia. Courtesy Mildred Stillman.

E. C. Rice, a master boatbuilder of Chesapeake Bay deck boats, stands in front of his home, the old Fleeton Hotel in Reedville. Rice ran the E. C. Rice and Son Railway at Fairport, and he and several members of his family owned and lived in the old hotel that had been converted to apartments. Courtesy Edwin W. Rice.

## C. H. RICE

*C. H. Rice was best known around the Chesapeake Bay as a builder of multipurpose boats, having built trap boats, purse boats, striker boats, skipjacks, and deck boats. The three skipjacks—*Somerset, City of Crisfield, *and* Caleb W. Jones—*are still oystering with the Maryland oyster fleet.*

*What many people do not know is that Rice built three deck boats:* Verna R., *built for himself in 1948 as a crab dredger; that same year, the 77-foot* Rebecca Forbush; *and in 1951, the 81-foot* G. T. Forbush. *Both* Rebecca Forbush *and* G. T. Forbush *were built with the double-deck pilothouse. These two large deck boats are two of just a few buyboats built from start to finish as double-deckers.*

The Rice family who lived near Reedville, Virginia, was much like the Wrights of Deltaville and the Smiths of Mathews County in that generations of each family were involved in building boats.

"My grandfather had the railway E. C. Rice and Son in Fairport, Virginia," says Edwin W. Rice, who lives just outside Reedville. "My dad, Charles Herbert Rice, my uncle Emory, and my uncle Luke worked for him. Our families lived at Fleeton in the Fleeton Hotel that had been converted into apartments. My grandfather, father, and uncles all owned an interest in the building. When my grandfather died in the 1930s, my uncle Emory took over the Fairport Railway and continued to build purse and

The builder C. H. Rice and members of the Forbush family of Crisfield, Maryland, are on deck the day *G.T. Forbush* was launched. Courtesy Edwin W. Rice.

striker boats for the menhaden industry and also deadrise boats.

"My Daddy later owned his own yard, C. H. Rice and Son Boatyard, and between the time he left my grandfather's railway and had his own yard he worked for the J. Howard Smith Company building purse and striker boats, and while there he laid a railway to haul the big menhaden steamers. Also, while working there, he laid down from a half model the framework for a menhaden steamer. According to all information I have been able to obtain it was the only menhaden steamer ever built from the keel up on Cockrell Creek. Mr. Harvey Smith named the steamer after my father, *Charles Herbert Rice*. A great deal of the lumber purchased when he ran this operation was sold to Virgil Miller when the Smith Company was sold, and Miller purchased Rice Marine Railway at Fairport, which was owned by my cousin Carl Rice. Carl built boats used as head boats for party fishing in northern waters, but was noted for building cruising style tugs, some of which were Charles Witholtz designs.

*Verna R.* is under construction at C. H. Rice and Son Boatyard on Cockrell Creek near Reedville, Virginia. Courtesy Edwin W. Rice.

Construction of the top deckhouse on the 81-foot *G.T. Forbush* is underway at C. H. Rice and Son Boatyard in 1954. Courtesy Edwin W. Rice.

*Verna R.* was built in 1948 by Charles Henry Rice of Reedville, Virginia, for crab dredging. She was named after Rice's second wife. Courtesy Edwin W. Rice.

"Dad worked at J. Howard Smith Company during World War II, and right at the end of the war ran the Reedville Marine Railway. When Mr. Butler, who owned the Reedville Railway, came back after the war, Dad started his own railway further up the creek. That's where he built the skipjacks and *Rebecca* and *G.T. Forbush;* remodeled two large mine sweepers into the fish steamers *Hiawatha* and *Pluck;* and built a lot of deadrise boats in the 42- to 43-foot range. He also built an oyster scow for Gus Forbush.

"I know he built three deck boats. He built *Rebecca* and *G.T. Forbush* and *Verna R.,* which he built for himself to dredge for crabs," says Edwin. "Mr. Will Pruitt dredged her for him at first and later my Dad dredged her.

"*Verna R.* was a nice little crab-dredge boat. She was 52 feet long. Dad named her after his second wife," says Edwin. "My grandfather, my father, and my uncle built a deck boat in the 1930s, and she was named after me. Her name was *Edwin W. Rice,* and she was built for a Mr. Libby up near Walnut Point who ran an oyster packing company. Uncle Emory built *E. Carl Rice* and I believe she was a deck boat.

"I was away in school when Dad was building *Rebecca Forbush,* but I was home and working when he built two of the three skipjacks in 1949 and 1950.

"His boatyard was right behind his house and I guess Dad was most noted for his versatility in boatbuilding. He was a master craftsman."

## JOHNSON MARINE RAILWAY

*One of the largest of the Chesapeake Bay buyboats was built in 1936. Appropriately named* Chesapeake, *she was launched at Johnson Marine Railway in Crittenden, Virginia, on a flood tide in the middle of the night.*

*Measuring nearly 100 feet long on the top deck,* Chesapeake *was the high-water mark in the history of Bay buyboats. She was built right after the Depression and just before World War II. There was a feeling of revival as the oyster industry peaked about this time. The trucking industry and the roads that would eventually take most of the freight business away from deck boats were still developing.*

*The oyster industry had grown since Civil War times to support several very large Virginia companies. One of those companies, J. H. Miles and Company of Norfolk, had Captain Lip Johnson build* Chesapeake.

*Captain Lip was one of the premiere deck boat builders on the Bay. He built deck boats from the start around 1900 until his death in 1944 at the ripe old age of eighty-one. He was one of*

Captain Lip Johnson built some of the largest deck boats on Chesapeake Bay. Arlene Matthews recalls that Captain Lip's wife, Mary, once asked him, "Why don't you dress a little better when you go down to the boatyard." Captain Lip replied, "Those who know me, know I can afford to dress better, and those who don't know me, I don't give a damn about." Arlene also recalls that Captain Lip had a "huge short-haired pointer" dog named Frank who followed him everywhere except when it got really cold, and then he would lie down by the big potbelly woodstove in the boatyard store. Captain Lip thought as much of Frank as he did of a lot of people. One night at supper, Captain Lip fed Frank a pork chop from the table. His wife told him not to feed the dog from the table and Captain Lip replied, "Don't worry, that pork chop didn't hurt me, I don't think it will hurt Frank." Courtesy Arlene Matthews.

This 1936 photo shows the three railways at Johnson Marine Railway in Crittenden, Virginia, where some of the largest deck boats on the Bay were built. A deck boat has been hauled on the railway to the far left; the middle railway has a yacht belonging to Poland and Company of Newport News, Virginia; and the third cradle has a small oyster boat. These boats were stuck on the rails for six weeks because of a winter freeze. Courtesy Arlene Matthews.

*the few builders on the Bay who built framed deck boats and laid the bottom planking longitudinally from stem to stern. Another occasional feature of Captain Lip's deck boats was the "hunting cabin." This design dates back to the coasting canoe era. Coasting canoes, which started to appear around the 1830s, were the second generation of log canoes on the Bay. According to M. V. Brewington's book* Chesapeake Bay Bugeyes, *there were four generations of log canoes—the open log canoe, the coasting canoe, the brogan, and finally the bugeye. With each generation, more boats were built to accommodate the Bay's growing oyster-dredge fishery. Brewington described the hunting cabin as "a cabin containing two built-in wooden bunks and a small woodstove at the forward end. The cabin occupied all the space between the washboards beginning just abaft the foremast and extending aft some six feet."*

*The hunting cabin on Captain Lip's boats took up the forepeak, running from just aft of the bow post to just forward of the mast. Several of Captain Lip's deck boats were built to carry supplies and passengers during the 1907 Jamestown Exposition as well as to tow barges in the Hampton, Norfolk, and Newport News areas. A larger cabin (the style of a hunting cabin) would be more useful on these boats than on a deck boat being used to fish a pound net or to dredge crabs, where space was needed to carry payload.*

*Whereas many Bay builders built from rack of eye, Captain Lip used half models and lofted his boats onto planks. His was one of the largest yards in the Bay region.*

When Lorenzo Dow Moger moved to Crittenden, Virginia, from Fox Hill to open a railway in 1894, he wrote that Johnson Marine Railway was already there.

Lepron Johnson was born in 1862 in Fox Hill. It is not known exactly when he moved to Crittenden near the mouths of the James and Nansemond Rivers and opened a railway/boatbuilding business on Chuckatuck Creek.

It turned out that Captain Lip (as Johnson was known up and down the Bay) had moved to a prime location. The James River seed oyster business was just downriver from him and large buyboats were needed to haul seed to private and public oyster beds throughout the Bay. Also, major seafood markets were located in Hampton and Norfolk, Virginia, not far from Crittenden. Captain Lip built some of the largest deck boats on the Chesapeake at his two railway locations on Chuckatuck Creek.

Captain Lip's granddaughter, Arlene Matthews, still lives in Crittenden and remembers her grandfather well. "When I was a little girl, I went to the yard most every Sunday morning with my granddaddy," she says. "When I was old enough to walk, he would come over to my house that was just down the street and he and I would go walking down to the boatyard.

*Edvina* was built in 1905 by Captain Lip Johnson of Crittenden, Virginia, and was owned for many years by C. R. Bagwell. Arlene Matthews, granddaughter to Captain Lip, recalls the time her husband was offered a job aboard the 52-foot buyboat by the Bagwell family. "Times might be tight," she said to her husband, "but I want you to know I didn't marry you from Friday night to Monday morning because that's the only time you'd be home." He wisely opted not to take the job. Captain Lip built boats similar to *Edvina* at his two boatyards on Chuckatuck Creek until his death in 1944. Courtesy Arlene Matthews.

He had a store at the boatyard with canned food, nails, paint, and other stuff. He had a candy counter and he gave me a bag of penny candy and we walked around the railway. The candy was my pacifier. I followed him around that railway and after he did what he was going to do, we went back home and he read the funny papers in the newspaper to me. To this day, I still love to read the funny papers.

"Granddaddy built yachts, sailboats, workboats, tugboats, ferryboats and buyboats. He had two railways and we'd say the first road went down to the upper railway and the back road went to the lower railway. They weren't side by side but they were close.

"Granddaddy employed twenty or thirty people at the little railway and that many again at the big railway. There was a blacksmith shop, machine shop, woodworking shop, and a large general mercantile store on the yard. He had lumber stacked everywhere on the yard and I fondly remember the sweet smells

Clifton Haughwout, yard foreman of the upper yard at Johnson Marine Railway, made the half-model and lofted *Chesapeake,* one of the largest deck boats ever built on the Bay. Courtesy Alese Haughwout Bailey.

On good-weather Sundays after working all week at the yard, railway workers would go down the hill to Johnson Marine Railway and sit around the general mercantile store at the railway in Crittenden, Virginia. Courtesy Arlene Matthews.

of all that wood. I think I'd like to live in a sawmill if it wasn't for the noise.

"When Granddaddy died in 1944, his girls [daughters] ran the yard for a while trying to collect all the money that was owed him," says Arlene. "There was an awful lot of money owing him, but he never worried about money. Thomas Hazelwood told me once that someone owed my Grandfather $60,000 and I told him that I bet my Granddaddy never lost a wink of sleep over it.

"People loved Granddaddy and when he died, there were grown men crying in the church. During the Depression, Granddaddy kept everybody going. If you worked for Granddaddy, you didn't go hungry. Now we didn't have a lot during the Depression, we had to make do, but Granddaddy would find a way to help those who needed help.

"The railway was like the country store on the corner in most towns," says Arlene. "At Granddaddy's store, all kinds of people would come by land and water to shop there. One of my uncles worked in the store. On Sunday afternoon, the benches in front of that store were filled with men smoking pipes and cigars and whittling on sticks. It was one of the popular places in town. When I got old enough, my mother would send me down the hill to the store for molasses and other things. I remember that barrel of molasses. It had a pump on it so my uncle could pump molasses into my jar," she says. "He had meats and all kinds of groceries. You got to remember that in those days a lot of people were still traveling by water and they would stop at Granddaddy's store to get stuff.

"Granddaddy built good boats and they were built to last. Ernest Wilson, who knew Granddaddy, said he would have his boat lumber cut in the winter when there was no sap and he air dried all the wood for a long time. That may have been the secret to his good boats.

Alese Haughwout Bailey's father was a foreman at Captain Lip's yard for many years. "My father was the foreman at the upper railway and his name was Clifton Haughwout," says Alese. "His ancestors were originally from Holland and they came over here when New York City was still called New Amsterdam.

"Some of his relatives were in the New York oyster business and they came down this way looking for oysters before the Civil War and that's why they settled in this area.

"There were three cradles on the upper railway, and in 1936 everything got froze in for six weeks. I also remember the 1933 storm. Water came halfway up the hill and floated all the boats off the rails. It did a lot of damage to the two railways.

"I remember a lot of the boats too and I surely remember *Chesapeake* because she was the biggest deck boat they ever built. I remember the night they launched *Chesapeake*," she says. "It was built on the lower railway and it was launched at night on a high tide. I was fifteen or sixteen years old and Mother, Daddy, and I and a lot of other people were there to see her launched.

"A man came by here about ten years ago and said he had the half-model of *Chesapeake,* and I asked him where he got it from because I knew my daddy had given it to Mr. [Rufus] Miles [of J. H Miles and

Company of Norfolk] right after the boat was finished and it was supposed to be in the office of the oyster house in Norfolk. He said he bought it in an antique shop in Nags Head.

"They never used boatbuilding plans that I know of for any of the boats. They just knew what they were doing. They would make the half-model and then take the lines from the model to draw [loft] the boat onto planks that were nailed together on the ground. They would use the drawings as a template to cut the pieces and shape the boat. They lofted the boat on the outside along that long shed that was down by the dock and I watched them a lot because I was always going to the yard to see Daddy.

"They also had a steam box where they would steam those boards to bend them. It was really crude. They had a boiler and they built a fire under the boiler to get the water steaming. There was a pipe from the boiler that went up into the box full of lumber and the steam would go into the box.

"When I was a child, it was a busy place and I think they were doing more maintenance in the 1930s than actually building boats but they built some," she says. "When Captain Lip died, the business didn't last too much longer.

"Daddy loved it down there and he had opportunities to go elsewhere but he never went and that tells you something about the type of man Captain Lip was. He was a decent kind of a man and his railway meant a lot to this little community."

## LINWOOD AND MILFORD PRICE

*James Crittenden of Amburg, Virginia, grew up just down the road from Linwood P. Price, who built some of the "prettiest" deck boats on the Bay. In 1930, right after the start of the Great Depression, Lin Price called upon his neighbor to try and help him out of a hole that he had dug himself into financially simply by not charging enough for his boats.*

*Over a forty-year span, Lin and his son Milford Price built over fifty deck boats and were arguably the most prolific and well-known deck boat builders on the Chesapeake.*

*The information in this section came from a November 8, 2002, interview with Crittenden at his farmhouse in Amburg, Virginia. He was ninety-two years old at the time.*

"I was coming out of church one Sunday morning in 1930 when Mr. Price called me to come back and talk with him. 'I want to see you a minute,' he said. 'I've

Captain Lip Johnson built the 55-foot *Ruby Chrystal* at his yard at Crittenden, Virginia, in 1924. This photo shows the vessel at Alton Smith's Railway at Horn Harbor, Virginia. Courtesy Mildred Stillman.

been watching you and I rented you a boat last year and you did all right with it. I know you got a whole lot more education than I have. How about you coming down to the yard and teach me how to make some money? I can build the boat but I can't make any money.

"I said, 'Mr. Price I'm just a boy but I know enough to know that you can't spend more than you take in,'" Crittenden said. "So when my vegetables were all in, I went to work at the yard as bookkeeper."

Lin Price was born July 29, 1888, in Amburg, Virginia. Public schools in Middlesex County, Virginia, did not start until about the year Lin was born, and in the beginning there were only elementary grades. It's fair to say that he probably received very little formal schooling. James Crittenden had gone to school for eleven years and attended Lynchburg College for a short while.

Price was in the Deltaville area when Ike Thomas brought his skills to the community and shared them with John Wright and others. "Mr. Price learned the deadrise construction from Ike Thomas and the first boat he built was for my father," says James. "It was a 30-foot long oyster boat. He built a few more small oyster boats and then Captain Al Ruark brought him a frame-built buyboat named *Virginia* to be enlarged. Captain Ruark talked to Mr. Price about cutting it in two and making it larger. I was just a boy then and Mr. Price was on Moore Creek in those days. He agreed to do it and he built a railway on the shore there. He took *Virginia* and cut her in two right in the center. I was a little boy and we would go down there and swim in the creek. I was more interested in watching people work than in swimming. I'd sit in the shade and watch. He cut that boat in half and after that he measured the railway 20 feet. He cut the railway in two, then slipped the back part of the railway and the boat down the hill 20 feet. He lined her up with a transit and built 20 feet in her middle. That was his start.

"He built some open boats on Moore Creek off the Piankatank River too. They were for pound-net fishermen from Mathews and Gloucester Counties, and the boats ranged between 42 and 45 feet long. He always built good, strong boats, but he also did something that no one else was doing, not John Wright, not anybody else.

"Mr. Price changed from John Wright and all the others and started using a large filler block to connect the sides and bottom at the chine. The other builders had the sides come down on 2-foot frames, like they do on all deadrise boats. Most fastened an extra double board to the chine, cut the frames so 2 inches would come over the top, and the sides and bottom were bolted to it. Instead, Mr. Price let the frame come down to the bottom; he bolted the board to the frame on the outside and put a 3½ inch chunk so he would have 5½ inches to bolt the bottom and sides to.

"People got used to that boat and that made him very popular," says James. "Soon after that [around 1923] he went to Fishing Bay because he was building big boats and he needed more water to get the boats in and out.

"When I got there, Mr. Price never had any money for himself," says James. "He was drawing about $25 a week and most of the time he would not pay himself. I've seen him go two months and not take a cent. He was paying $4 a day to carpenters and $5 and $6 a day to caulkers. Captain George Benson

was the head caulker. He and his brother had been caulking boats at Humphrey's Railway on Carters Creek, but work got slack over there so they came over here.

"Mr. Price got a break in 1926 and 1927 when he got two orders from W. E. Valliant Company, a fertilizer company that hired him to build the 74-foot *Del-Mar-Va* and the 97-foot *Marydel*. [*Marydel* was named for the states of Maryland and Delaware and was one of the largest deck boats ever built on the Bay.]

"*Marydel* cleared 150 tons and everybody all over the Bay was talking about what a beautiful boat she was," says James.

"The best boat that he built when I was there was for Cliff Evans from Crisfield, Maryland. Cliff was the ugliest human being that you have ever seen on this earth. He would joke about it and say, 'I am an unfinished specimen of humanity.'

"He had bad feet and could hardly walk, but he had learned to make money. He wanted everything around him to be pretty. He was about forty years old when I first knew him and he married this girl who was about twenty-eight and she was a beauty queen. He kept her in Cadillac cars and she'd drive from Crisfield over to Price's to see him.

"When I first met Cliff in Washington, D.C., he had a boat named *City of Crisfield* and he hauled fish to Washington in her. I'd see him when I was there selling watermelons. It was Prohibition and rum-running was a big thing in those days and one of those rum-runners offered Cliff $20,000 for *City of Crisfield*. Cliff was all about money so he said he'd sell it but he had to be paid in cash or gold. They paid him $20,000 in $100 bills. *City of Crisfield* was a frame boat that carried about 60 tons at the most, but she was pretty. Everything Cliff had was pretty.

"After he sold *City of Crisfield* around 1931, he came over to see Mr. Price to get him to build him a boat. I was sitting right in the office when he came and Cliff said, 'Lin Price, I've sold *City of Crisfield* and I want a boat that will carry 80 tons. I want everything to be in style—nothing ugly about her.'

"Mr. Price said, 'Well, Cliff, I haven't built but one ugly boat in my life and that wasn't my fault.'" [Price was referring to *Ruth S.*, which he built for Captain Johnny Stiff in 1927. Price claimed Stiff changed the lines on her in the early morning hours when he was away from the yard. However, most admirers of Chesapeake Bay deck boats consider *Ruth S.* to be a

At Lin Price's yard on Broad Creek, buyboats were sawed in two. The sections were pulled apart, and the gap was filled in with wooden planks and beams to make the boats longer. Courtesy Wessie Price.

good-looking boat, particularly when she was owned by Charlie Pruitt of Tangier Island.]

"'I want it good and I want the best materials in her that money can buy,' says Cliff.

"Mr. Price gave him a price that was way too low. He took so much pride in building his boats right, but he couldn't get the price right. He had a man by the name of Walter Hurley who had gone to Baltimore as a young man and had built rowhouses there after World War I. He was a good carpenter and Mr. Price got him to build the pilothouses on the boats. People talk about the pretty houses on Price boats—well, Walter Hurley was the main man involved in that. Man, he could build a pretty house.

"When Cliff's boat was finished, he put a Caterpillar engine in her. He brought it down himself from Baltimore in the back of a truck and we hooked her up. She even had a sail on her and we hoisted it up on her before she left the dock. They were taking pictures of her with the sail up. Her name was *Betty Ann* when she left but he changed it several weeks later to *Virginia Estelle*.

"I worked for Mr. Price from 1930 to 1933 and during that time Mr. Price built five or six deck boats, 65 to 80 ton boats, in a row. He would build three boats in one year and had all three going at the same time. He got $3,600 for the entire boat [a 65-foot deck boat] not including the engine. There was $2,100 worth of lumber in them. After a year, I got so I could figure what it was going to cost. Mr. Price didn't want to be worried with the cost of things. He studied his work night and day as he built his boats, and he wanted every one to be better than the one before.

"The largest part of my job was to check the sheets of materials used in the buyboats. I had to have

Linwood and Milford Price of Deltaville built *Island Star,* originally named *Frances,* in 1925. The Prices are considered by many to have been the most prolific builders of Chesapeake Bay buyboats on the Bay.

This Coast Guard identification license is one of just a few photos in existence showing Linwood Price in later years. Courtesy Wessie Price.

lumber, spikes, pipe, caulking, cotton, red lead paint, hardware, and many dozen more things ready as the new boats needed them. Materials had to be ordered from Baltimore to come to North End Wharf by steamboat, and then I went down in the truck and picked them up so they would be on hand as each job came in.

"After a couple months or so, I got pretty good at it and almost learned from memory just what I had to have for the size boat that was being built.

"When Milford, his son, came along, he was good with figures and he helped Mr. Price a lot. Milford knew whether he was making money or not and, like Mr. Price, he was a good boatbuilder.

"Mr. Price was born right here in Deltaville and he had two brothers who worked for him every day that I was there," says James. "John Wright and Mr. Price learned to build boats from the same man and Mr. Wright thought Mr. Price was trying to get work from him. It wasn't so. Captain John didn't have but maybe one or two men helping him and Mr. Price had twenty-five men. When Captain John built *Iva W.,* it took him two years to do it. We thought she was going to rot where she was before he finished her.

"Don't get me wrong, Captain John built a good boat, but he didn't have the help that Mr. Price had. I don't know why Captain Johnny [Ward] did not come to Mr. Price for his boat, *Iva W.* Captain Johnny's brother Will Ward had *Virginia Belle* built by Mr. Price [in 1923]. I think that was the first boat Mr. Price built when he went to Fishing Bay. Captain Johnny and Captain John lived so close that maybe he felt he had to go to Captain John. Anyway he got a good boat in *Iva W.*

"The boatbuilding business was a good business because it was year-round work. When the weather was bad there was shop work and Mr. Price always had the boys building skiffs. It was hard to find year-round work in those days.

"Mr. Price only used a blueprint one time in his life and that was for a yacht, but all the deck boats were built from his head. Most of the wood came from Baltimore and the decking came from Norfolk. I remember one of the last loads of lumber we got at Fishing Bay. It was cheap because of the Depression and because there was so much lumber coming in from the West Coast. He bought a boatload of 2½ inch thick by 24- to 36-foot long siding and bottom boards for $27.50 per thousand feet and a 16-inch by

16-inch by 65-foot long keelson for $250. We usually paid $500 for a keelson. The catch was they wanted a certified check and they wanted us to provide a boat to come up alongside their boat to offload the lumber. Captain Tom Johnston went to Baltimore in *Louise J.* and got all that lumber.

"Mr. Price did not convert many boats over from sail to power but he did do *H. H. Conway* on Moore Creek for Captain Johnny Ward. She was a sailing schooner. Mr. Price changed her over from a schooner to a powerboat without hauling her out of the wa-ter. He laid her over on the shore, took the masts and all out of her, and converted her over. I went down to North Carolina and got a truckload of pine flooring and he built the pilothouse out of that."

Lin Price died in 1957 and his son Milford ran the Broad Creek yard until he sold it to Virgil Miller in the 1970s. Price had first built boats on Moore Creek, then at the Fishing Bay yard, then back at Moore Creek when he lost the Fishing Bay yard, and finally at Broad Creek. He and his son were two of the most prolific buyboat builders in the Chesapeake.

*Throughout Maryland and Virginia, boatyards took part in the process of converting sailing vessels to powerboats. One of the more active yards in the Bay region was Deagle and Son Marine Railway in Deltaville, Virginia. Lee Deagle bought the yard and twenty-eight acres on Fishing Bay in 1935, and much of his early work dealt with converting sailboats to powerboats.*

*Unfortunately the master mechanic and railway man passed away in 1989 before this book was started. His son Ed, however, ran the yard with his father for many years and continued to do so for several years after Lee died. He recalls clearly the way it was when internal-combustion engines took the place of wind and sail. Deagle's is a good example of a Chesapeake Bay yard that took advantage of the changing times and profited from the switch from sail to motor power.*

*Powerboats would eventually replace traditional sailing vessels, but the changeover was not abrupt. Steadying sails were still used for years, until engines were developed that were powerful enough to control the boats in heavy seas. Once the larger engines were available, the sails on buyboats were taken down and the era of sailboats used for commercial freight came to an end.*

# 2: THE SWITCH FROM SAIL TO POWER

The problem with the sailing schooner or bugeye was that wind or lack of it could keep a vessel from reaching her destination in a timely manner. An engine-powered deck boat could haul freight from point A to point B within a reasonable and scheduled time frame.

The change from sail to power was completely due to the evolution of the compact internal-combustion engine. Steam engines had been successfully used in boats since 1786 when John Fitch built the first workable steamboat. However, steam power required a large boiler that limited its use to large boats. The average Chesapeake Bay fisherman was working in a 30- to 40-foot workboat—too small for a steam engine. The larger schooners and bugeyes might fit a boiler in the hold, but there would be no room for cargo or payload.

It wasn't until the very early twentieth century that gasoline and diesel engines became commonplace enough that sails began to fade and the engines took over as the main source of power for Bay boats.

At first there was a gentle transition from sail to power. Many captains were skeptical of the new-fangled motors, and understandably so. They cautiously approached the conversion of their boat, which so directly affected their livelihood.

Consequently, the first installation of engines in sail-powered boats changed the appearance of the boats very little. For a short period, engines were installed aft of the centerboard trunk with a long shaft extending aft from the engine to the prop. The boat retained all its original sailboat features including masts, booms, and rigging.

Later, confidence in the internal-combustion engine grew as did the realization that a powerboat could generate more income than a sailboat. The masts, rigging, and centerboard trunks were taken out of two-masted schooners and bugeyes and the standard single mast-and-boom configuration of a traditional buyboat was installed. A deck boat–style pilothouse was also added, but many of the boats continued to show major characteristics of sailboats. Longheads, bowsprits, and outside rudders remained. Bay maritime historian Robert Burgess referred to those early converted boats as "hybrids." As the transition continued, bowsprits and longheads were shortened and finally removed. Many boats carried the schooner-style stern with a large wooden rudder throughout their career as powerboats, while others had a different style stern added.

Other variations could be seen on the oyster dredge fleet of sailing vessels on the Maurice River on Delaware Bay. An early photo in Donald H. Rolf's book *Under Sail—The Dredge Boats of Delaware Bay* shows

Sail-powered bugeyes were converted to power on a regular basis. *Ida Lula* still has her outside rudder from her sailing days. She is an early example of a bugeye conversion. Note the entrance to the engine room. Instead of a full cabin behind the pilothouse, she has a small engine room compartment, a typical style on many early conversions. *Ida Lula*, owned by George L. Smith and Brothers of Sharps, Virginia, was built in 1885 at Somerset County, Maryland, as a sail-powered bugeye. The mate aboard the boat, Harvey Smith, is standing in the pilothouse door. Courtesy James Smith.

two-masted schooners with bowsprits and longheads cut off but still carrying two masts cut down to about half size. The masts and sails ensured a return to port if the engine should fail.

Those with sentimental feelings for the old sailboats looked at these new, often less-than-pretty hybrids, with disgust, but the larger schooner hulls made good powerboats and an average size schooner could carry 7,000 watermelons compared to 4,000 hauled by a 65-foot deck boat. A powered schooner and bugeye could also carry more seed oysters, oyster shells, fertilizer, lumber, grain, coal, road materials, livestock, and other bulk freight.

A new era in maritime history had come to the Chesapeake Bay. And out of this new era came the motor-powered buyboat.

## DEAGLE'S BOATYARD

Ed Deagle of Deltaville, Virginia, was a boy in the late 1930s roaming around his father's railway on Fishing Bay. He watched as some of the largest sailing vessels on the Chesapeake were converted from sail to motorized deck boats.

Lee Deagle, Ed's father, was owner and operator of Deagle and Son Marine Railway. Ed's grandfather, who was also named Ed, was a pioneer in the building of deadrise workboats in the Bay area in the early 1900s, about the time watermen began to switch from log canoes to cross-planked, box-style deadrise boats.

During the 1920s and early '30s, Lee owned a small railway and machine shop located near the public boat dock on Jackson Creek. He made a living doing general repair work on boats and motors and converting sail-driven log canoes to power. The conversion work on these smaller log canoes laid the foundation for Lee to step up to the conversion of larger schooners and bugeyes at his new yard on Fishing Bay.

Ed recalls some of what went on during those early years, "Oh yeah, the Old Man [Lee Deagle] did a lot of conversion work, and what I liked about it

RICHARDSON OYSTER HOUSE AND BOATS. WEST POINT, VA.

Taken around 1915 at George Richardson's Oyster House on the York River in West Point, Virginia, this photo shows two bugeyes that have been converted to power. Some twentieth-century maritime historians referred to these early motor-powered vessels as hybrids because even though they were converted to power, they still had obvious features left over from their sailing days. This particular photo shows a progression of the conversion process. The bugeye on the left carries the original raked mast that was installed when the boat was built as a sailing vessel, stepped forward of the forepeak house. Bugeyes carried two masts so the aft mast of this boat has been removed. She still carries the original bowsprit and longhead on her bow and an outside tiller-style sailing rudder on her stern. Note the top of the mast which was painted white, a standard look on many Bay sailing vessels. On the boat at the right, both original masts have been removed and a shorter, vertical (not raked) mast has been added aft of the forepeak house. The bowsprit has been shortened and the stern appears to have been reconstructed. She looks a little more like the traditional Bay buyboat. Later conversions removed the bowsprit and longhead and different styles of sterns were added. After a while, almost all sailing features were removed. Courtesy Chesapeake Bay Maritime Museum, photograph by R. F. Hargrave, Jr.

were the yawl boats. I was a boy roaming around there and once motors were put in the big boats, they [the owners of the boats] didn't need yawl boats anymore. They would take the motors out of the yawl boats to use or sell and put the boats up on the shore to die so I got all of them. I had yawl boats everywhere. [Powered yawl boats were used to push and pull sail-powered vessels when there was no wind. Most ev-

ery boat converted by the Deagles had a small yawl boat that came along with it.]

## *Chase* (Former Rumrunner)

"The largest boat that we converted over from sail to power was *Chase*. She was about 124 feet long and had been built in Yarmouth, Nova Scotia, in 1921. When she came in here around 1944 somebody else had already taken her [sail] rigging off but we changed her over to power. F. C. Haislip of Harryhogan, Virginia, owned her. He owned a lumber mill and used her to haul wood to Baltimore.

"She had so much draft though that he couldn't get her in the shallow creeks where he was cutting wood. The boat was drawing about 10 or 12 feet of water. My daddy took her and cut the bottom right off her and you'll never guess what he found. She had two bottoms in her. One was a false bottom that left enough space between [it and] the real bottom for plenty of hidden cargo to be stored. She had been used to run rum during Prohibition in the 1920s.

"So the Old Man went in there, pulled both bottoms out of her, framed her right inside the hull; and built a boat inside of a boat. She had a new bottom and keel and we got her down so she only drew about 6 feet of water. We put two engines in her and built a house on her and she was ready to go."

Robert Burgess in his book *Chesapeake Circle* said *Chase* was originally named *Kirk and Sweeney*. She had lived an interesting life prior to arriving at Deagle's. She had been used for running bootleg rum from the Caribbean to Bronx, New York. She and her rum-running crew were eventually captured and the United States Coast Guard confiscated the boat. She was used as a training ship until she incurred severe damage in a 1938 hurricane. Then, *Chase* was sold back into the private sector and was used to haul lumber for many years. She was finally laid to rest to be used as a breakwater at Gratitude near Rock Hall, Maryland, in the early 1960s.

It was not unusual for motor-powered schooners and bugeyes to be used in running illegal spirits during Prohibition. The bugeye *Norma,* built in 1901 by O. Lloyd of Salisbury, Maryland, was converted to power in 1922. Shortly thereafter, the vessel and her crew were caught with $100,000 worth of whiskey and Scotch malt. The United States Coast Guard captured the rumrunners near Salisbury and took *Norma* to Baltimore, where the liquor was confiscated.

## Sarah, Betty I., and *Ida B. Conway*

"The old man converted most of the Conway boats," says Ed. "*Sarah Conway, Betty I. Conway,* and *Ida B. Conway* were three that we converted over to power."

Ed Deagle worked and managed Deagle and Son Marine Railway on Fishing Bay along with his father Captain Lee Deagle. Now retired, Ed builds models of the boats he used to repair. *Bogue Sound* was a frequent visitor to the yard.

Lee Deagle converted many of the Bay's sailboats to motor-powered deck boats at his yard on Fishing Bay. Courtesy Becky Lengua.

*Sarah C. Conway* is shown not long before she was converted to power at Deagle and Son Marine Railway near Deltaville, Virginia. Courtesy Dr. A. L. VanName, Jr.

We did a lot of work over the years for the Conways and on the boats when they were sold later on. [Harvey Conway was the patriarch of the noted family who owned the Conway fleet of sailing vessels. He was from Cambridge, Maryland.]

"The first boat that I remember we completely tore apart and put back together was *Sarah Conway*.

We took the mast, rigging, and everything right out of her. I got the yawl boat out of her and used it for a long time around the yard.

"Most of the sailboats were already partially dismantled by the owners when they came here. Most of the masts and riggings were taken out before they got here but *Sarah [Conway]* sailed in here. I can't re-

Shown here moored at Ocean City, Maryland, in February 1986, the motor-powered *Sarah C. Conway* sank March 6, 1986, in the ocean off Atlantic City, New Jersey, at the ripe old age of 114 years. She was working in the hard clam fishery when she capsized and was lost at sea. The United States Coast Guard rescued four crewmembers.

member yesterday but I can remember that day. She was a beautiful picture coming into Fishing Bay under sail.

"She was owned by Calvert Evans of Cambridge. He brought her down here in 1935. I'll never forget it because I was so impressed with him. He was a young man and handsome and I know that sounds kind of funny but I wondered what he was doing on an old boat. Most captains were old and weathered by that time. He came in, anchored, and came ashore in his yawl boat.

"I'll always remember this story.

"He told my daddy, 'I want to convert her to a powerboat but I don't have any money, Captain.'

"That was 1935 and the Old Man had only had the place for a few months. So the Old Man said, 'Well, I don't [have any money] either.'

"Calvert said, 'Well, Mr. Deagle, if you feel you can do it for me, you will be paid. I promise you that.'

"The Old Man said to him, 'I believe you will.'

"So, we pulled the mast, rigging, and everything out of her and put a Regal engine in her and put the

house on her. Calvert took her away and it wasn't long before he paid Daddy in full.

"After that Calvert Evans was one of the best customers we ever had. No one hauled *Sarah Conway* but Daddy during the years he [Evans] had her. Then there was the time she sank at his dock in 1957. Calvert and his mate Pete were running phosphate rock on *Sarah* from Baltimore to Seaford, Delaware, and picking up a load of grain on the return trip on the Nanticoke River. On this particular trip he stopped off at his home in Vienna, moored at his dock, and went up to his house to spend the night, leaving the cook and his dog asleep in the pilothouse. That night a tugboat came through pushing a barge, and ran right up her stern and pushed through to the pilothouse. *Sarah Conway* sank, drowning both Pete, the old mate and cook, and Calvert's dog Sport. He got the boat up, brought her to us, and we rebuilt her again.

"He later sold her to Captain Rick Salvage of Ocean City, Maryland. Rick used her to go offshore in the Atlantic Ocean dredging clams. She got caught in

Even after her conversion, the schooner-style stern on *Sarah C. Conway* remained intact.

*Harriet C. Whitehead* gave Captain Lee Deagle his start at his new boatyard. She was the first boat he rebuilt when he moved to the Fishing Bay yard in 1935. Courtesy Dr. A. L. Van Name Jr.

a snag that pulled her over, and she sank and was lost in 1986.

"We also converted *Betty I. Conway*. She had been stripped, so there was no sail on her. Captain Buck Sherman owned her. We rebuilt her and put a new house on her. Captain Buck had already pulled the rigging out up in Cambridge.

"To convert these boats, we would bore the shaft log; back aft where the sternpost comes down, we'd take that old big rudder off and we had a boring bar that we would bore a hole right through, then we'd put a sleeve in it for the shaft. The bearing would pass right through the end of the sternpost and a lot of times my daddy would cut the sternpost off and put in one that went all the way through to the deck for more stability. Then you moved your rudder stop back aft of the wheel. We had to make the house. We made a trunk or raised deck and the house would set on that. We put a double-decker house on *Betty I. Conway* and *Sarah Conway*."

*Sarah Conway* was built in 1872 as the *A. H. Schulz* in Baltimore, Maryland. *Betty I. Conway* was built in Stony Point, New York, in 1866 and started life as the two-masted schooner *George S. Allison. Ida B. Conway* was built as *William Layton* on the Nanticoke River in Maryland in 1873. She was converted by Deagle in 1947 and was renamed *John J. Crouch*.

## Harriet C. Whitehead

The schooner *Harriet C. Whitehead*, built in Waterford, Connecticut, in 1892, was converted to power during World War II in Cambridge, Maryland. *Whitehead* was one of the largest schooners on the Chesapeake at 120 feet long. Although Deagle's did not convert her to power, she was the first boat Lee Deagle rebuilt at his new yard in 1935, and it set the stage for many conversions in years to come.

Ed recalls the story of the first job his father had. "When *Whitehead* first came, the cradle on our railway was off the track," says Ed. "Daddy had just bought the railway but didn't have money enough to pay any men to help him. The railway was also in disrepair. So, Daddy told the men in the neighborhood that any man who wanted to come work should come in, and when he got some money from the *Whitehead* job he would pay them. He also told them that if they came right away, he'd guarantee them a job as long as they wanted.

*Mollie V. Leonard* was the second largest bugeye built on the Bay. F. Cantwell of Cambridge, Maryland, built her in 1904. She was the first bugeye on the Bay to have a patent stern installed. Courtesy Dr. A. L. Van Name, Jr.

"A crowd of men came here, pulled the tracks up, and jacked her up and got the roller boxes back under the cradle," says Ed. "When *Whitehead* came in, she was so wide she wouldn't go between the two piers between the railway. So, Daddy had to pull the docks up.

"I've heard this story so many times. *Whitehead* was the first large boat he had ever hauled. Daddy pulled the boat up and when he started to haul her the [cross] ties [on the railway] started breaking. You see all these old sailboats were hogged. A hog is when an old boat starts bending from the stem to the stern and it droops.

"When you know how much hog you got, you can go in there and block her up on the cradle so when she comes out of the water she comes down on the railway and the weight is evenly distributed on the cradle. The old man didn't know how much she was hogged and she was sitting so all the weight was on the bow and on the stern and there was no weight in the middle, so when he started to haul the boat and it got to the hog, the boat would drop down and the force of the boat broke a cross tie on the railway and damaged the boat. Finally, I think she broke two or three, and on the last one she broke the old man's

nerves, so he gave up and screamed, 'Stop her right there!' He thought he was going to ruin the boat and his railway too, and he wouldn't have money to get her back overboard.

"So, he walked around shore and went over to Ruark, Virginia, where there was an old steamboat dock and ferry on Fishing Bay and where there was a little store where an old man named Ruark sold Arrow beer. Daddy sat down in the store and drank two beers to get his nerve back.

"He walked back around here and when he got about halfway over here the beers started taking effect, and he yelled, 'Take her ahead'!

"By that time the tide was up and she floated with the tide until she came down and sat on the cradle.

"The joke was that those two cans of beers brought her right up on the hill.

"After that job, he was able to pay his first-class caulkers forty cents an hour and that was top wages. He also kept his promise and several of the men stayed and worked at the railway the rest of their lives."

*Harriet C. Whitehead* was later lost at sea in a hurricane after leaving the West Indies with a load of sugar.

The planked bugeye *O. A. Bloxom,* built in 1901 by J. T. Marsh of Solomons, Maryland, was at Deagle's railway in Deltaville in 1991 for repairs. Her round stern was installed at Deagle's in 1948.

## A. Booth

"We had one boat come in here the year the Chesapeake Bay froze solid. It must have been 1938. It was a boat called *A. Booth* and it had come in before the freeze but we couldn't put her on the railway because we already were working on one," says Ed. "That winter Fishing Bay froze solid as far as you could see and when we finished the boat we had on the railway we couldn't get it off to start *A. Booth* and besides *A. Booth* was stuck in the ice. So Daddy took a crew of men with crosscut saws and sawed a wide groove of ice out right up against the bank and they floated *A. Booth* up close to the bank. We literally rebuilt that boat standing on the ice.

"There was this old big oak tree on top of that hill. [Ed pointed over towards the railway. The giant oak tree is still standing.] They ran the halyard from the tree to a donkey engine on *A. Booth* that had been used to pull the sails up. They used the engine to help raise the boat up and we tilted her over by pulling on that tree. We were able to rebuild and frame one side of her about two or three feet below the waterline. After we replaced the planks and frames, we caulked her, painted her, let her back down in the water, then pulled her up on the other

side and did the same thing. I remember that. That was a job."

T. Kirby, a Baltimore oyster packer, built *A. Booth* in 1880 in Talbot County, Maryland. During World War II she was converted to power [not by Deagle's] and was operating out of Miami, Florida, in 1947. She was finally sold and moved to Costa Rica.

## Bugeye O. A. Bloxom

*O. A. Bloxom* was built in 1901 at the James T. Marsh Shipyard on Solomons Island, Maryland, and was first named *Nora Phillips.* A 1908 listing of documented working vessels on the Chesapeake described *Nora Phillips* as a two-masted sailing bugeye, 75 feet long and 21 feet wide.

During her early years, she was used to haul grain and lumber up and down the Bay. Captain Harry Porter of Kent Island, Maryland, was captain of her around 1922 when she was converted to power. A diesel engine and a small pilothouse were installed and she was used mostly to buy oysters. Her name changed in the 1940s to *O. A. Bloxom,* after which she was bought by Ballard Fish and Oyster Company of Norfolk. She was used by Ballard to buy James River seed from public beds and

This close-up look shows the patent stern configuration on the bugeye *John Branford*. The patent stern was invented and patented in 1908 by Captain Joseph E. Robbins of Cambridge, Maryland. Courtesy Dr. A. L. Van Name, Jr.

to harvest seed and to dredge market-size oysters from Ballard's private oyster grounds. Ballard had one of the largest shucking houses in the Bay region with over two hundred shuckers.

In 1948, *Bloxom* arrived at Deagle's for a complete rebuilding. She still had the bugeye-style stern and bow—pointed at both ends. Deagle's installed a round stern on her and cut her in two and lenghtened *Bloxom* to 84 feet.

Deagle's also installed patent sterns on bugeyes. In 1908 Captain Joseph E. Robbins of Cambridge, Maryland, invented and patented a design that provided a means for supporting the pipe davits on the bugeye's pointed stern. It was originally just framework, but later planking was installed between the frames to give more deck space, wrote Robert H. Burgess in *Chesapeake Sailing Craft*. Ed says many bugeye owners wanted a round stern but the patent stern required less structural change to the boat and was less costly.

"The story goes that when the owner of *O. A. Bloxom* asked the Old Man what his boat would look like with a round stern, he sat down on a fish box up on the hill, took a stick, and drew a picture on the ground of how the boat would look," says Ed. "And then he had his men do it."

In 1991, *O. A. Bloxom* was back at Deagle's for a final going over before leaving for Florida, where she was going to be used to haul frozen food and other supplies from Ft. Lauderdale to the West Indies.

## OTHER CONVERSIONS

### Bateau *Nannie*

*Nannie* was a prime example of a small sailing bateau converted to a powered deck boat. She shows that not all the conversions involved large, over-70-foot sailboats. Deagle's did not do the conversion on *Nannie*, although the work was done at the same yard when Linwood Price owned the Fishing Bay boatyard in 1919.

According to the book *Family Histories of Middlesex County*, David Andrew Taylor was born May 15, 1847, in Accomack County, Virginia, on the Eastern Shore. Captain Dave left the Eastern Shore as a young man and sailed to Stingray Point near Deltaville. There he met Nannie Elizabeth Saunders. They fell in love and were married on April 18, 1872. Captain Dave owned three sailing vessels that he used to haul

Logged and planked bugeyes were built throughout the Chesapeake Bay region. *O. A. Bloxom* was obviously a planked bugeye as the stem-to-stern bottom planking is visible in this photo.

Near Deltaville, Virginia, Linwood Price converted the bateau *Nannie* to power in 1919. She was a good example of a small sailing vessel converted to power. She measured only 45 feet long. This photo of her stem line was taken in a winter freeze in 1981 on Lagrange Creek at Remlik, Virginia. She was owned then by J. W. Ferguson Seafood and was being used to haul and dredge for oysters.

lumber, railroad ties, and other cargo. He owned a two-masted schooner, *Elizabeth Ann,* a three-masted schooner, *Lillie O. Wells,* and a sailing bateau that he named *Nannie* after his beloved wife.

The documentation on *Nannie* says the boat was converted to power and rebuilt by Price in 1919. There is no mention of where the boat was originally built, but in 1981 then owner of *Nannie* J. W. (Buster) Ferguson said he thought she was built on the Eastern Shore of Virginia.

In 1919, the square stern of *Nannie* was rounded, and her first engine was installed. In 1981, the original square stern configuration was still visible within the round stern.

That same year, said Robert Taylor of Deltaville (grandson of Captain Dave), his grandfather used *Nannie* to haul oysters, watermelons, and potatoes to Washington, D.C., and Baltimore.

Taylor says *Nannie* was originally a 36-foot bateau, powered by sail. She was cut in two by Price and lengthened until she reached 53 feet in length.

Taylor can remember being aboard *Nannie* as a boy, sailing up the Bay toward Baltimore with a cargo of potatoes. The auxiliary sail was tight with wind.

"She had a square auxiliary sail that helped to keep her steady," says Taylor. "There was an old 14

Near the wharf of Marshall's Oyster House in West Point, Virginia, in the late 1920s, two deck boats are drying their sails. The boat to the right of the town's flour mill is the converted bugeye *A. W. Ruark*, then owned by George K. Carlton of West Point. The other boat is a deck boat used as a tug to tow barges full of logs from Elizabeth City, North Carolina, to a veneer plant in West Point. The boats had evidently been through a storm, and the sails were wet. They were raised in an effort to dry them out to prevent mildew and rot. Courtesy Van Name/Perry collection.

hp Regal engine in her with a 1:1 ratio, straight drive, and a 30-inch by 30-inch prop. My grandfather ran a many a watermelon and potato on her," he says.

Ferguson bought *Nannie* in 1941 and used her until his oyster business closed in the late 1980s. A new 3-71 Detroit Diesel was installed for power in 1981, the fourth engine Ferguson installed in her. After one winter of dredging with the Regal, a Chrysler Imperial was mounted and, in later years, two Chrysler Crowns were installed at different intervals.

## Schooner *Lula M. Phillips*

Built in 1877 at Oxford, Maryland, the sail-driven schooner *Annie M. Leonard* became the powered deck boat *Lula M. Phillips*. As a sailing schooner she was rebuilt in Bethel, Delaware, in 1913. She was converted to a powered deck boat in the 1930s.

Lynn Perry of Urbanna, Virginia, knows some of her history because his grandfather bought her at public auction in the 1920s to settle an estate. Lynn wrote a short history of *Phillips* as he recalled it in 1996.

"My grandfather Vandallia Perry was president of the Peoples National Bank in Salisbury, Maryland, from 1903 to 1923. The schooner *Lula M. Phil-*

*lips* was to be sold at public auction to settle an estate.

"Captain George Carlton of West Point, Virginia, wanted the schooner and knew of the sale, but had to take the steamboat from West Point to Baltimore and the train from Baltimore to Salisbury. As a result he did not arrive in time for the sale. My grandfather met Captain Carlton at the train and asked if he was still interested in *Phillips* as he had bought her but would have no trouble getting his money as several people were interested.

"Captain Carlton wanted the boat and thanked my grandfather for what he had done for him. I was living in West Point with my parents and when my grandfather would come to visit, Captain Carlton would often take a group of us out for a sail on the York River.

"Captain Carlton employed Captain Snow Parsons of Chincoteague, Virginia, as master of *Phillips,* and for a number of years she was used as a buyboat to buy oysters from James River hand tongers. The boat then was used to run oysters from the James "up the beach" to Rhode Island. In the early 1930s, Captain Carlton had *Phillips* converted to a powerboat. He used her to haul oysters from James River to Rhode Island until he sold her to Captain Will Ward of Deltaville in the mid-1930s.

Winegar's Marine Railway in Lancaster County, Virginia, was a busy place in the 1920s. A deck boat at the dock has a sail raised to dry it out. Courtesy Cathy Winegar Davenport.

The boats mentioned in this chapter are representative of the types of boats that were converted from sail to power. The appendix of this book shows over 150 sailboats that were changed, and there were probably twice that many or more. Yards up and down the Bay were involved.

## MOTOR-POWERED BUYBOATS UNDER SAIL

*I was well aware that even after motors were installed, for a while sails were used on the Bay buyboats. There are, however, very few photos of deck boats with "steadying sails" raised, so when this project was first conceived, I felt it would be difficult to find good representative photos showing sail and motor used together in the early years.*

*One of the first places I went to look was in the photo collections of Lynn Perry and Dr. A. L. Van Name. Both photographed many of the sailing vessels that came and went in West Point, Virginia, where they grew up in the 1920s. Flipping through album page after album page at Lynn's home in Urbanna, Virginia, I saw schooners, rams, and bugeyes under sail or moored in a harbor, but no "combination" boats. I was*

*about to give up when we came to the very last page of the last album.*

*"What's this?" I asked.*

*Lynn looked over my shoulder and said, "Oh yeah, I had forgotten about that."*

*The photo showed two deck boats with sails raised to dry after a storm. The boats are moored at the dock at Marshall's Oyster House in West Point sometime in the late 1920s.*

*"Doc took that one probably at the end of a roll that he needed to finish off," says Lynn. "He was probably out in his skiff with his camera after a schooner that was underway."*

*Sometimes those last frames at the end of a roll prove to be the best frames. Since sail and power were used together for such a short time period, Dr. Van Name's end-of-the-roll photo shown in this chapter documents a time in Chesapeake Bay maritime history that is seldom mentioned and rarely seen.*

## Lynn Perry

Lynn Perry sailed aboard several of the old sailing schooners and watched as motors replaced sail. In a 2001 interview at his home in Urbanna, he recalled that both sails and motors powered the early deck boats.

"*Lula M. Phillips* was one of the first schooners that I remember being converted over to power," says Lynn. "It was around 1929 or 1930 and she was owned in West Point. *W. J. Matthews* was [converted] after that in 1934 but they were two of the first that I remember. Prior to that, John Wright in Deltaville and others were building these box boats, as they called them. They were deck boats under 65 feet long. If they were 65 feet or over they had to have a licensed captain so they were building them around 62 to 64 feet and that's why so many were built just under 65 feet," he says.

"The converted-to-power schooners could take as much in one load as the little freight boats could take in two or three loads," says Lynn. "The schooners were in demand but the little boats were freighting too and had as much work as they could do. They usually carried one sail that they called a steadying sail. It helped keep the boat steady while underway. Converted schooners also kept a sail. When converted over to power, schooner masts were pulled out and a smaller mast and boom was installed for a smaller gaff-style sail. The mast had a dual purpose. It was used to carry the sail but it was also used to hoist tubs full of oysters up from the smaller oyster tong boats onto the deck of the buyboat.

"Early gasoline engines were not powerful enough to push the schooners very fast so even though there were motors early on, it took a while for them to get big enough to push a schooner. Prior to 1900, the sailing schooners had to have men in the crew to raise the sails, get the anchor up, and the yawl boat was powered by a pair of oars and they would row the lines ashore [if the boat was unable to land at a dock, men on shore would pull the boat ashore] and if they had a fair tide they could put the yawl boat out with a couple men with oars in it under the bow for steerage to help get her underway.

"Once the engine came out, they put one on deck and used it to raise the anchor and sails and they also put a pumping engine on them. All the old boats leaked so this eliminated hand pumping. This also eliminated about two crewmembers. Prior to engines there was a captain, mate, two crewmembers and a cook aboard the schooners. After the deck engines came along, two crewmembers were eliminated.

"The first [motorized] yawl boats had single cylinder, up to 7 horsepower engines with no clutch. They were two-cycle [burns oil and gas together] and

Taken in the 1930s, this photo shows a deck boat loaded down with freight and its sail raised. Courtesy Betty Burton.

you could hear them pop, pop, popping way off in the distance, but they would run all day long. They were dependable.

"Then gasoline engines got a little more advanced. They built a four-cycle engine, just like in a car, with a clutch. They started at 12 horsepower and went up to around 24 horsepower. This is when the conversions of schooners and the construction of new deck boats sort of took off.

"Not all schooners could be converted over," he says. "The hull had to be strong enough to support doing it. If the hull was old and hogged, it wouldn't work. *Lula M. Phillips* had a good hull and *W. J. Matthews* was all right. These boats were used to run seed oysters from the James River up to Providence, Rhode Island, for many years and they were great competitors. They were used as buyboats for oysters but they were also used for freighting lumber, grain, and railroad ties."

*W. J. Matthews* was originally the schooner *Dorchester*, built at Madison, Maryland, in 1882.

## Captain Paul Pruitt

The late Paul E. Pruitt of Urbanna, Virginia (and formerly of Tangier Island) worked as a young man with his father Captain Edward Pruitt of Tangier Island aboard a seven-log deck boat named *Three Brothers*. She was built in Poquoson, Virginia, in 1922 and

The late Paul E. Pruitt, captain and owner of the deck boat *P. E. Pruitt,* bought his sails from a sailmaker in Crisfield, Maryland, the same year he had the boat built—1935. *P. E. Pruitt* is presently at Rock Hall, Maryland, moored in front of a restaurant that is named P. E. Pruitt.

*Iva W.*, built in 1929 by Captain John Wright of Deltaville, Virginia, for his neighbor Captain Johnny Ward, carried 105 square yards of sail. About 1945, when motors were powerful and dependable enough for watermen to no longer need a steadying sail, Captain Johnny did away with his sail. He was one of the last captains to do so. Courtesy Robert W. Jensen.

named after Captain Ed's three sons, Paul, Charlie, and Stanley. Paul later owned the 59-foot *P. E. Pruitt,* and both boats carried a sail and an engine.

In a 1985 interview, Paul said the traditional buyboat had a square sail measuring 16 feet on the gaff. "It was a lot prettier than a sharp [jib-headed] sail," says Paul, who had his sail for *P. E. Pruitt* made at a loft in Crisfield. "We'd hoist it sometimes going across the Bay," he recalls. "But those sails were right much trouble. When there would come a hard summer rain, they'd mildew if we didn't get them up soon to dry.

"When we got decent power, most everyone stopped using sail," says Paul. "It would help, though, to keep the boat steady and to keep her from rolling. It also helped her go."

In addition to her sail, P. E. Pruitt had a three-cylinder, 36-horsepower Lathrop—"one of the best ever made," according to Paul. "I once ran her from North Carolina to Baltimore in thirty-eight hours freighting watermelons, and she was steady plucking."

## Captain Johnny Ward

In 1928, the late Captain Johnny Ward of Deltaville, Virginia, had Deltaville boatbuilder John Wright build the 60-foot buyboat *Iva W.* In a 1985 interview, Captain Johnny said he had Wright build the boat for $2,350—not including the engine, sail, and the wheel in the pilothouse.

"I paid twenty-two dollars for this wheel, and he made the spool and stand," says Captain Johnny. A brass plate on the mahogany wheel read "American Engineer Co., Philadelphia, Pa."

"I've put in many an hour on this wheel," he said. That was obvious from the smoothly worn wooden handles. Shiny brass handles had replaced two of the wooden ones that had broken off.

There was a clear tone of pride in his voice when he talked about his *Iva W.* "You see all that trim in here [inside the pilothouse]. That's all white oak, and when it was new it was just as bright as a silver dollar.

"Before I had this 115-horsepower Caterpillar installed, I had a 60-horsepower Atlas engine and used an auxiliary sail in *Iva W,*" he says. Before the Atlas, Captain Johnny had a four-cylinder Regal engine, which also required the use of sail.

"There was 105 yards of sail on her, and I kept the sail until around 1945 when I put the Caterpillar in her. The sail had rotted, so I decided not to buy another one."

## Captain Melvin Ward—Sails in a Bathtub

Captain Johnny's oldest son Melvin recalls clearly when sails were used on deck boats. Melvin was captain and mate aboard many of the boats his family owned, including *Muriel Eileen, Ruth S., Nora W.* (originally named *Amanda C.*), *Ward Bros.* (earlier named *Andrew J. Lewis*) and two named *Thomas W.,* which had been *P. E. Pruitt* and *Midland;* and there were others.

"All my father's boats had sail in the early going and we used them practically all the time," says Melvin. "You take *Muriel Eileen,* she had one. If you were going to Baltimore, and you were to put up your sail in a fair wind, she would steer better. It would give us a little bit more speed but the main thing was she would steer better and keep the boat steady.

"Daddy would get his sails made in Baltimore. There was a sail loft near Vane Brothers ship chandlers and that's where Daddy had his sails made. [Vane Brothers was located on Pratt Street in Baltimore and was one of the largest ship chandlers on the Bay.] When we got more power in the boats, sails were more hindrance than they were good. It was some trouble to put them up and they had to be dried after every storm because they would mildew and rot.

"Once a year, sails had to be taken off the boat and my father would take a 16-foot skiff, fill it with lime water, and soak the sails in it for several days. It would bleach the sails out white. It was like a big bathtub. It would take the mildew and all the stains out and make them look like new. My father did not like stuff looking bad. He did this in the off-season, right before watermelon season started in June. That was the time we would paint the boats up too."

Once engines were large enough to power the deck boats loaded down with freight, the auxiliary sail began to disappear. Many captains, however, kept a sail handy just in case there were problems with the engine. In case of a breakdown, a sail could help them get close enough to shore to get some help. However, when the sails rotted out over time and engines became more reliable, they were not replaced and thus ended a short era on the Chesapeake Bay when sail and motor worked together.

*I was aware at a fairly young age that a group of small log canoes had been built specifically for engine power. There was one on Urbanna Creek that I admired well into the 1980s. These motor-powered log boats were the last generation of log canoes. Though the original canoes dated back even prior to English settlement, this last group of boats never carried a sail and were powered by motor. The era did not last long as cross-planked-bottom deadrise workboats became the vessel of choice for most Bay watermen.*

*However, log canoes were built in the Poquoson, Seaford, and Dare areas of Virginia on a steady basis well into the 1940s—the last one being built in Poquoson in 1988. When I started research for this book, one of my first thoughts was that large log boats, other than log bugeyes, had been built specifically as powered deck boats. I was right.*

# 3: LOG DECK BOATS

The Chesapeake Bay log canoe was the earliest workboat used in the New World. Log boats, made from single trees, were being built and used by Indians when the settlers arrived in 1607. At first, early colonists used one- and two-log canoes as much for transportation as for working the water.

The development of the Bay log canoe as a commercial workboat is closely tied to the oyster fishery. When the colonists first came to America, oysters were in such abundance along shorelines that settlers, Indians, and slaves could walk out into the water and pick up enough for mealtime. As the population began to grow, oysters along the shore became depleted to the point that small canoes were built and used by watermen to work in deeper water.

Hand tongs were introduced on the Chesapeake around 1702, and by 1760 a professional oyster fishery had come into being in the Bay. The vessels of choice for those early fishermen were dugout log canoes, sharp at both ends, perhaps 18 to 20 feet long. Colonial oystermen supplied taverns, inns, and individuals in local communities with shellfish.

The coming of the New England schooners altered the business methods on the Bay. The oyster fishery in the northeast was far more advanced than

that of the Chesapeake and by 1800, New Englanders had overfished their own waters and were looking to the Chesapeake to supply seed and oysters to replenish grounds off Long Island and elsewhere.

First, the New England schooner captains bought oysters from Bay tongers. But this process was too slow, so they introduced the oyster dredge to the Chesapeake Bay and caught what they wanted in a hurry. The dredge changed forever the way oysters were caught in the Bay, and it was the reason for the development of the next generation of log canoes, the coasting canoe, which evolved to meet the specific needs of Bay watermen. Fishermen had used open log canoes for years, but as they ventured farther from home and began to use the heavy dredge to harvest oysters, the need for a larger boat was obvious. The 20- and 25-foot boats were too small, and demand grew for 35- and 40-foot canoes. M. V. Brewington described the coasting canoe in his book *Chesapeake Bay Bugeyes* as a 35- to 40-foot vessel with a tiny hunting cabin in the bow.

Brewington also described the brogan as the next stage in log canoe development. "The characteristics which distinguished the brogan from the canoe were solely size and interior arrangement. The hull had grown to an average length of 40 to 50 feet. In her construction the washboards had become real pieces of deck and the open body of the canoe had been divided by bulkheads and covered with hatches."

The log bugeye was the next development in sailing log boats. These boats were over 50 feet and made from at least seven and possibly up to thirteen logs. Brewington wrote that bugeyes had framed topsides and were carvel-built and planked up to the deck. The entire body was decked over except for a small cabin forward of the hatches. Even though Virginia builders were extremely active in log canoe building and built a few bugeyes, Maryland builders excelled in building the larger log and planked bugeyes.

Though not mentioned by Brewington, the last stage in log canoe development on the Chesapeake was the motor-powered deck boat, which was made two different ways. These engine-powered log boats were not converted bugeyes, but were log hulls—45 feet and over—made from seven or more logs. The boats were powered by early gas engines and carried a traditional deck boat steadying sail.

Boatbuilder Joe Conboy worked for Milford Price at Price's yard on Broad Creek in Deltaville in the early 1960s, and he also built boats for many years on Robinson Creek near Urbanna, Virginia. While at Price's he worked on several log boats. Conboy says the hulls of the powered log boats were built identical to the traditional Chesapeake Bay log canoe.

For instance, in the case of a five-log canoe, there is a center keel log with two garboard logs attached to the keel log and two bilge or chine logs attached to the garboard logs. Chunks are used to lengthen the hull from the bilge log to the stem and stern. The larger log boats simply had more logs. Some boats had as many as thirteen logs.

Virginia log buyboats were often called "chunk boats." When watermen call a log boat a "chunk boat," they are referring to chunks of wood used as "raising wood" (side planking), which raises the height of the sides. On Virginia boats chunk side logs or planks are laid down on top of the chine log and are attached to knees that abut and are attached to the chine log. Once the first layer of chunks is laid, a second layer is then laid on top of the first and so on until the proper height is obtained. Side chunks are the same width as the top of the chine log.

Another feature of frame and box-built deadrise buyboats pertains to chunk construction and goes

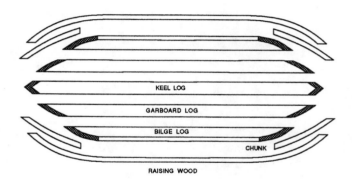

This drawing shows the general construction of a five-log canoe with chunks installed in the bow and stern. Some of the largest log deck boats were built with thirteen logs. Virginia-built vessels were called chunk boats because of side chunks used to raise the sides. Drawing by Ray V. Rodgers III.

back to that heritage—a chunk-built round stern. This style of construction is a throwback to log canoe building and is similar to the process of building chunk sides on large log boats. It consists of a number of chunks of wood layered to shape a round stern. Once the bottom layer is attached, the next layer of chunks is positioned so that the top chunk covers the seam where the chunks abut on the bottom layer. Watermen refer to this style of stern as a chunk stern. Most round stern deck boats have chunk sterns, though a few have staved sterns.

K. T. Smith of Smith Marine Railway in Dare, Virginia, says he worked on Virginia and Maryland motor-powered log boats at his family's vintage 1842 railway. He confirmed that most Virginia-built boats were chunk built, but Maryland builders, who knew a lot about planks from building planked bugeyes, built hulls from logs and used 2½-inch thick planks for sides. Notches were cut in the logs so frames could be fitted and side planking could be attached flush to the outside of the chine log. Neither style was unusual at his railway and he worked on as many plank sided log boats as chunk sided. "It just depended on where the boats were built," he says. "If they were chunked, we knew they probably were built in Virginia, and if they were planked they came from Maryland."

Throughout the nineteenth century, Bay boatbuilders used logs instead of board planks in boat construction because there was very little sawed lumber. Before gasoline-powered engines and electricity

Chunk construction on round sterns like this one on *Nellie Crockett* was a throwback to log canoe days. Most Virginia-built round-stern deck boats had a chunk-built stern.

were available, sawed lumber had to be pit-sawed by hand. Pit-sawed lumber was made by digging a pit and having one man in the hole and another man up top to work a two-man rip saw. Although there was a lot of waste using logs to build boats, it was less time-consuming and less work to cut down a tree for a log than to pit-saw enough planks for a boat. Sawed lumber was available by the 1920s, when powered log deck boats were being built. However, construction of these boats was confined to areas where log canoe building was a tradition, which played a role in the continuation of log boatbuilding.

It should also be noted that there are advantages to log vessels. Logs are thick and tough. When oysters, fish, and crabs were stored in a boat's hold, a metal shovel would hardly dent a log bottom, whereas over time a shovel might damage a planked bottom. In addition, log boats were lower to the water, making it better for oyster and crab dredging, because high-sided deck boats required more time and effort by watermen to fish and empty the catch onto the deck. Along with this, log boats could do everything else that a deadrise deck boat could do.

The motor-powered log deck boat marked the end of a maritime era on Chesapeake Bay that predated English colonization. Although fewer of these boats were built than cross-planked deadrise deck boats, these unique boats are very much a part of the history of Bay buyboats.

## STEVE PRUITT

"There were right many of those log or chunk boats on the Bay," says Steve Pruitt, who was born and raised on Tangier Island. "We called some of the canoes chunk canoes. The sides, bows, and sterns were made from chunks of logs and put together just like a jigsaw puzzle. There were others with planked sides. We just called them log boats. The plank sided log boats were built in Maryland."

### Early Log Boats

"Most Virginia log deck boats were built down in Poquoson, Dare, and Seaford," says Steve. "One that came from that area was *F. D. Crockett*. She was named for her owner, Ferdinand Desoto Crockett of

*Facing page: Dewey* was built in 1912 at Elliott, Maryland. Here she is in 1966 as part of the Tangier Island, Virginia, crab-dredging fleet. Note her stem line as compared to that of *Nellie Jane,* a box boat built in 1939 near Deltaville. The stem on *Dewey* is oval whereas the stem line on *Nellie Jane* is almost vertical. A close inspection of *Dewey* also reveals stem-to-stern side planking, a characteristic of Maryland-built log buyboats. Courtesy Lewis Parks.

This photo of Tangier Harbor in 1949 shows several buyboats. The double-ender log boat *Mary Jane*, second boat in the slip behind the handprinted "Tangier Island, Va.," was carrying a bowsprit. Some early log boat builders installed a bowsprit on these motor-powered log deck boats for looks and also to provide more tie-down space for lines. Courtesy Lewis Parks.

Seaford. He owned a lot of oyster shore down that way and he was my grandmother's brother.

"*Three Brothers, Edward M., Ethel L.,* and *Mary Jane* were all log boats around Tangier Island. Wallace Pruitt of Onancock owned *Edward M.* He was originally from Tangier. *Edward M.* had a log hull and a beautiful round stern on her. She was used for crab dredging in the wintertime and hauling watermelons in the spring and summer. *Three Brothers* was not as pretty because the stern was so long and it stuck way out. *Ethel L.* was a round stern canoe and she had a pretty stern too.

*Mary Jane* was a log boat and she was pointed on both ends. The early ones were double-enders or pointed on both ends but in later years they put round sterns on them. I don't think *Mary Jane* was ever under sail even though she carried a short bow-

sprit for a while. I think even after sail was gone, some builders continued to put a short bowsprit on the boats for looks as much as anything else. [*Mary Jane* was built in Salisbury, Maryland, in 1909 and would have been one of the early powered log boats.]

"*Mary Jane* was named after Mary Jane Wheatly and she recently passed away in a home up in Baltimore," says Steve. "Charlie Wheatly owned *Mary Jane* and he ran crabs in her from Dymer Creek on the Northern Neck of Virginia to Crisfield. She was on Tangier forever and used for a lot of different things. She also ran passengers and freight.

"Another log boat was *Lizzie* and no one on Tangier wanted her because of her name. You wouldn't want to go into Tangier with a boat named *Lizzie* because they would make fun of you bad. There was *Web* and *Dewey. Web* was a chunk boat but another one,

This 1966 photo of *Mary Jane* shows that the bowsprit seen on the 1949 Tangier Harbor photo has been removed. The boat was used on Tangier Island to haul passengers and supplies. The open, high rail that runs around the entire boat is typical of a deck boat used to haul passengers. Also, the boat has been "placed in a coffin": the spots along the hull reveal that metal has been installed either to keep ice from damaging the hull while underway in freezing weather or to help stop it from leaking. Courtesy Lewis Parks.

*Dewey,* was a plank sided log boat built in Maryland. She had a round stern." [*Dewey* was built in 1912 at Elliott, Maryland, by Lyman Ewell and measured 55 feet 2 inches. Watermen on Tangier and Smith Island owned *Dewey* at different times.)

## Old Point

"*Old Point* was another one. A fellow on the Eastern Shore owned her at one time. One day, I was over on the railway at Fairport, [Virginia] and the *Old Point* pulled up. When he [the captain] shot up to the dock in *Old Point,* he must have been two-thirds drunk because he ran right into the dock," says Steve.

*Old Point* is still alive and is one of the feature displays at the Chesapeake Bay Maritime Museum in St.

Michaels, Maryland. Their research states that J. G. Wornom of Poquoson built *Old Point* in 1909 for J. I. and George C. Wainwright. The Wainwrights must have owned her for just a short while because she was owned and worked by the Bradshaw family of Hampton, Virginia, from 1913 to 1956. The Bradshaws used *Old Point* to dredge crabs in the winter, freight fish in the summer, and haul and plant seed oysters from the James River during the fall.

In 1956, *Old Point* was sold to the Old Dominion Crab Company, which used her for winter crab dredging. At some time after 1956, *Old Point* suffered a fire in the bow that destroyed the forepeak. Some charred frames are still visible; the damaged portion of her logs was filled with Portland cement. This was a typical cure for boats with damaged or soft wood, but often times not a long-term cure. In 1968, *Old Point* was sold to Norman F. Williams, who changed her name to *Miss Terry*. She passed through several other ownerships, being used for freight and excursions in the Caribbean until Mr. and Mrs. Richard C. Du Pont donated her in 1984 to the museum.

## Working on Log Boats

Steve Pruitt worked aboard several of the log boats on Tangier. His first job during the summer between his eighth and ninth grades in school was aboard the chunk canoe *Lester*. "*Lester* was owned by Elisha [Lish] Pruitt, and he and his son Wallace were on the boat along with me," says Steve. "We would buy fish from fish trappers [pound-net fishermen] down near Reedville and haul them to the fish dock at Washington. There we would huckster the fish at the dock.

"We would live on the boat for two weeks and make two trips from Reedville to Washington before going home for a weekend. *Lester* was a double-ender about 45 feet long." [*Lester* was built in 1912 in Poquoson, Virginia.] "We bought shad, herring, carp, trout, bluefish, rockfish, and spot and we would sell the carp to Jews and Chinese. The rest of the fish most everybody would buy.

"Captain Lish and Wallace slept in the pilothouse and I stayed by myself in the forepeak," says Steve. "It was quite an experience, for a boy like me.

"I also worked on my brother's boat. He owned a log boat and I crab dredged on her. He had *J. P. Moore*. She had a log hull and had been a sailboat but she worked just like a motor-powered log boat. [*J. P. Moore* was originally a bugeye, built in 1888 in Poquoson, Virginia, by builder J. P. Moore.]

"Log boats were good crab-dredging boats because they were low sided but they were not very good sea boats. There wasn't much deadrise in them. They were a little flat so the boats didn't handle as good in rough seas as a regular deadrise deck boat. They were good working boats but they wouldn't turn quick. Draketail deck boats wouldn't turn good either."

## Paul Pruitt Worked Aboard *Three Brothers*

During an interview in 1985, Captain Paul Pruitt of Urbanna talked about working on his father's log deck boat. "My father, E. S. Pruitt of Tangier, owned *Three Brothers*. She was a 55-foot Poquoson round-stern log boat with a 14-foot beam powered by both a two-cylinder 24-horsepower Lathrop engine and a sail," says Paul.

"*Three Brothers* was used by my father to buy oysters, crabs, and fish. We bought fish from haul-seiners near Crisfield and pound-net fishermen from New Point, Virginia. I remember the time we bought 330 bushels of fish and iced them down in the hold with seven tons of ice.

"Before Daddy started the E. S. Pruitt fish house in Baltimore, we would sell our fish there to the dock off *Three Brothers*. Later Daddy opened the fish house and then we would haul fish in *Three Brothers* to the store. They passed a law so we couldn't sell fish from the boat. Daddy then rented the fish house for ten dollars a week, which made it even better for us because everyone else had to quit."

During the summer crab season, the Pruitts freighted hard crabs from New Point to Cape Charles, and in the winter they would haul oysters from the Potomac and Rappahannock Rivers to the John Handy Company in Crisfield. This establishment was a large shucking plant that used a thousand bushels daily and was serviced by no fewer than four buyboats.

When Paul's father died in 1940, the E. S. Pruitt fish house in Baltimore closed and *Three Brothers* was sold.

## K. T. SMITH OF SMITH MARINE RAILWAY

K. T. Smith was born in 1926 about the same time Alexander Gaines and Smith's father and uncle were building log deck boats at Dare, Virginia. Sitting beneath a large trawler at his railway on March 12, 2003, Smith talked about log boats.

"Captain Alex Gaines was across the creek, not far from here, and he would put all the logs together and would start up the side and then he would float the hull over here to our railway and we would finish the sides, decks, and pilothouses. *F. D. Crockett*, *Catherine*, and *Edward M.* were three log boats that he built.

"My daddy and uncle, John and Kirby Smith, also built log deck boats. The first log boat they built was *Isle of York* in 1925. She was about 50 feet and she went to Ocean City, Maryland. Another one they built was *Ethel L.* and she was built in 1927.

"Captain Alex built right many and Captain Joe Moore built *J. P. Moore* in 1888, but she was a bugeye," says Smith. "There were right many log boats on the Bay. Some were built in Poquoson and right many were built up around Solomons, Maryland, but the Maryland design was different from the Virginia boats. The Virginia log boats kept on with logs or chunks right up the sides. The Maryland boats were built so they were shaped like a clamshell. The hull was almost flat, and then they put timbers [frames] into the logs and would use 2½-inch thick planks for the sides.

"There was a pile of those boats around. *Old Point* was a seven-log canoe. *F. D. Crockett* and *Ethel L.* were made from nine logs. I put a many a piece in *Old Point.* When I first remember *F. D. Crockett,* she had a 50-horsepower Lathrop for power. She was used for freighting fertilizer, pigs, and watermelons. Everybody raised pigs back then and there was a pigpen right on the deck of *F. D. Crockett.*

"There are two log deck boats right over there sunk," says Smith. "When the tide's down you can see the Palmer engine in one out of the water. One was named *Lewis Felber* and the other one was *Alice Walker.*

"Alex Gaines was the last one around here to build log boats. He passed away in the 1940s. He and his brother Tom worked right here at the yard. I remember that Captain Alex would come to work in the middle of the coldest days of the year with just a light jacket on. We had another man working at the yard by the name of Ben Riggins and he used to say, 'Captain Alex's mother must have been an Eskimo.' We had a good time at the yard." Smith laughed.

## F. D. Crockett

Ron Turner of Poquoson, Virginia, owns *F. D. Crockett* and is in the process of restoring her. Ron is the great grandson of K. T. Smith's father, John Franklin Smith. "Alex Gaines must have been a pretty sophisticated boatbuilder," says Ron, pointing to the stern. *F. D. Crockett* has a beautiful fantail stern and the hull is made from nine massive logs.

"When she was first built she was in the business of freighting cargo. Particularly before the bridges were built across the James and York Rivers, the deck

K. T. Smith's father and uncle built log deck boats at their railway in Dare, Virginia. Today, K. T. runs the yard that was started by his family in 1842.

Smith Marine Railway was well versed in repairing and building log boats. This 1920s photo shows *J. P. Moore,* a log bugeye built in Poquoson, Virginia, in 1888, at the railway in Dare, Virginia. Courtesy K. T. Smith.

The log deck boat *F. D. Crockett* was built for and named for Ferdinand Desota Crockett of Seaford, Virginia, in 1924. The boat was built near Dare, Virginia, by Alex Gaines.

boats moved most of the freight around here. She was a packet boat until bridges came and the roads got better; then most of the boats went to crab dredging." The 10-inch by 10-inch white oak dredge post has been removed from *F. D. Crockett* but the dredge post step in the keel is still visible. Turner says she was still being used to dredge crabs about ten years ago [1993].

"Captain Purdy Green was captain of her for forty or fifty years. He is buried at Providence on Wolf Trap Road and there is a full picture of this boat cast into his tombstone," says Ron.

"Captain Gaines built it straight across the way from Smith Railway in Seaford. They rolled her over and rowed her across the creek where Kirby and John Smith and Captain Gaines put the deck and cabin on.

"I tried to get this boat for years," says Ron. "First I heard 'she's for sale but you can't buy her.' I had to wait my turn—the watermen just weren't through with her yet.

The stern on the log boat *F. D. Crockett* has a fantail shape.

"When I got *F. D. Crockett*, the pigpens were still in the hold. They would fill the hold with pigs, and I've been told they used wire fencing up on deck to contain smaller pigs. They would go around to all the farm piers and pick up pigs, five here or ten there, and haul them to the processing plant at Smithfield, Virginia, up the Pagan River. The buyboats would all arrive with a boatload of pigs.

"We hear more stories about watermelons than anything else. She would hold 3,500 watermelons, 500 bushels of potatoes, and also bagged fertilizer. The James River Bridge was built around 1929 so most everything that went up the Pagan River in those days went by deck boats.

"*Old Point* and *F. D. Crockett*, I think, are the only log boats of this type still alive," says Turner. "When we got her, she was about sunk. The barnacles were about eight inches thick up the topside."

By 2003, Ron had stabilized the boat and was in the process of refurbishing the classic Chesapeake Bay log deck boat. *F. D. Crockett* is believed to be the largest remaining log deck boat on the Bay built specifically for power. She measures 62.8 feet overall.

*Sometime around 1945, before I was born, Captain Otho Smith laid the two-masted sailing schooner* Kate Tilghman *to rest on Rosegill Bank on Urbanna Creek. Even today, parts of the old vessel's centerboard trunk can be seen at low tide.*

*By 1958, when I was old enough to go out on the creek, enough of the old schooner was visible for a child's imagination to dream of it out on the waves with sails filled with wind. As children, my friends and I would run up and down her decks, jump on her cabin top, and dream of pirates and gold.*

*I recall going home one day after having been aboard her and Mrs. Cora Marchant, my next-door neighbor, asked where I'd been. I told her I was playing on that old boat. "You best stay off that old freight boat before you get hurt," she said. That was the first time I'd ever heard the term "freight boat."*

# 4: DECK BOATS AS FREIGHT BOATS

Throughout most of the Chesapeake region at the turn of the twentieth century, roads and highways were still primitive at best and bridges across the wide rivers and the Bay itself had not been built yet. The waterways and boats were still the primary means of transporting passengers and freight. The terms "freight boat" or "Bay freighter" or "packet boat" were commonly used up and down the Bay to identify the boats that hauled freight.

Hauling freight in motor-powered deck boats was simply an extension of the freighting business that had been done under sail. The Chesapeake Bay deck boat became the tractor-trailer of the waterways.

Some of the freight hauled by the deck boats and the sailboats that had been converted to power consisted of coal, fertilizer, lumber, cordwood, oysters, oyster shells, grain, watermelons, cans, canned produce, livestock, and other farm produce.

Oysters, grain, and farm produce came from isolated country landings and were hauled to Baltimore, Washington, Norfolk, Hampton, Richmond, Annapolis, and other commercial centers. Coal, fertilizer, cans, barrel staves, and other manufactured goods were hauled from cities on return trips to the small towns and countryside landings throughout the Bay.

Deck boats were used by steamboat companies and others who wanted to haul freight from isolated docks that did not handle enough freight or passengers to warrant a large steamboat coming and going. This could mean hauling anything from passengers to muskrat pelts to live chickens in coops.

Several regions had specific needs too, as was the case in the lower Bay and Smithfield, Virginia, on the Pagan River. Before the James River Bridge was constructed in the late 1920s, hogs were hauled from farmers' piers throughout the lower Bay by deck boats to the processing house at Smithfield.

Powered deck boats were also used by Tangier and Smith Islanders and by people in other isolated regions to transport groceries, lumber, automobiles, and whatever else was needed from Crisfield, Maryland, or Reedville, Virginia, or elsewhere.

The watermelon trade was also a throwback to the days of the sailing schooners, and powered deck boats took over much of that business too. Many Bay deck boats were used to freight watermelons in the summertime. From late June until around the first week in September, boatloads of watermelons went to Washington and other towns, but Baltimore's Long Dock, just off Pratt Street, was the primary center of the watermelon trade. There were so many boats there, forty-five or fifty at peak season, that they rafted three or four deep and lines would curve around the end of Long Dock.

*Alice & Annie* is at Diggs Wharf on the East River in 1926. This boat carried passengers and freight from the North, Ware, and Severn Rivers and connected with the Norfolk steamer at an East River wharf. *Alice & Annie* was built in Perrin, Virginia, in 1922. Courtesy Chesapeake Bay Maritime Museum, Herman Hollerith Collection.

The shouts of "come aboard, come aboard" echoed across the water as each boat captain tried to entice potential buyers to purchase his product. "Melons! Melons! They are sweet, red, and ripe Congos and Georgia rattlesnakes. Melons! Melons!" They would yell from the boats.

Wholesale dealers from Philadelphia and every town and village near Baltimore would send a horse and wagon or a truck to buy a load. Some would arrive as early as 2 A.M. After wholesalers got their fill by midmorning, individuals would come down to the boats and buy a melon or two. Buyers would walk from one boat to another comparing prices and quality—punching melons and asking skippers to thump them before making their final choice.

Farmers and boat captains would often bring their families along, partly to help sell melons but also for a vacation to Baltimore. They would sleep and eat right on the boats. Many had relatives living in Baltimore. It was a time when friends and family could visit. The summer watermelon season was a special time and created fond memories for those who were there.

Some information in the lead-in to this chapter on the watermelon trade was taken from an interview with Captain Homer Pruitt of Tangier Island, published in an August 23, 1964, *Sun Magazine* article. Homer Pruitt was owner of the deck boat *Bessie L.* and a longtime buyboat captain.

## STEVE PRUITT

Steve Pruitt recalls how the watermelon business worked. As a boy in the 1930s, Steve would go with his father in the summertime on the deck boat *Elsie Virginia* from Tangier Island to North Carolina to pick up a load of watermelons and bring them back to Long Dock in Baltimore.

## Running Watermelons

"The watermelon season was in July and August for us," says Steve. "The first trip and sometimes the second trip of the season was to Edenton, North Carolina, at the mouth of the Chowan River. The next trip was usually to Coinjock, North Carolina, and then we would buy around the Bay until the season was over.

"On the Bay we would load watermelons from Deltaville, Virginia, on the lower Bay, to Bennett

Before bridges were built across the rivers and Chesapeake Bay, boats like *Secret* hauled passengers and freight here and there. Note the scalloped canopy to keep the sun off passengers. *Secret* was built in Portsmouth, Virginia, in 1916. Courtesy Sam Richardson.

Landing on the Nanticoke River on Maryland's Eastern Shore.

"When we went to Edenton there were brokers down there that owned these warehouses and they would sell you a load of watermelons or you could haul them for the broker on commission.

"I was just a boy and we'd go down there on the boat and there was this one broker who had a son about the age of me and we'd run around together. I'd eat at his house every day for dinner. We didn't have much to eat on the boat.

"The other way we bought was to buy a whole field. Daddy and his brother Charlie Pruitt, owner of *Marion Sue Handy,* would buy a field of watermelons from a farmer and split the load up.

"When we got a load to Baltimore, we did what we called 'legging' watermelons. We would get off the boat and stop a car and sell a watermelon or two. Then there was the Safeway [grocery store]; they would buy them by the truckload and we'd soon get rid of our load. I used to hate to see the big trucks coming because I liked to spend time in Baltimore. I liked East Baltimore Street and I'll tell you the truth, there wasn't any mission school there. For an island boy, there was a lot of action.

"Boats like *Elsie Virginia* would carry about 4,500 watermelons," says Steve. *Elsie Virginia* was a 55-foot deck boat built by Lin Price in 1922. "There were three grades of watermelons. There were selects, primes, and culls. The culls were loaded on the quarterdeck alongside the outside walls of the pilothouse aft. We would stow the selects and primes in the hold. We had to handle each watermelon one at a time by hand. In the hold, we would put a row down and put a row on top until the hold was filled. Then we filled the deck. There was a rack built on the deck like a corral. The rack would go from the forward cabin to the aft end of the pilothouse. When we left [North] Carolina and all that freshwater, our decks would just about be in the water but when we got up to Norfolk in salt water, she lifted right out of the water. [Salt water has more buoyancy than freshwater.]

"It would take us thirty-six hours from Edenton to Baltimore. We would always stop in Norfolk and fuel up," says Steve. "There used to be a house barge that would lay off shore at anchor. It had a diesel tank and a gas tank. You could go alongside and fuel up right there in the harbor.

"In later years, instead of going to Carolina to get our watermelons, we went to the Market Place at night right there between Pratt and Baltimore Streets [in Baltimore]. There was a big fish and produce market. We would go there and buy trailerloads of watermelons but we couldn't load them at Long Dock where we tied up. We had to go down to Curtis Bay and load them on at night; then we would go back to the Market Place to sell.

"A lot of times we would buy a piece of a trailer. Sometimes it was just 2,000 watermelons but we made good on it because we didn't have the cost of running back and forth to North Carolina.

"When we were selling them off the boat, it didn't make any difference what kind of watermelons you had if a customer wanted a North Carolina, Georgia, or Florida melon, we had it whether it had come from France.

Tangier and Smith Islanders and people from other isolated areas of the Bay hauled all kinds of freight back and forth. This particular load on *Nellie Jane* included an automobile. Courtesy Lewis Parks.

"I started running watermelons as a boy in the 1930s with my father, but in the 1920s and before, I heard the old-timers speak of running watermelon from Delaware, through the Delaware Canal in [sail-powered] schooners and bugeyes."

## Running Grain

When Steve got older he captained *Carol Ann*, which had been built in 1873 by Zac Layton as the two-masted schooner *William B. Layton*. She was later renamed *Ida B. Conway, John J. Crouch,* and finally *Carol Ann*. She was under motor power as *John J. Crouch* and *Carol Ann*.

When Steve was her captain, she was owned by Arthur Eubank of Lewisetta, Virginia. "He owned *Carol Ann* and *Eugenia*. I was the last one on the Chesapeake to run *Carol Ann*. Shortly after my last trip, she went down in the islands [West Indies] and she didn't last long. She went to pieces. She was 106 years old when I ran her. A fish boat ran into *Eugenia* right off Windmill Light and sunk her.

"The house on *Carol Ann* was like a hotel. She had a big old house on her. I'd love to have that steering wheel off her. It was one of those big wheels where you'd have to walk it over. You could put your feet on the spokes and walk her around.

"I was captain of her the first year I got my pilot license so it was around 1956. I ran grain—corn, soybeans, oats, and barley. I'd go up to Snow Hill [Maryland] for corn and that's where I'd have my problem, getting across that bar at Saxes Island, trying to get out of Pocomoke Sound over into the Pocomoke River.

"If the tide was low I'd just run her ashore and wait for high water," says Steve. "I'd get to Snow Hill and get a load of corn. I'd also go to Salisbury and Kinsale [Virginia]," he says.

"The grain season runs a long time because a lot of farmers hold their corn until it gets good and dry. Some farmers would dry the grain themselves and hold it for a long time." he says. "When I ran *Carol Ann* for Captain Arthur, we cut the cost of operations down the middle. We paid expenses and we would share up at Christmas time. After Christmas, he'd send me to Norfolk and I'd pick up the last load of corn in that year and I'd take it to Seaford, Delaware, on the Nanticoke. I started hauling in the fall and he gave me money to operate with. He knew how many trips I made and what I got and I put down what I used."

Although it might appear in this 1981 photo that the deck boats *Nora W.* and *Ward Bros.* are waiting in line for a load of corn at Southern State Granary on Urbanna Creek, the boats have actually already off-loaded seed oysters in the Rappahannock River. *John W.* is loaded down with corn. Deck boats hauled grain until the larger steel-hulled Bay boats like *John W.* took over the business.

## MELVIN WARD

Family legend has it that two seafaring brothers with the last name of Ward sailed from "up north" into the Chesapeake Bay in the early 1800s. One settled in Guinea Neck in Gloucester County, Virginia, and the other at Crisfield, Maryland. Over generations, most of the Ward men worked the big boats. When sail was the main means of transportation, they freighted in schooners, bugeyes, and rams, and when power came they worked the deck boats.

None was more renowned than Captain Johnny Ward of Deltaville. His oldest son Melvin speaks of the days when the Ward family owned a fleet of Bay buyboats.

## A Little Bit of Everything

"The deck boats were the trucks of today. We hauled watermelons, oysters, a little bit of everything," says Melvin at his home in Urbanna, Virginia. "Our family came from Crisfield. My grandfather and grandmother lived

there and my father was born there. All the Wards of Crisfield were seafaring men. My grandfather, Henry Ward, owned the bugeye *Louise Travers*. She was a sailboat when he first had her and he converted her to power. She had a sharp stern with a patent stern rig on her.

"My grandfather put *Louise Travers* under power, but when he got old he gave her to his son Maurice. The first time Daddy came to Deltaville he was on *Louise Travers*. They came over here junking. They were buying old, rusty plow points and scrap iron. If they had a big old plow or something, they would hoist it onto the boat with falls on the mast. They would put it in the hold and haul it to a foundry in Baltimore or Washington. Those were the days when it was hard to get hold of a dollar. They would go around and farmers would bring old pieces of plows down to a landing. My grandfather had a big old skiff and they would paddle to a big farm. One place they paddled to was at Stingray Point, and that was how my father found Deltaville.

"My grandfather also ran watermelons and lumber in *Louise Travers*. My father ran watermelons, tomatoes, shell lime, oyster shells, oysters, and potatoes in *Iva W.*, and I ran watermelons, grain, shell lime, and oysters in 'little' *Muriel Eileen*. She was the first boat I ran, and after her I ran *Ruth S.* and *Ward Bros.* Daddy bought *Muriel Eileen* from a fellow in Gloucester [County]. The first load of watermelons I hauled in her I got from Edenton, North Carolina. I logged them out of Edenton and took them to Baltimore. I went down the Intracoastal Waterway and went on up Albemarle Sound to get to Edenton. I bought my first load from a man named Francis Ward. I will always remember his name because it was my first wife's name too.

"I bought his whole patch of watermelons from him. He was a farmer and he cut them and he charged me so much apiece. I went there and told him I wanted the whole patch and he brought the watermelons to the rails." [The farmer was responsible for getting watermelons to the "rails" of the boat, and the captain and crew were responsible for loading the boat.]

"A cull cost us 12 cents apiece, while primes cost a quarter apiece. There was a public dock there at Edenton and all the boats could load there. A prime watermelon weighed around 22 pounds and a 12-cent cull in those days is the size of one worth about $3.50 today.

"We liked to buy the watermelons and sell them ourselves because we could make a whole lot more. We'd pay 12 cents for a cull and could sell it for 25 cents. If the market was right, we could make a few thousand dollars selling the watermelons ourselves compared to $150 a farmer would pay us to freight them. But, we couldn't always buy a patch so we would freight for the farmers too. We needed to keep the boat working so we did what we had to do. The last load of watermelons I ran was in *Muriel Eileen* for Bob Jackson and Harold Revere.

"When I took watermelons to Baltimore, there was a commission merchant at the dock there and he would help me sell the load. A & P grocery stores were big customers in those days. Sometimes they would buy the whole load.

## Grain and Shell Lime

"I hauled a little grain in *Ruth S.* and *Muriel Eileen* but the bigger boats were better for grain," says Melvin. *Muriel Eileen* would carry only about 1,900 bushels of wheat and we were getting about 12 cents a bushel to haul it. So you didn't get much money. If it took two weeks to make the delivery, you might get a tiny small week's work. It wasn't anything to amount to much. *Ward Bros.* carried about 5,000 bushels and *Nora W.* would carry about 5,500 bushels, so we could make some money off that.

"I ran shell lime [oyster shells ground up] for farmers on *Muriel Eileen* and that was worse than wheat. *Muriel Eileen* would carry 60 tons and we got $1.50 a ton. I'd go get a load at Crisfield and haul it up to Layton's Wharf on the Rappahannock River and I'd get $90. By the time I took out for gas, grub, and pay for the help, I didn't make nothing hardly.

"The small boats were good for watermelons and crab dredging but we realized we needed bigger boats to make any money freighting. That's when we got *Ward Bros.* and *Nora W.*" (*Muriel Eileen* measured 58.3 feet by 18.1 feet; *Ruth S.*, 60.3 feet by 17.7 feet; *Ward Bros.*, originally *Andrew J. Lewis*, 69.6 feet by 21.2 feet; and *Nora W.*, originally *Amanda C.*, 74.5 feet by 23.5 feet."

## Memories as a Boy

"One of the times I went to Edenton with my daddy on *Iva W.* was when I was a small boy," says Melvin. "That time he was going after potatoes in wooden barrels and he would put them in the hold and on deck. We would dock at a public dock and children would be swimming off the freight boats that were rafted to the docks waiting to be loaded.

"Well this little girl jumped off the boat that was furthest out and she must have hit something on the bottom because she broke her neck. It was a pitiful sight for a boy like me to see a girl die like that. It really hit me. They carried her across *Iva W.* to get to the dock and she looked so pitiful.

"The trips down the Intracoastal Waterway were slow going and there were a lot of mud banks with children swimming and jumping in the water. I remember it with Daddy and when I went by myself too, the kids would yell for us to give them a watermelon. Daddy would say, 'Go back on the stern and get a couple culls and throw them to those boys and girls.' I remembered that when I was freighting and I would always throw a cull or two to the kids. They would swim off there and get the melons and break 'em open on the riverbank and have a small feast. It was fun to watch the children play. There wasn't much else to do on the boat."

Seed oysters were the main freight of many Chesapeake Bay deck boats. *Lula M. Phillips* and *Iva W.* are loaded down with seed in Urbanna Creek around 1975. The little *Gracie Lee* was owned by Alvin Daniels of Urbanna and was used in the Rappahannock River haul-seine fishery. Courtesy W. C. Hight Collection.

## JAMES CRITTENDEN, FARMER AND CAPTAIN

James Crittenden, ninety-two, of Amburg, Virginia, started his long career as a crop and vegetable farmer hiring boats to haul his watermelons and potatoes to Washington, D. C., and Baltimore. During one season he leased a boat and captained it himself.

"When I was a boy, the boats were just part of everyday life," says James. "Everybody knew somebody who was involved in Bay boats. We called them Bay boats or freight boats in those days. Now people refer to them as buyboats or deck boats. Years ago, I heard them called runners or run boats.

"The summer before I graduated from high school, I raised about two acres of watermelons. Tom Crittenden, my uncle, had about four acres and we bought another two acres of watermelons from my uncle Wallace Crittenden. We hired a boat owned by Captain Ed Pruitt from Tangier Island. He came over to Deltaville to buy a load of watermelons and couldn't buy any, so we hired him for $100 to carry our watermelons to Washington, D.C.

"That was some experience! I learned, with my uncle's help, how to sell watermelons and I worked at it night and day for four days until I sold them all. The retail customer seemed to like seeing a young boy selling.

"But the best thing about the trip, to me, [was when] late at night after everyone had stopped buying, ten or twelve boat captains would get together, bring something to the dock to sit on, and tell all kinds of stories. I learned so much about the Maryland and Virginia Eastern Shore from them.

"The other thing I remember about that first trip was when we got to Alexandria, it was beginning to get dark and the captain had never been up the ten miles from Alexandria to Washington and his friend told him to steer straight for the flag staff on the Capitol building in Washington. So we could see the lights on the Capitol very plain and he headed the boat directly to it and in about an hour we came right up alongside Eleventh Street Wharf where all the produce boats unloaded.

"We had another connection to the boats too. My daddy had grown up with Captain Dighton Taylor and at one time he was the leading Bay boat operator on the Chesapeake. Captain Taylor was born in Deltaville but he got in some trouble as a young man and had to leave. He had a sail canoe that he used for oystering, so he sailed that canoe to the Eastern Shore and stayed there his entire life," says James. "He went over there with maybe $10 and that canoe. When I knew him he was one of the richest men on the Eastern Shore.

"Daddy would always tell me if I ever got into trouble on the Bay get hold of Captain Taylor. He owned the Bay boats, *Myrtle Virginia, C. E. Hopkins,* and *Agnes Sterling*. Captain Lip Johnson built *Myrtle Virginia* and Dighton claimed he built *C. E. Hopkins* himself but I think he hired some carpenters and was the overseer on the project. *C. E. Hopkins* was a small boat. She would carry about 55 tons. *Myrtle Virginia* would carry 900 barrels of potatoes. I don't know her exact tonnage. Lin Price built *Agnes Sterling*. He built her for Captain Johnny Sterling of Crisfield. Captain Johnny was a boat broker, but if he couldn't sell the boat right then he would use her to haul oysters or potatoes or whatever. Somebody before long would buy her and Captain Johnny would have another one built. Price built *Agnes Sterling* and *Joyce Sterling* for him and three others that I know of. It may have been more.

"When I started running potatoes to Washington on Bay boats, Captain Taylor had an Irish potato contract with Sanitary Groceries, a big chain in those days. Safeway from the West Coast later bought it out. He always made sure we had a market for our potatoes when we got to Washington.

"I started young raising watermelons and potatoes and I hired boats to take them to Washington and Baltimore. Of course, I'd go along to sell my stuff. It was common practice for the farmer to go along because all the boat got was the cost of freight, which was about $100 to $125 a trip. Once in Washington, the farmer had to make sure his goods were sold properly. You could also sell a patch of watermelons to a Bay boat captain, but I never did that. You make more money selling yourself.

"One year I ran a boat myself. Mr. Linwood P. Price [Deltaville boatbuilder] had taken a boat in on

a trade, *James J.*, and I couldn't find a boat to haul my stuff. I rented *James J.* from him and hauled my crops myself. She was a small boat, about 35 tons. I couldn't get no one to run her and I could run the Potomac River as good as anyone, night or day, so I decided to do it myself.

"My problem was that I didn't know anything about engine repair," says James. "I was scared to take the chance going up the Bay without knowing anything about fixing engines so I hired Howard Hudgins to go along. He was a young man just starting out, like me, and Mr. Price was building a boat for him. Howard didn't have anything to do until the boat was built so he decided to go with me. We got along fine on the boat and we made a half dozen or more trips.

"That boat came with a 36-horsepower Sears Roebuck engine and Howard looked after the engine," he says. "One trip in *James J.* was to Baltimore. We didn't usually go to Baltimore because there was a 10 percent commission fee on what we sold there. But we went there to sell my watermelons because Mr. Bernard Wood, who owned a tomato-canning factory, needed tomato cans from Baltimore; so I brought a load back.

"The funny part about that trip was that Howard wasn't feeling very good so as we were leaving Baltimore he asked me to take him to Stampers Bay Landing on the Piankatank River, which was close to his home. I agreed and he went to sleep.

"Well, I came on out Patapsco River by Seven Foot Knoll Light just as the light went on. That boat was fast. She'd run steamboat speed so I got on down the Bay before morning light. I saw Stingray Point Light and I knew what that was but I'd never run up the Piankatank River in my life. So, I woke Howard up and told him to get up here.

" 'What's the matter?' he asked.

"I told him, 'I don't know the first thing about the Piankatank. I see a lot of lights but I don't know what they mean.'

"He said, 'You can run up Baltimore Harbor and down the Bay in the middle of the night but you can't get in the Piankatank River. Now that's something else.'

"We both laughed over that thing.

"I hired one boat one time that could carry 8,000 watermelons," says James. "I don't remember her name but a man from Accomac on the Eastern Shore had her. She was a big converted bugeye. He put a piece in her and turned her into the powerboat. I paid him $150 to carry that load.

"Most all I carried were to Washington, but I had Captain Dea Ailsworth in *Lillian T.* carry a load to Baltimore one time. I ran into a time when Washington was filled up with cantaloupes and watermelons and it was taking over a week to sell a load. So I come back and got a load on *Lillian T.* and I decided I'd try Baltimore. It was filled up in Baltimore too but I got rid of them.

"I've made as little as $10 off a boatload of watermelons and as much as $1,600. It was like anything else; when there were plenty of watermelons the price would be down and when there weren't many around you could make some money.

"I hauled a lot of potatoes to Washington in thirteen-peck barrels. I'd buy the barrels from Callie Butler or Cleveland Payne and fill them with my potatoes. In most areas where potatoes were grown, there were several barrel makers. I got so I used Cleveland Payne more because I starting hauling staves for him in my truck.

"I used Captain Dea Ailsworth in *Lillian T.* and Captain Johnny Ward in whatever boat he was using then to haul my potatoes. Johnny Ward and I went to Baltimore with a load of my potatoes one time and we got there at dark. I sold them that night, and we unloaded them and were back on the Bay by daylight.

The first year I started farming after I left Lin Price's boatyard was in 1933. The first load my uncle and I sent to Washington we got $4.50 a barrel. The next load we got $4.75 a barrel. We had some left but didn't have enough for another load so Jessie Hurd put some on and they went to Baltimore and sold them for $5.00 a barrel but they had to pay the 10 percent commission fee. *Lillian T.* would hold about 500 barrels of potatoes. We put them everywhere you could stick one. *Myrtle Virginia* would carry 900 barrels. When she came up to the dock, you could hardly see Captain Taylor's head in the pilothouse because the barrels were stacked so high.

"I enjoyed that part of my life," says James. "It was fun being in the city and out on the boats and it was a break from everyday farm life at home."

*My great-grandfather and grandfather, Jeter and Raymond Blake, sold oysters to buyboats on the Rappahannock in sail-powered log canoes. My grandfather worked the water until he retired in the early 1970s.*

*Buyboat was a part of my vocabulary from the early years of my life.*

# 5: DECK BOATS AS BUYBOATS

The term buyboat goes back long before gasoline and diesel engines. The first buyboat on the Bay was probably a one-log dugout canoe used by Native Americans to paddle out into a cove or creek, where they would use fish or oysters to barter with English colonists or other Indians.

There was, however, not much need for buyboats in the early years of the seafood business during the development of colonial Maryland and Virginia. In those years, virtually all plantations and towns were situated on or near a body of water. Slaves could easily be used to work the Bay for its fish and shellfish, and the less wealthy could catch their own seafood with relative ease.

But, with the coming of more settlers and the forced relocation of the Native Americans away from the coast, the nation began to spread inland. As centers of population and commerce evolved, fewer and fewer people had the capability to catch their own seafood. Many began to purchase fish, crabs, clams, and oysters from local watermen, either directly off their boats or from the back of an ox cart or horse-drawn wagon.

Then a few entrepreneurs began buying wholesale from watermen and selling retail to the general public. Some had their own storefronts, while others had large boats that they filled with fresh seafood pur-

chased from pound-net fishermen or shaft tongers. They would then carry the product back to a dock in a city or town, and sell it to anyone willing to pay the price. Washington, D.C., Norfolk and Hampton, Virginia, and Baltimore, Maryland, seafood markets "down on the docks" grew out of this practice.

As fish, crab, and oyster sales began to expand on the Bay, oyster shucking houses, crab picking houses, fish canning and pickling houses, soft-crab shedding facilities, and various other seafood facilities grew throughout the Chesapeake.

These early processing plants were often some distance from the rivers and coves where particular species were harvested. And, in those days, watermen were working the Bay in 25- to 40-foot sail-driven log canoes, boats that were certainly not suitable for carrying heavy catches over long distances on a daily basis. Even for short distances, watermen were dependent on fair winds and friendly tides to get them to market and then home. A still day or a strong running tide could keep a man from reaching his market in a timely fashion.

Land transportation was primitive at best and roads were poor. A trip to market some sixty miles overland was completely impractical for a waterman with a load of fresh fish and no ice or refrigeration to keep it from spoiling. A better means to gather and

Buyboats bought from fishermen using boats of all sizes. This 1920s photo on the Corrotoman River shows a skiff full of fish being sold to a buyboat. Courtesy John Wilson.

transport seafood was needed. The buyboat was the answer to this need, and it played an important role in the development of the Bay's fishing industry. It also played an important role in the Bay's overall economy as the boats were used to haul more than just seafood.

The following stories give us some insight into the watermen's day-to-day life and the way motorized deck boats were used as seafood buyboats. The boats were used to buy just about every kind of seafood from watermen working in just about every kind of boat from sailing skipjacks to hand-sculled skiffs.

## RAKING CLAMS ON PERRIN CREEK

Carter Smith was born in 1923 in Guinea Neck in Gloucester County, Virginia. His father Luther worked the water. Luther worked in the spring and summer as a pound-net fishermen for $15 a week in the Fox Hill area of Hampton, Virginia; in the oyster fishery on the York and Rappahannock Rivers in the winter; and raking clams during the off-seasons near his home on Perrin Creek at the mouth of the York River.

As a child Carter helped his father rake clams and they sold to a buyboat that came from the Eastern Shore almost every day. "We came up the hard way, you better believe it," says Carter. "My first memories are of going out with my daddy and raking clams.

"We would sell them to a guy by the name of Burley Ward. He would come over in a buyboat regularly from the Eastern Shore and buy our clams."

"We would take a garden rake and go around the marshes, anywhere then, and catch all the clams you want," says Carter. "I was about seven or eight years old. Captain Ward came most every day and would buy from the entire neighborhood.

"We were getting about half a cent apiece for a clam and by the time we caught three or four hundred we were getting good extra money," says Carter. "In those days a couple dollars would go a long ways. There were nine of us in the family—seven girls and two boys—and Daddy had us all raking clams. We liked it though because it was fun wading around in the marsh.

"There was a place Captain Ward would come with his boat and everybody in the neighborhood who caught some clams that day would take them down to the boat.

"It might seem like a little bit of money but it helped us out a lot to get through hard times," says Carter. "When we had a few clams we were always glad to see Captain Ward come."

## *MUTT* AND *JEFF* AND CODFISH

*Sometime around 1996, I was introduced to Swainson Hudgins, then eighty-seven, of Mathews County, Virginia. Swainson had been an outlaw waterfowl market hunter in his youth, and I wanted to get historical information on how he made duck decoys and gunning lights.*

*I interviewed him at his home at New Point, Virginia, and when we finished I went home. When I got home, I realized I'd left my tape recorder at his house so I drove back down and we talked some more. The story of the buyboats* Mutt *and* Jeff *came from that second meeting.*

There are specific years that every old-timer on the Chesapeake Bay remembers, such as the Great Freeze of 1917–18 when the Bay froze solid for fifty-two days, or the August storm of 1933 when the entire Bay region flooded for days.

The year 1931 was the year that codfish were caught in great numbers in the Chesapeake for the first and only time in memory. Everyone working the water then remembers that as the "Year of the Cod."

Swainson and his father were working a pound net off New Point when they started catching large numbers of codfish. "That was a bunch of fish that come in here and worked their way on up the Bay," says Swainson. "We caught a lot but outside [further out] nets near the middle of the Bay caught ten times as many codfish as Daddy and I caught. They didn't stay in here long—maybe a week. It was a once in a lifetime thing because all the old, old watermen had never seen anything like it and I've never seen anything like it since.

"We got three cents a pound for those codfish," he says. "I'll never forget it, we sold to a couple of Maryland buyboats that came down from Crisfield every day.

"The boats were owned by the same company and one of the boats was named *Mutt* and the other *Jeff*," says Swainson. "I guess after the funny-paper characters.

"One of the boats was big and long, like Jeff was big and tall, and the other was small and short, like Mutt in the funny-paper script.

"*Mutt* would come one day and the next day *Jeff* would come down here," he says. "That was something, all those codfish. We thought we were going to make big money off them but three cents a pound was all we got."

Phillips Packing Company out of Cambridge, Maryland, owned the buyboats, *Mutt* and *Jeff*. The firm had a custom of naming its buyboats after comic-strip characters. Two others were named *Andy* and *Popeye. Merchant Vessels of the United States* shows that *Jeff* was built in 1923 at Honga, Maryland, and was 64.7 feet long. *Mutt* was built in Cambridge, Maryland, the same year as *Jeff*, and she is listed at 67 feet long. However, Robert Burgess in his book *Chesapeake Sailing Craft Part I* states that *Jeff* was a converted two-masted schooner built in 1888, first named *Richard Cromwell* and later *Harvey H. Conway*, after the patriarch of the seafaring Conway family of Cambridge. He wrote that Phillips Packing Company in Cambridge bought *Harvey H. Conway* and renamed her *Jeff*. Perhaps, the firm named two boats *Jeff*, and if indeed it was *Harvey H. Conway* buying codfish it would clarify Swainson's story of a very large boat named *Jeff* and a smaller one named *Mutt*.

## DECK BOATS SELLING TO BUYBOATS

Buyboats were used extensively in the spring, summer, and fall pound-net fishery. Large seafood firms from all over the Bay would send boats to buy, particularly in areas where pound-net fishing was lucrative, like Mathews County, Virginia.

Thomas E. Owens's grandfather and father, Henry and Everett Owens of New Point, Virginia, sold fish to buyboats belonging to Ballard Fish and Oyster Company out of Norfolk, Virginia.

The Owens family fished numerous pound nets and owned several deck boats that they used to haul and catch fish. The boats were moored side by side, and Owens boats would sell fish to Ballard's. The Owenses owned the deck boats *Thomas E., Ellen Marie, L. R. Smith,* and *Lavenia H.* Ballard would send *William Somers* and *Irene & Pearl* from Norfolk to buy fish.

"My grandfather worked right on the pound line in about 40 feet of water," says Tommy. "They had two or three nets at the middle ground, southeast of New Point Lighthouse. In later years, they went across the Bay and set trap nets just above the cement ships and they caught a lot of fish." The pound line is the furthermost point in Chesapeake Bay where pound nets are allowed. The gear is not allowed in the main channel of the Bay.

"Years ago there was a buyboat that would come every day from Norfolk and moor right off from Chesapeake Seafood at Sand Bank Wharf. They tied up to a pole out there in the water and bought from the pound-net fishermen. Sometimes it was *William Somers* and other times it was *Irene & Pearl*. Captain Jimmy Temple ran *Irene & Pearl*. We would tie our boats right up to the buyboat and cull our fish on a culling board, weigh the fish on old scales, and grade and separate the fish into wire baskets. A basket of fish weighed 50 pounds. Then they would pass the baskets to men on the buyboat and they would put the fish in a hold, ice them down, and take them to Norfolk.

"When Ballard's buyboats came here they had their own ground-up ice. When you handed the basket of fish to the man he would put trout all together in the hold, then put spot all together in another location, and then put croaker all together. As he put fish in the hold he would reach over and shovel ice over the baskets.

"Then later on, the buyboats stopped coming and we took our fish to Sand Bank Wharf. Walter Garrett owned the wharf and he would provide us with ground ice. He had an ice plant right there. When the roads got better, trucks started taking all our fish. Then we started using wooden boxes that would hold a hundred pounds of fish. They would put the fish in cold storage or put them on refrigerated trucks and run them to Norfolk, Hampton, or

Pound-net fishermen working deck boats also sold to buyboats as this 1955 photo of *Thomas E.* and the buyboat *Irene & Pearl* (belonging to Ballard Fish and Oyster Company) reveals. Fish are being culled and separated into species and grades and placed in wire baskets that each hold fifty pounds of fish. The culling board is on the deck of *Thomas E.* Note the wire baskets. Later, fishermen used boxes that held a hundred pounds of fish. Courtesy Thomas E. Owens.

Baltimore. They got them to market as quick as they could."

## SELLING SCRAP FISH TO *P. E. PRUITT*

Robert Rollin Hudgins of Port Haywood, Virginia, worked aboard several of the deck boats in winter and summer. He also sold oysters to buyboats in the winter and fish in the summer when he worked for his uncles, Henry and Walter Armstead on *L. R. Smith.*

"She was an open boat and she stayed an open boat until the day my grandfather went out of business," says Robert. "Captain Henry Owens bought the boat. He decked her over and made a crab dredge boat out of her.

"I started when I was eleven years old working for my uncles. They sold market fish to *Irene & Pearl* and after we finished with market fish we would sell scrap fish to Paul Pruitt on *P. E. Pruitt.* Paul would pay 5 cents a bushel most of the time. Once in a while we would get 6 cents for a bushel. Scrap fish was fish too small for market. A lot of the fishermen would shovel them back overboard but not my uncles. If they had two to three hundred bushels it added up.

"Paul carried the fish back to Tangier and Smith Islands, and would sell the fish to crab pot and trot-line fishermen. He had a good business going and we appreciated the extra money. We would just shovel them overboard if we didn't sell to Paul."

## SELLING A FEW OYSTERS

### The James and Rappahannock Rivers—Roosevelt Wingfield

After the Civil War and into the twentieth century, the Bay's oyster fishery offered work for anyone willing to go out and tong them. A bushel of oysters was worth the same for a white man as a black man. Roosevelt Wingfield, seventy, remembers well when there were plenty of oysters and the oyster grounds on the James and Rappahannock Rivers offered work from October to June 12.

Roosevelt was born November 25, 1932, to Lucy and Edgar Wingfield. He grew up near Tuck's Ferry Road at Stormont, Virginia, just a short distance from the Piankatank River, not far from where his ancestors had lived for generations as slaves.

He quit school in the tenth grade, as many young men did in those days, to make a living and help support his family. His father worked in local sawmills and Roosevelt tried that trade for a short time, but he preferred working the water. As a boy he culled oysters for Willie Brooks on an old draketail-style workboat. Many young boys in the Bay, white and black, culled oysters at some point as a way to help support their families.

Roosevelt got married in 1951 and went to work for his father-in-law, Sterling Ward, on a log canoe named *Shamrock*. From September to February, he worked the Rappahannock River, hand-tonging market-size oysters and selling oysters to the J. W. Ferguson Seafood house in Remlik, Virginia, and also to several buyboats.

From March through June 12 every year for eighteen years, Roosevelt and his father-in-law would go to the James River on *Shamrock* and harvest seed oysters, which they would sell to market boats.

"When we worked the Rappahannock we mostly sold to Buster Ferguson of J. W. Ferguson Seafood, but we also sold to Randolph Ashburn on *Thelma Earl* and Paul Pruitt on *P. E. Pruitt*.

"There were other boats out there too but even though a boat might come from across the river with a flag raised, we were very cautious about selling to other buyers because we felt it was better to have a market every day than a few more dollars a bushel for one day. If you were loyal to that buyer, he would buy from you every day even when he didn't need many oysters.

"Now we would sell to Paul Pruitt and Randolph Ashburn when Buster didn't need many oysters. We felt we could sell to Paul because he carried his oysters to Crisfield and places like that, and Randolph bought for Buster sometimes. But we would not sell to Clyde Green, who owned *Grace,* because he sold to Kibler Parker and Boyd Hurley who were competitors of Buster's and we were Buster's boys."

Parker owned a shucking house on Parrotts Creek just a couple creeks away from Ferguson on Lagrange Creek, and Hurley was on Urbanna Creek, both on the Rappahannock River.

"Clyde didn't need to buy from us anyway because he had his own group of men who sold to him," says Roosevelt.

This was common throughout the area. Sometimes generations of oystermen sold to the same boat. For instance, James Ward, captain of *Nellie Crockett,* bought oysters from tongers in the same families who had sold to his father and grandfather.

| J. W. HURLEY & SON |  |  |  |
| :-- | --- | --- | --- |
| DEALERS IN |  |  |  |
| FISH, HARD AND SOFT CRABS |  |  |  |
| Urbanna, Va., ............. , 195...... |  |  |  |
| **Bought Of** |  |  |  |
| ........ lbs. Small Rock ........@.......... lb. | $.............. |  |  |
| .......... lbs. Medium Rock......@............ lb | $.............. |  |  |
| ........ lbs. Large Rock ...... @.......... lb. | $.............. |  |  |
| ........ lbs. Croakers ............@.......... lb. | $.............. |  |  |
| ........ lbs. No. 1 Spot ...@.......... lb. | $.............. |  |  |
| ........ lbs. No. 2 Spot ......@.......... lb. | $.............. |  |  |
| ........ lbs. Medium Blues ...@.......... lb. | $.............. |  |  |
| ........ lbs. Large Blues ........@.......... lb. | $.............. |  |  |
| ........ lbs. Buck Shad ......@.......... lb. | $.............. |  |  |
| ........ lbs. Roe Shad .......... @.......... lb. | $.............. |  |  |
| ........ lbs. Jacks ............... @.......... lb. | $.............. |  |  |
| ........ lbs. Herring ............ @.......... lb. | $.............. |  |  |
| ........ lbs. Large Grays ......@.......... lb. | $.............. |  |  |
| ........ lbs. Medium Grays ....@.......... lb. | $.............. |  |  |
| ........ lbs. Pan Grays ...@.......... lb. | $.............. |  |  |
| ........ lbs. Salmon Trout ..@.......... lb. | $.............. |  |  |
| ........ lbs. Flounders ..........@.......... lb. | $.............. |  |  |
| ........ lbs. Cats ...@.......... lb. | $.............. |  |  |
| ........ lbs. Carp ................@.......... lb. | $.............. |  |  |
| ........ lbs. ...@.......... lb. | $.............. |  |  |
| J W. HURLEY & SON |  |  |  |
| By ........................ |  |  |  |

Boyd Hurley of Urbanna bought fish on the buyboat *Walter Boyd.* This 1950s accounting sheet from J. W. Hurley and Son Seafood tells the kinds and grades of fish that buyboats and fish houses were buying.

"The James River was the same way. When my father-in-law and I would go to James River to tong, seed oysters were sold mostly to Achilles Rowe on *John Branford.* I grew up not far from where Mr. Rowe lived and I would see him at the country store as a child. He was a nice man.

"When I got grown and started going to James River with my father-in-law one of the first boats I saw there was *John Branford* and Achilles knew me and after that we were his oystermen. We always had a market when *John Branford* came. We'd tong all day until we'd see her mast coming under the James River Bridge and then we headed that way. We could tell her from way off in the distance because she looked different from the other boats. [*John Branford* is a sail-powered bugeye built in 1900. When Roosevelt

*Margarett* is buying oysters on the Rappahannock River in the 1960s. Note how the mast and booms are rigged so the captain can buy from two boats on each side. On a few of the larger boats, a captain could buy from eight boats at once—two forward and two aft on each side of the boat. A vessel had to be 80 to 100 feet to accommodate eight boats. Courtesy John Frye.

was selling seed oysters to Achilles Rowe, she had been converted to power. She's still alive today working in the Atlantic Ocean hard clam fishery.] Achilles looked after the boys from the Rappahannock. It was the same way for the boys from Tangier Island or those from Guinea Neck [Gloucester County, Virginia] or Bull Island [Poquoson, Virginia]. They all sold to captains they knew and who were from their area. The boats had their own markets and sometimes oystermen would sell market and seed oysters to the same captains.

"There were black men who captained buyboats, but they bought from the people they knew too. It wasn't a race thing as much as it was who you knew or who you had been working with.

"When *John Branford* wasn't there we'd have to sell to other boats, and they would buy from their main oystermen first and if they needed more then they would buy from us.

"I've seen as many as 150 buyboats working the James River. We knew who would buy from us and we also knew which captains had whiskey on board. There was one captain who kept plenty of Old Quaker whiskey in a cabinet. He would sell it to you at cost to get you to come sell your oysters to him. My father-in-law and myself were beer drinkers but we had a mate who

loved that Old Quaker. When *John Branford* wasn't there, he'd worry us to death to sell to this one boat. When we did the first thing he'd do is buy a pint from the captain and drink it before we would get back to Little Boat Harbor.

"We'd drive down to the James River in a 1941 Ford on Sunday evening, stay until Wednesday evening, drive back home, and come back early Thursday morning and work until the weekend. We slept right on the boat but there wasn't much room. *Shamrock* had a small cabin so the three of us had roll beds. There was a stove for cooking in the cabin so there wasn't much turning room.

"We would go out about 6 A.M. and start oystering. Along about 3:30 or 4 o'clock we would start selling to the boat," says Roosevelt. "Achilles could unload four boats at a time, two on each side, but there were boats unloading eight at a time. *W. J. Matthews* was long enough she could work two boats, side by side and fore and aft on each side. She could unload eight boats at a time. I remember her because a black man was her captain for a while and he never ever made a mistake with a tally. [*W. J. Matthews* was a two-masted schooner that had been converted to power.]

"A tally board was used by the buyboat captain to keep the tally, but we also kept a tally ourselves," says Roosevelt. "Say a buyboat was unloading four boats and we were the second boat. When they would get to us and we unloaded our first measure he [the captain] would say 'two is a one' and make a mark on the tally board with a pencil. We were the second boat and we unloaded one bushel. The second bushel would be 'two is a two.' For each bushel he marks it on the tally board and when he gets to five bushels he yells 'two is a tally' and draws a tally mark through the four marks and starts on the next tally.

"I kept tally by placing an oyster shell in a bucket for each time he yelled tally for our boat," says Roosevelt. "When we were unloaded, I counted the oyster shells to make sure his figures were like mine.

"Achilles used an old board to keep tally on and at the end of the day, he would take a piece of sandpaper and sand the marks off. We were paid cash or stock money as it was called on the boats, and the price changed regularly but on average we were paid about 50 cents for a bushel of seed.

"I enjoyed working the water but I don't miss it now," says Roosevelt. "I hate to see the oysters all gone and I appreciate what I got out of it. I bought two homes from oyster money, but I had to work real hard. I don't owe the river nothing and she don't owe me nothing."

## SONNY HINES—JAMES RIVER OYSTERMAN

As a boy and a young adult, Sonny Hines of Smithfield, Virginia, oystered the James River. In April 2003 at his home in Smithfield, he talked about his life as an oysterman on the spat-rich James River and about some of the buyboats that he saw there. Sonny now builds recreational boats, but he is a sixth-generation James River waterman.

"My family—grandfather and father—owned workboats and oystered the James River. We had one oyster boat called *Let's Go* and my grandfather owned *Laura*," says Sonny. (Sonny's grandfather was Ernest Franklin Hines, nicknamed "Big Pokey." His father was Ernest Melvin Hines, nicknamed "Little Pokey.")

"We would shaft tong for seed oysters, and when we were ready to sell we would look for a buyboat with a flag on the rigging, which told us which boats were paying more for oysters. But most of the time my grandfather would put out to the buyboat with

The day this photo was taken, *Grace* was paying a little more than the other buyboats for oysters. Note the flag or towel flying on the forward mast line as mate Dick Burrell fastens the lines. The flag told tongers that Captain Clyde Green of Remlik, Virginia, would pay them more for their oysters. Courtesy Marie (Green) Stallings.

the lowest freeboard if there was only a few cents difference.

"If it wasn't much difference in price, we could catch a load; get it off quick to a low-sided buyboat, get back out, and go back to work," he says. "During the peak season, I've seen as many as 125 buyboats working and the James River was loaded with oyster boats.

"The first of the season there were a lot of oysters. There were so many oysters out there people would hardly believe it today. We were working 14- to 16-foot long hand tongs. We worked on top of the rock during the first of the season in October and part of November. Then later we worked the edges or tucks of the rock.

Ben Wormeley unloads oysters from the hold of the buyboat *Grace*. Captain Lepron Johnson built *Grace* in Crittenden, Virginia. Note the Virginia measure (tub) used to get oysters to and from the boats and to and from the buyboat to the dock. A Virginia measure was a little more than a bushel of oysters. Also, note the cabin forward of the mast. This is called a hunting cabin and is a throwback to an early style of cabin that was found on brogans and coasting canoes. This style of cabin had a step up across the entire boat, all the way forward to the stem. The step up is in view and is forward of the rail. Courtesy Jonesey Payne collection.

"When a northwest wind came along, it would blow and roll oysters off the top of the rock under the edges, or what we called tucks, and those boys from up the Bay hated working tucks. You have to work them kind of sideways [from the boat]. On the forward part of the rock—the upper riverside—a long slope comes back and there is a quick drop off. A storm would make those oysters roll across the top of the rock and they would fall over the slope—just like falling off a cliff. Oysters would be under the tuck so thick and if you could stay on them you could catch a pile of oysters. You had to work it on an ebb tide to keep on the rock, because on flood tide you would be backing up to it.

"Wreck Shoal, White Shoal, and Dog Shoal down near the James River Bridge were rocks that ran up the river on the channel side. So you wanted an ebb tide with a little bit of northern or southern wind to keep you around on the rock depending on which side of the river you were on. Sometimes we would anchor just forward of amidships to kick the boat around and that would keep us on the edge of the oyster rock.

"It's just a shame that no one will ever see the river like it was again. I've seen hundreds of boats roll out of Deep Creek before light in the morning [going to work]. They would keep coming right on out till 7 or 8 o'clock, one right after the other. Buyboats would be in there too, but most of the buyboats would moor in Little Boat Harbor.

"*Earl* and *Pattie May* were two buyboats that worked the river regularly. Herbert Sadler ran *Pattie May* and he mostly bought up the river. We had different areas in the river that grew different types of oysters. Up the river around Burrell's Bay, on what we called the Three Mile Reef and some called Long Reef, an oyster grew that was small and single and it looked just like shell corn in the fall of the year. It was the prettiest stuff you have ever seen in your life. It would count anywhere from 800 to 1,000 oysters to a tub and it was just picture perfect. The inside of the shell was just as pearl white as it could be. They were just beautiful oysters and it was nice working up there.

"When we wanted larger oysters and those that were bunched together, we looked down the river around the James River Bridge and Ballads Marsh. The oysters had a few mussels on them and that helped fill a tub. Those pretty seed oysters grew anywhere above Jones Creek to a line across to Deep

*Iva W.* and *Lula M. Phillips* are loaded down with seed oysters purchased from James River oystermen. Courtesy W. C. Hight Collection.

Creek, up the river. That's what the buyers wanted to buy because the yield was so much better. They didn't like those down-the-river oysters.

"My grandfather oystered and sold to sail-powered buyboats. I heard him talk about the sailing vessels coming to buy oysters. It was such a romantic era. My grandfather would look to see if any of the buyboats were flying a flag on the forward mast, and if they really wanted the oysters they would be flying two flags. [Two flags meant the captains were paying top dollar for oysters.] Grandfather would keep his eye on that boat. Sometimes they used a towel for a flag, sometimes a red flag, and sometimes they would run an American flag up the mast to let the boys know they wanted our oysters bad. All morning long there would be one buyboat right after another coming on the grounds. It was really something to see all those boats, putting out oysters and listening to the tallyman calling tally. Boy, it was an exciting time.

"The first day of oyster season was just like a big carnival. Everybody was down at the creek tuning engines up and we couldn't sleep the first couple days before the start of the season. We would spend those first days before the season opened talking about what we were going to do, and we would go out and do what we called 'try the rocks.' A couple weeks be-

fore the season opened, we would run downriver, race around, and try the rocks [tong a few to get a good location as to where to start on the first day of the season]. Even after trying the rocks, we were usually just as confused as to where the best place was to start. It was just an exciting time though and I miss that excitement as much as anything about it.

"My grandfather was a wise man and he would try to bring it all into perspective when he would say to me, 'On the first day of oyster season the world is full of money but every year you must remember you have bad weather [when an oysterman can't work], Christmas, and taxes to take that money.'

"I started culling oysters as a boy when I was so short I had to stand on two automobile tires that we used for bumpers to reach the culling board. Then Granddaddy got me a fish box to stand on. I culled for my father and grandfather as a boy.

"At the first of oyster season seed oysters would bring 50 cents a bushel. The cheapest my daddy ever got was 25 cents a bushel. Around 1948, the union tried to go into it. They tried to unionize a bunch of fishermen and oystermen. I was thirteen years old when they tried it, but that didn't work.

"Buyboat captains would always fuss about slack measures, cribbing the tub, and shells [mixed with good oysters]. I always say if they were doing their job they would not have to worry about shells and slack measures. All they would have to do is not buy slack measures or shells and it would stop.

"One day my brother and I were working on our private beds and *J. C. Drewer* came along. [*J. C. Drewer* was a 65-foot buyboat built by Linwood Price and Co. in Deltaville, Virginia, in 1929.] We decided we would sell to her and when we off-loaded our oysters Captain Vernon Drewer, Sr., said all he had in stock money was coins. He said, 'Son, I'd pay you boys off in coins if you want them, but I know you don't want to fill your pockets with coins. I'll pay you next week.'

"I said, 'No you won't! We will take the coins.' He paid us off in quarters, dimes, and nickels, and that bought groceries that week. *J. C. Drewer* was a 1,500 to 1,800-bushel boat. We had several 5,000-bushel boats. One 5,000-bushel boat that I remember coming in here was *Sarah Conway*. She had been a sailing schooner converted to power. I think the captain's name was Luke Parker and his son-in-law who worked as mate was named Hap. [The over-80-foot *Sarah C. Conway* was built in Baltimore, Maryland, in 1872 and was a sailing schooner before being converted to a powerboat.]

"Some of the other boats that worked the James River were *Thomas F. Jubb, Zeph S. Conover, Sterling, John H. Miles, Fisherman,* and *Chesapeake*," says Sonny.

"Most of the time we sold to Ballard's boat [Ballard Fish & Oyster Co. of Norfolk] *Zeph S. Conover* because Ballard always kept a boat in the creek. My uncle, Harry Minga, captained it and his crew consisted of his father Marvin Minga and his two brothers Cappy and Frog Minga. They knew our boat and they knew the boats that sold to them. Well, in the wintertime, they looked out after us when the market was slack or the weather was bad. We seldom ever sold to a Miles boat during the season. [Miles was the other large seafood dealer out of Norfolk.]

"In the winter the upper Bay, where a lot of James River seed oysters were planted, would freeze and the buyboats could not plant so they would stop buying until the rivers thawed. Also, a large number of the smaller planters would run out of money, reducing the competition for seed. The large planters like Miles and Ballard bought all through the year, so naturally if you wanted steady market you had to sell to them.

"Like I said it was an exciting time. All the creeks and guts around here were filled with watermen liv-

ing on their boats. Oystermen from all over the Bay came here, and there were local watermen too. Locally, there was a group from Deep Creek and there was a group out of Jones Creek. There was a group from Rushmere. A lot of the group from Rushmere worked the shipyard and navy yard at night and worked the water by day. There was always market up there. The buyboat *Pattie Mae* worked up there most of the time.

"There was a group that came to Jones Creek every year, and I would go down there in the evenings. Watermen from Saxes, Tangier, and the Rappahannock River from up the Bay would come there and moor at nights. I have seen the creek blocked from side to side with oyster boats. From the bridge all the way to the dock, boats would be moored anywhere from five to eight deep. All the watermen would congregate at the service station, and as a kid I would sit down and listen to them talking. It was an experience. I wasn't familiar with the Tangier and Saxes island dialect, and the Guineamen were even worse. At first I had a hard time understanding. I got so I could understand them pretty well and the same ones would come back every year so I got to know some of them.

"It was a wonderful place to grow up. I honestly miss those times. I never thought I'd see the oysters and all those boats go. It's hard to believe that my generation might be the last to have heard a tallyman call out a count or see as many as five hundred oyster boats working the James."

## TANGIER ISLAND BUYBOATS

Steve Pruitt worked aboard several Bay buyboats buying fish, crabs, and oysters. He grew up on Tangier Island, where many of the boats were used to buy year-round for seafood dealers in Maryland and Virginia.

## Buying Oysters

One of Steve's first jobs was with his uncle Alfred Pruitt on *David Goldstrom* buying oysters on the Potomac and Rappahannock Rivers for a Deal Island, Maryland, oyster shucking house.

"*David Goldstrom* was a good one. My uncle kept her spotless. When we were working the Potomac River, we would harbor in Colonial Beach, Virginia, and when we were working the Rappahannock we would tie up in Urbanna.

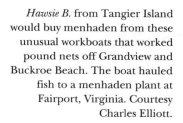

*Hawsie B.* from Tangier Island would buy menhaden from these unusual workboats that worked pound nets off Grandview and Buckroe Beach. The boat hauled fish to a menhaden plant at Fairport, Virginia. Courtesy Charles Elliott.

"When it was time for the tongers to knock off we would run out in the river and drop anchor. The tongers would come alongside. Most of the time we unloaded two boats, one on each side, but sometimes we unloaded two boats on each side. That worked us right good. The man on the inside boat had to grab that offshore tub from the outside boat and let it come up to me. I was the dump man. We dumped them on deck, usually not in the hold.

"My uncle bought oysters for Carl Hoffman of Wenona on the lower end of Deal Island. He would pay top dollar if you got him good oysters. When we went to Potomac River, he wanted Cedar Point oysters. He didn't care what you paid for them. They were slow-growing oysters but if you could get a bushel of three-inchers they would shuck a gallon and that's what he wanted.

"Cedar Point is on the Maryland side of the river just below the Potomac River Bridge, right across from Dahlgren Proving Grounds. Each day we would check with a watch boat that would tell us if we could go across because they always tested those guns. We had to stop each day and get permission to go over and buy oysters.

"When we were buying my uncle would stand up there with a tally board and a pencil tied to it on a string. A tally board was a piece of wood about 12 inches wide. It was cut so it fit good in his hand. I still have my daddy's. It's been sanded so many times.

"It would take us a couple days to get a load and once we got loaded we would head on over to Deal Island and off-load at the shucking house," says Steve.

"We also worked the James River seed season. We would go to the James and if we were going to pay a little more, my uncle would put up an American flag to let tongers know we were paying more. Some of the boys would put up a towel or any old kind of rag. We would do that with the Cedar Point boys for market oysters too. All the tongers knew what that meant. We would load about every day from the James and we ran seed to the York River and to the Rappahannock River. My uncle worked for several different growers who had their own oyster grounds.

"He also carried plenty of stock money in the pilothouse to buy oysters with because he had to pay tongers every day. We'd go to Crisfield sometimes and tie up and leave the boat for awhile and we never had anybody try to take stock money from us. Very rarely did you hear of that happening," says Steve. "The only boat I knew that had a safe on her for stock money was *Hawsie B.* and Clarence Christie owned her. He sold her to Ulysses Thomas and he used her to buy scrap fish [menhaden] from pound-netters down off Buckroe Beach and Grandview. They had the funniest boats. Every one of them had scows [blunt on both ends] and their shaft was on a universal joint."

## Buying Fish

The pound-net scows Pruitt mentioned were designed to be pulled up daily on the beaches of Grandview and Buckroe. The strong surf along these beach areas was not conducive to the building of small piers to moor traditional-style workboats. Therefore, the surf scow evolved to accommodate the needs of a very lucrative pound-net fishery in that area. Sails powered early scows, and rudders and tiller sticks were designed to be removed when the boats were hauled ashore. The steering rig was held in place by sockets. When power came, fishermen kept the same type of steering and tiller system, but the prop shaft and propeller presented a problem. Fishermen had to come up with some method of raising the shaft and propeller when they hauled the boats up—often loaded down with fish—onto the beach.

To remedy this problem, watermen installed a universal joint in the shaft. Also attached to the shaft was a handle that extended up through the boat. An L-shaped adjustable metal strut was designed to hold the shaft in place and allow it to be raised and lowered. The scow used by these fishermen was not used anywhere else on the Chesapeake, and it was an unusual boat. Although market fish were hauled to shore, boxed, put on a trolley car, and carried to Hampton fish houses, buyboats from around the Bay bought bait and scrap fish from these fishermen on a regular basis.

"I worked on *Hawsie B.* some too, and we hauled bunkers to McNeal Dodson Company [menhaden plant] at Fairport," continued Steve. "I don't know what the fishermen were paid because that was between the factory and the fishermen. The fish were unloaded with an elevator. They would lower the elevator down into *Hawsie B.*'s hold and men would shovel the fish to the elevator. The elevator led into a hopper and when it was filled it was considered one thousand fish."

## Buying Crabs

"The first year my brother got *Lora Lee,* we bought crabs out of Hampton and hauled them to Crisfield," says Steve. "Every spring of the year the boys from Tangier would go down there at the first of crab pot season.

"It was different from what it is today. Each crabber didn't have but a hundred pots each but the crabs were so thick we would have two or three hundred barrels every day acoming up to Crisfield.

"We would deliver to each one of the buyers in Crisfield. Say, we would put off Marshall Pruitt's thirty-five barrels to Ted Riggins, a crab buyer, and then we'd go to another one and put off thirty barrels of sooks. We were running all night. We were paid a dollar a barrel freight and most days we had three hundred barrels of crabs. Those old wooden barrels held a hundred pounds of crabs. Back then that was a good day's work. The fish house would pay the crabber and we would collect freight.

"I bought seafood on *Lora Lee, Elsie Virginia, Stewart Brothers, Three Brothers,* and *J. P. Moore.* "When I started, I was a small boy on *Stewart Brothers.* I was a third man without pay but I had to go every summer with my daddy.

"I started on the water and I spent my life on the water." Besides the many commercial fishing boats he worked aboard, Steve was captain of an oil tanker for many years and was captain of *Miss Ann,* a cruise yacht for Tides Inn in Irvington, Virginia.

*The double-deckhouse buyboat that I remember as a child coming into Urbanna Creek was the big Muriel Eileen. When she was moored in the creek, I'd ride up close by in my 12-foot flat-bottom skiff and my eyes were always pulled to her grace, size, and beauty.*

*Her top deck towered over other boats and her clean, bright look—she was always freshly painted—made her stand out over all the other workboats in the harbor. She was a Baltimore company-owned boat and was always well maintained.*

*I thought even then that she was special with those impressive double deckhouses but it was years later—after I had seen Sarah Conway at West Ocean City, Maryland, in 1986 (just weeks before she sank in the Atlantic), and Coastal Queen at Deagle and Son Marine Railway in Deltaville in 1996—that I realized just how unique the double-deckhouse buyboats were on the Chesapeake.*

# 6: DOUBLE-DECKHOUSE BUYBOATS

The double-deckers were some of the largest buyboat-style boats on the Bay. Several of the Conway schooners were given double deckhouses when converted from sail to power. (Harvey Conway and his sons of Cambridge, Maryland, owned a fleet of schooners in the early part of the twentieth century. Harvey named the boats after members of his family.) *Sarah Conway, Ida B. Conway, Betty I. Conway,* and *Ruth Conway* all ended up with double deckhouses.

These larger boats, most over 70 feet in length, were often used for freighting on the Chesapeake and Delaware Bays. Many of these boats were worked between the Caribbean and the Chesapeake and were at sea for long days and nights, or they ran regular runs throughout the Bay region to Baltimore or Norfolk. The double houses provided comfortable living conditions and also allowed payload to be stacked high on deck above the lower deckhouse. The pilothouse was located in the upper house, which allowed the helmsmen to see over the payload. The lower deckhouse provided a galley and room for lodging.

There were few of these boats around in comparison to the number of deck boats. Even in the heyday of the buyboats, most double-deckers started out as either large sailing vessels or single-house buyboats and were converted to double-deckers. The few vessels built from the start as double-deckers were built mostly for large fertilizer, oyster, or vegetable packing companies. The two largest deck boats built on the Bay were *Marydel* and *Chesapeake*. At 97 feet 9 inches long and 24 feet 9 inches wide, *Marydel* was built by Linwood and Milford Price of Deltaville, Virginia, for W. E. Valliant and Company, a fertilizer distributor from Laurel, Delaware. She was built with a double deckhouse in 1927. *Chesapeake* was 92 feet 9 inches long and 24 feet 9 inches wide. She was built in 1936 at Lepron Johnson's yard in Crittenden, Virginia, for Miles Oyster Company in Norfolk. She was an oyster-dredge boat and carried a double deckhouse.

Perhaps the large converted sailing schooners were the first to have the double deckhouses but these boats were awkward looking. (Note the photo of *Sarah Conway* in chapter 2.) However, the second deck on the larger Bay-built buyboats often provides a graceful, charming profile on the water. Along with the large stable platform, this attracted some to consider for the first time converting these boats to pleasure craft.

## BIG *MURIEL EILEEN*

One of the most interesting double-deckhouse buyboats is the big *Muriel Eileen*. William C. "Bill" Hight of Urbanna, Virginia, recalls the vessel with great fondness

Few deck boats started out with double deckhouses. This photo shows *Ruth* being cut in two at Humphrey's Railway in Weems and having a second deckhouse installed. Many times, builders pulled the single house off and used it as the second story of the double decker. They built the bottom level from scratch. Courtesy Ted Haynie.

and has researched its history. "I have been interested in the boat for many years," he says. "I knew the boat as a child in the late 1940s and early 1950s. I also knew the man who captained the boat from about 1928 to 1967—Captain Lee McNamara.

"There were two deck boats named *Muriel Eileen*. These girls—one named Muriel and one named Eileen—were the daughters of a man named R. E. Roberts of Baltimore, Maryland. Roberts owned the Lord Mott Company in Baltimore and Morattico [Oyster] Packing Company of Urbanna."

Lord Mott was a vegetable canning and oyster packing company that was founded in 1836. The company owned many large boats over the years. One of the most famous was the schooner *Chesterfield*.

"The first *Muriel Eileen* [also known as the little *Muriel Eileen*] was owned by Captain Willie Brown who was a very prominent man in the Achilles/Bena [Virginia] area in a community known as Guinea Neck. He lived near Sages Creek, which is right at the mouth of the York River. [The boat had a different name when Captain Brown owned her.]

"One of the main boatbuilders in that area then was J. W. "Big Jim" Smith," says Hight. "Jim Smith and his son Sidney built the little *Muriel Eileen* in 1926 and then built the big *Muriel Eileen* in 1928.

"Captain Willie Brown put a 50-horsepower Regal engine in the little *Muriel Eileen* and used her to haul lumber and freight for a little while. He sold the boat to R. E. Roberts in January of 1927. Mr. Roberts named the boat after his daughters Muriel and Eileen, but because the boat was not big enough for his needs Roberts sold it in July of 1928.

"Mr. Roberts, however, liked the boat and knew she was well constructed so he got the Smith brothers to build him a bigger boat and also named her *Muriel Eileen*."

Thus there were two boats with the same name. Over time, even though they were owned by two different people, the boats became known around the Bay as big *Muriel Eileen* and little *Muriel Eileen*.

"In 1934 Roberts and his Lord Mott Company purchased old West Urbanna Steamboat Wharf and adjacent land that had been part of the old 'Lang' Nelson Hotel property. The August storm of 1933 was the final nail in the coffin for the steamboat era on the Chesapeake. The storm destroyed many of the piers on the Bay and badly damaged the West Urbanna Wharf. The steamboat era was just about over anyway, but the storm hastened its demise.

"The firm bought the property and opened a vegetable canning factory and an oyster packinghouse

*Ruth* shows off her new double deckhouse. Joseph C. Jett of Menhaden Company, a menhaden plant in Reedville, Virginia, owned the boat. Jett used the boat to haul bagged fish meal on deck and fish oil in tanks in the hold to Baltimore, Maryland. The little girl is Ruth (Jett) Haynie; the boat was named after her. Courtesy Ted Haynie.

at the end of the wharf. Over time, the pier and wharf were filled in and replaced with an oyster shell causeway. The oyster shell road led to the canning factory and an oyster shucking house that was built over thousands of oyster shells.

"Around the time the big *Muriel Eileen* was completed, Captain Garnett Belfield of Coles Point, Virginia, and Lee McNamara, his mate aboard the Lord Mott–owned schooner *Chesterfield,* were busy hauling produce and oysters on the old sailing schooner for Lord Mott. Shortly after the big *Muriel Eileen* was completed in 1928, McNamara was named her captain.

"The new boat was a bigger boat than the little *Muriel Eileen* even without a double deckhouse. The big *Muriel Eileen* started out with a single deckhouse. Mr. Roberts used his new boat to haul finished products to Baltimore such as canned spinach, peas, and tomatoes. He also hauled live hogs and oysters to Baltimore and would haul empty cans, sugar, and other items associated with the canning factory from Baltimore to the Lord Mott plant at West Urbanna.

"Mr. Roberts loved the boat but she was still not quite large enough. By that time, there were builders taking a boat at its widest point, cutting it in two, adding footage by using sister keelsons and new frames and tying everything together," says Hight.

"So in 1935, Mr. Roberts took the big *Muriel Eileen* over to Weems, Virginia, to Humphrey's Railway and had her lengthened from 59 feet to a documented 78 feet 8 inches long. [From stem to stern, however, the vessel was 85 feet 1 inch long. Customhouse measurements were waterline measurements that do not take into account the extension of a stern or a raked bow stem.] When she was lengthened they took the boat out of documentation and put her back in the customhouse at 48 gross [28 net] tons with a beam of 20 feet.

"They also lifted the pilothouse and the captain's stateroom and mate's quarters right behind the wheelhouse off the boat and built a new house, then put the old pilothouse and quarters back on top of the new house. This new house contained a galley and quarters for Mr. Roberts and his family. He would sometimes use the boat for pleasure to vacation and travel around the Bay. She had a lot of canvas and rope netting that held suitcases, and youngsters would even sleep in the netting on a cool summer night," says Hight.

"She also became an important link between the two offices in Urbanna and Baltimore. She hauled lumber, building supplies, paint, sugar, and all sorts of stuff related to running a canning factory. She was

This side view of *Muriel Eileen* shows the layout of the double deckhouses. Courtesy W. C. Hight collection.

also like a courier boat for the two offices. She would carry letters, office supplies, and other communication between Baltimore and Urbanna. She was a vital link between the two offices for thirty-seven or thirty-eight years," says Hight.

"I've seen the big *Muriel Eileen* come into Urbanna Creek from Baltimore with boxes of cans halfway up the window of the wheelhouse. This was when she had a double deckhouse," says Hight. "I always knew when she came directly from Baltimore because she had a Baltimore scum line still on her, but I also knew if she was coming because she was loaded with boxes of empty cans up on deck. She would carry around 4,400 boxes of finished canned products in her hold and all finished product was hauled in the hold. When cans were on deck, it meant she was arriving from Baltimore."

## Oyster Business

The big *Muriel Eileen* was also used in the company's oyster business. "Lord Mott was big into the oyster business. One reason for the Virginia plant was to capitalize on the Virginia oyster," says Hight.

"Lord Mott Company leased seed oyster grounds from the state of Virginia on the James River and leased planting grounds on the Rappahannock River.

"The big *Muriel Eileen* and a smaller buyboat named *Elsie Louise,* also owned by Mr. Roberts, would go down to the James River during the seed harvest season. *Elsie Louise* was built in 1914 at Humphey's Railway and was later converted into a snapper rig boat to harvest menhaden for bait for crab pot fishermen.

"They went to the James River to dredge and buy seed oysters from tongers and bring them back to grounds leased by Morattico Oyster Packing Company, which was owned by Lord Mott.

"*Elsie Louise* would dredge for oysters and her crew would load the oysters on *Muriel Eileen* and when she was loaded *Elsie Louise* would buy from tongers until she was loaded down and they would both come on down the Bay. They would load *Muriel Eileen's* hold and pile seed up high on deck and she would carry about 3,000 bushels. That's about what the converted schooners would carry on deck because I remember that *Lula M. Phillips* carried that much on deck.

"The seed was planted on Lord Mott grounds on the Rappahannock and then during harvest, *Muriel Eileen* and *Elsie Louise* were used to dredge for market-size oysters. Market-size oysters were taken to the oyster packinghouse where they were shucked, packed, and iced down. When they had a load they were put on *Muriel Eileen* and taken to Baltimore to market. It was about a twenty-hour trip to Baltimore from the plant in Urbanna."

## Jingle and a Gong

Many of the larger deck boats, like the big *Muriel Eileen,* were engine-room controlled, said Hight. Early power plants were primitive and did not have the capability to shift into reverse and forward from the pilothouse, so when the direction of the boat needed to be changed, the engine controls would be changed from down in the engine room. Also, there were many types of crude starting and stopping devices, and these were located on or near the motor in the engine room. Therefore, a full-time engineer was required on these boats.

For years, menhaden steamers and Bay steamboats had used a bell system to instruct the engineer as to what was needed topside. That same system of a "jingle and a gong" was used on the buyboats, and the boats that used it were known as "bell boats." The bells signalled instructions to the engineer. For example, one gong would mean "come ahead," and two "a little more gas."

Throughout the Chesapeake, there are wonderful stories of what happened when the bells failed or the engineer took a catnap and captains and mates resorted to stomping the floor to instruct him to slow down, or stop the engine to put her in reverse. If all the docks had been torn down according to the stories told about bell boats, it's surprising there was a single dock left on the entire Chesapeake Bay. These types of accidents were actually very rare. Engineers aboard the boats were second in command to the captain and were usually highly experienced at their job. The captain and engineer were often full-time employees on boats like the big *Muriel Eileen,* whereas the crew changed from season to season and year to year.

The system of using signals with a jingle and gong worked, but when starters, transmissions, and clutches enabled a pilot to handle engine controls from the pilothouse, the engineer's job on Bay deck boats was eliminated.

## Keeping Her Fit

"Mr. Roberts kept his boats fit," says Hight. "When they had down-time at the plant, Mr. Roberts would

The gong and jingle off the big *Muriel Eileen* is part of W. C. Hight's collection of buyboat memorabilia. The gong, *left,* and the jingle were used before pilothouse controls existed. An engineer in the engine room was signaled by the captain from the pilothouse when to shift into reverse and forward, when to speed up and slow down, and when to start and stop. As a backup when the bells would not work, some captains used a "stomp-the-floor" system.

get the men to work on his boats. He would have men paint *Muriel Eileen* in the heat of the summer standing in a skiff while in the water. They would paint the sides from the copper line up to the guardrails. They would stand in skiffs, tied alongside *Muriel Eileen* in a real protected area [in a deep-water cove or at the head of a creek so the boat would stay still as they worked]. Then they would scrape her and paint her right there in the water.

"Then she would go to the railway and they would paint the bottom, recondition the propeller, and put all new zincs on. Keeping the topsides painted was a hedge to keep her in good shape and keep the railway bill down."

## The Day She Sailed from the Bay

Captain Lee McNamara was at Lord Mott dock in Urbanna the day *Muriel Eileen* was sold to the clamming operation. Earl Mills, manager of Lord Mott, and his son Bobby were standing next to him as it

Model-makers have found the double-deckhouse buyboats fun to build. This model of *Muriel Eileen,* made by the late Granvill V. "Fritz" Coleman in 1997, is owned by W. C. Hight.

*Andrew J. Lewis* is an example of a double-decker that started life with two houses but was converted later to a single-house deck boat. Built in 1929 at E. C. Rice and Son Boatyard in Fairport, Virginia, *Andrew J. Lewis* became *Ward Bros.* in 1952 when Captain Johnny Ward of Deltaville bought the vessel and had Lee Deagle at Deagle and Son Marine Railway convert her to a single pilothouse deck boat. She is still alive under the name *Crow Brothers* at Tilghman Island, Maryland. Courtesy Edwin W. Rice.

sailed away. George Mills recalls what his father and brother heard and saw on that day.

"It was my dad, Bobby, my brother, and Captain Lee, all standing on the dock at Lord Mott. *Muriel Eileen* sailed east out of the Rappahannock and as she was going down the river, Captain Lee looked at the boat and said to my father and brother with tears in his eyes, 'There goes my boat and there goes my life.'

"It really did end a wonderful chapter here on the Rappahannock."

## COASTAL QUEEN

*One of the better-known Chesapeake Bay deck boats is* Coastal Queen. *I first did a story on her in the August 15, 1996, issue of the* Southside Sentinel *and had no idea then of her fame. All I knew was she was one pretty double-deckhouse buyboat.*

*During the research for this project, longtime friend Joe Conboy introduced me to the book* The Inside Passage *by Anthony Bailey, published in 1965. Bailey's book chronicles a trip along the inland waterway up the East Coast of the United States aboard* Coastal Queen.

Boatbuilder A. G. Price built several large buyboat-style vessels on the banks of Hudson Creek off the Little Choptank River on Maryland's Eastern Shore. In 1928, Price built the 65-foot single-house vessel named *A. G. Price.* She was named after the builder himself, who ran a small boatbuilding shop with no railway. Typical of many early builders, when he finished the boat, Price pushed and rolled the buyboat from the shore into the water with poles greased down with wax, and beef tallow. Bailey writes that one of the boats owners later tracked down a ship carpenter who worked on the boat in 1928 for 25 cents an hour, which was low wages for those times. Most yards paid about $4 a day [ten-hour days] or 40 cents an hour for a good carpenter, but it did vary from yard to yard and area to area. She was built of Eastern Shore pine and her planking was 2¼ inches thick. As *A. G. Price,* she was used to buy oysters from skipjacks and from smaller tong boats out of Cambridge, Maryland.

She was used as a commercial buyboat until 1958, when boatbuilder Slade Dale bought her for $10,000 and completely rebuilt her, installing her double deckhouse in the process. Slade took *A. G. Price* to Ralph Wiley's yard in Oxford, Maryland, and there he rebuilt her into *Coastal Queen* in about a year.

The old workboat was converted into a luxury cruiser and was used by Slade to carry passengers through the inland coastal waterways from Florida to New Jersey. Although she has new owners, *Coastal Queen* is still going strong in 2003 and is one of the finest examples of a double deckhouse anywhere.

Anthony Bailey described the layout of the double deckhouse in his book *The Inside Passage:* "The two-story deckhouse stands above the engine room.

At the fore end of the first, or main, deck level is the saloon, with armchairs, bookshelves, and dining tables, with windows all around and both a door and hatch into the galley. The galley contains stainless steel sinks, a big electric freezer and refrigerator, and a modern electric stove and oven.

"More companionways lead to the promenade deck above. The staircase aft comes up to a sort of back porch, or veranda, covered with a permanent scallop-fringed awning. There are three well-furnished staterooms. Stateroom C is a bed-sitting room complete with two beds, two armchairs, built-in chest of drawers, and a separate toilet and shower. There is a connecting door to the pilothouse."

The boat is now owned by three old college buddies from Yale and she is equipped with a helicopter pad, elegant staterooms, and all the conveniences of a modern yacht.

## Stories from *Coastal Queen*

Many Chesapeake Bay buyboats have gone south to the West Indies and made trips back and forth to the Bay region. A story told to skipper Deacon Nelson by a former skipper of *Coastal Queen* happened while the boat was moored near the Bahamas late one night.

"The skipper heard some movement in the water around the *Queen*," says Deacon. "He looked through a porthole and saw a man shinnying up the anchor line with a pistol in his mouth.

"The captain had an Uzi [gun] on board," says Nelson. "He ran out, and with the butt of the gun knocked the pistol and the man into the water.

"He then pointed the Uzi at the man and some other men in a skiff and told them he was going to shoot. They hightailed it. When it was over he noticed there wasn't a clip in the gun."

In one of his own stories, Nelson was the skipper of *Coastal Queen* when he and a mate had crewed the vessel to the Bahamas. "I had gone ashore and left our mate [a young woman] onboard," he says. "She was down below taking a shower when she heard someone on deck. She came out in a bathrobe with a .38 [caliber gun] underneath her robe. She told the men who were there to pirate supplies that the captain was below and they better leave. They told her that they watched the captain leave and they knew she was alone. She pulled out the .38 and fired the gun. Those boys left in a hurry."

*I've always been aware that small buyboats were around. As a boy growing up in Urbanna, Virginia, in the 1950s, I often saw a line of buyboats rafted off the Standard Oil Dock on Urbanna Creek. The old* John Branford, *a converted sail-driven bugeye, and the big* Muriel Eileen *with a double-decker pilothouse were frequently there along with a little deck boat named* Gracie Lee.

*The other boats towered over and beyond* Gracie Lee—*she was only 46 feet in length. I knew she was built for haul seining but it was many years before I realized how unusual and unique these little boats were.*

# 7: THE SMALLEST BUYBOATS

There were literally just a handful of buyboats built for the Chesapeake Bay haul-seine fishery. These boats were less than 50 feet in length and built usually light; they were the smallest of the Bay buyboats.

These 38- to 49-foot boats were built mainly for spring and summer haul seining but were also used in the winter crab-dredge fishery and to buy oysters in the winter oyster fishery.

The haul-seine fishery is one of the oldest fisheries in America. George Washington used haul seines at Mt. Vernon to provide food for his plantation. He also sold herring and shad to domestic buyers in the colonies and shipped on consignment to the West Indies. The haul seine was one of the earliest gear forms used in the Chesapeake region that enabled fishermen to catch large numbers of fish.

The fishery is a shoreline fishery but the way nets were worked from colonial days to modern days changed. This change eventually led to several fishermen building buyboat-style boats in the late 1940s. Specific traits were built into these boats to accommodate the fishery and the results were a few of the "sweetest little boats" on the Bay.

Early haul seiners worked their nets by attaching one end of a net to shore, extending the other end out at about a 45-degree angle from shore, then sweeping the fully extended net toward shore and trapping the fish between the shore and the net.

This method was widely used by colonial fishermen and in later years as well. It was a convenient fishery because nets could be worked in close to shore in small skiffs. Two or three skiffs and plenty of hands could handle the water work and a horse-drawn wagon down on the beach could haul the catch to market or to a nearby fish house for salting.

In the early years, fishermen tied one end of the net to a tree stump on shore, paddled out in a skiff full of net, and fed the net out into the water. Once the net was out, men on shore—in the water and in skiffs—would pull the net full of fish into shore.

When power came, fishermen used motor-powered skiffs to extend the net out and had a donkey engine on shore to pull the net loaded with fish to shore. Also, larger motor-powered boats were often used to tow nets and gear and to carry the fish to market.

The traditional haul seine, however, had its limitations. When big catches were landed, fish were able to escape over and under the net and bunt. Also, fish would often suffocate and spoil before fishermen were able to get all the catch out of the net and to market. Refrigeration and ice to keep fish from spoiling were not available in the early years of haul seining.

Deck boats were used to tow fish seine skiffs full of fish and ice back to the fish packing house. Courtesy Grace Daniels.

A revolutionary change came to the haul-seine fishery around 1938 when Earl Hudgins of Mathews County, Virginia, invented the detachable purse pocket in the haul-seine bunt. This enabled fishermen to drive the fish into the pocket and close it so fish would not escape.

This meant that fishermen no longer had to bail fish from the net in close to shore. With the new system, fishermen were able to set a net in 3 feet of water (up close to shore), make a set, close the pocket, detach it from the main net by untying lace lines and unsnapping snap hooks, and then haul the pocket full of fish into deeper water where they would empty it at sunrise, all without getting on the shore.

It was a more efficient way of fishing because it did not allow fish to get away. Also, if a net was so full that watermen could not handle the entire haul they would simply close the pocket, carry what fish they could handle to market, then go back and open the pocket to get the rest later.

Also, no longer were fishermen tied to working a long, straight, beach shoreline. Shorelines with trees and other obstructions were not considered fit for haul seining prior to 1938, but the purse pocket or purse bunt, as some called it, extended the area watermen could work.

With this new development, the haul-seine fishery flourished for over twenty years and some fishermen made "big" money. The new net along with tremendous hauls of croakers during the 1940s and 1950s made some fishermen the wealthiest folks in town. They built new homes, bought new cars, and built new boats. A few of those fishermen built deck boats. The new method of fishing required a boat powerful enough to drag 10,000 pounds of fish in a purse pocket and several skiffs loaded with gear out into deep water all at one time.

Haul-seine deck boats were less than 50 feet in length and were built of 1½-inch thick planking. This made the boat lighter and enabled it to get in close to shore where haul seines are worked. Most buyboats used in other types of commerce were built with 2-inch thick planking or thicker, and most were over 55 feet in length.

Interestingly, haul-seine deck boats were only occasionally used to carry fish. Their main purpose was to haul the net full of fish still in the water and the seine skiffs out into deeper water. A line was attached to the top of the mast on the buyboat and the other end to a cleat on the bow of a skiff. Another line was attached to a cleat on the forward bulkhead of the skiff and the other end to the net that was in the

Some of the largest catches ever recorded on the Chesapeake came in the 1940s when haul-seiners landed some enormous schools of fish on the Rappahannock, Potomac, and York Rivers. Small boats were loaded down with fish and were towed to the docks by Bay deck boats. Courtesy Grace Daniels.

water. This method of hauling was used because it kept the net on the bottom and the fish safe as it was dragged into deeper water.

The haul-seine buyboat was also a product of affluent times. The haul-seine fishery was a nighttime fishery. Large and small schools of fish have a tendency to swim close to shore after dark. Before the purse pocket, watermen would work all through the dark of night and into the next morning to empty their nets to keep fish from spoiling. The purse pocket allowed fishermen to haul nets into deep enough water where there was plenty of oxygen to keep large numbers of fish, in a close bunch, alive and fresh for market.

Once nets and skiffs were secure out in deeper water, watermen could bunk down for the night and fish the net in the morning light. With crews of five and six men and sometimes more, a large, comfortable boat with room for several bunks and a large gal-

ley was a convenience that a few good fishermen could afford in the late 1940s.

## CAPTAIN WILLIS WILSON

*In 1948, Willis Wilson of Deltaville, Virginia, and his partners, Lennie Callis and Charles "Charlie Fred" Montgomery, had Deltaville boatbuilder Captain Johnny C. Weston and his son Earl build a 49-foot deck boat for haul seining and crab dredging. They named the boat* Dolphin.

"My first big boat was *Dolphin*," says Willis. "I owned two 40-foot deadrise boats before that. I had *Dolphin* built in 1948. Captain Johnny Weston and his son Earl built her for me. [The Westons built boats in Deltaville, Virginia, from the 1940s to the 1960s.] I paid $2,250 for the hull. It was another $275 to put the pilothouse on her and at that time the government had a whole bunch of barges with 6-71 GMC engines for sale. So we went to Norfolk and bought a barge with the engine, prop, steering wheel, shaft, tanks, and all that stuff," he says. "We brought it back to Deltaville and took it up to Lee Deagle's and put it on to her.

"We built her for haul seining and crab dredging," says Willis. "We had been using a purse haul seine for about three years. Lennie, Charlie Fred, and myself owned the haul seine together. We were using my little boat to work it with. I had a 40-foot [deadrise] bateau.

"You see, we haul seined in the fall, spring, and summertime, and patent tonged and hand tonged (for oysters) in wintertime. Then about 1948 oysters started dying and it got so we weren't making enough money in the winter. So we started thinking about building a boat for haul seining that we could also use in the winter crab-dredge fishery. The best way to crab dredge then was from a deck boat working two 6-foot dredges, one on each side of the boat. Later, the boys figured out how to work two 6-foot dredges from the stern of a 42-footer and that has just about killed the deck boats.

"In 1948, you could make $100 to $150 a week crab dredging," says Willis. "We made plenty of money in the spring and summer fishing but it wasn't always enough to last. Before we got *Dolphin*, Charlie Fred and I would oyster—hand tong and patent tong—in the winter, sometimes making as little as $10 to $15 a week. Lennie bought oysters around [from other

*Gracie Lee* was owned by haul-seiner Alvin Daniels and used in the spring and fall to fish. In the winter the boat was used to buy oysters. Courtesy Grace Daniels.

watermen, wholesale] and would sell them retail. He wasn't really doing much and neither were Charlie Fred and me. We needed something steadier in the winter. So we put our heads together and decided to build *Dolphin*.

"We gave Captain Johnny and Earl the order along about July and they had the boat finished by the first of October. She was 49 feet long by 15 feet wide and she had a 16-foot long house on the back of her.

"We built her small for haul seining but big enough to go crab dredging. Now we couldn't do as good [dredging for crabs] as the fellows who had them great big deck boats [sixty foot and over]. We didn't have the power and the big boats could tow a dredge better.

"Everybody was towing two 6-foot dredges but I could only tow 100 feet of chain and they were towing 125 feet, which meant they could get a longer tow. I'd say that on a given day when a big deck boat would catch a bushel of crabs to a tow, I would get two-thirds of a bushel to a tow.

"But the advantage we had was that *Dolphin* was small enough that Charlie Fred and I could work it with just the two of us," says Willis. "The big boats had to have a captain and two crewmembers and it took a

bigger engine to run her. We didn't catch as much but it didn't cost us as much to work either. I got so that in later years [1975–80] I worked it by myself.

"*Dolphin* was great for haul seining," says Willis. "We had a 30-foot boat for carrying the net in, a 20-foot skiff for carrying the winding engine and rope, and a 16-foot skiff for us to use for getting from here to yonder. We used *Dolphin* to tow all that to where we were going to haul, whether it was upriver or across the river.

"After we got to where we were going to fish, about 4 or 5 P.M., Lennie would usually cook dinner and we would eat. *Dolphin* was a good comfortable boat. The reason Lennie became the head cook was because he never could mend nets but Charlie Fred and I were good at it. So, when Lennie was fixing dinner, we would find holes in the nets and mend them.

"Lennie was a good cook. We had regular stuff to eat. For supper we had boiled fish and hot dogs and hamburgers—regular stuff. We had a fish box we had rigged up for an icebox and would keep the food down in that to keep it from spoiling.

"Breakfast was always fish and for lunch we would make a sandwich. We most always had fresh fish and I never got tired of it because it always tastes better on the boat. That was most of the menu; the only time we

*Dolphin* was built for haul-seining in 1949 using 1½-inch timbers instead of traditional 2-inch, to give her less draft so she could fish in shallow water. Courtesy Betsy Hudgins.

Captain Willis Wilson worked a haul seine in the 1940s out of Deltaville, Virginia, and had a deck boat built for haul-seining.

didn't eat fish was when we weren't catching any and that wasn't often.

"After we had supper we laid there until it was time to run [the net] out," says Willis. "We would mend nets, sleep, read, and joke around until the tide was right.

"To pull a haul seine you have to tow it with the tide. You have to lay there until the first of the flood tide, and then you run it out in the river on an approximate 45 [degree angle]. After the net is all run out, we had a 55-fathom line tied to the seine boat and fastened to the seine. Then we had a rope from the seine boat to the top of the mast so it would sweep over the pilothouse. We towed all that with *Dolphin* until we would cut towards shore, hit bottom, and could go no further.

"Then we would turn the seine loose, back off, and anchor. When we thought the net was full of fish, we would haul it in with a donkey engine and winch with a [5 horsepower International engine] in a 20-foot skiff. As we would haul, the fish would swim into the purse pocket. When the pocket was full of fish, we closed the purse pocket and untied it from the main net. *Dolphin* was used to haul skiffs and the purse pocket full of fish into deeper water.

"When I started haul seining, I was towing the net out with the 5 horsepower donkey engine in a skiff. When I finished I was hauling the net with a 6-71 Detroit Diesel engine and would wind it to shore with a six-cylinder Chevy engine.

Virginia law requires that a haul seine be no longer than 500 fathoms. "All good watermen sneak over a little tiny bit," says Willis with a laugh. "I've never known a good waterman not to sneak over a little bit. Not too much though!

"The big [purse] pocket on the end of the net would hold about 100 boxes of fish [10,000 pounds]. We would pull it off in deep water around 2 or 3 o'clock in the morning and then we would go aboard the boat and go to sleep. We would sleep until sunrise or around 5 A.M. and then get up and start bailing fish out of the purse pocket. We did not bail the fish into *Dolphin*. All the fish went into a 16-foot skiff that would hold 17,000 pounds. We would use *Dolphin* to haul the skiffs full of fish to market or a large buyboat would come and get the fish from us.

"When everybody got more net and more power to pull with, fishermen started catching enough fish to justify building big boats. But the main thing was,

we could work her year around. *Dolphin* was a little tiny bit too big for haul seining but she worked out all right. She had a whole lot better sleeping and cooking quarters. The pilothouse was up on deck and we could put windows down and open doors to catch a fair night breeze. It was good sleeping out there, I'll tell ya that."

On the other hand, *Dolphin* was a little bit too small for crab dredging. "After a few years, Lennie got sick and I bought him out so I owned two-thirds of *Dolphin*. We worked like that for a number of years. Then Charlie Fred bought a 50-foot deck boat named *Rebecca Ann*. The Walden Brothers [of Deltaville, Virginia] built her for themselves to crab dredge and didn't like the work so Charlie Fred bought her. I bought him out so I owned all of *Dolphin* then."

In 1980 after thirty-two years of working *Dolphin*, Willis sold his boat to Captain Dick Parks, a Tangier Island waterman, for $15,000 and went to work full time at Montgomery and Wilson Railway in Deltaville.

Willis and Charlie Fred started the railway on Broad Creek near the mouth of the Rappahannock River in the 1950s, just to maintain *Dolphin* and *Rebecca Ann*. Over time, watermen began coming by and the business grew into a full-time job. Willis was still running the railway in August of 2001 when this interview took place. He has since retired.

*Some of the largest buyboats built in the Chesapeake region were built for the large oyster companies on the lower Bay. Perhaps the grandest of all was* Chesapeake, *a 100-foot vessel built for Rufus Miles of J. H. Miles and Company of Norfolk.*

*Morris Snow of Bavon, Virginia, ran* Chesapeake, Ocean View, Mobjack, York Spit, Fisherman, *and other Miles boats. He also personally owned the deck boats* Linda Carol *and* Harold. *He graciously agreed to this interview and in his soft-spoken way provided knowledge of the boats that only a great skipper like himself could know.*

*Ed Payne and Robert Roland Hudgins also contributed to the portion of this chapter that describes dredging; both worked as mates aboard oyster dredge boats in Virginia's dredge fishery. The late Captain James Ward provided information on planting seed; he owned* Nellie Crockett *in 1985.*

# 8: OYSTER FISHERY

Chesapeake Bay deck boats were used extensively in the oyster-dredge fishery and to haul and plant seed oysters. The boats would still be working today if the Bay's oyster fishery had not collapsed.

## DREDGING

The oyster dredge was introduced into the Chesapeake area around 1800 by northern oystermen whose oyster grounds in New Jersey, New York, and Connecticut were depleted from overharvesting. They came south looking for oysters to replenish their own stock and to meet the growing demand for oysters in large northern cities.

Before this time, Maryland and Virginia watermen were harvesting oysters as they had done since colonial days with scissor-like hand tongs. A good hand tonger could catch thirty to forty bushels a day. A good crew aboard a large dredge boat with four dredges could catch forty bushels with one lick.

The early dredge boats were sail-driven schooners, skipjacks, and bugeyes. Because the dredge was so effective, Virginia and Maryland enacted laws in 1811 and 1820 respectively to outlaw the dredge and out-of-state shipments of oysters.

Maryland legislators eventually voted to allow dredging as long as the vessel was powered by sail, and in the 1890s Virginia authorized Lieutenant James Bowen Baylor of the United States Coast and Geodetic Survey to conduct a survey to establish 143,000 acres as public oyster grounds and another 110,000 acres to be set aside for private growing. This survey would play a significant role in the development of the Chesapeake Bay deck boat on the lower portion of the Bay. Virginia's law allows private growers to use dredges on grounds leased from the state, and when motor-powered boats came along the state allowed their use on private oyster beds. As the business grew throughout tidewater Virginia, the need for more and larger boats to catch and haul thousands of bushels of oysters to market also grew. The Chesapeake Bay deck boat provided the platform for catching and hauling these oysters.

Maryland's law prevented motor-powered boats from being used in the dredge fishery, but deck boats were used as buyboats by oyster packers to purchase oysters from watermen working in the state's sail-powered skipjack fleet and the hand tong fleet. Buyboats hauled oysters back to Maryland shucking houses.

Some growers had a fleet of deck boats as was the case of J. H. Miles and Company, who leased over 8,000 acres of oyster grounds from Ocean View to Mobjack Bay.

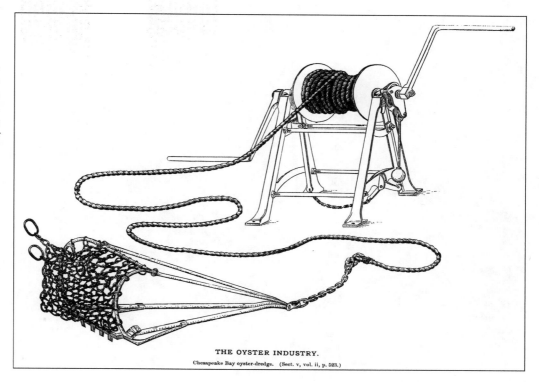

Before power, hand winders were used to haul oyster dredges to the surface. Motors and winches made life easier for oystermen on Bay deck boats. From Goode's *The Fisheries and Fishery Industries of United States.*

**THE OYSTER INDUSTRY.**

Chesapeake Bay oyster-dredge. (Sect. v, vol. ii, p. 523.)

Many deck boats were built for the oyster fishery but several large boats, ranging from 70 to 100 feet, were built primarily as dredge boats. The largest at 100 feet overall was *Chesapeake.* The vessel was registered at 92 feet 9 inches long and 24 feet 9 inches wide, with a 7-foot draft. She was not the largest deck boat built on the Bay but she was the largest built for dredging oysters.

## CAPTAIN OF *CHESAPEAKE—* MORRIS SNOW

"I was captain of *Chesapeake* and several other buy-boats. I hate to see the old buyboats go by the way, but there's nobody to work on them any more because the old woodworkers are gone," says Captain Morris at his home on Davis Creek in Mathews County, Virginia. "*Chesapeake* was a frame-built boat [stem-to-stern bottom planking] and I think she was the second-largest dredge boat ever built on the Bay. She was built down on Chuckatuck Creek by Captain Lip [Lepron] Johnson in 1936.

"I took care of Miles oyster beds all around and I worked *Fisherman* for a while. She was a big boat too. She was originally 75 feet long by 25 feet wide. Lip Johnson built her in 1921. Captain Rufus wanted her

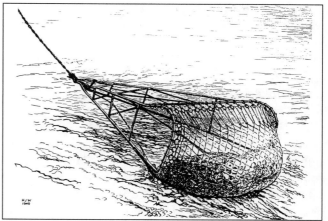

Oyster dredge. Courtesy Virginia Institute of Marine Science.

bigger so he had her cut in two and added 26 more feet. That made her 101 feet long but it weakened her structurally so bad that she couldn't carry as many oysters as he wanted. So he decided to build *Chesapeake.* He wanted this boat to be just right so he went himself down to Georgia, selected pine trees for lumber, had it cut and milled, and had it stacked on a train and brought back to Virginia. It was 3-inch-thick Georgia pine. Man, you talking about some pretty wood that was something to look at. The

For a while, *P. E. Pruitt* was named *Thomas W.* and worked in the winter crab-dredge fishery. The way the dredge boat is rigged—with a dredge post supporting two blocks and with chains running from the post to the dredge—is the way most oyster-dredge boats were rigged and worked.

mast came from the West Coast and it was 57 feet long.

"*Chesapeake* had 3-inch thick Georgia pine planks on the inside sheathing and 3-inch sheathing on the outside and she had an old Fairbanks-Morse engine in her. She was a big boat and she had a direct reversible engine, which meant you couldn't take her out of gear except by cutting the engine off. I had to start her in gear because the whole motor reversed, but I had learned her like a book. I had the engineer stop the motor and shift the cam to put her in reverse or forward—she didn't have a clutch. Ninety percent of the old boats were like that. *Chesapeake* was a nice rig. She was very dependable. She was first class.

"She was a double-decker and was built that way. Most of the double-deckers had the second deck added. The pilothouse was on the upper deck and there were three bunks on that deck. The galley was in the lower deck. The forepeak had plenty of bunks because when we were dredging we carried fourteen men in a crew. There was a potbelly coal stove in the forepeak and the boys could bank her so she would

work as good as a stove with a thermostat. They'd bank her at night and the next morning she'd still be hot as a firecracker. They learned it.

"We cooked right on the boat and we'd eat a plenty. We had a regular cook on *Chesapeake*. Boy, I tell you what, none of those restaurant cooks had anything on that dude. He was a black man out of the Mobjack area and he could solid cook. He'd be standing around at 11 o'clock and I'd say to my mate that cook better get on the ball or we won't have nothing to eat today. Boy, when 12 o'clock came and he'd ring the dinner bell, it was ready for you. He knew what he was doing.

"Lord, the coffee was good too. I'd be up in the pilothouse on the upper deck just off South Hampton Avenue when he'd start that coffeepot and that smell would drift up top. Lord, there's no better smell in the world.

"We'd back out from the dock about 3 A.M. down in Norfolk to go to the oyster grounds. Some days we'd finish by 6 P.M. It was a long day everyday. We didn't work Saturdays. Sometimes we would load in

*Mobjack* is one of the largest deck boats left on the Chesapeake Bay at 72 feet by 25 feet. Note the Bobcat loader on deck that is used to off-load seed.

four hours or so, get back to the dock and unload, and go right back out to Pig Point on the Nansemond River and dredge up another 1,500 bushels.

"We could load 5,400 bushels of seed oysters on *Chesapeake* and 3,400 bushels of market-size oysters," says Morris. "We worked four dredges at a time and every time her dredges came on deck we would take on 50 bushels. With fourteen men on deck and four dredges, boy, there was something going on. We'd take on about 12½ bushels to a dredge. In about four hours you could load her down with 3,400 bushels as pretty as you want to look at.

"Captain Rufus had a shucking house with 500 shuckers so we needed to keep them busy. I bet you could go to Norfolk now and you couldn't find five shuckers. Most of them were black women. There were two kinds of shuckers. There was the stabber

*Chesapeake* was the largest deck boat ever built for the oyster-dredge fishery and the second largest deck boat built in the Bay. Lepron Johnson built her for Rufus Miles of Norfolk, Virginia, at Crittenden, Virginia, in 1936. She carried a fourteen-man crew and hauled four dredges at one time. When she was used as an oyster buyboat, she could unload eight boats at once. Courtesy Dr. A. L. Van Name, Jr.

and the hammer. The hammer shucker had a hammer and shucking knife. They'd hit the beak of the oyster with the hammer, break it, and stick the knife in. The stabber opens the oyster by stabbing into the beak.

"Captain Rufus had 8,000 acres of oyster ground. He had 101 plots [of oyster grounds] measured into squares in Mobjack Bay alone. To mark the plots, four buoys marked the corners of every square and we had a number on the southwest corner of every square. So, that's how we knew what to dredge or plant on and we kept track of what we were doing that way. We had learned the grounds so well that the old boat would almost go there by itself. In those days, there was no radar or anything and we'd run sometimes in the middle of the night. All we had was a compass and leadline. We knew about where all the boats were and what time the traffic was coming in. We knew when the Bay Line steamers were coming and going and we'd look out for them. They were pretty things coming up and down the Bay. We stayed on our side of the channel. We felt safe even if we weren't.

"One thing about *Chesapeake,* if you pointed her in a direction she went straight as a gun barrel. You could turn her loose and aim her for something and she would go right to it. If I were needed on deck or something, I would just set the wheel where I wanted and go out on deck. On most of the old boats I had to use a becket [steering string] when I left the pilothouse. [One end of the becket was tied to the side of the pilothouse and the other to the wheel to keep the wheel from turning by itself.]

"*Chesapeake* had to stay out in deep water because she was drawing 8½ feet of water. I could only work her on grounds at Cape Henry Hole, Mobjack Bay, or off Ocean View. She couldn't go up in the creeks and all. She was a better boat loaded because she didn't roll about. When she had a couple thousand bushels of oysters on her she was real steady.

"One of the darnest things I ever saw was when I was taking oysters up to Captain Sam Bailey in Leonardtown, Maryland, one time in *Ocean View.* I was loaded down with 2,900 bushels. We had dredged oysters up from the Nansemond River, near where [former Virginia] Governor [Mills] Godwin was from. I was going towards the mouth of the river when I saw all these hogs in the water. There were thousands of hogs and they were feeding on oysters off the bottom. They were taking the oysters up on shore, cracking

them with their teeth, and eating the meat. There were just so many oysters everywhere. It's hard to believe that the oysters are gone. It's unbelievable.

"We would catch more than just oysters," says Morris as he held up a fossilized crab. "We caught this at Cape Henry Hole. I guess this is thousands of years old. We also dredged up pistols. Once we dredged up two pistols at one time. The boats coming from overseas weren't allowed to have pistols aboard so they would throw them overboard at the mouth of the Bay. We caught two in one day and one of them we fired before we got home.

"One of my favorite times on the boat was Christmas time. The crew was mostly black and Captain Rufus always let the crew have all the oysters they wanted for Christmas. 'Just help yourself,' he would say. We'd go out and catch a mess and they'd start shucking right on deck and somebody would break into song. They'd sing and shuck and just have a good ol' time. A lot of the boys would mix a bucket of oysters and clams. They shucked for the engineer and for me too. It was a special time of the year and a happy time.

"When the oyster business started going down in 1964 or 1965, the big boats were sold for ocean clamming in New Jersey. *Chesapeake* would have done fine up there in the ocean because she was a frame boat with a round bilge, but those little deadrise boats 65 feet and under couldn't stand the pounding long in the ocean."

"When *Chesapeake* went to New Jersey, she eventually caught fire and burned. The old engine in her would fill up with carbon. It was a two-cycle, two-stroke engine. She had oil in the base and a dirty old pump. Oil would drip down in an oil pan and it was supposed to pump the oil out of the pan until it was dry; but it didn't always do it.

"When carbon built up in the manifold, it would get real hot and catch the oil on fire. It had a 14- to 15-inch exhaust pipe going up through the cabin and if you didn't get the fire out quick it would go up through the exhaust. I think fire went up the exhaust pipe and caught the cabin on fire. We had similar things happen but we always caught it before it went too far.

"*C. F. Miles, Oysterman, Fisherman, Chesapeake, Ocean View, York Spit,* and *Mobjack* were just some of the Miles boats. *C. F. Miles* was a logged bugeye built in 1909 and made from thirteen logs. She was 75 feet long and 22 feet wide and was built in Oriole, Maryland. Linwood and Milford Price built *Mobjack* in 1946 in Deltaville, Virginia. After *Mobjack,* Price built *Ocean View* for Miles. Alton Smith built *York Spit* in 1949. I also ran the old *Julian* for Emory Kellum of Weems [Virginia].

"I captained a lot of boats but I also owned two. I owned *Linda Carol* and *Harold*. Alton [Smith] built *Linda Carol* but Sidney Smith from down in Guinea Neck put a pretty round stern on her. In the early years there were square stern, V-stern, diamond stern, and draketail sterns on deck boats. There was also the ducktail stern on the bugeyes. In the pound-net fishery, the V-stern worked well. It was just like being on the bow because the men could lean right up against a pole and work the pole into the bottom. They could work from either end. There were also draketail stern deck boats built up around Hooper Island.

"Captain Rufus offered me a job in the office once but I always wanted to be on the boats. My name was on all of the captain's papers for all of Miles's boats, which meant I could run any of them but I went on the 50-foot *York Spit* and was on her for nearly thirty years. She was a wonderful, heavy boat and she was my favorite. You didn't have to worry about weather with her.

"I've been out on the Bay in some bad weather too," says Morris. "One night we had *Ocean View* loaded down with 3,000 bushels of oysters when we ran into a bad storm. We were up near Wolf Trap. I could see Smith Point Light thirty miles away and I could see a bad storm was coming. It hit us hard and we had a big, heavy refrigerator on deck. It turned that refrigerator over on deck but the boat was heavy with all those oysters so we went right through the seas. Boy, Milford Price put plenty of wood in her too. The boat was built flat but Milford was a good builder."

## ED PAYNE: ONE DREDGE SEASON WAS ENOUGH

Around 1948, Ed Payne got a job aboard *Elsie Louise,* a deck boat owned by Lord Mott Company and captained by Captain Rob Williams of Urbanna. In the spring, he got a job dredging seed with Elmer Shores and sold seed oysters to the buyboat *Muriel Eileen*. He recalls some of what went on that winter and spring.

"We were dredging Morattico Packing Company's oyster grounds in the *Elsie Louise,* from Morattico Bar

*Island Star* is dredging oysters in the Rappahannock River in 2001 for Virginia's Oyster Replenishment Program. Note the dredge is being hauled from the mast and boom.

all up and down the Rappahannock River," Ed says. "We caught 450 bushels just about every day we worked. We'd go back to the factory and shovel them out in wheelbarrows.

"It was just me and Johnny Hodges out working on deck and it was hard, cold work. I told Johnny, 'You might have to do this but I'm just a youngster and after this winter it would be it for me.'

"They paid me $35 a week. I'd work all day and then have to shovel those oysters out. It was hard work. Now the black folks rolled the wheelbarrows. They would roll the empty wheelbarrow down a plank onto the boat, and Johnny and I would shovel the oysters into the wheelbarrow, and they would roll it into the plant.

"We would leave early in the morning. Most of the time we worked right on Morattico Bar or we dredged on Balls Point. It wasn't a long run for us. Rob Williams would always take his time. He was never in a hurry. We set around and talked as he went up river. When we would get there he'd say 'all right, boys, let's get 'em.'

"This was on private grounds so we didn't cull nothing," says Ed. "There was a dredge on each side and when we'd bring in a dredge, we'd dump it, throw the dredge overboard, and shovel the oysters back to the pilothouse on deck. There were boards up on the sides so we could pile the oysters up high in front of the pilothouse and all the way to the stern.

"It took us about four hours to catch 450 bushels with two dredges," says Ed. "Catching them wasn't the problem, it was unloading that took the time. We never missed a day for weather either. It could be blowing a gale, pouring down rain, or snowing. It didn't make any difference. We went!

"On board Rob would do the cooking and run the boat. She didn't have a door from the pilothouse to the galley so he had to go out the pilothouse door, out on deck, and go around back to the galley door. There were two bunks in the pilothouse and they were stacked over top of one another so the one in the top bunk had to crawl up from the bottom bunk to get to the top.

"That spring *Elsie Louise* went to James River to dredge seed oysters and I went too, but not on her. I got a job with Elmer Shores on a 38-foot round-stern deadrise and we dredged for seed and sold our oysters to the other Lord Mott boat—*Muriel Eileen.*

"We would catch 65 to 70 bushels a day and hoist them up on *Muriel Eileen*'s deck," says Ed. "I was making a lot better money. I was making $250 a week so it was a whole lot better than the $35 a week I was making that winter on *Elsie Louise.*

"We had a good time on the boats. They was good old days. It was hard work but being young like that—joking around and playing around—it wasn't bad."

## ROBERT ROLAND HUDGINS— SNOWBALL IN THE FOREPEAK, STEALING THE COOK'S PIE, AND MORE

Robert Roland Hudgins of Port Haywood, Virginia, was sixteen years old when he first got a job as a deckhand on the oyster dredge boat *William Somers.* Linwood Price of Deltaville built *William Somers* in 1923. She was registered at 58.6 feet by 16 feet by 5.8 feet and was owned by Ballard Fish and Oyster Company of Hampton, Virginia.

"It was the coldest time in the world and we would ride down to Hampton in the captain's car," says Robert. "You see we lived on the boat during the week and would go home on weekends. The captain was Lesley Brooks and he had a 1940 car with no heater. It got mighty cold riding down to Hampton and it was cold on the boat.

"Aboard the boat were the captain, engineer, a cook, and four deckhands to work the two dredges. *William Somers* was engine-room controlled. She had a big Buda diesel engine in her and she was a pretty fast boat for those times.

"In those days, most dredge boats were engine-room controlled meaning the engineer would turn the engine off and on and shift it into forward or reverse from down in the engine room. Say they wanted to go into reverse; the engineer would have to stop the engine, shift the cam to reverse, and then start the engine back up. The captain inside the wheelhouse would use bells to tell him what to do. There was a gong and jingle. They would start her up and the engineer would stand by for instructions. There was a pulley in the wheelhouse attached to the bells for the captain to use to direct the engineer. Each sound signified what to do. One gong meant 'come ahead' and two meant 'a little more gas.' A jingle meant 'wide open' and when the captain jingled and pulled a gong right after, the engineer was supposed to slow her down. I used to know all the signals but I've forgot some of it. I know if the engine was in neutral and the captain hit two gongs it was to stop the engine.

"One fellow was engineer on *Margaret.* She was a Ballard boat that we called little *Margaret.* She was going in Cape Charles one time and the captain rung the bells for the engineer to slow her down and go in reverse so they could go into a slip. The engineer got confused so he ran up on deck and yelled to one of the mates 'what did he mean?' The mate said, 'I don't know but you better back the son-of-a-bitch up before we run through the dock.'

"I remember my first trip. There were four men in the crew and we lived down in the forepeak. It was the coldest time of the year. I was the youngest one of the crowd. We slept aboard her all week and would come home Saturday evenings. It started out cold but I got used to it. The first day I wasn't used to it though. It was blowing and the wind would pick up the water and it would freeze right to my oilskins. *William Somers* would dip her stem and water would almost freeze before it would get to the dredges. We were shoveling oysters and I thought with all that freezing and rough weather, we would surely go in; but we didn't. We stayed out there until we got a load of oysters and we carried them to Norfolk to Ballard's oyster shucking house.

"After the first week, I said I'd never go again but I worked aboard her for four seasons. There was a coal-fired potbelly stove in the forepeak where we were sleeping. The first night, we burned all the coal on the boat and had to burn one of the bunks to keep warm. There were five bunks and just four of us so we broke the empty bunk up and burned it up. We got more coal before we left that morning.

"We kept the stove stoked up and tried to keep it hot, but sometimes she would go out in the night and it was real cold when we woke up. The cook had it better than us. The galley was in the aft end of the pilothouse. He cooked and slept back there. He had it more comfortable than we had. The captain and engineer had it better too; they slept in the wheelhouse. They had oil burners that burned all night to keep them warm. We could have kept the coal stove going all night but we couldn't get up. We had so many covers on us and once we got tucked in and got warm nobody wanted to move.

"*William Somers* pulled two dredges, one on each side of the boat, and there were two men working a dredge. We dumped the oysters from the dredge on deck. The dredges were heavier than a crab dredge but they were 5 feet wide, whereas a crab dredge in those days was 6 feet wide. As soon as we'd get the dredge empty and overboard, we would shovel oysters up in a pile on deck and the captain would have pulled the other side up; and by the time they were finished, he was pulling ours up again. There wasn't much idle time, I'll tell ya that.

"There were plenty of oysters then and we would dump the dredge and shovel oysters back towards the house. We didn't put any oysters in the hold. We piled them up on deck and on a hatch that was over the hold. We would start back next to the wheelhouse and work forward. By the time we got her loaded we hardly had room to shovel. We weren't that long load-

ing a boat either. We would leave to get on oyster grounds at daylight from either Norfolk or Hampton and be back by midafternoon and sometimes sooner. Ballard's shucking house was in Norfolk. Most of the work we did was on oyster grounds that were inside York Spit Light, off of Poquoson.

"I've heard old-timers talk about pulling an oyster dredge with a hand winder. That's what they did in sailboat days but we had it good. We used the motor to haul the dredges to the surface. I can't imagine the hard work in pulling a dredge up by hand. It was hard enough just being out in the elements, dumping the dredge when it got up on the boat, and shoveling all those oysters. We talk about how important motors were as transportation, they also helped to haul the dredge up and down.

"The food on *William Somers* was delicious," says Robert. "Of course I was young and I would eat anything and all I could get. You would think being on an oyster dredge boat with all the oysters in the world, we would eat a lot of oysters, but we didn't. Once in a while, we would have fried oysters. We ate in the galley. It wasn't very big so we ate in shifts. The captain and engineer would eat first and then we would eat by twos. It was an all white crew then but one year we had a black cook. He was a real good cook.

"The cook grubbed up every weekend and whatever we needed he got. He could make real good pies and I remember once he put a pie out on the window ledge to cool off and we stole it and ate it down in the forepeak. He complained to the captain that we were a bunch of pirates. It wasn't all work; we had some fun out there too.

"I didn't think I would like the work at the time but it wasn't so bad," he says. "At night after we would get all the oysters off, we would clean up a bit and go to downtown Norfolk. We wouldn't stay very long. It was down on East Main Street Norfolk in prewar [World War II] days. It wasn't a very safe place but we went in a group so it wasn't so bad. East Main Street had burlesque shows, tattoo parlors, barrooms, and you name it. As a sixteen-year-old, it seemed like a real wild place.

"Another thing I liked was when we worked close to home. Ballard had some grounds off of Horn Harbor near home and we would come up here and clean up the grounds in *William Somers*. There weren't many oysters there but we kept the grounds clean by running the dredges over it. We would come into Horn Harbor [near Port Haywood] at night and tie the boat to a stake. We carried a skiff on the boat and we would scull to shore and go home at night. I liked being home in my own bed. Sometimes we had to break ice in the creek to get back on the boat in the morning.

"Ballard also had a lot of grounds on the Eastern Shore of Virginia and we would carry seed oysters to Kings Creek right at the mouth of Cherrystone Inlet," says Robert. "We would dredge the seed up on the western shore of the Bay and carry it over there and plant it.

"There wasn't much spare time except at night and when we were going across the Bay. Most every night we played cards in the forepeak by the light of oil lanterns. We slept a lot when we were going to the Eastern Shore. Sometimes when we were going over to Kings Creek, we would pick out some large oysters and shuck several quart jars. There were times when we had to wait for a real high tide to plant seed and would stay over there for a week or so. During that time we would get off the boat and walk to a town or community and sell the oysters we had shucked for a little extra money.

"Another time, we went up to Moon Shipyard in Norfolk. They had to do some work on the boat and a bad snowstorm came up," says Robert. "It paralyzed Norfolk, Portsmouth, and everywhere. We woke up that morning and the snow had come down through the booby [forward] hatch and there was a little pile of snow on the floor. As a joke, I made it into a snowball and threw it at my buddy who was still half asleep. That day we took the oyster shovels and walked up the street and started shoveling people's walks and driveways. We made more money doing that than we made with our wages. It was rough times but we thought it was good. I got $35 a week and Ballard was furnishing oilskins and boots and food. I liked getting the oilskins because I used them in the spring working pound nets. When I started fishing pound nets I thought I was doing pretty good when I made $50 a week.

"Ballard had several boats that he used to oyster dredge but he also used them to run fish during warm weather," says Robert. "They had *Inez,* [little] *Margaret, O. A. Bloxom,* and *W. A. Ballard.* Miles Oyster Company had bigger boats. They had *Chesapeake* and she had four dredges on her. She was the biggest I ever saw."

Robert worked on *William Somers* for four winter seasons before he "graduated" to crab dredging in the winter months. He dredged crabs aboard the deck boats *Harold* and *Elizabeth D.* and worked pound nets on *L. R. Smith* when she was an open boat. She was later decked over.

"When I graduated to crab dredging, I worked on *Elizabeth D.* and *Harold* with my uncle, and Garnett Godsey was on *Beryl Marie.* He was out there dredging too. One time he had trouble with a mate not coming to work. The mate said it was blowing so hard that day he figured Captain Garnett wouldn't go out, so he slept in. Garnett told him if you come outside and the wind is blowing so hard it knocks you down on the ground one time, you get up and come on to work. If it's blowing so hard it knocks you down on the ground a second time, you go back in the house."

Another time Robert was aboard *Elizabeth D.* with his uncle going across the Bay to Cape Charles when Captain John Haywood of Guinea Neck came along in *Thomas W. Carroll* and wanted to race. "Haywood's boat was supposed to be a fast boat but *Elizabeth D.* was fast too. They both had GM 6-71 engines and they got to racing up Cape Charles channel. This other fellow and I went up in the forepeak and then we heard my uncle yelling to get up on deck. I thought we were slowing her down with our weight forward but the gas lever broke and he couldn't slow her down or stop her. So we went around in circles in Cape Charles Harbor until we finally had to cut the gas off to her and then it took her a while to stop."

The oyster dredge is still used today in the much-depleted Virginia oyster fishery. On occasion, the state of Virginia calls upon deck boats and other boats to dredge shell and seed as part of the state's Oyster Reef Restoration Program. However, very few private growers are willing to put a great deal of money into planting seed oysters today only to have them die because of MSX and dermo, two deadly diseases that have decimated the state's oyster industry.

## BUYING AND PLANTING SEED AND SHELLS

Chesapeake Bay deck boats provided an ideal platform for hauling and planting seed oysters and shells. The history of growing and planting seed in America goes back to the mid-1700s, long before the existence of gasoline and diesel engines and modern deck boat–style vessels.

The business grew out of the New England oyster fishery. By the mid-1700s, oystermen on Cape Cod

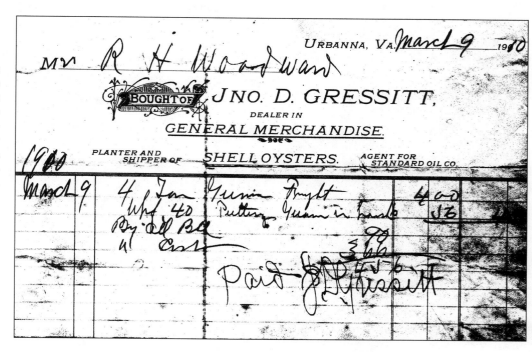

Many people other than oystermen also grew oysters. This 1910 billhead tells that Jonathan D. Gressitt, who ran a general merchandise store in Urbanna, Virginia, was also an agent for Standard Oil Company and a planter and shipper of shell oysters. Courtesy Bettie James.

had depleted their natural oyster beds by overharvesting, and they began taking small oysters and planting them on local oyster beds, thereby "growing oysters."

After seeing the success of New England growers, Bay oystermen began to plant and harvest oysters. This grew into a large business and buyboats were hired to travel to the James River, purchase seed oysters from hand tongers, and carry seed back to be planted on private oyster grounds. Many entrepreneurs became oyster planters and they were not necessarily oystermen. For instance, Jonathon D. Gressitt was an owner of a general merchandise store in Urbanna, Virginia. A 1910 flyer for his store described him as a "Dealer in General Merchandise, planter and shipper of shell oysters, and agent for Standard Oil Company." Located at Bowlers Wharf on the Rappahannock River, C. P. Garrett and Son was an oyster packing house that was also involved in the finfish and crabbing fisheries. T. A. Jones of Saluda, Virginia, was in the lumber business. His billhead read in 1910 "T. A. Jones, dealer in All Kinds Sawed Lumber, Planter of Rappahannock River Oysters." Many individuals also leased oyster grounds and the family oyster beds were as revered as the family home place by some. These private growers provided work for hundreds of buyboats. In addition, the states of Virginia and Maryland hired boats

to buy seed from James River and plant it on public oyster rocks.

The spring season for harvesting seed from the James was a busy time. In the heyday of the oyster fishery, oystermen recall seeing seventy-five to a hundred buyboats lined up purchasing seed on James River from hand tongers in hundreds of smaller deadrise workboats. After purchasing seed, buyboats would haul oysters to the many guts and tributaries of Maryland and Virginia and sometimes farther north to Delaware and New Jersey on Delaware Bay. A colorful history evolved when Virginia passed laws to limit the sale of seed to other states. The price of seed escalated in those states, so much so that many buyboat captains would haul loads of oysters in the darkness of night and in a thick fog to dodge the law.

The success of the Chesapeake Bay buyboat is tied closely to the Bay's oyster fishery. The oyster fishery provided wintertime work for many of the boats. As trucks and good roads began to take the freight business away from deck boats, many captains and owners turned to the oyster fishery to provide work for their boats.

## CAPTAIN JAMES WARD

"My daddy, Captain Will Ward, was eleven years old when he started working for my grandfather, Captain

T. A. Jones of Saluda, Virginia, was a dealer in all kinds of lumber in 1910, but he also was a planter of Rappahannock River oysters. Courtesy Bettie James.

motorized deck boats registered in the federal Historic Landmark Program. She received this designation in 1994.]

"Daddy went to the fifth grade and then quit to work on the boats," says James. "Grandfather would sail with my father from Crisfield to buy seed oysters on the James River, but in those days he was also using his boat to haul loads of potatoes in hundred-pound sacks, tomatoes in bushel baskets, watermelons, and lumber."

James's father, Captain Will Ward, was born in Somerset County, Maryland, on December 4, 1896. Captain Will visited Deltaville in 1923 to have boatbuilder Linwood Price build him a boat. There he met his future wife Virginia Harrow. Captain Will named his new boat *Virginia Belle* in honor of his fiancée. They were married and Captain Will worked *Virginia Belle* for a number of years before buying *Lula M. Phillips. Phillips,* originally named *Annie M. Leonard,* had been built in Oxford, Maryland, in 1877 as a two-masted sailing schooner.

"I went to work on *Lula M. Phillips* full time when I came out of the service in 1946," says James. "Besides hauling seed oysters, we were hauling lumber, grain, and whatever else we could find. The war changed our business a lot. Trucks began hauling many of the things that we hauled. In fact, later on, about the only thing left for us were seed oysters. What lumber we were hauling came from Totuskey Creek on the Rappahannock River. It would take three and a half days to load up, twenty-four hours to get to Baltimore, a day to unload, and about twenty-two hours to get back to Totuskey for another load. We'd always unload on a Friday and go right back. It didn't make any difference then if it was Saturday or Sunday, we'd work right on through. Daddy had a 75-horsepower

William Henry Ward of Crisfield, on the sail-driven bugeye *Louise Travers,*" said James in a 1985 interview aboard his buyboat *Nellie Crockett.* [*Nellie Crockett* is still on the Chesapeake Bay and her home port is now Georgetown, Maryland. The 65-foot deck boat was built in 1925 by boatbuilder Charles A. Dana of Crisfield, Maryland, for Andrew A. "Shad" Crockett, who named the boat for his daughter. James Ward purchased the boat in 1955. Today she is one of just a few

This 1985 photo of *Nellie Crockett* shows her loaded with 1,852 bushels of seed. The seed oysters were purchased from oyster tongers on James River and planted on grounds in the Rappahannock River for a Water View, Virginia, oyster grower.

Fairbanks engine that was a lot bigger in size than the 450-horsepower I've got in *Nellie Crockett*."

James bought *Nellie Crockett* in 1955. "Captain Shad Crockett of Tangier Island had her built in Crisfield. He was hauling the same things my father and grandfather would haul—potatoes, tomatoes, watermelons, lumber, and seed oysters. I'll tell ya the truth; this ol' boat has been a good friend. A many a time, I've come down the Bay on those rough nights, ice making up on the rigging and deck, but she's always brought me home. I don't load her down, though, in the wintertime. I carry about 1,850 bushels of seed in the winter and about 2,000 in the spring. The oyster season lasts from the first of October until June 15. You've got to be careful in the wintertime because ice builds up on the boat when it goes up and down. I've seen six inches of ice on deck and that's a lot of weight. It pays to be conservative with a load in cold weather." The season for market oysters ran from October to March and the season on seed oysters ran from March to June 15.

James bought and planted seed the same way his father did and his father before him. He would buy all his oysters from hand tongers and mostly from those on the James River, but he did buy oysters from tongers on the Piankatank and Great Wicomico Rivers too. Traditionally, these three Virginia rivers produced the majority of the seed oysters used on the Bay. Their salinity level is perfect for producing seed, but not particularly good for growing oysters to market size.

"I know I plant seed the same way as it's been done for a hundred years. There are new ways of unloading. Some take a high-pressure water hose and blow them off the deck, while some growers have conveyors on barges that scatter the seed, but I do it the ol' fashion way of broadcasting it with strong backs and shovels," says James.

## Buying Oysters

"I generally spend Saturday cleaning up the boat after a haul, so by 3:30 A.M. Monday morning I'm on the boat making ready to go. I get outside of Jackson Creek about 4:15 A.M. and it takes me about five and half hours to get to Deep Creek on the James River. If I've got a fair tide it doesn't take quite that long.

While at the wheel of *Nellie Crockett,* Captain Ward steers the vessel so that every corner of the oyster grounds receives some seed.

Seed is broadcast over the grounds by shovel on *Nellie Crockett.*

When I get to Deep Creek, I go to the dock there to fuel up, buy ice and food, and by 10:15 A.M., I'm at my spot, all anchored, ready to buy oysters.

"I've got several tongers that sell just to me. Some are old-timers who sold to my father. I'm real lucky to have good oystermen to buy from. You take a good day; I can buy 1,000 to 1,100 bushels of seed. But most days, I guess we average 500 bushels, so it takes three or four days to make a load. I got a power hoist, which my grandfather didn't have, to haul the measure up on deck. They used to haul the seed up in a measure by hand from log canoes, hoisting it up with block and tackle.

"On *Nellie Crockett* I can unload four boats at once, two on each side. There were a few boats that could handle eight at one time but they had to be over 90 feet long because there would be four boats on each side, two side by side near amidship and two side by side in front of those. They did the same thing on the other side to make eight. You couldn't do that with a 65-foot boat."

## Planting Seed Oysters

On an October 9, 1985, trip, after loading 1,852 bushels onto *Nellie Crockett* from Deep Creek, James arrived at 1:00 A.M. on a Friday in Urbanna to pick up a crew of six men and wait for high tide. The load was to be delivered to private grounds leased by Donald Morton of Water View near Punchbowl Point on the Rappahannock. These are relatively deepwater beds, eight to ten feet at high tide, which offer plenty of depth for *Nellie Crockett* to maneuver. [She draws 5 feet light and 7 feet loaded.] At 8:30 A.M., the captain and crew left Urbanna on a rising tide.

On the way, James explained that because of the depth of the water, seed could be broadcast from the deck of *Nellie Crockett.* The large buyboat cannot touch bottom while seed is being spread because if mud is stirred up it could cover the oysters and cause them to die. Therefore, in many areas farther upriver on the Potomac, Coan, and Patuxent, three small boats are generally used to scatter the seed. There oysters are off-loaded from *Nellie Crockett,* placed on smaller vessels (sometimes just skiffs), and spread across the beds by about a dozen men. "The small boats are able to get up in the corners and in areas that *Nellie Crockett* can't go, but in deep water I can do it as well as the small boats," says James.

On arriving at the mouth of Parrotts Creek, James placed a call to Morton on his VHF radio, notifying him that *Nellie Crockett* and her crew were ready to deliver. Shortly thereafter, Morton arrived in a runabout to assist James in the unloading. They both stayed in the pilothouse as he directed *Nellie Crockett* across his 14½-acre oyster rock.

The vessel circled back and forth across the beds as the six men (three on each side) shoveled seed oysters into the Rappahannock. With only an occasional break to light up a cigar, the men worked for an hour and a half steady until the load was all overboard. When oysters were delivered and payment made, *Nellie Crockett* headed back to the James River to load up once again. James's ledger book showed Morton paid him one dollar a bushel or $1,852 for a load.

James Ward died in 1989 and his son Jimmy inherited the vessel. Jimmy, who is the Commonwealth's Attorney in Middlesex County, Virginia, sold the boat. However, he kept James's log and ledger books and the boat Bible given to James by his wife Anne St. John Ward on Christmas of 1962, all of which tell something of the career James and *Nellie Crockett* had together on the Bay.

## Ledger Book, Logbook, and Bible

The first page in the worn ledger book is dated 1959 and from October 1 to December 31, Ward hauled seed for J. H. Miles and Company of Norfolk, Virginia. During that fall, Ward and *Nellie Crockett* hauled 24,288 bushels of seed to Miles's oyster grounds on Mobjack Bay and off Ocean View. From October 1 to November 13, he received 75 cents for every bushel hauled and from November 18 to December 31, he received $1.00 a bushel. For his work, he received $3,923.99 from Miles.

The rest of the ledger book has each year listed, the date, location and number of bushels of each haul. His best year was 1984, when he hauled over 70,000 bushels of seed and received $71,676 gross. During the 1960s, his best year was 1969 when he grossed $16,034 and hauled about 32,000 bushels. The best in the 1970s was 1979 when he grossed $67,023 and hauled over 70,000 bushels of seed for the year. Usually, a buyboat captain paid tongers half

The logbook, ledger, and boat Bible of *Nellie Crockett*. Courtesy Jimmy Ward.

of what he received for a bushel of seed from a grower. For instance, if James received 30 cents for a bushel of seed from a grower, he would pay the tonger 15 cents a bushel. Over the years, James received anywhere from $1.00 a bushel to 30 cents a bushel. Captain Melvin Ward of the little *Muriel Eileen* recalls paying 5 cents for a bushel of seed oysters in the 1940s. That meant he received 10 cents a bushel from the grower.

A typical year was 1970 when *Nellie Crockett* and James grossed $11,183 and hauled forty-five loads to customers up and down the Bay. The ledger shows James's first load was for Enock Hutson on January 23. He received $340 for delivering 1,150 bushels, or 30 cents for a bushel. That year, he hauled for Hutson from January 10 to March 7 and made nine hauls all together. On March 17, he hauled a 1,617-bushel load for James Verlander near Water View, Virginia. He received $529 for that load. His largest load of 3,265 bushels went to Warren Denton Company on September 16. He received $653 for that load. *Nellie Crockett* could hold about 2,100 bushels on deck and when it was over that amount it meant James loaded the hold and deck with seed. That year, he also hauled for Francis McNamara on the Piankatank River, Virginia Marine Resources Commission, Potomac River Fisheries Commission, J. C. Lore and Son of Solomons, Maryland, C. M. Lewis, Miles Oyster Co. of Norfolk, and James Kirk of Laneview, Virginia.

J. S. Darling and Son had a marine railway and was an oyster planter and packer. In 1959, the company paid 18 cents a bushel for oyster shells. Courtesy W. C. Hight collection.

James's logbook is also revealing. Inside the front cover is "Christmas 1974" indicating it was probably a gift. The first trip with the new logbook was from Deep Creek on James River to Bowlers Wharf on the Rappahannock River. It is dated October 9, 1975, and gives the times he reached certain points. He reached Old Point at 4:55 A.M.; Wolf Trap at 8:20 A.M.; Stingray Point at 10 A.M.; and Towles Point at 11:45 A.M. The book gives times, course, amount of time from one location to another, and a few remarks.

For instance, on a trip from Solomons, Maryland, to Deltaville, Virginia, on April 15, 1977, he wrote "fair tide" and "from W. H. Harris Seafood, light" which means he had unloaded and was headed home without a load. On a trip in July 9, 1980, from Newport News to Saxis his only remark was "flood tide." On a trip from James River to Crest Shoals on June 10, 1983, his remark was "turn 25 minutes above No. 6," and on a trip from James River to Smith Creek, Maryland, he wrote "bell buoy in river above Smith Creek."

Along with the ledger and logbook, James's boat Bible was also part of his son's collection. The cover of the Bible has engraved in gold "Nellie Crockett" and on the inside cover it states, "Presented to James H. Ward by Anne St. John Ward," his wife. The date was December 25, 1962.

The Bible showed obvious signs of being a boat Bible as water has stiffened and wrinkled the pages. It made every journey with James aboard *Nellie Crockett*, and its very presence on the boat speaks to the captain's faith.

## HAULING SHELLS BY BARGE

Oyster shells are planted on oyster beds to help develop nurseries for growing oysters. The shells act as a clutch for oysters to breed and grow on. Chesapeake Bay deck boats are used to haul oyster shells to oyster beds. Some boats carried shells on deck but as revealed here, boats were also used to tow and shove barges full of shells to oyster grounds.

William C. "Bill" Hight purchased one of the old Morattico Packing Company buildings just outside of Urbanna. In an upstairs room of the building, he discovered numerous old records concerning the firm. One was a letter to an insurance adjuster in Baltimore concerning a claim. It shows that deck boats were used to tow barge loads of shell to oyster grounds.

The papers included a bill from J. S. Darling and Son of Hampton, Virginia, dated June 22, 1959, to Morattico Packing Company of Urbanna, for 814 bushels of oyster shells. The cost of the shells was 18 cents a bushel for a total of $146.52.

The letter was to Clarke Langrall of Baltimore from Morattico Packing Company.

At about noon on Tuesday June 23, 1959, our powerboat *Elsie Louise,* captained by Robert Williams, was leaving the small boat harbor at Newport News, Virginia. This powerboat was handling a scow owned by the State of Virginia, which was loaded with approximately 1,000 bushels of oyster shells valued at 18 cents a bushel.

Due to close quarters in the harbor the scow was tied along the starboard side of the powerboat and would be strung aft on a towline upon reaching open water. As the two vessels left the outlet to the small boat harbor, a sea or wake from some large vessels caused the scow to overturn, dumping its cargo of shells in the water and landing bottom up on the starboard side of *Elsie Louise.*

The impact of this action knocked a 3-horsepower gasoline driven pump, valued at $225, from the deck of *Elsie Louise,* broke a casting on the dredge chain guide mounted on the starboard rail, totally damaged the powerboat anchor, and stove in two planks on the deck of the scow.

Mr. Woods, superintendent of Davis Boat Works in Newport News, sent a tug out and towed the two vessels, which were still hooked together, to his yard. After obtaining authority . . . he extracted the two vessels and righted the scow. The charge for this service was $59. He was then instructed to repair the two deck planks of the scow at a cost of $45.

Captain Robert Williams was instructed to check *Elsie Louise* for further damage. *Elsie Louise* is now in service in the Norfolk area. The vessel will soon be hauled for normal maintenance and will be further inspected for hidden damages. Because of a slight separation of the deck of *Elsie Louise* from the king plank near the mast, there is some fear that there may be further damage to the hull of the vessel not yet disclosed.

It was fairly common practice for deck boats to pull or shove barges full of oyster shells and sometimes two deck boats were used to tow one barge. When it was blowing, the boat or boats towed or pulled the barge from the front, but when it was a clear day, deck boats "shoved" the barge from the side. The deck boat and barge were tied together side by side.

In an interview with Terry Haydon, who captained *Mary E. Haynie,* he recalls towing a 28-foot by 100-foot barge that held between 7,000 and 8,000 bushels of oyster shells. He would buy shells from a shucking house in Colonial Beach, tow the barge full of shells from there to the Piankatank River, and plant the shells on private oyster grounds. The shells were blown off the barge by a high-pressure water hose.

Terry also recalls seeing the deck boats *Nora W.* and *Ward Bros.* towing together a 28-foot by 120-foot barge that held about 10,000 bushels of shell. He said it was not an unusual practice for two boats to pull a barge. One boat would be out front with stern lines tied to the bow of the other boat. The second boat's stern lines were tied to the barge.

The oyster seed and shell business kept many of the Chesapeake Bay buyboats working through much of the twentieth century. As the oyster industry declined, it also marked the decline of the Bay deck boat as more and more were without work.

*The growth of the pound-net fishery throughout the Chesapeake did as much as any fishery to create a demand for deck boats, particularly in the 1920s and 1930s. Larger boats are still used in the deepwater pound-net fishery while smaller ones, often referred to as trap boats, are still used in shallow-water fishing. Boats are geared up differently depending on whether they are used in deep or shallow water.*

*The first section of this chapter is about the trap boat* Martha Virginia *that was owned by Eddie Gaskins of Ophelia, Virginia. Eddie fishes shallow-water pound nets (25 to 35 feet of water) in the Potomac River and Chesapeake Bay, and over the years* Martha Virginia *was often around when my camera was clicking. She was typical of many trap boats used in the shallow-water pound-net fishery.*

# 9: POUND-NET FISHERY

The introduction of pound nets to the Chesapeake enabled fishermen to catch large quantities of fish and provided a use for Bay deck boats. In the mid-1800s and early 1900s, strong markets for fish in the Bay area grew, and fish houses in Crisfield, Baltimore, Norfolk, Hampton, and elsewhere would send out large buyboats up and down the Bay to purchase fish. Also, pound-net fishermen needed larger boats with a sturdy platform to carry thousands of fish and to haul the heavy and awkward gear that was used to set the nets. Many deck boats were built specifically for pound-net fishermen.

## ORIGINS OF POUND NETS

The actual origin of the pound net has been lost to time. However, it is known when and how the gear was introduced into the Chesapeake Bay region. The pound-net fishery started to expand on the Bay around 1870. R. Edward Earll, in his description of the Spanish mackerel fishery on the Chesapeake in 1887, gave an account of how the pound-net fishery started.

One of the first pound nets on the Chesapeake was introduced by fisherman George Snediker of Gravesend, Long Island. Snediker is credited with bringing the pound net to the Delaware and Chesapeake Bay regions.

Earll wrote that in 1875, Snediker went to New Point Comfort, Virginia, and constructed a large pound in the waters of Mobjack Bay for the purpose of taking shad and other species. It was there that one of the most colorful stories surrounding the pound net on the Bay survived time and is still told today in the New Point area.

Earll wrote:

The fishermen of the neighborhood [at New Point] being wholly unacquainted with the pound net, were very jealous of the stranger that came among them with such destructive apparatus. They watched Mr. Snediker's movements closely for several weeks, and after seeing the enormous quantities of fish taken by him, at once informed him that he must take his traps and leave the county.

[When Snediker refused] to comply with their demands, a number of them sawed off the stakes of the pound even with the water and carried the netting to the shore, assuring Mr. Snediker that if he attempted to put it down again they would destroy it. Seeing it was useless to continue the fishery here, he decided to seek some more favorable locality.

*Linda R.* is a good example of an open trap boat. She is not considered a deck boat because the house/pilothouse is actually set on the ceiling or floorboards of the boat. On a standard deck boat, the house/pilothouse is built up on deck and decks extend fore and aft of the house. When Bay fishermen refer to trap boats used in the pound-net fishery, they can be either a deck boat or an open boat like *Linda R.* Many early trap boats started life as open boats and were converted to deck boats. *Linda R.* was used for years as a trap boat by longtime Gwynn's Island, Virginia, fisherman Wilson Rowe. Alton and Lennie Smith of Susan, Virginia, built her in 1936.

Prior to leaving, he sold the stakes that remained in the water to a local fisherman, who secured from the stakes the design of the pound and in a short time had one properly arranged for fishing. The local fishermen also destroyed this, but not until enough had been learned to convince them that pound nets could be used with great profit, and within a year from that time twelve pounds were fishing in Mobjack Bay. In 1879 the number more than doubled and by 1880 every available site was taken up. Often three, or even four, nets were placed in line, the leader of one being attached to the outer end of another, for the purpose both of economizing on space and of securing the fish that might be passing at a distance from the shore.

Snediker, on leaving New Point, went to the Eastern Shore and became associated with one of the most popular fishermen of the region, in this way hoping to prevent any organized opposition on the part of the resident fishermen against the use of the pound.

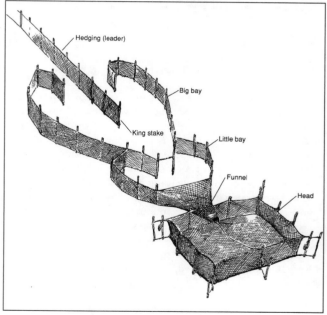

The pound net was not extensively used in the Chesapeake until after the 1870s. Bay deck boats have been used in the fishery and are still used today. Pound-net fishing is one of the few fisheries left that still offers work for Bay deck boats. Courtesy Virginia Institute of Marine Science.

Henry Owens of New Point, Virginia, owned the trap boat *Ellen Marie* when this photo was taken. She is an open boat here but was later converted to a deck boat. Owens used the boat in the pound-net fishery. Note the pile driver (ladderlike structure) used to drive poles into the bottom. Tommy Owens, Henry's grandson, described how it worked: "The boats had certain jobs. For instance, *Lavenia H.* and *Ellen Marie* were used mostly to set pound poles. There was an 850-pound maul on the pile driver that was mounted on her side. On the western shore of the Bay we could drive poles down with the driver, but on the Eastern Shore nets we couldn't get them down with just a driver so we tied a 12-foot length of 1-inch pipe to a hose and attached the pipe to the bottom of each pole using nylon string. The string was something we could pop loose from the pole when we got the pole down far enough into the bottom. Even with an 850-pound maul we had to pump a lot of water through the hose to pump and drive the poles because the bottom was so hard. It didn't take long to do because Granddaddy had so many men. If we had pretty weather we could drive all the poles for one net in about four days. Sometimes it took right much longer because we had so much maneuvering to do. We could set so many poles and then the tide would change and the men would have to pull up anchors. There were anchors stuck around in every direction to keep the boat still while the poles were set. We had a good crew of men. Once we got the hedging in a straight line, we could move right along." Courtesy Thomas E. Owens.

## Swainson Hudgins Tells the Story

This story was further expanded in 1995 when Swainson Hudgins of New Point, then eighty-two years old, gave an oral version as told to him by his grandfather.

Swainson started working a pound at the age of twelve with his father and grandfather and fished for seventy years. "I will tell you what I was told about Snediker and I know it's true because my grandfather told me this story. He helped run Snediker away from here.

"It was 1874 when Snediker first showed up here," says Swainson. "He come and got his spot at New Point to set his net. He worked out of Davis Creek. He went to work setting poles and net and the first day she was run full of fish.

"All we had then were gill nets and when the men of New Point saw how many fish he caught, they told him to move on or else. The first day he didn't move so my grandfather and several others went to him again and told Snediker he better move or else.

"On the third day, they went down to the shore and the net was still there. They all went home, got their axes and guns, got in their boats, and met out by the net. They chopped the poles off to the water and pulled the net up and threw it on the beach.

"Snediker went and got the law and all the men of New Point got summoned to appear in court at Mathews Court House," he says. "My grandfather said that the commonwealth attorney was a man named Donovan and he talked the judge into trying one fisherman and the punishment would go to all.

"Well the one fisherman was found guilty and when they set bond, all the men of New Point rushed to the front of the court, pushed the sheriff and commonwealth attorney aside, turned over a big old coal stove in the floor, and made it clear [that] to take the whole bunch would mean a fight.

"After that Snediker gave up, dropped the charges, and left. No one from around New Point ever heard of him again and nobody went to jail.

"They were rough times then," says Swainson. "It was just ten years after the Civil War had ended. I don't think there was a whole lot of law in Mathews County then. I don't think what law there was wanted to mess with that bunch from New Point either. So, it was probably best for everyone that Snediker left and never came back.

"You know what happened next. We got the pattern from the poles that we'd chopped off," says Swainson. "I was born in 1912 and started fishing full time in 1924. I fished some before that. I went with Granddaddy—I called him Pa—and my daddy. I can remember when there were 200 to 300 nets off New Point extending miles out into the Bay. Old Snediker did us a favor by bringing the pound net because a lot of fish were caught after that.

"We used to sell fish by the bushel and the most fish I remember selling from one catch was 1,500 bushels. [A bushel weighed 80 pounds so Swainson caught 120,000 pounds of fish.]

"The most I ever heard of being caught in one night was 3,000 bushels [240,000 pounds]. It would take days to get that many fish out of a net. They'd tie

*L. R. Smith* was built for pound-net fisherman Henry Armstead in 1926 by Lennie Smith. When this photo was taken, probably in the 1940s, Henry Owens of New Point, Virginia, had just purchased the boat. Note the small pilothouse aft and an engine cover built forward of the pilothouse to protect the motor. As watermen needed to spend more time and go longer distances on the boats, pilothouses and houses became larger and more elaborate. Courtesy Thomas E. Owens.

the bunt off so the fish couldn't escape and fish it daily until it was all empty."

## EDDIE GASKINS AND *MARTHA VIRGINIA*

*Martha Virginia* was converted to a deck boat in 1940 in Deltaville, Virginia. Interestingly, the vessel was originally built as a standard Chesapeake Bay deadrise workboat with the house forward and motor aft of the house. She was an excellent example of a small deck boat used in the pound-net fishery. These boats are also referred to by some as trap boats. Another term in the Chesapeake region for a pound net is a trap net. Trap boats are small deck boats or open boats used in the shallow-water pound-net fishery where fishermen work nets in 20 to 35 feet of water.

*Martha Virginia* was registered at 39 feet long, 11.9 feet wide, with a draft of 3.6 feet. Over the years she was a workhorse, but in 2001, time and work had taken her life and she was no longer considered fix-

Deck boats are used as work platforms to lay out and set pound nets in the spring. Eddie Gaskins and crew aboard *Martha Virginia* are setting a net near the mouth of the Potomac River.

able. So, Gaskins pulled her engine, gear, and gas tanks, dragged her up on shore, and burned her.

## Her Life as a Deck Boat

"She was longer than 39 feet," says Eddie. "The customhouse measures from the bow to keel and doesn't include the amount of distance created by the horn timber. She was 45 feet or more in length. [A horn timber is attached to the keel aft and extends the length of a boat by 3 to 6 feet.]

"I got *Martha Virginia* from Nelson Mitchell. Nelson ran a good-sized trapping rig in the Potomac River and Chesapeake Bay. In 1974, I was fishing crab pots in the summer and dredging crabs in the winter. I had heard that he wanted to sell his trap rig so I went to see him. It was in May.

"Nelson said to me, 'I don't want to sell right now but after the spring season you come talk to me.'

"So near the end of the spring season, I saw him down at the fish house and he asked me if I was still interested in buying his nets, stands, and *Martha Vir-*

Originally an open trap boat, *Peggy* was built in 1925 by Harry A. Hudgins of Peary, Virginia. She was later converted into a deck boat as pictured here. She is still alive and is owned by Kim and Gretchen Granberry. Courtesy Kim Granberry.

*ginia.* He said, 'My wife Virginia and I want to go on a trip to Louisiana to see my son.' His son was working in the menhaden fishery down there. 'Why don't you take the rig and fish it the rest of the season and I'll split things up with you,' he said to me.

"I took my pots up and while he was down south I worked the traps for two weeks and done real good. The four nets I worked those two weeks were right inside the mouth of the Potomac River. Nelson had some real good stands.

"When he came back he asked me, 'What do you think about it?'

"I said I wanted to buy it but I could tell he really didn't want to sell right then. He told me to go ahead and run the rig for the next two weeks. I fished it two more weeks and by then I could really tell he was not ready to get out of the business. It was a time in his life when he knew he should retire but he didn't want to. When you get older you understand that better than when you are young.

"So, I said to Nelson, 'I've got a lot to learn about this business; what do you think about me buying half now and we stay in partners the rest of the year and then at the end of the year we can talk again.

"He jumped right at that. So what was supposed to be a five-month partnership ended up being about

a four-year partnership. It was a good learning experience for me and it was good for both of us. Nelson had been fishing forty-four years so he knew the business backward and forward," says Eddie.

"Nelson had one trap he had fished [continuously] for forty-four years and that was the Wood Yard," he says. [Most fish trap sites on the Chesapeake are given names by watermen. The same names are still used today for sites that were first started in the 1880s. Eddie fishes the Betty, Nineteen Footer, Charlene Smith, and one called the Big Boy. These nets have had the same names for decades.]

"*Martha Virginia* came with the rig. She was an old boat when I started. Nelson bought her from a man in Deltaville who was using her to carry fishing parties. She had a cabin on the front when Nelson got her. I was a boy, twelve or thirteen years old, when Nelson bought her and he took her to Addison Cockrell's Railway [Cockrell's Marine Railway in Heathsville, Virginia]. They took all the decks and cabin off the front and put the wide decks and cabin aft. A lot of people don't realize that some trap boats were converted from large standard workboats.

"I was up there at the railway on my bicycle and Nelson didn't have the throttle hooked up just right but *Martha Virginia* was ready to go home," says Eddie.

This photo of *Martha Virginia* shows watermen lowering a pole to be set in the bottom.

"He said, 'Come on, ride with me down the river. I want to take the boat home. I'll let you steer and I'll work on the throttle.' I lived real close to Nelson and he put my bicycle in the boat. I stayed right there and steered her up the river and in the creek, while he worked. That was the first time I was at the wheel of *Martha Virginia*. I thought I was something.

"That summer after I got out of school he came after me. I was thirteen and he said, 'Come on, help me this summer.' I worked with him until I finished high school; then I went on my own and worked crab and eel pots until Nelson offered me the business.

"When Nelson got out of the business, *Martha Virginia* was getting in right bad shape around the horn timber, shaft log, and mast. I took the mast out of her and took her down to Rice's Railway near Reedville. Raymond Bray and his brother hauled her right up in the house. The railway went up into a house and they cradled her and took the entire shaft log and put a whole new stern into her. I fished her a few years like that.

"She still had the original bottom on her so a year or two later, I took her to George Butler at Butler's Railway [Reedville Marine Railway] in Reedville. He knocked the bottom off from in front of the engine up to the mast and he put a new bottom to her.

"I carried stakes with her, pulled skiffs full of nets, and carried fish in the hold," says Eddie. "In the spring we had brakes on her to carry stakes. [Brakes are made from two large—often 10-inch by 12-inch—beams, one placed forward and one aft across the sides, extending out over the water. Two pipes extending upward at the end of each beam hold pine fish stakes in place as *Martha Virginia* hauled stakes to the fishing grounds.]

"We really worked the boat. In the spring we drove stakes off her and when we got the last net out we would take the brakes off her and the hoses and the driver off her. [Water hoses and the driver were used to pump and pound the poles into the bottom.] "Once we got those off, we went to fishing in her.

"We fished all summer and then we would switch off and use *Bobbie*. We would send *Martha Virginia* down to George Butler's for repair and we would work *Bobbie* for a while. He would paint her and caulk her up. We had two boats so we would switch them around and when *Martha Virginia* was finished at the railway, *Bobbie* would go. Having two boats really worked out well for us. Later, my brother got *Manfred L.* so we had three deck boats.

"In the fall of the year, we used them to draw stakes out of the bottom. We had to take the stakes up

Deck boats are used to tow seine skiffs, like the one shown, to and from fishing grounds. Note the brake mounted across the stern of the deck boat.

when the fishing season was over. We had a nice stake-drawing rig on her. It's a piece of 6-inch by 6-inch or 8-inch by 8-inch oak beam that comes along the gunwale from the back of the cabin and extends out over the bow stem by about 18 inches; a pulley goes through the end and a cable goes through the pulley and you have a grip chain on the end of the cable. There is probably 12 feet of slack. Then your other end hooks to the winder through a block and tackle. We throw the grip chain over the pole, get a hold on that, and you come ahead on it [and pull the pole out of the bottom]. Sometimes the poles are in the bottom so far that the bow of *Martha Virginia* would go down three or four feet in the water. It would pull her down so much that the wheel [prop] would come out of the water.

"We had such a good rig that other pound-netters got us to draw their poles," says Eddie. "One year we drew over 1,000 poles from Lewisetta to Reedville for ourselves and other fishermen.

A pole driver run off hydraulics is used to pound trap poles into the bottom of a river or bay. Eddie Gaskins is keeping the pole straight as his crew guides the driver over the top of the pole.

The deck boat *Bobbie* is a modern-style deck boat with a traditional house/pilothouse configuration. She is used in the Potomac River pound-net fishery.

"The most fish we ever got on *Martha Virginia* was 30,000 pounds (300 big boxes). She was loaded and her decks were to the water. That was in 1975 when the down-run herring came in the Bay. [Down-run herring are herring that have gone to the headwaters of the rivers, laid their eggs, and are coming back out of the rivers to the Bay after the spawn.]

"It was also the year when there were a lot of bluefish in the Chesapeake Bay. What we think happened is that the Bay was loaded with bluefish and as the down-run herring were coming out of the Potomac River, they ran into those bluefish. This forced the herring to congregate at the mouth of the river to keep away from the bluefish in the Bay. Bluefish feed on other fish.

"It has never happened since but that year we loaded up with herring. Most of the time down-run

Brakes are installed on deck boats, as shown on *Manfred L.*, to carry trap poles in the spring to fishing grounds and to bring poles to shore in early winter when nets are dismantled and the fishing season is over. *Manfred L.* was built in 1922 in Denbigh, Virginia, and is still working on the Bay in 2003.

The hold on a trap boat is often used to haul payload. The hold of *Martha Virginia* is loaded with spot caught in a pound net.

A fish tub full of spot is hauled to a culling table on shore. The fish are culled and boxed for market.

herring leave by the first of May but that year they stayed here until the tenth of June. That was the last year we have had a big run of herring."

## Another Big Catch

"In the early 1980s, fishing was bad one year, and I was having trouble paying the crew," says Eddie. "We just weren't catching any fish. We went up one morning to fish two nets in the Potomac and two nets in the Bay. The shallow net was in 20 feet of water and there wasn't much there. So we went to the deeper net in 28 to 30 feet of water. When we pulled her up there was a whirl in her [fish churning] and that was unusual. We pulled her up some more and she had a load of the most beautiful [gray] trout you have ever seen. They ran seven to eight fish to a carton. [A carton holds 50 pounds.]

"This was on a Saturday so we took about half or two-thirds out of the net that day in *Martha Virginia* and we got a good price for the fish," he says. "Well on Sunday we don't fish but I decided I'd go look at the net and I met my brother Jimmy [Gaskins]. He had just come from the net that was named Big Trap. He was excited and he said, 'You got to go down there and look at that net, she's full of fish.'

"I said, 'No, Jimmy, you know she's not full. Now don't fool me.'

"We went down there and there were so many fish the fins were stuck out of the water. There was nowhere for another fish to get into that net. I slacked the pocket funnel up, threw him a piece of line, and we tied it off so none could get in or out. She didn't need any more to get in right then," says Eddie. "We fished on her Monday, Tuesday, and Wednesday. By Wednesday, we were getting her down some. So I opened the

Sometimes unusual fish were caught in the nets. This 485-pound jewfish caught on the deck boat *Thomas E.* in 1955 was captured on film. The fish was caught at York Spit Light. This was not, however, the most unusual fish caught by the Owens family. A prehistoric fish dead for thousands of years surfaced in one of their nets. Tommy Owens described this fish: "This old black man who worked for my granddaddy for fifty years told me this story. His nickname was "Old Jelly" but his real name was Will Forrest. He told me that back in the late 1940s, off on the middle ground (southeast of New Point Lighthouse in Chesapeake Bay) on a pound line, they were fishing when something got caught in the hedging. Jelly went to get it out of the net. He thought it was an old sea turtle but it wasn't. It was the greatest looking thing he had ever seen in his life. He said it was bigger than any hog he had ever seen. It had a funny-looking nose and a fan-like collar all around its neck. There were thorns sticking out of its body and a long tail that looked like a rudder on a boat. In later years, I saw that fish on the Discovery Channel and it was a prehistoric fish. Jelly said it was rotten and must have come out of the bottom. Nobody believed him much, but I did, and I'll believe him until I go to my grave." Courtesy Thomas E. Owens.

funnel back up. We fished her Thursday and on Friday and she was filled back up with bluefish and trout.

"That was the best week I ever had. We caught 1,000 cartons that week, about 50,000 to 60,000 pounds," he says. "The next week it went back to what we were doing before—practically nothing. But that week made my season.

"I hated to get rid of *Martha Virginia* but she got down and she sunk at the dock. The only time she sunk

the entire time I had her so I decided last August [2001] that I wasn't going to fix her. I took the motor out and all the other things. The one thing that hurt her most was that one year we were late [in the season] driving stakes and getting the driver off the boat. I was busy handling bait. We didn't take her to the railway like we normally had done. We got a lot of rain that year and freshwater will rot her quicker than anything. She sat there with no paint on the deck and that hurt.

Loaded to capacity, *Seven Brothers* entered Dymer Creek in 1963 with 90,000 herring in her hold. Courtesy Andrew Simmons.

"I pulled her up the river to Cockrell's Railway and we hauled her. I knocked a board out of the bottom to get water from out of the inside and a few weeks later we burnt her up. I hated that. It almost broke my heart but it just cost too much money to fix her."

The fate of *Martha Virginia* was typical of many deck boats. When the cost to fix it up was too much, the boat either went to the burn pile or to Davey Jones's locker.

## DEEPWATER POUND NETTING: *SEVEN BROTHERS*

As the pound-net fishery grew, fishermen began to install nets in deeper water—40 to 60 feet in the Chesapeake Bay. More fish were caught in deeper water and poles and gear were longer, larger, and heavier. The size of the equipment, coupled with the fact that watermen would be working in the Chesapeake Bay where rough weather was a regular occurrence, created a need for larger deck boats.

Watermen soon found that 55- to 65-foot deck boats worked well in the Bay's deepwater pound-net fishery and other fisheries. A typical example of a deck boat built for deepwater pound-net fishing was the 60-foot *Seven Brothers*. The vessel was registered at 59 feet 8 inches long, 16 feet 4 inches wide, 4 feet 1 inch draft, 28 gross tons, and 17 net tons.

From the 1920s to the mid-1960s, *Seven Brothers* stayed in the same family and was used in the spring for the deepwater shad and herring pound-net fishery. She was also used during the off-seasons to freight watermelons and other produce to Baltimore and coal and other items on return trips.

In the 1970s, '80s and early '90s, she was sold several times and was rigged and used in the Bay's snapper-rig fishery (purse nets) to harvest menhaden for the crab pot bait business. Her last home port was Cambridge, Maryland, where she was being used to plant seed oysters. Her last owner bought her in May 2001 to convert her to a pleasure boat, but when she was on her way to Chesapeake, Virginia, for the start of a two-year restoration project, she was run aground. The weather was too rough for anyone to attempt to save her and, tragically, she sank on May 6.

From the day she was launched near Foxwells, Virginia, in 1928 to the day she died off Stingray Point in 2001 (incidentally just a few miles from Foxwells), *Seven Brothers* was a commercial fishing boat.

Nets were hauled to the surface by manpower. The large skiff used by fishermen to haul the pocket full of fish to the surface is called a "tow-bat" in the Mathews County area. It is called a bateau throughout most of the rest of the Bay region. It was towed behind the large deck boats. Courtesy Thomas E. Owens.

## Early History

William E. "Capt. Billy" Simmons of Kilmarnock, Virginia, and his wife Chowning Simmons raised seven sons and four daughters. Captain Billy was born in 1865. He grew up to work the water and was soon fishing four deepwater pound nets in the Chesapeake's strong spring shad and herring fisheries. His first boat was an open dory but in 1925 he raised enough money to have boatbuilder Gilbert S. White of Foxwells build him a 60-foot buyboat that he named *Simmons*.

*Simmons* was used extensively in the spring pound–net fishery. Captain Billy worked his nets from February to May. Fish were hoisted out of the pound head into the hold of *Simmons* and hauled to a fish canning/pickling factory at the mouth of Dymer Creek just down the creek from where the boat was moored. Captain Billy had a steady market for his catch near his home. The rest of the year he farmed land and hauled watermelons and freight to Baltimore with his boat.

Fishing was good, and William and Chowning made a good life for themselves. They built a two-story farmhouse just outside of Kilmarnock, and William built a small school on the property and hired a schoolmaster to educate his children.

When grown, several of the boys decided to follow the water and in 1928 Stewart and Wroten Simmons had White build them a boat. They named it *Seven Brothers* after the seven Simmons sons of Captain Billy and Chowning. The vessel remained in the family until 1964, when she was sold to be worked in the menhaden purse-net fishery.

## Andrew Simmons

Stewart's son Andrew, sixty-seven, lives in a brick house next door to the old Simmons home place on Dymer Creek. Andrew was mate aboard *Seven Brothers* as a young man growing up, and captained her for four years in the early 1960s. Although emphysema has slowed him down in hot weather, he still goes patent tonging for clams in the cold-weather months in his 42-foot deadrise workboat.

"*Seven Brothers* was a good boat for what we were doing with her and she was very typical of the type of deck boats being used in the deepwater pound-net fishery," says Andrew. "She would hold 90,000 herring and 100,000 bunkers (menhaden). Herring were a little heavier than bunker.

"There were just a few of us fishing those deepwater nets in Chesapeake Bay. All we'd fish for were

Fish were hauled from the pocket of a pound net onto the boat and into the hold of the deck boat by way of a dip net. Courtesy Thomas E. Owens.

herring and shad and mostly just herring. We had twelve head [men] in a crew. We'd eat breakfast and dinner on the boat.

"Our stakes were 80 to 90 feet long, 12 to 13 inches across the stump [base]. We were fishing in 50 to 60 feet of water," he says. "We'd try to set our nets out when the dogwood would bloom. That's when the herring run would start. We did all right; I'll tell ya that. I'm not saying this because he was my daddy but my daddy [Stewart] and Odell Fitchett were the best fishermen on the Bay at that time." Fitchett also worked deepwater pound nets in the spring and he worked *Jennie Dare,* a 66-foot deck boat that White built in 1926.

## Bay Rowe

In 1963, Bay Rowe, fifty-three, was a teenager spending the summer at his grandmother's home in Ocran, Virginia. One of his summer jobs was to get up at 4:30 A.M. and work aboard either *Simmons* or *Seven Brothers.*

Andrew Simmons served as captain on *Seven Brothers* in the early 1960s. His father and uncle had the boat built in 1928.

On May 6, 2001, *Seven Brothers* was foundering on Stingray Point bar in Chesapeake Bay and by Monday morning, May 7, much of her hull and top work had been torn to pieces and washed ashore.

Carlyle Simmons was one of the seven Simmons brothers and he worked with his father, Captain Billy, on *Simmons* until his father died. Then, Carlyle took over *Simmons* and was captain of her. However, Andrew Simmons says that the family would work together to take stakes up after the spring run of herring, and often times Carlyle would take the larger *Seven Brothers* instead of *Simmons*. Rowe would work on whichever boat Carlyle was working that day.

"I worked for Carlyle Simmons on *Simmons* and on *Seven Brothers*," says Rowe, who is now manager of the Wilson Trucking Company at White Stone, Virginia.

"They worked deepwater pound nets and fished for herring and shad," says Rowe. "They'd sell to a

canning factory that would pickle and can the fish. When I got to my grandmother's towards the last of May or first of June, the fishing season was just about over. All their revenue-producing fish were caught in March, April, and May.

"My job was to help pull stakes and nets up once the season was over," says Rowe. "The stakes were pulled, rafted, towed home, and hauled up on the river bank. I was the raft man. If a pole got loose from the raft, I would run across the raft of [floating] poles and pull it back together or swim to the pole and bring it back.

"I was just a boy but I looked forward to getting up and going to work," he says. "One of the colored boys had an old car with a hole in the muffler. When he'd go by my grandmother's house, it woke me up every morning.

"When I heard the boat had died, it took me back to those days," he says. "I was surprised she was still alive because she was old when I worked aboard her. Old wooden boats like *Seven Brothers* just have a good feel to them that you don't get from any other type of boat.

"I'll tell you one thing, she's had a many a fish in her hold, because that family [Simmons] were some of the best fishermen on the Bay," he concluded.

## Roland George

Roland George, seventy-five, of Ocran, Virginia, bought *Seven Brothers* around 1970 and owned her for over two decades. He used her in the pound-net fishery and later rigged her as a snapper rig to catch menhaden. He sold her around 1990 and works a steel-hulled snapper-rigged boat today.

When the Simmons family owned her, *Seven Brothers* would hold 100,000 menhaden. George raised the deck and sides so the boat would hold 110,000 menhaden in her hold.

"One day I overloaded her with menhaden and I was coming into Cockrell Creek when a breeze picked up," says George. "She nearly went over and would have but two company [menhaden] steamers came up beside me—one on each side and knocked the breeze down. I was able to make it to the dock wedged between those two boats.

"She was a well-built boat," says George. "If Gilbert White had the [electric] tools people got today he could have turned a boat out in a week. Everything on *Seven Brothers* was made with hand tools and you've never seen a prettier wheel.

"I read in the paper that the man who lost her on Stingray Point said when he had his hands on her wheel bringing her down the Bay that he felt like he had his hands on history," says George. "We may have lost *Seven Brothers,* but we didn't lose that wheel. Before I sold her, I took that wheel out and made a coffee table out of it. Gilbert White never made a prettier wheel and I'm glad I saved her. The wheel that man had his hands on cost me $29. I'm so thankful I took this wheel off before I sold her. I've been offered $500 for her, but I won't sell her.

"When I heard the boat went down it hurt me a bit inside, because when you work a boat every day on

Fortunately, the original wheel from the wheelhouse of *Seven Brothers* was not lost when she sank. Former owner Roland George removed it to make a coffee table for his home in White Stone, Virginia.

the water, you grow fond of the fact she helps you make a living and that she brings you home every day, sometimes in the worst of weather. Even after you sell 'em, you don't forget those things."

## The Day She Died

On May 6, 2001, the Chesapeake Bay lost one of its oldest remaining buyboats when *Seven Brothers* sank just a few hundred yards from the place where Captain John Smith nearly lost his life in 1608. A stingray had jabbed its spine into Smith's arm, which is why the point of land is named Stingray Point.

It was actually known in 1608 as Stingray Isle, leading one to assume there was an island near the point of land that ends the 40-mile-long county of

Middlesex, Virginia. In 2001, there was no sign of an island but shoal waters reach out from the point for a couple of miles into the Chesapeake Bay.

On May 5 strong northeast winds were pushing 5- and 6-foot seas across a wide span of water leaving any inexperienced mariner with a delusion that there was plenty of water across the shoal.

Frederick Ramsay of Charlotte, North Carolina, had just purchased the vessel from George Chance of Cambridge, Maryland, and was bringing it to Chesapeake, Virginia, for a two-year restoration. Chance had been using *Seven Brothers* to haul seed oysters in the State of Maryland's oyster replenishment program.

Ramsay bought the boat to restore it and convert it to a pleasure boat, just as many of the other buyboats on the Bay have been converted to pleasure craft.

Ramsay had reservations to dock on Broad Creek near Deltaville, Virginia, on the night of May 5, but missed the mouth of the Rappahannock River and motored into the Piankatank River. Finding no place to moor, he decided to backtrack to the Rappahannock. This was a fatal mistake for *Seven Brothers* as Ramsay and his crew of two ran her aground on Stingray's shoal point.

The seas pounded against her stern and turned her sideways. Water gushed over her sides as pumps could not keep up with the abundance of seawater. Ramsay and his crew were rescued by the Coast Guard and the boat was left to the sea. On Sunday, *Seven Brothers* was still intact, but efforts to get her off the shoal failed as seas pounded everything and anything that came close. By Monday morning, the vessel had broken into pieces and was gone from sight.

For seventy-three years, she was worked hard and she died hard as the northeast wind drove seas against her hull. But even as she began to break there seemed to be some peace surrounding her death—as if, just maybe, she came home to die.

*As far back as the 1920s, Chesapeake Bay deck boats were used in the menhaden fishery as "snapper rigs." I first went on a snapper rig in 1986 when I was asked to do a story for* National Fisherman *on the menhaden bait fishery. Although the vessel I went aboard was a converted Maine sardine carrier, I knew that traditional Bay deck boats were being used in the fishery. I was not, however, aware of the role the boats played in the spring herring and shad fisheries.*

# 10: MENHADEN, HERRING, SHAD, AND FISH CUTTINGS

The start of the modern menhaden fishery came to the Chesapeake region in the 1860s when skippers came down from New England to catch menhaden in an effort to supply a growing national fish-oil business. Oil extracted from menhaden was used as lamp oil and as an ingredient in paint. It was also used for tanning leather and for making soap and rope. For generations, coastal communities depended on whale oil as their main source of oil, but as early as 1811, oil was being extracted from menhaden. It was much safer to harvest fish than whales.

One of the first menhaden fishermen to arrive in the Bay area was the so-called "father of the industry on the Chesapeake," Elijah Warren Reed of Brooklin, Maine. Captain Reed set up a kettle menhaden plant near Old Point Comfort and began to harvest menhaden by the thousands. Later, he moved his kettle plant to the Northern Neck of Virginia. The town of Reedville, Virginia, is named for him, and the fish he came to catch made it one of the wealthiest towns in America.

During the first quarter of the twentieth century, Reedville had the highest per capita wealth of any town in the United States, and in 1912 there were eight large plants in and around Reedville. These plants had large "company" boats, first powered by sail, then by steam engines, and finally by gasoline and diesel engines. Small "snapper rigs" owned by independent fishermen also worked the Bay. Some sold their fish to the large fish companies while others, especially in later years, developed their own markets, selling menhaden for bait to blue crab fishermen working crab pots and also to recreational hook-and-line fishermen.

There are still large World War II vintage company boats (over 100 feet) working the Bay, and into the 1990s Chesapeake Bay deck boats were still used by snapper-rig fishermen. Before the introduction of modern-day gear and spotter planes, snapper and company rigs worked two purse boats and a striker boat. Some snapper fishermen worked two deck boats, one to carry payload and tow purse boats and another to accommodate the large crew.

Purse boats were used to set and haul purse nets and to haul loads of fish to the surface. Prior to the 1960s, there were as many as twenty to thirty men in the two boats to haul the bunt to the surface, while the striker (or driver as he was also called) was in the small striker or drive boat and would lead the two purse boats to the fish.

A snapper rig's single purse boat is alongside the deck boat *(not pictured)* using its power block to harden up the catch.

In the 1950s Mario Puretic of San Pedro, California, invented the power block to hoist nets in and out of the water. The number of men required for a crew was then cut significantly, and with the utilization of airplanes to spot fish the need for a striker was eventually eliminated. Modern-day snapper rigs use only one deck boat and one purse boat, while the large company boats still use two.

Deck boats were used in a variety of ways in the menhaden, shad, and herring fisheries. When large numbers of shad, herring, and menhaden were being caught in pound nets, deck boats were used as runners between the nets and the factories in Reedville. The boats would be loaded down with fish from the pound nets and would carry the payload to the factory. Many of the larger converted schooners and bugeyes were also used to haul fishmeal and fish oil to market before trucks took over that job.

## STEVE PRUITT: SNAPPER RIGGING WITH TWO DECK BOATS

"For a couple summers in the mid-1930s, my uncle and my daddy used their boats together as snapper rigs," says Steve. "They used *Mary Sue Handy* as the carry-away, the one they bailed the fish onto, and my father built a house over the forward hold of *Stewart Brothers* to make enough room for the crew to sleep. They didn't come home every night so they lived on the boat, and it took a right big crew to work a purse net.

"They had two purse boats and the first year they rowed [the purse boats] around the fish, but the second year they installed a Model B engine in one of the purse boats. It was a four-cylinder car engine, and they also had a little striker boat. There was no engine in the striker boat.

"When purse boats were rowed there were two oars and two men to an oar and the oars were 16 feet long," he says. "You better have had a good seine setter because he had to throw the net overboard with arms full. It was hard work.

"The whole process was hard work and I guess the money wasn't there for them to keep doing it. There was a lot of labor involved," says Steve. "After a couple summers, they went back to hauling crabs and other things."

## HAULING FISH CUTTINGS

Ted Haynie of Reedville, Virginia, used his deck boat *Namu* in the winter crab-dredge fishery, hauling passengers and freight from Reedville to Tangier Island in warm weather and in the spring hauling fish cuttings from a herring cutting house to the menhaden factories in Reedville.

One of the oldest fisheries on the Bay is the spring herring fishery. America's first president, George Washington, and other tidewater Virginia plantation owners caught herring and shad in the early spring in haul seines. They had fish houses on shore where the herring were gutted, salted, and cured. The fish were barreled and shipped to the West Indies in exchange for rum, pineapples, and other products from the islands.

Tidewater Virginians and others developed a taste for salt herring. The fish, along with cornbread covered with homemade butter and molasses, became a breakfast staple for many families. Large commercial cutting houses became common in many tidewater communities in the late 1800s, but by the middle of the twentieth century, salt herring had become more of a specialty food and no longer a staple. In the 1950s and through the 1970s, small herring houses were scattered about the Chesapeake Bay region with several located on the Northern Neck of Virginia near Reedville. Pound-net fishermen supplied herring to these houses as millions of fish were caught starting in late March and continuing through the spring herring run.

In 1957, aboard *Namu,* Ted hauled cuttings for Treakle's Cutting House at Palmer, Virginia, on Antipoison Creek. He also used *Namu* to run fish from pound nets to the fish factories in Reedville.

"A man from Milwaukee bought all the herring from Treakle's," says Ted. "He shipped the herring back to Milwaukee where he made pickled herring with wine sauce and sour cream. He had a big business. I hauled the cuttings [the rest of the fish not used in the curing process]. There were several boats doing that in those days. McGinnes was another cutting house right next door to Treakle's and the deck boat *Hawsie B.* hauled from that house."

At the cutting house, the herring were gutted, the heads were cut off, and the body of the fish was placed in brine. Fish roe was cut out and packaged. "There were machines to fillet the fish but the gutting and beheading was done by all these colored people. There must have been a hundred of them working in each house," says Ted.

In the fish house, there were big tanks filled with brine. The term used for placing fish in brine was to "strike the fish," thus some used the name striker house instead of the term cutting house. Herring were struck in two tanks. The first tank was used primarily to get the blood out of the fish and the second was used as a secondary cure. The fish were then barreled and shipped by truck or train to Milwaukee where the final pickling process and canning or jarring took place.

"We dumped the cuttings right in the hold of *Namu* and I would carry it to the menhaden factory at Reedville and they would make it into fish meal. When I got to the factory, they had a pump and would pump it all out of the hold.

"There were a lot of herring in those days and you don't see people catching fish like that anymore,"

Deck boats hauled fish cuttings from fish packing houses like Fairport Packing Company to menhaden processing plants near Reedville, Virginia. Courtesy Dr. A. L. Van Name.

says Ted. "The pound-net boys would set their nets in late February and early March. They would catch Labrador herring in early March but they didn't want too many of them because, for some reason, people don't like a meaty salted fish.

"Odell Fitchett had deepwater pound nets off there in 40 and 45 feet of water and he would be loaded with herring. When the herring house wasn't running, I would lay *Namu* up against Odell's net on a Saturday, and I would load every last one she would carry and bring them right on to the factory to make meal and oil from. There was a lot of shad too. There was one trap off Windmill Point that caught more shad than any other net around. I've seen him catch 5 to 6 tons of shad a day. I hauled from his net too and I've come up the Bay with many a shad.

"At the factory, I got paid $1.00 for 1,000 fish. The factory had a sectioned-off dump [container] at the dock and each section would hold 750 pounds. They considered 750 pounds to be 1,000 fish. There were four sections on the dump and each time a section filled up with cuttings, I got $1.00. I've had as many as 200,000 fish on *Namu* and I got $200 for the load."

A suction hose from a hydraulic fish pump is lowered into the net full of fish, and the menhaden are transferred to the hold of the deck boat.

## HAULING FISH MEAL AND FISH OIL

"Before they started hauling fish meal in bulk, it was hauled in burlap sacks by deck boats," says Ted. "Most of the big freight boats like the Conway family boats—*Sarah Conway* and *Betty I. Conway* and others—freighted a lot of fish scrap [meal] and fish oil from Reedville to Baltimore. My father-in-law, Joseph C. "Joe" Jett owned *Ruth*, a double-deck buyboat, and he would do the same thing.

"The Conways must have had a contract with the McNeal Company [menhaden plant in Reedville] because they hauled fish scrap and fish oil for them all year long," says Ted. "They would carry fish scrap and fish oil to Baltimore and bring back salt, fuel oil, coal, and whatever else the factory needed to operate. The

fish scrap was put in burlap bags and piled on deck and covered over with canvas. The fish oil was pumped into tanks in the hold.

"My father-in-law did the same thing with *Ruth* because he had family in the business," says Ted. "After a while, he got some shares and eventually ran the Menhaden Company. The Jett family owned it.

"Fish scrap is a high-protein feed ingredient used in poultry and hog feed," says Ted. "The fish are cooked and pressed and then put through a dryer. It [the dried fish] is stored in a scrap shed and it has to be turned several times or it will catch fire. Then it goes through a grinder and it is reduced to an ingredient just like flour. You don't see any bones or anything. It has the consistency of corn meal and years ago they used to bag it and sew the bags up. There wasn't anything like shipping meal in bulk by truck. Now you wouldn't think of bagging it. Today, it goes in a dump trailer.

"In the late 1940s and early 1950s, I remember *Betty I. Conway* coming to Reedville almost every week to freight meal and oil," says Ted.

"There was another boat named *Armistead*. Reedville Oil and Guano Company owned her. She was an old boat with a steel hull with wood fastened over the steel. She was a converted lightship and I think she was an old Jersey beach schooner. She was shaped just like if you took a watermelon and cut her lengthwise. She had a double-deck pilothouse and had the galley in the lower deck. They put steam in her in the 1940s but the boiler took up too much room so they put a one-cylinder Fairbanks-Morse in her later on. She must have been 90 to 100 feet long.

"I worked on her one summer and she had two tanks in her hold for fish oil; bags of fish scrap were piled up on deck, and we hauled canned tomatoes from a tomato-canning factory owned by Reedville Oil and Guano Company. We would take mixed loads and I think a lot of freight boats hauled mixed loads. We hauled everything to Baltimore. The cans of tomatoes were in a box unlabeled. They were later labeled with a brand name of the broker who bought the tomatoes.

"When we unloaded in Baltimore we would go load the boat with salt and other things for the factory."

## *NAMU:* A MENHADEN EXPERIMENT

*Namu* was not originally built as a Chesapeake Bay deck boat. The vessel was built as an experimental

*Elsie Louise* is shown before she was converted into a replica of an old wooden menhaden fish steamer and renamed *Georgeanna*. Captain Rob Williams is painting the sides of the boat from the skiff. Many deck boat owners did this to keep the railway bill down. Courtesy Carroll Davies.

menhaden boat, started by Joseph C. Jett of the Menhaden Company.

Jett was looking for a way to cut down on the amount of labor used to haul the nets to the surface. This was before the power block was developed in the 1950s and before experiments with smaller purse nets in the 1970s led to working nets with smaller crews and only one purse boat. "There were about thirty-four to thirty-six men to a crew before the power block and Joe was looking for a way to fish without the men," says Ted. "His idea was that one small deck boat would make the set and a few men could load the big boat like *Ruth* with the fish.

"*Namu* was originally built with the cabin forward and a big turntable net on the stern. Joe had the long-leaf pine shipped in from Georgia. He tried two or three things that did not work out and he went into the hands of the receiver and he lost the place. When Menhaden Company was sold, *Namu* was about 80 percent complete. The new owners

*Elsie Louise,* built in 1914 in Irvington, Virginia, has had a major facelift. Here she is as *Georgeanna*. She was converted and used as a snapper-rig vessel by her owner, Captain Wesley "Dootsie" Walker.

Snapper rigs used one purse boat, like the one shown, whereas two purse boats were used by the much larger menhaden company boats.

hired Herbert Rice to complete the boat. Rice and the owner got the same idea and rigged her up with the purse net aft. Rice tried it all that summer but couldn't get it to work so he let some boys crab dredge in her that winter. Finally, he put her up for sale and I bought her. The forward house was already off and I put a new house aft on her, like a traditional deck boat. She made a great deck boat," says Ted.

## MODERN SNAPPER RIGS

As recreational hook-and-line fishing and the crab-pot fishery grew in the Chesapeake region, the demand for reliable sources of fresh bait also grew. For a period of about fifteen years from 1974 to 1989, a few Bay deck boats found new life in the menhaden bait snapper-rig fishery.

*Seven Brothers, Marie, Yeomac,* and *Elsie Louise* were four boats used in this small but effective fishery. Roland George worked *Seven Brothers* for about six years in this fishery. Jimmy Kelley owned *Marie* and *Yeomac.* Kelley also converted a Maine sardine carrier named *Nereid* into a snapper boat. Captain Wesley "Dootsie" Walker converted *Elsie Louise* into a replica of an old menhaden steamer with the wheelhouse

forward. Walker also added a refrigerated fish hold and changed her name to *Georgeanna,* after his late wife.

One of the first to gear up was the now defunct Kelley Seafood of Northumberland County. In a 1986 interview, Kelley said he decided to get into the bait business in 1974 to meet the needs of local blue crab fishermen. He started buying menhaden from pound-net fishermen on the Eastern Shore of Virginia and block-freezing the fish. "This just didn't work, because we never knew how much bait we were going to get," he says. "So, we decided to try and catch our own."

During the early years of his bait business, Kelley used *Yeomac,* a 65-foot deck boat. He strung a two-hundred-fathom purse seine, rigged up a purse boat, and started catching menhaden. His was one of the first small purse seines seen on the Bay in many years.

At the same time Kelley was getting into the bait business, Roland George was already using *Seven Brothers* to work pound nets and was selling baitfish to crabbers. He too began experimenting with a small purse net and a single purse boat. Over time, Kelley, George, and others figured out how to work the nets.

"We tried several different types of nets in the beginning," says Kelley. "I even bought nets from the big companies, but they didn't work real good for us be-

A snapper-rig purse boat makes a set. A sea anchor holds one end of the net to the bottom, while the boat encircles the fish with the rest of the net.

cause of the deep bunt. You see, all of our fishing is done right here on the Bay, and we don't need a deep net." The large company menhaden boats fish in deeper waters of the Bay and in the Atlantic Ocean.

Kelley and others designed a shallow-water net that has a tapered bunt so when the net is pulled in tight, all the fish are up, ready to be sucked on board.

With the exception of the nets, the gear is basically the same as that on the larger company-owned steamers. When the bigger vessels make a set, they begin by casting off two 40-foot aluminum purse boats that are lashed together, each carrying half of a huge net. The 40-footers are directed—as a pair—to a school of fish by a spotter pilot flying high overhead. At his signal, each purse boat splits away and begins to run in a large semicircle. In the process, the twine zings over the side of each boat, followed by the purse line, which runs through rings at regular intervals along the bottom of the net.

When the circle is completed and the purse boats are linked once again, a hydraulic winch or "cathead" is used to drop the "tom" overboard. Made of lead, the tom weighs about 1,000 pounds; it slides down the

purse line, both anchoring the end of the line and holding the net on the bottom. As the tag end of the purse line is wound up on a purse boat winch, the lower edge of the net bunches up against the tom, closing the seine and preventing the escape of the encircled menhaden.

The tom is then hauled up, and the power blocks on both purse boats begin to draw in the net, reducing the size of the circle. When the net is as tight as the power blocks can make it, the steamer comes alongside.

When the larger vessel is in position, the purse boats form a triangle, with their sterns against the big boat and their bows against each other. A gaff hoist is lowered, lashed to the twine, and hauled up to tighten the net further. Finally, a fish pump hose is lowered into the net, and the menhaden are transferred to the fish hold aboard the steamer.

Snapper-rig operations have modified this system somewhat to reduce cost. The biggest difference is their use of just one purse boat, which approaches the school, drops a sea anchor to hold one end of the net, and then continues to circle the fish while feeding

Roland George of White Stone, Virginia, worked *Seven Brothers* in the Bay's snapper-rig menhaden fishery for several years. Note the crow's-nest ladder up against the mast and the galvanized pump and trough up against the house, used to pump fish from the net into the hold. Courtesy Robert W. Jensen.

the seine overboard. And, since the nets used by the snapper rigs are smaller than the seines carried by the company-owned steamers, the leadline itself keeps the twine on the bottom during pursing, thereby eliminating the heavy tom.

## ROLAND GEORGE AND *SEVEN BROTHERS*

"I actually bought *Seven Brothers* from David Winegar of Winegar's Marine Railway to work pound nets, and I used her for that for several years," says Roland. "I shifted over to snapper rigging in the 1970s. First I was fishing pound nets on Monday, and then Tuesday I'd purse net and Wednesday pound net and so on for the rest of the week. Later on, all I did was purse net with her.

*Yeomac* was built in 1924 by T. W. "Tom" Wright in Deltaville, Virginia. Kelley Seafood used her in the snapper-rig fishery. Note that a coffin has been applied to her hull. A coffin is a protective covering made of felt material and metal, which is nailed to the hull to keep the boat from leaking.

"In the early years we worked from year to year experimenting until we got the purse net thing right. We didn't have much choice because we couldn't afford to go with the big [company] size boats so we kept working with the small boats.

"The pound-net business was a killer because one day we would get $1.25 a pound for gray trout and the next day we got 6 cents a pound. You don't get much for baitfish but you get about the same amount all the time and you catch more.

"There's a good bait market too with crab potters and hook-and-line fishermen who use chum to catch fish," says Roland. "There's a lot of demand for menhaden so the price doesn't jump around a lot.

"The other thing about pound-net fishing was there were big labor costs. We carry a five-man crew on the snapper boats. We needed more for pound netting.

"When we first started we used a ladder-type crow's nest attached to the mast to spot fish, but now we use spotter planes like the company boats, and it has made a world of difference. We don't spend near as much fuel running around looking for fish.

"The hold on *Seven Brothers* would hold 112,000 menhaden and it generally took three sets to fill up the entire hold," says Roland. "When we first started we bailed the fish out with a dip net but later we installed a pump and pumped the fish from the nets into the hold."

Roland sold *Seven Brothers* in 1990. He and his son still work a snapper rig but they now work a large steel-hulled boat. "I hated to get rid of *Seven Brothers*. God, I loved that boat, but I needed a boat that would hold more fish and I needed a refrigerated hold.

"If I could have found something she could do to help me make a living I would have kept her forever; but I couldn't."

Fish are pumped from the bunt of the net into the hold of *Seven Brothers*. Courtesy Roland George.

With a load of fish in her hold, *Seven Brothers* is on her way to home port. Courtesy Roland George.

*The Ward brothers—Melvin, Floyd, and Milton—spent their working lives aboard the boats, and their father Johnny Ward was known all over the Bay for his association with buyboats.*

*On March 18, 2003, I appropriately held the final interview for this book on Captain Johnny's dock on Jackson Creek in Deltaville, Virginia, talking with his three sons about crab dredging.*

# 11: CRAB DREDGERS

About the same time as motor-powered deck boats came on the Chesapeake scene, Virginia began licensing dredge boats for the harvesting of blue crabs. It was the winter of 1904 but the exact year watermen began dredging crabs is unknown. Surely it was before the turn of the twentieth century and legend has it that a waterman working an oyster dredge out of Hampton Roads ventured a little too far over into the Bay's channel and brought up a lick full of sooks (female hard crabs). This eventually led to Virginia's winter blue crab fishery.

Along about the end of autumn, the Bay's female crab population, after mating, begins its long migration to the lower Bay. Female crabs cannot tolerate low salinity at low temperatures, so as winter weather lowers water temperatures, the sooks move into deeper, warmer water and burrow into the bottom. The result is that a large percentage, about 85 percent of the winter harvest, consists of female crabs.

For many years, Bay deck boats were the main vessel of choice for most crab dredgers. Since the work was done in deep water and in the winter, deck boats provided a large, stable platform; room for a galley and comfortable overnight accommodations; and a larger engine that allowed fishermen to pull dredges from both sides at one time.

It took a while for Bay watermen to figure out that a standard deadrise could also pull two dredges at once. More watermen owned 40- to 45-foot Chesapeake Bay deadrise workboats than 55- to 65-foot deck boats. For years, watermen in the smaller boats pulled just one dredge from the side. When they figured out how to pull two dredges off the stern of the smaller boats, watermen began building deadrise workboats in the 50- to 55-foot range with a wider beam. This allowed room for a larger, comfortable house and for two dredges to be worked off the stern with relative ease.

Interestingly, this led to yet another name for the boats as owners of smaller deadrise crab-dredge boats referred to deck boats in the crab-dredge fishery as "mast boats." The last deck boats built in any numbers were built for the Virginia crab-dredge fishery in the 1940s, '50s, and early '60s. The use of the smaller deadrise workboats in the crab-dredge fishery marked the end of the era of Chesapeake Bay deck boats as commercial fishing vessels.

## THE WARD BROTHERS

Captain Johnny Ward's story is well documented in this text. He owned a fleet of Chesapeake Bay buyboats and in the 1940s he started turning the boats

*Delvin K.* was rigged for crab dredging on Davis Creek in Mathews County, Virginia, in the mid-1990s. Note how the dredge is mounted on the side. Courtesy Cloyde W. Wiley III.

over to his sons, Melvin (Mel), Floyd, and Milton (Mit).

"The first boat Daddy rigged up for crab drudging was *Lagonia*," says Floyd. "I don't know when that was but it was fairly early. [*Lagonia* was a log deck boat built in 1913 in Poquoson, Virginia, and was Captain Johnny's first large boat. He bought it used.] The first year he didn't make enough money so he stopped doing it for a while. The early years of crab drudging, the "back creekers" from Seaford and down that way controlled the drudge business. They didn't want Daddy or anybody else getting in the business and they made it hard on him." In the early years of crab dredging, the market for winter crabmeat was small so watermen and buyers in areas like Seaford and Poquoson were able to control the market. As time passed, crab buyers from Crisfield, Maryland, and other areas around the Bay began buying winter crabs, which took the control of

the market away from the lower Bay watermen and buyers.

"We know Daddy was drudging crabs before I was born," says Mel, the oldest son. "I'm seventy-seven years old. When I first started it was all deck boats drudging crabs except for a few boys out there in small boats hauling one drudge from the side. They had a small 4-foot-wide drudge that they pulled from the side because they didn't have any power. They had 25-horsepower Palmers and Model A Ford engines—that kind of stuff—and they couldn't pull but one drudge. Deck boats were bigger and had more power."

"It was a lot of boats in the early years with side rigs," says Mit. "Those boys from Tangier Island were out there in small boats pulling one drudge. The main boats to crab drudge with were deck boats."

"A boy got drowned out there in one of those side rigs," says Floyd. "They had a lot of mussels in the drudge bag and they reached down to grab the bag

The captain and mates aboard the smaller deadrise crab-dredge boats referred to the larger deck boats as mast boats. This shows the contrast between the two styles of boats. *Ward Bros.* is pulling dredges from the sides, whereas the smaller deadrise vessel pulls two dredges from the stern. It is obvious why some called deck boats "mast boats" as suggested by the towering mast. A boom is not used in the winter crab-dredge fishery.

and it pulled them overboard. The boat started going in circles. People saw them fall overboard and went and got one but the other one drowned before they could get him."

"We all started drudging on our own about 1945," says Mit. "That was the year Mel took over the little *Muriel Eileen* with that little Fairbanks-Morse engine."

"That was about the time we started trucking crabs to Crisfield too," says Floyd. "Before that Daddy would run *Iva W.* night and day. He would drudge all day and haul crabs to market all night. He used *Iva W.* as a buyboat too because he would buy from other drudgers. We would load the truck and if we had a lot more crabs I'd drive the truck and Daddy would haul the rest to Crisfield on *Iva W.* The truck would hold 325 barrels.

"We got the truck so Daddy would not have to go up and down the Bay at all hours," says Floyd. "Daddy was born in 1902 so he was forty-three years old when we started trucking. Before that he ran all his crabs by boat to Crisfield."

"I started out in *Ruth S.,*" says Mit. "I ran her for six years and then Daddy sold her to Charlie Pruitt of Tangier Island and we bought *Nora W.* and I ran her. *Ruth S.* had a Fairbanks in her that Daddy took out of *Muriel Eileen.*"

"The three of us owned *Thomas W.,*" says Floyd. "We had two named *Thomas W.;* one was *P. E. Pruitt* and the other was *Midland.* Paul Pruitt from Urbanna had sold *P. E. Pruitt* to some fellow in Reedville and we bought it from him. We didn't keep *Pruitt* long, maybe four or five years.

"Crab dredging season ran from December 1 to the last of March. There aren't many deck boats working now. There is one now tied up at the head of Little Creek named *Ella K.* She's the only one still working that I know of and there were a hundred or more out there at one time.

"There were thirty or forty deck boats working right out of Cape Charles," says Mel. "Crisfield could solid pick a crab. We have handled as many as 500 barrels of crabs in a night. We couldn't do it every night

The final nail in the coffin of the Chesapeake Bay deck boat came when Virginia watermen figured out how to tow two dredges from the stern of the smaller Bay deadrise boats. The use of the smaller boats was more cost-effective than working the larger deck boats. This realization, along with the decline of the oyster fishery and the development of a modern twentieth-century road and highway system, meant there was no more work for the Bay deck boats.

but when there was a glut we handled that many. We would haul 200 to 300 barrels a night right along to the Crisfield picking houses. Now we weren't catching all those. We were buying too."

"I remember the time Mel caught 102 barrels and we knocked off at 2 P.M.," says Mit. "Daddy had gone to Florida and hadn't gotten back and Mel was in *Iva W.* It was the first time he had crabbed *Iva W.* by himself."

"That day, the drudge would come up out of the water and crabs blew right out on deck and there were so many the crew had to shovel them up and pile them right up against the pilothouse. They were so clean they looked like they came right out of a crab pot," says Mel.

"You take 102 barrels, that's a right good pile of crabs," says Mit. "We filled up all the barrels in short order, so we made a pen out of the barrels to keep the crabs from getting away until we got to the dock and

*From left:* The Ward brothers of Deltaville, Virginia, are Melvin, Floyd, and Milton. The brothers were captains of several deck boats from the 1940s until they retired in the 1990s.

*Ward Bros.* is named after Melvin, Floyd, and Milton Ward of Deltaville, Virginia. Sons of Captain Johnny Ward, the brothers grew up knowing they would be captains of Chesapeake Bay buyboats. The 70-foot *Ward Bros.* was originally *Andrew J. Lewis,* built in 1929 at Fairport, Virginia. She was built as a double-deck buyboat but was converted to a single deck boat by Captain Johnny Ward, who also changed her name.

got more barrels. We would throw them over in the pen so they wouldn't escape."

"I've sold crabs for as low as $1.50 and that was the night we had 500 barrels and that was a good run," says Floyd.

"The day we caught 102 barrels we got $6 for a barrel, the next day $5, the next day $4 . . . right on down until we got $1.50 for those 500 bushels," says Mit. "That must have been around 1951."

"We sold to the Crisfield dealers," says Floyd. "Booker Ward, Bud Tawes, Mel Colburn, Earl Dize, and the Drydens. Booker Ward in the summertime could pick 100 barrels a day at his picking house."

"The crab houses used to have a 25-barrel limit per day on crabs and the state put us on a limit," says Mel. "We had ten to twelve boats working for us. Tommy King of New Point in the boat *Sadie,* he sold to Daddy for a long time. The *Gloucester Beauty* was another one.

She was a pretty little boat, that *Gloucester Beauty,* and was owned at Onancock one time. *Squirrel, Old Point, Oysterman,* and *Willie M.* were some other boats that we bought crabs from. Sonny Brooks of West Point, Virginia, owned the *Willie M.* He crabbed for us."

"I'll never forget Sonny," says Floyd. "I was out there one day when I tore a dredge and here he come. He stopped drudging, got on my boat, and helped me fix that drudge. That's the way he was."

"By golly, he was a good man. I broke a chain hook on my drudge one time and I didn't have a spare," says Mel. "Sonny stopped, came aboard, and told me I could take one of his hooks. He didn't have an extra; he was going to cut himself out of a day's work drudging to give me that chain hook. I'll tell you this whenever he had a need, I'd stop whatever I was doing, even if it cost me a day's work, to help that man."

"We helped one another out there. One time a waterman was drudging crabs in *Frederick H. Ayers* when something happened to his engine and she was broken down for two or three days. So every day each boat would bring in a barrel each for him so he could make a day's work. We tried to look out for one another," says Floyd.

"My daddy's brother Howard Ward of Crisfield ran some of my daddy's boats. He ran *Walter Bailey*, *Edward P. Parkins*, and *Sophie A. Durm*," says Mel.

"I don't think he ran *Edward P. Parkins* but one year," says Mit. "She was in such bad shape. They used to say, you see her coming, you untied to get out of her way because she was in such bad shape."

"Now this is the truth," says Mel. "Howard got in bad shape, he had children and couldn't make a dollar, so Daddy bought the bugeye *Sophie A. Durm* for him to work, but she needed an engine. Uncle Howard came over and asked Daddy where the motor was for her. Daddy said we got to go to Guinea [Neck in Gloucester County, Virginia] to get it.

"They went to Guinea and walked down on a dock and Howard asked Daddy, 'Where is the engine?'

"Daddy pointed down in the water to a boat that was sunk with an engine in it and said, 'There she is right there Howard,'" says Mel. "They got her up and used her for years in *Sophie Durm*.

"Daddy also bought *H. H. Conway* when she was just about in sail," says Mel. "Milford Price changed her over to power."

"Daddy made a lot of money in the early years when he was running crabs in *Iva W.*," says Floyd. "He had the market cornered because nobody wanted to run night and day like him. When the trucks got into it everybody could deliver crabs."

"When you drudge all day and run all night and you make a dollar a barrel off 200 barrels, you are making $200 while everyone else is sleeping," says Mel. "The end of the week you had right much left over.

"Everybody knew Daddy. I went to Smith Island several years ago and stopped at a place to get a soft crab sandwich, and I guess I look like Daddy because someone asked me if I was related to Johnny Ward. When I told them who I was you would have thought I was a movie star.

"It's funny how a man could get a reputation by just plain working hard," says Mel. "And that was my daddy."

The deck boat *Iva W.* is underway on Chesapeake Bay towing two dredges. The dredge post located amidships holds the combined weight of the chain and dredges.

## TED HAYNIE OF REEDVILLE AND BIG JIMMIES

Ted Haynie of Reedville, Virginia, worked the deck boat *Namu* in the crab-dredge fishery from the 1950s through the 1980s. He recalls this story when he and his mate set on a large mess of jimmie crabs.

"I crab dredged in *Namu* all over the [Virginia portion of the] Bay in the winter. I'd start working out of Davis Creek [lower bay] and as it wound down I'd move further towards home [from Reedville to Windmill Point]. In those days [1960s] there were what we called gang crabs. I could go out and catch 25 barrels in twenty minutes and go home, but after a while, we pretty much wiped them out and they would get scarce. When this happened, we would move closer to home and work. We pretty much had it all to ourselves because the boats working out of Davis Creek wouldn't come here unless it really got bad towards the mouth of the Bay.

"One winter right before we moved from Davis Creek to Reedville, we got into a mess of jimmie crabs. Most everything we caught crab dredging was females, but not this time. It was a severely cold winter

A two-man crew empties the dredge bag of crabs on the deck boat *Iva W.*

and I think the ice and cold drove a lot of big jimmies down from out of Maryland to deeper water here in Virginia.

"No one else was around and we were fooling around up near the Old Station in 60 to 65 feet of water. It's what people now call the Cell. It was just about time to pull the dredges in and go home when we hit a lick of crabs in that deep streak of water just before you get to the Old Station. We caught almost all jimmies. We took another lick and did it again. All we got were jimmies. That night I took those few jimmies back to Davis Creek and sold them to a buyer there on the dock.

"I had an old colored fellow working with me named Pike Lee. [Normally, three men work a crab dredge boat—a captain to steer the boat and two crewmembers to dump and handle the dredge as it comes aboard.] Pike and I worked the boat and dredges without another mate because he and I could get more money that way and he was good at it. I ran the boat and would come out of the pilothouse and help dump crabs out on deck after each lick and get the dredge back overboard. It wasn't so bad on *Namu* because she was only 60 feet long, but I used to work along *Nora W.* and she must have been 85 feet long. Sometimes she was worked with two men too. The

man in the pilothouse would have to run out on deck, help dump the dredge, and run back in the pilothouse. He had to take off running like he was in a football game.

"We'd done so good, I told Pike the next morning we were going to be there at daylight. Next morning, we went up there and worked that deep hole in the blackest mud you have ever seen in your life and there were plenty of crabs. We had baskets stacked up on deck with nothing but jimmies. There must have been 75 or 80 baskets and 45 barrels of sooks. I told Pike we aren't going to Davis Creek tonight. We are going to Reedville. [Davis Creek in Mathews County was where most crab-dredge boats moored and worked from. Virginia Marine Police made regular crab limit checks there. Ted and Pike were way over the catch limit.] I was worried too they might be checking at Reedville but they weren't. Melvin Smith of Smith Point Seafood came down to the dock and he saw all those jimmies. I knew Melvin wouldn't say anything to the law because he wanted all the jimmies he could get. They were worth something then and he was glad to have them. I had hardly gotten home when my phone rang. It was Odell and Clifford Lawson [crab dredgers] and they would never tell you anything about where they were crabbing. They wanted to know where I got those jimmies! Melvin Smith had called them because he wanted more of those big crabs. I told them I was kind of down the Bay, over here and there, and did everything I could to keep them from knowing where I was.

"Well, the next morning when I came out of the creek, there they were in their boat waiting. They must have stayed up all night waiting for us. That day, I didn't go near the spot but later in the week they kept watching us like hawks until they finally found it too. The word spread quickly and the Davis Creek boats came too when they heard about the jimmies. It was a hard place to work though. The mud was thick and black and stones all over the place. We had to handle a lot of stone.

"When you were catching crabs, it was hard to keep it a secret."

## LIFE ON A CRAB-DRUDGE BOAT: STEVE PRUITT

Steve Pruitt grew up on Tangier Island and worked the water with relatives at a fairly young age. Winter crab dredging was a steady job for Steve and he recalls what life was like aboard a crab-dredge boat.

"The first year I crab drudged I worked with my daddy and my brother on *Elsie Virginia,* and the next year I worked with my brother Winnie, who had bought the deck boat, *Lora Lee.* Later I worked on *Three Brothers* and *P. E. Pruitt.*

"Winnie was just a little late—he was supposed to have been a slave driver," says Steve with a laugh. "Everything on that boat of his had to be spotless. He didn't do it himself now, but he made me do it. He made it awful miserable for me. He was good to me too."

"Winnie bought *Lora Lee* from the United States Coast Guard. Her number was *CGR 1207* and she had been confiscated from a bunch of rumrunners out of Carolina during Prohibition days. Her first name had been *M.V. Chadwick.* She was caught loaded down with railroad ties and corn liquor under the logs. The Coast Guard confiscated her and fixed her up real nice.

"She was one nice boat. She had hot water steam heat all through her. The Coast Guard kept confiscated boats for twenty years and then they would either rebuild them or sell them. When my brother got out of the service they had these boats for sale under the GI bill so only veterans could bid on them. He was

While waiting for another lick, this crewman aboard the crab-dredge boat *Iva W.* washes down the decks in December of 1985.

bidding on a steel-hulled boat named *Black Rock.* He wanted it to go deep-sea trawling.

The Coast Guard decided to keep *Black Rock* so he ended up with *CGR 1207. Lora Lee* had a lot of brass on her. She had eighteen pieces of brass in the pilothouse and I don't know how many pieces in the bedroom. The drawers had brass handles and the desk pulls were all brass and every piece had to be shined and Winnie wanted it to look like it was brand-new. All of her interior in her pilothouse had been sealed with cedar and I had to wipe that down with furniture polish. When you walked in there it smelled just like you were inside a cedar chest.

"Boy, Winnie wanted it right and a lot of the captains were like that too. Now you take Charlie and Paul Pruitt on *Three Brothers* and *P. E. Pruitt,* they were particular. Charlie, oh my gracious, I don't care how

Wooden barrels were used to contain crabs before plastic barrels were available. For years, Chesapeake Bay deck boats hauled barrel staves from Baltimore to barrel makers throughout the Bay region, and the finished barrels were often hauled by deck boat to crabbers. In this 1940s photo, the crew of the deck boat *Marion Sue Handy* has just off-loaded some barrels at a wharf on Tangier Island. Courtesy Lewis Parks.

good I made my bunk up or how good I scrubbed her up after work it was never good enough. He didn't do it to hurt my feelings. He just wanted it to his standards and nobody could do it that good. Every morning I'd get up and make my bunk up and he would come behind me doing something to it. We learned early to make our bunks. I never got out of a bunk in my life that I didn't make it up. Charlie would never say anything to you about it. He was just too good. He would just come behind you and fix it but I knew how he operated and tried to keep things the best I could. It didn't matter how good I scrubbed the deck down after a day's work, he was going to come behind me and do more. I don't care how long you scrubbed. If he saw a broom straw on deck, he'd pick it up.

"The food was good on the drudge boats. The cooks weren't gourmet cooks or anything but we ate good. We'd catch a rockfish sometimes and we'd have stewed rock with mashed potatoes. We caught a lot of flounder in the drudges and they were good to eat. Sometimes we would get a pair of [wild] ducks from home [Tangier] on weekends. Then we would have stewed duck with Irish potatoes and turnips. That was good. You get that gravy on your thumb, you would almost bite your thumb off.

"The Coast Guard had made the cabin real comfortable on *Lora Lee* and there was a seating area with cushions all around so in the evenings after work all the boys from the other boats would congregate there," says Steve. "Winnie didn't want all those people on board because he didn't smoke for one thing and most all the boys smoked, plus he didn't want them making a mess. We didn't miss many days for bad weather and I think it was because Winnie didn't want all those boys sitting around and messing up his boat. She was the only deck boat on the island that had a bathroom. Every other boat I worked on I used a bucket in the engine room or I went over the monkey rail.

"Winnie was a smart man. When his son Bill decided he would quit school, Winnie took him crab dredging." [Bill Pruitt is the current commissioner of Virginia Marine Resources Commission.] "We'd work the foulest bottom he could find and put out more chain than he needed to work us harder. It was load after load of crabs and rocks. When school opened up, Bill was the first to enroll. Winnie knew what he was doing.

"I'll tell you this, *Lora Lee* held the record for the most barrels caught in one day and that was 124. We were right down at Pickett's Hole catching 5 barrels to a drudge. We were down there on hard bottom offshore off Kiptopeke, just south of Cape Charles where those cement ships are. Those gang crabs were on a hard, sandy bottom. You couldn't work on those crabs but a couple days because you would tear them up so bad. In that sand, we would pull the backs off them.

"As far as I know, that was the record and we got $2.00 a barrel. That was good money then. Then we were harboring at Cape Charles. We would leave Tangier on Sunday night late or Monday morning real early, work all week, and come home on Saturday. We would live right aboard the boat, get up at 5 o'clock and get our breakfast. If we were drudging a long way away, like down around Lynnhaven or somewhere, we left real early in the morning.

"Two of us worked on deck and my brother ran the boat. I worked aft. I was the one who turned the dredge when she came up upside down. I was the one that hooked her when she went overboard and I culled crabs under the chain. That's the most dangerous place on the boat. If you hit a hang [catch something that breaks the chain], men have been killed when the chain breaks loose. I've seen barrels cut right half in two. A lot of people would cull over the chain but that's not smart. I've seen a drudge get hung up in an old ship and break the chain and fly right through the pilothouse.

"My brother Winnie was the best waterman I've ever seen in my life when it came to handling a boat," says Steve. "On a foggy day you won't see Winnie dredging crabs in Virginia, he'd slip up into Maryland [which was against the law]. Brother William had a book that he kept. He knew what the tide was doing and knew how long it took him to get from one place to another on a flood tide. He could go up in Maryland and catch crabs. We'd put the crabs in the hold, so no one would know what we had. We did that in Virginia too. We'd put a few on deck, the amount that was a normal day's catch, so no one would know for sure what we had caught. You didn't want them following you the next morning. You didn't tell anyone what you had done, particularly if you'd done good.

"We were up in Maryland one day when we saw *Nellie Jane* get caught up near Crisfield by the Maryland police," says Steve. "We hightailed to get below the Virginia line at Smith Island as hard as we could go. They chased us but they didn't catch us."

One of the most dangerous places to work on a dredge boat is under the dredge chain culling crabs.

## WILLIAM WRIGHT: PATENT DIP AND DREDGING OFF THE STERN

William Wright was involved in the very early years of crab dredging on the Bay. He grew up in Deltaville, Virginia, in a boatbuilding and waterman's family and as a boy he worked with his father Ladd Wright aboard the converted-to-power bugeye *Sophie A. Durm.*

In the early years of dredging with small engines, experiments involved pulling a dredge off the stern of a deck boat, but as engine power increased, it was soon discovered that two dredges could be worked from the sides.

William recalls pulling a dredge from the stern of *Sophie A. Durm* and working a patent-dip trotline from the deck. A patent-dip trotline was developed around 1910 and it eliminated the need for a hand dip net when trotlining for hard crabs. Its use on deck boats was probably limited, but William's story shows the gear played a part in the history of Bay deck boats. Certainly, the low-sided log deck boats and converted–to-power bugeyes would provide a good platform for working this gear.

"I liked following the water with Daddy," says William. "We would work the sea side of the Eastern

Shore. We lived on the boat and worked right off Smith Island, Virginia, at the mouth of the Bay.

"We moored right at the end of Fisherman's Island and there were eighteen to twenty boats there with us. We caught as many as 50 barrels of crabs a day and we got $1.00 a barrel. I've sold them for as little as 25 cents a barrel," says William.

"At first, we were in a 41-foot bateau that Daddy and I built together in the yard. Later Daddy bought *Sophie A. Durm*. We patent-dip trotlined off her side and dredged for crabs off her stern on the sea side of the Eastern Shore.

"There was a group of us working together and we had the largest boat," says William. "If there wasn't any buyboat market on a day, since Daddy had the largest boat we would load everyone's crabs on *Sophie A. Durm* and haul to the Hampton [Virginia] market.

"*Sophie A. Durm* was a big boat, and if the tide was low we had to go out into the ocean to come in the Capes to get inside the Bay," he says. "She was sharp on both ends and didn't have a patent stern. A northeast storm came up in 1926 when Daddy had a boatload of watermelons on her bound for Washington. He went in the Coan River [a tributary of the Potomac River] to get away from the wind and anchored with two anchors. The wind was so bad, though, that it blew him up on a bar and he couldn't get off so Daddy sold her to Captain Johnny Ward. He got her off the bar and brought her back to Deltaville. He wanted a round stern on her so he hired Daddy and me to take the pointed stern off and put a round stern in her. We did it, and it took us away from dredging crabs."

*I did not realize until I was about three-quarters of the way through this project that the trip I made with Captain Johnny Ward in 1985 aboard the buyboat* Iva W. *was a watermark event for this book. Though most of the interview appears in* Harvesting the Chesapeake—Tools and Traditions, *it would be a travesty not to include some of Captain Johnny's own words in a book on buyboats.*

*Captain Johnny was to deck boats what Harvey Conway was to Bay schooners. Captain Johnny was the patriarch of a family who ran a fleet of deck boats for over seventy years on the Chesapeake. His life spanned almost the entire era of motor-powered deck boats and he spent his whole life aboard the boats. He was named after Captain Johnny Sterling, his uncle, from Crisfield. Johnny Sterling brokered deck boats on the Bay and named several of the boats after family members. He would keep a boat for a short while, sell it, and have another built.* Agnes Sterling, Joyce Sterling, *and* J. E. Sterling *were just a few of the boats he had owned.*

*A portion of the 1985 interview is in this chapter along with stories from others who remember Captain Johnny Ward. Captain Johnny died at his home in Deltaville on December 14, 1998, at the age of ninety-six. The day he died, his beloved deck boat* Iva W. *was moored at his Jackson Creek dock behind his home.*

# 12: A DAY ABOARD *IVA W.*

The fog drifted lightly across Davis Creek in Mathews County. The Virginia air had a cool edge to it, but it seemed more like early spring than December 13. It was 4:00 A.M. and Captain Johnny was down in the engine room of his boat, greasing the Caterpillar engine and preparing for a day of crab dredging on the Bay. Captain Johnny had performed this task many times in the years that he owned the 65-foot *Iva W.*, built in 1929.

*Iva W.*, named after Captain Johnny's wife, sat by the dock in the fog and stillness. Then, one after another, the sounds of cranking engines broke the morning silence as the string of crab-dredge boats prepared for their journey out to the Bay.

Two deckhands arrived at 4:05 A.M. and Captain Johnny, clad in blue bib overalls spattered with white paint and wearing a red hat with a Southern States logo above the brim, came up the ladder to meet the crew.

After a quick good morning, the men slipped the lines from the mooring piles. In single file, the dredge boats slowly moved out the creek toward the Chesapeake.

The two hands scurried back into the heated galley, which is warmed by the exhaust pipe that extends from the engine up through the galley and the roof. When the engine's running it keeps the galley good and warm. Captain Johnny turned on a small light

over his compass and flipped his depth finder on as he steered *Iva W.* out into the darkness.

Above his head was a new $3,000 radar unit, but Captain Johnny kept looking at his compass and depth finder. "Yeah, the boys talked me into putting that thing in here," he says, motioning to the radar. "But I know nothing about them. I'm sure they're fine if you know how they work, but if you don't you might just as well pitch 'em overboard," he says with a slight chuckle.

Captain Johnny leaned over the wheel to get a close look at the compass. "A fellow gave me this compass when I had the boat built," he remarked. "I had it rebuilt in Norfolk once, but that's all I've ever done to her."

Captain Johnny was born in 1902 and comes from a long line of Chesapeake Bay watermen. Born and raised in Crisfield, he quit school at thirteen and went to work on his father's 75-foot sail-driven bugeye. "Daddy bought shucked stock oysters from around the Bay and seed from the James River. He would also haul watermelons, lumber, and whatever else he could find to haul.

## CAPTAIN JOHNNY REMEMBERS

"My daddy taught us a lot about working the water. He would always tell us what a load would bring and

Captain Johnny Ward, eighty-three years old in this photo, is at the helm of *Iva W.* Captain Johnny died in 1998 at the ripe old age of ninety-six. He worked the Bay most of his life and was known as a hard driver from one end of the Chesapeake to the other.

what it would cost him. I remember he would charge $45 freight for a load of watermelons hauled from Gloucester County to Washington, D.C., or Baltimore. One of the things he taught us was how to sound the bottom, and when that leadline hit the bottom you best let him know the water depth quick. I think he knew his boys would all be working the water one day. There were nine of us, five girls and four boys.

"I was about sixteen when I bought my first boat. It was a little 40-foot frame boat with a little engine. Daddy said I'd never make any money in her because she was too small, but I ran her hard. I made a daily trip from Crisfield to the Piankatank River, up past Freeport Landing, to buy soft crabs. I'd take them back and sell them to a buyer in Crisfield. I had to get up early to make the trip every day and I slept on the boat. There wasn't any house on the boat so I'd wrap up in a piece of canvas with just my nose hanging out. That was to keep the mosquitoes from taking me away," he mused. "I'd sleep there all night until a night watchman would come around and tap on the canvas with his billy."

"He'd say, 'Time to go Johnny.'"

As the CB blared overhead and the captain watched his compass, he continued to talk of those early days. "When I was eighteen years old [in 1918] I bought *Lagonia*. She was about 50 foot and was a log canoe. [*Lagonia* was built in 1913 by James H. Moore in Poquoson, Virginia, which was a center for log canoe building in those days.] I started out buying clean-culled oysters in her during the winter and I'd buy fresh fish from pound-netters and haul them to Gwynn's Island in the spring and summer.

"I've had many a boat," says Captain Johnny with a tinge of an Eastern Shore accent. "I've run just about everything there is to run. In the 1930s, I ran watermelons from North Carolina to Philadelphia in the old *Edward Parkins*." One after another, he listed the boats he had owned.

"Lands, if you were to put them all in a pile, that would be one big pile of boats!" He said. One of the most famous of Captain Johnny's boats was the old converted-to-power schooner *H. H. Conway*. "I bought her and had a heavy-duty 175-horsepower Fairbanks-Morse installed in her. She was named after the famous skipper, Harvey Conway. [Conway was the founder of the legendary Conway Fleet, which the old captain assembled from the 1880s until his death in 1931. Legend has it he started with all he owned in a twelve-pound flour sack, but was a millionaire when he died.]

It was in *Lagonia* that Captain Johnny first started dredging for crabs. "The first time I went adredging was in 1926. I couldn't make enough that first year to pay two men $12 each a week," he says. "I was getting $1.50 a barrel for my crabs.

"I had to give it up or starve. One week, I lacked $10 at the end of the week for paying off the men," he says. "I went home and asked Iva, my wife, if she had any money. She had $10, so I paid off the men and headed for Crisfield, dead broke."

Shortly after that, Captain Johnny began buying oysters from the James River and selling to buyers in Crisfield. The first oysters he bought cost him 40 cents a bushel and he sold them for 80 cents.

Off in the distance, the lights on the other dredge boats could still be seen. Captain Johnny opened the pilothouse window so he could see better and the cool breeze chilled the house. He lit a small heater.

Behind the pilothouse, inside the house of *Iva W.*, a picture of Jesus Christ sitting on a hillside hung on the wall. Next to it was a photo of Captain Johnny's

Captain John Wright of Deltaville, Virginia, built *Iva W.* for Captain Johnny Ward in 1929.

wife inscribed "Love, Iva—1948." Across the way was a picture of an ocean liner identified as "The North German Lloyd flier *Europe,* sister ship of the *Bremen,* the two fastest afloat."

Three bunks cluttered with an assortment of gear from life jackets to line extended from the floor to the ceiling. A chart rack loaded with charts was neatly placed overhead and a medicine cabinet hung from the wall. It contained everything from nuts and bolts to a bottle of Bufferin.

"We've been a lot of places together," he says of *Iva W.* "I've been from Cape Charles to Crisfield in weather when the Old Bay Line steamers wouldn't come out on the Bay.

"Many a night my daddy would check down at the dock in Crisfield to see if I'd come in. He'd say, 'I know Johnny didn't come up the Bay because my house was shaking from the wind.'

"But they'd tell him at the dock, 'Johnny's landed the crabs and be damn if he ain't gone back for more!'"

During the crab-dredge season, Captain Johnny would dredge all day and then buy from other crabbers. "I had fifteen boats working for me and after I'd load up with crabs I'd haul to Crisfield at night, and be back the next morning dredging again.

"I'd work six days a week, night and day. The engine never got a chance to cool off," he says. "I'd go home on Sunday morning and be back out on the Bay dredging Monday morning. A lot of people have asked me how I could do it, but I was young then, and that made a whole lot of difference.

"After a while, all I did was work crabs. I'd buy in the spring, summer, and fall and then dredge in the winter. I've seen a many a crab in my life, I have. Once, I guess it was in the early 1930s, I went into Little Creek, right off from Lynnhaven Inlet, to buy crabs from some patent-dip trotliners. You know, there weren't any crab pots around then. I don't know what happened but that night they struck a gold mine of crabs. That day, I bought 460 barrels of crabs and all the other buyboats were loaded up too. I had to dump them loose in the hold to get them all on the boat. I'd never seen so many crabs in my life.

"Well that glutted the market and my buyer told me I could go back but I could only pay $3.00 a barrel. I had been paying $4.00 a barrel. The rest of the buyboat captains decided to go ahead and rig up for dredging because it was the middle of November, but I decided I'd try to make another load because I knew there were plenty of crabs there.

"When I got down there, I told the boys I could only pay $3.00 and they all laughed at me and said 'no way.' So, I told them to go ahead and find another market. Well, I knew Hampton was glutted, just like Crisfield, so I decided to wait and see.

"There was a little beer joint there near the shore and all the crabbers were in there beering up. I went in and sat down to have a beer and it wasn't long before they came to me and asked if I'd clean them out for $3.00 a barrel.

"Yep, that was one time it paid to wait around. I was always one to take a chance. It didn't always pay off, but most of the time it did.

"I've bought crabs for as little as 50 cents a barrel from down in Guinea Neck, but most of the time it was around $1.50 when I first started.

"I've done more than just run crabs in her. In 1929, I ran watermelons from North Carolina to Baltimore. Then, I had an old Regal gas engine in *Iva W.* It would take four hundred gallons of gas for that trip. That was right bad, but fuel oil wasn't but 4½ cents a gallon. I got $90.00 a load to make the trip and I paid a man $6.00 to go with me. So, it cost me $18.00 for fuel and $6.00 for labor. I made about $60.00 a load when you figure food and everything. The next year I changed to the 60-horsepower Atlas and she only burnt two hundred gallons a trip. So, it saved me some money."

At daybreak, Captain Johnny stepped into the wheelhouse and pulled a string that was hooked onto a bell in the galley. It was a signal for the crew to come forward and ready themselves for work.

All the windows were lowered on the pilothouse, and Captain Johnny asked one of the crewmen if he could see buoy 36 in the channel. The crew included Floyd Johnson of Newport News, who for the past twelve years has crab dredged in the winter, and Franklin Forrest of Mathews County.

"Check that dredge to make sure there's no hole in the twine," says Captain Johnny. Sure enough, there was a hole. The captain came out of the pilothouse, got down on his knees, and mended the hole.

When everything was ready, the dredges on the starboard and port sides were dropped overboard one at a time. "We caught our limit of twenty-five barrels day before yesterday," says Captain Johnny. "Yesterday we had sixteen barrels and six baskets of jimmies.

The price for crabs was $18.00 a barrel for females and $11.00 a basket for jimmies. They were also catching some conchs, which were bringing $6.00 a basket. Captain Johnny has sold crabs for as little as 50 cents a barrel and as much as $66.00 a barrel.

Besides the prices, Captain Johnny has seen other changes since 1926. "When I started, I had a 25-horsepower Palmer in the log canoe and we could only use 5-foot-wide dredges," he says. "Now we have plenty of power, and the law allows 7-foot-wide dredges."

Another change on the Bay is the competition. "There are ten times more crab dredgers on the Chesapeake than when I started," he commented. "There are over two hundred licensed dredgers from Virginia and now they're letting Maryland crabbers come down here."

Captain Johnny moved over to a rope on the side of the pilothouse. When he pulled down on the rope, the 175-foot chain connected to the dredges began to reel in. As the dredge moved up from the bottom, Captain Johnny slowed the throttle down and continued to pull down on the rope. A towing post (dredge post) amidships holds the combined weight of the chain and dredge. Hung on the top of the post are two large steel blocks through which the chain passes. After passing through the two towing blocks on the post, the chain runs belowdeck and around a toothed sprocket, which is driven off the main engine. Two 3-foot stop chains are also attached to the towing post and by tension they keep the chains from going out farther than the skipper desires. These chains are secured by one of the hands who hooks a two-pronged catch link into the long chain when Captain Johnny signals him.

One of the crewmen picked up a 2 × 4 "turning stick" and, as the dredge surfaced, he used the board to straighten the dredge so the open end fell against the boat, which kept it from coming aboard backwards. Captain Johnny then moved the rope back and forth, and the dredge went up and down in the water, washing the mud out of it. Once the dredge was on deck, the two hands shook the contents onto the deck by grabbing the two large rings attached to the twine dredge bag.

The catch was not what the captain or crew had anticipated. There were a few crabs, a conch, and some sponges. "I've never seen anything to beat that," grumbled Captain Johnny. "It's not very good."

The dredge was released, and the chain clanked against the horizontal and vertical rollers on the side. The crewmen sorted the female crabs and placed them in a barrel. The jimmies and conchs were put in baskets, and the horseshoe crabs and sponges were tossed back.

After each lick the crew hosed and washed the work deck. The second dredge did not yield much more than the first.

At 10 A.M., Captain Johnny and his crew had only two barrels, and the licks seemed to get longer and longer. "When you have to take long licks like this they don't amount to nothing." It was between ten and twenty minutes a lick.

After each lick, Captain Johnny asked the crew to check the cotton bag for holes. (A chain bag is on the bottom of the dredge and the cotton bag is above it.)

The skipper said some days they catch over a bushel to a dredge. It takes three bushels to fill a barrel. "We really need to catch a bushel a lick to do much," he says. "I've seen it when we've caught a barrel in a lick. That was some good days."

During the day, there were few breaks in the routine, except in between licks, "Today's a nice day, but some days there's ice all over the deck, and when it's cold, it ain't so nice," the captain said of the weather.

For lunch, each crewman had a sandwich and a piece of fried chicken reheated on the stove in the pilothouse. They ate in the galley. The galley walls on *Iva W.* are tongue-and-groove beaded paneling painted green. An old wooden-spindle "Sunday school" chair with gray paint wearing off the seat and a newer model folding chair are nearby.

Between licks, the crew would sip on a cola, take a smoke on a cigar, or get a drink of water from the old water barrel mounted on the stern against the galley wall. The barrel is a classic-style container typical of those on the old sailing vessels that were a part of Captain Johnny's youth. "I picked her up in Crisfield off one of the old boats. I've got a new-style barrel at home, but I like the way the water tastes from that old wooden one," he says.

Captain Johnny and his crew continued to work the dredges, and several licks yielded a bushel of crabs. As other boats came near, conversations could be heard over the CB. Occasionally, Captain Johnny would ask, "What are they saying? I can't hear all that rumbling."

When the day was just about over, *Iva W.* had harvested its worst catch in a week. There were eight barrels of sooks and six baskets of jimmies. Captain Johnny radioed one of his sons on the dredge boat, *Thomas*

Secured to the galley wall, this string ran from the bell to the pilothouse. Captain Johnny pulled the string and rang the bell to let the crew know it was time to go to work.

*W.,* to come and pick up his catch and crew because he was going home to Deltaville.

Generally, he'd take his crabs back to Davis Creek to be sold, and the crew and Captain Johnny would be back dredging on Saturday. "It's just not worth the effort," he says.

Before the crew left, Captain Johnny paid them each $392 for a week's wages. The crew is paid according to the catch. The boat gets 40 percent off the top each week. The expenses are paid, and what's left is divided evenly between Captain Johnny and the two crewmen. This method of pay is used by many of the dredge boats.

After the crabs were loaded onto *Thomas W.* and his crew boarded her, Captain Johnny headed for home. Cruising up the Bay, he began talking again about his years on *Iva W.* "I've learned a lot about life

Captain Floyd Ward aboard *Thomas W.* takes Captain Johnny's crabs from *Iva W.* Floyd carried his father's crabs to market, while Captain Johnny took *Iva W.* home to Deltaville. The barrels hold three bushels of crabs.

working the water," he says. "Once I brought an old man from Crisfield to Deltaville because he was having a boat built here. His name was Jim Hurley and we ran into one bad storm. Mr. Hurley went up in the forepeak and he got banged up right bad. I'll never forget what he said to me when we got him out. He said, 'Johnny, the Good Lord looks out after boys, but when you get to be old, you have to look out after yourself.' I don't think I exactly knew what he meant by that then, but now that I'm older than he was at the time, I think I know what he meant.

"A lot of times we put in seventeen-hour days, and that's hard on an old man," he says. "But I guess it's something that just gets in your bones. It's hard to give up. I'll do it until I just can't do it any more."

With the sun down and the stars out, Captain Johnny pulled up to his dock in Deltaville. "Well, we're home one more time," he says.

## STORIES OF CAPTAIN JOHNNY

*"When John Wright built* Iva W., *he built her to John Ward's specifications and I mean he put some fasteners in her. Of course John Ward had to have the boat right because he was out on the Bay when it wasn't fit for a porpoise. That is the truth too."* —Steve Pruitt of Sunnybank, Virginia.

## Captain Johnny's Autopilot

About halfway home one day when I was out on the Bay with Captain Johnny, he asked if I'd take the helm so he could clean up the deck from the day's work. I agreed and he pointed to a specific tree on the shoreline miles down the Bay. "Now you head her to that tree and it will take us home," he said to me.

Well, there were hundreds of trees along the shoreline and exactly which one he was referring to I could not tell, but I had the general direction in my mind and felt comfortable taking the helm.

So Captain Johnny went out on deck and began to wash and scrub her down. Meanwhile, I was left in the pilothouse to keep *Iva* on course, but I soon found that I had a problem. *Iva's* steering ropes were extremely slack and when I'd turn the wheel hard to get the slack out of the line, the then fifty-eight-year-old boat would suddenly turn sharply. When I would turn her back she'd do the same thing. So there we were zigzagging down the Bay.

After a while, Captain Johnny came into the pilothouse and asked, "What the hell is wrong with you, mate? Look out the way!"

So I quickly moved out of the way.

The old captain reached for a string or a becket as watermen call it. It was coated in dirt and grease and was about the size of kite string. One end was tied to a nail on the pilothouse door trim and the other end dangled loose behind the door. Captain Johnny took the loose end, held it in his hand, looked down the Bay toward that all-important tree, got *Iva* on course, and then tied the loose end of the string tight to the wheel.

When he was set, he said to me, "All right, mate, this becket will take us home. You come on out on deck and help me."

He and I went out on deck and cleaned her up nice.

When we were about finished, I looked up and saw Jackson Creek buoy dead ahead. If Captain Johnny hadn't taken the helm from that string, *Iva* would have run right square into the buoy.

"I told you that becket would take us home. Didn't I?" he said to me with a grin and patted me on my back.

## Compass, Alarm Clock, and Leadline

One of the first Bay terms I learned from interviews with Elmer Crockett of Tangier Island in the early 1970s was the meaning of the term "hard driver."

"I'll tell you one thing, Captain, that boy was one hard driver," he would say with his Tangier accent, meaning that the skipper of a particular vessel worked his boat hard in all kinds of weather conditions.

I don't think anyone would disagree that the king of the "hard drivers" on the lower Chesapeake Bay was Captain Johnny. The late Hugh Norris in recorded interviews told the next two stories on his front porch overlooking Jackson Creek around 1987. Captain Hugh first went to work aboard a sailing schooner in 1910 and continued as mate and captain aboard many different vessels until marriage cut his sailing career short in 1928. He worked the water and built boats in his backyard thereafter in Deltaville. He lived right down the lane from Captain Johnny and he knew him well.

"Captain Johnny was a hard driver and he made a fortune in that 65-foot boat [*Iva W.*]. He would go out and crab dredge all day long starting at 3 or 4 A.M. and when he was done he would go to Cape Charles and buy crabs from the other dredgers. They'd go home and go to bed but not Captain Johnny. He'd load the hold of *Iva W.* with barrels of crabs, run every night to Crisfield, and be back in the early morning to dredge some more. In the wintertime, he ran her through snowstorms and northern winds coming down the Bay. Just think what he put that boat through and what he went through.

"All he had for navigating was a small compass, an alarm clock, and a leadline. He didn't know what a fathometer was. He never knew what a radar was. He'd come out of Crisfield in pitch-black darkness, set his course by compass, and set his alarm clock for so much time. When the alarm clock started ringing he knew it was time to set another course.

"Finally Captain Johnny got old and was still dredging and making that run to Crisfield. It worried his sons who were dredging crabs in their own boats out there. So they talked him into buying a truck and hired a man to drive the crabs to Crisfield. Still he kept on dredging and the boys talked him into putting radar on *Iva W.* He didn't like it for nothing and swore he'd never use it. Then one day coming home from dredging he turned the radar on and set her for Jackson Creek. Damn if he didn't run right square into Jackson buoy and knocked the buoy over."

"Next day, he pulled the radar out of her."

## Haggling over Watermelons

"Sometime in the 1930s, Captain Johnny was hauling watermelons to Baltimore in *Iva W.* and had a load on the boat at the dock that he had agreed to purchase from Calvin Butler, Sr., of Bushy Park, Virginia," says Hugh.

"When Captain Johnny and Calvin were ready to settle up on the cost of the watermelons, they got to arguing over the price. Calvin was a great big man and Captain Johnny was shorter and smaller.

"Old man Calvin said, 'You little short S.O.B. I can buy and sell you anytime.'

"Captain Johnny jumped down off the boat and got right under Calvin's chin and looked up at him and said, 'You big son-of-a-bitch. I can buy you and won't have to sell you.'

"That was Captain Johnny."

## Which Half of the Boat Do You Want?

William E. Wright also recalls a couple stories on Captain Johnny. "This is a true story because Raymond Perry was on *Iva W.* and he saw and heard every bit of

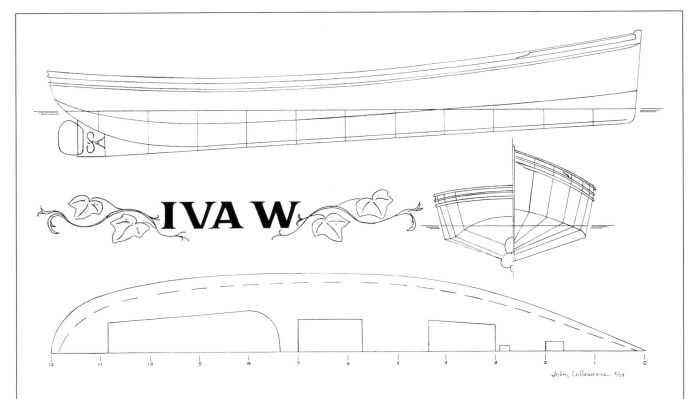

# IVA W

*Iva W.* was built for Captain Johnny Ward in 1929 and he owned the boat until his death in December 1998. The boat was sold out of the Ward family in 1999. She has been converted to a pleasure boat and now sports a double-deck pilothouse. She is registered at 55.4 feet by 16.5 feet by 4.9 feet, gross 30, net 20, and her hull number is 229217. Drawings by John Collamore.

it," says William. "Captain Johnny left out of the sea side [of the Eastern Shore of Virginia] one evening in a storm. He was loaded with crabs going to Crisfield and he got up above Cape Charles and it [weather] really got bad.

"Everybody on the boat was being thrown all around and the crew was scared to death. Captain Johnny yelled back in the galley where the crew was 'which end of the boat do you boys want because she for sure is going to break square in half.'

"Raymond was standing close to him in the house and after a while Captain Johnny started laughing. 'You reckon they really think she's going to break in two, Raymond?' he asked."

## Making $500 a Day
## When $500 Was Like $5,000 Today

"Johnny made all the money in the world and I know it," says William. "In the 1920s, '30s and '40s, he would crab dredge all day. When he was finished he would fill *Iva W.* up by buying barrels of crabs from the other dredgers.

William worked aboard the deck boat *C. E. Wright* with his father Ladd Wright and sold crabs to Captain Johnny. "He would pay us $1.00 a barrel and that's all we got from any local buyer. I've gotten as little as 25 cents a barrel. Then Johnny would take off to Crisfield where they were paying $5.00 and $6.00 a barrel for crabs. He'd go all night long and be back on the crabbing grounds the next morning ready to go again.

"He did this every day during the crab-dredge season and the engine in *Iva W.* hardly ever got cold," he says. "He was probably clearing $500 a day when the average man working a job then was lucky to make $40 a week.

"He just didn't seem to have any fear of the Bay. He had the guts to go out on the water anytime. I mean he would go out when those big Bay steamers

154

weren't out there because it was too rough; Johnny was out there. He was probably the most successful deck boat captain on the Chesapeake Bay."

## Opening the Drawbridge

Morris Snow of Mathews County, Virginia, recalls that Captain Johnny had to open the drawbridge at Crisfield himself because the bridgetender wasn't there at the time of morning he got there.

"Captain Johnny would get to Crisfield so early in the morning that he would have to tie *Iva W.* to a wharf, open the drawbridge himself, go through the draw, tie his boat back up, close the drawbridge, then get back on his boat and go to the crab house. Once he got his crabs off the boat, he'd head back out and many a time he had to open the draw on the way back," says Morris.

The unusual drawbridge connected Main Street in Crisfield with the small island of Jersey. Captain Johnny would have to open the drawbridge each night to get to the seafood houses on Main Street. (See *Chesapeake Bay and Tidewater* by Aubrey A. Bodine.)

## That Radar Didn't Help Much

*In 1992, Paula Johnson of the Smithsonian Institution and David Taylor of the Library of Congress in Washington, D.C., visited Deltaville on a field study of boatbuilding. They visited Captain Johnny down at his dock on Jackson Creek. I was along and recorded this story by Captain Johnny.*

"One time when I was out in the Bay dredging crabs my grandson John Melvin [Ward] was in *Ward Bros.* and I was in *Iva W.* It was getting nasty and it was getting as thick [foggy] as it could be. John Melvin said, 'Daddy John, let's come on and go. It's time to go. It's getting nastier all the time.' [All the grandchildren called Captain Johnny "Daddy John."]

"I said, 'I'm coming along in a minute. I want to fill this barrel up and as soon as I fill up with hard crabs, I'll come along.'

"'You ain't got no radar and we got radar, why don't you come on with us?' said John Melvin.

"I said, 'Well if they don't move Jackson Creek or fill the Piankatank River up, I can get in there all right.'

"I may have stayed there five more minutes. Then, I opened up on her and put her on a right good run. I passed them but they didn't see me. I came on in and tied her up to the dock.

"When they did come, I said, 'That radar didn't help you much.'

"John Melvin said, 'Yeah when you left there, you put her in the corner' [meaning he had throttle wide open].

"Well, I just ran what she's supposed to run. I told them."

## A Pint of Whiskey and He Could Work a Mule to Death

Steve Pruitt was aboard *Elsie Virginia* crab dredging in the Chesapeake Bay during the winter. He and his father would sell crabs to Captain Johnny. "I've loaded a many a barrel of crabs from *Elsie Virginia* onto *Iva W.*," says Steve. "Captain Johnny was a hard driver and people wondered how he kept a crew. He would dredge all day, buy from us at the end of the day, haul his load of crabs to the buyers in Crisfield, and be back dredging before most of us would get back out there the next morning.

"Well, he had one old colored fellow named Willie who stayed with him for a long time. After they loaded the crabs on *Iva W.*, they were off to Crisfield to sell the load. Willie knew the Bay as well as Captain Johnny. He obviously had been out there for a lot of years.

"Every night when they got to Crisfield Captain Johnny would give Willie a pint of whiskey to work on. Willie would get that pint of liquor in him and after that he could solid handle some crabs. Captain Johnny would work a mule to death and when they were going back down the Bay Willie would take a long nap. When they got back to the dredging grounds, Willie was ready to go again," says Steve. "Captain Johnny knew how to get the most out of his crew. He figured the cost of a pint of liquor a day for Willie was well worth it."

*Chesapeake Bay buyboats were used in many different ways on the Bay. The boats were extremely vital to the isolated Bay communities of Tangier Island, Virginia, and Smith Island, Maryland. Deck boats carried high school children from Ewell, Rhodes Point, and Tylerton to Crisfield; hauled home fuel oil and gasoline; carried a circus elephant to and from Tangier; brought the first telephone lines to Tangier; and carried passengers, groceries, and other goods on daily runs.*

# 13: BUYBOATS ON THE ISLANDS

Buyboats had many jobs. These short stories and reflections from those who knew the boats tell a great deal about the ways Chesapeake buyboats were routinely and in some cases unusually used and worked on the islands.

## *PEARL FAYE:* "THE PEARL OF MY LIFE"

Todd Parks of Tangier Island worked as a boy and a man aboard *Pearl Faye,* a 65-foot long by 16-foot wide buyboat his father bought in the 1960s to freight soft crabs between Tangier Island and Crisfield, Maryland. [*Pearl Faye* was built in 1928 on Fishing Bay at Price's Railway in Deltaville and was originally named *Lillian T.*]

Todd's father, Richard "Dick" Burton Parks, Jr., used *Pearl Faye* as a soft crab carrier from Tangier to the crab packing houses in Crisfield for forty years. "What Dad used to do was get the soft crabs from watermen at home [Tangier] and ferry them to Crisfield to the crab house in *Pearl.* On the return trip he would bring hardware, passengers, and groceries for the stores on the island," says Todd. "In the wintertime, he'd use her to buy oysters or go crab dredging, whichever he could make the most money at.

"When Daddy bought *Pearl,* she was named *Lillian T.* and he got her from up in Maryland. That's about all I know of her history. Daddy bought her in

the 1960s and worked her for about twenty-five years. He would take crabs to the buyers at Crisfield and sometimes to Onancock. The first deck boat he had was about 45 feet long and was called *Ellen Virginia,* but it got so they were catching so many crabs that he was having to make two trips a day so he bought *Pearl* which was larger.

"Daddy died in 1992 and I always have thought that when he lost that boat he lost his will to live," says Todd. "*Pearl* got so old that Daddy couldn't keep her up and we had some wind one night and she sunk to the dock [at Tangier]. It broke his heart and two or three years later he died."

The boat was named after Pearl Faye Parks, Todd's mother. "When Daddy got the boat, we were all telling him what to name her and he said 'I already know what I'm going to name her.'

"'What's that?' we asked.

"He looked at my mom and said, 'I'm going to name her after your mom, Pearl Faye, the pearl of my life.'"

## THE GREAT CHESAPEAKE BAY ELEPHANT FLOAT

*Lewis Parks's house in Richmond, Virginia, is full of old memorabilia of Tangier Island where his mother and father were born*

*Pearl Faye* hauled soft crabs from Tangier Island to Crisfield, Maryland. In this 1980s photo, she is moored at Crisfield beside a converted-to-power navy barge. After World War II, several Chesapeake Bay watermen purchased tow barges from the government and installed an engine, house, and waist. The boats were used for dredging oysters and planting seed oysters.

*and raised. Trunks under his bed are full of old newspaper and magazine articles that reveal some interesting uses for Bay deck boats. One event that he remembers was the arrival of Pasha the elephant, who came to the island with Roberts Brothers Circus as part of "the great elephant float." It brought fun and joy to the island children.*

"I remember when the circus came to the island in 1977," says Lewis. "I was twelve years old and the thing I remember the most was when a man wanted to take a picture of two children on the elephant and me and a friend were chosen to get up on its back. It was exciting for a young boy.

"There were all kinds of newspaper articles written about the circus coming to the island and I've collected several over the years."

The *Richmond News Leader* carried a cartoon with a picture of an elephant on a deck boat and the headline read "The Great Elephant Float." The story stated, "The coming of Pasha and her friends has been billed as 'the great Chesapeake Bay elephant float' . . . [the elephant] is the first to travel by fishing boat to an is-

land. Pasha, a 2,775-pound, eight-year-old from Thailand, will be loaded on the 65-foot boat *Ruth S.* at Crisfield for the fourteen-mile trip across the Bay.

"But that's not all.

"Joining the 8-foot-long star attraction will be two ponies and at least five dogs, and on two other boats, 15,000 pounds of electrical equipment and props, Max Bertel (a seventy-six-year-old clown), and more than thirty other performers and crew."

In a later *News Leader* article the headline read "Circus Overwhelms Tangier." It stated, "It took the dredge boat *Anthony Klein* three trips from Crisfield to carry all the animals, performers, and tons of equipment needed for the two performances by the Roberts Brothers Circus.

"Before the last boat was unloaded, a 1½-ton member of the troupe—Pasha, the performing pachyderm—had already become an island favorite. Pasha was the first elephant to set its big foot on the tiny island."

Yet another story, headlined "Tangier Welcomes Its First Circus," states, "The circus, which has been

157

This early photo of Tangier Island, Virginia, shows deck boats in the harbor. The boats played a major role in the lives of residents of Tangier and Smith Island, Maryland. For many years, the boats provided the main transportation to and from the islands. Courtesy Lewis Parks.

performing in towns all along the Eastern Shore, set sail from Crisfield in the afternoon and arrived on the western side of the isolated island.

"Grover Charnock, a member of the volunteer fire department which is sponsoring the circus, said there would be no parade because the island's flimsy bridges might not support Pasha.

"There's not too many places that could hold an elephant," said Carnock. "We've got small bridges that have signs on them: 'two-ton capacity.' If the elephant went through, they'd have a devil of a time getting him out of the salt mud."

Pasha made it to and from Tangier without a hitch and, Lewis says, she was the hit of the show. "I was just a boy but I'll always remember getting up on that elephant. That was something. We felt like we were in the city."

## A JOURNEY TO A NEW HOME

*Just how far back a person remembers can often become the topic of debate. I recall when I was a teenager, a family member showed me a family photo and asked if I recognized anyone. I immediately recognized Miss Lizzie Sadler, my great-great-aunt. "You don't remember her because you were hardly two years old when she died," he said to me.*

*I didn't argue the point, but I remembered Miss Lizzie picking me up in her arms and just about smothering me with her hugs. I remembered her face, her smell, her touch, and her love for me. When she died she left me all her worldly possessions, which included a marble-top dresser and a three-quarter spool bed. I treasure them to this day and I knew Miss Lizzie.*

*Terry Murphy was three years old when his family left Tangier Island bound for a new life in Urbanna, Virginia, aboard the Chesapeake Bay buyboat Beryl Marie. Some say he was too young to remember the trip but he says he does and I believe him.*

"My mother and father were both from Tangier Island," says Terry. "Daddy was born in 1914 and mother was born in 1929. There was right much difference in age. Daddy's father fought in the Civil War for the Union Army. He was real young when he was in the war and he was in his late 60s when Daddy was born.

"The Murphys came to Tangier much later than my mother's people. Daddy's people were Irish and there were a few Irish names on Tangier, like Murphy, Dailey, and Thorn. My grandfather went to work on a [sailing] oyster-dredge boat and ended up on the island. A lot of Irishmen that would come into Baltimore ended up on the dredge boats. [During the last half of the nineteenth century and first quarter of the twentieth century, Irish immigrants found work at the docks in Baltimore on oyster-dredge boats. It was one of the roughest, toughest jobs to be found, and the captains were often unscrupulous. Once the season was about over, many a mate lost his life to the boom rather than being paid for his work. Some were given the choice—the boom or be left on an isolated Bay island. This may have been the way the Murphy family found Tangier. "Paid with a boom" was a term used when an unsuspecting oysterman was not looking and the boom swung across the deck, pushing him overboard.]

"My mother's maiden name was King and her relative was one of the British soldiers who occupied the island during the War of 1812," says Terry. "Down in Canaan where we lived, the British were stationed and I guess he met my great-grandmother there. That's how the Kings got to Tangier.

"Daddy was a career army man who had gone in service in 1930 and during World War II was captured by the Japanese and survived the Bataan Death March and prison camp and the war.

"I was born in 1959 and he stayed in the army until 1960 and then we moved back to Tangier. He took his big Studebaker [car] to the island, which was too big for the narrow roads. They rolled it up in the marsh with pound poles and it's still over there. He had to have his car. Then hurricane Donna came along and water came up in the house. I think that's why they decided to leave.

"Anyway, I was three years old in 1962 when we left and Tangier was the only world to me then. I remember my uncle brought his small workboat up the ditch at Canaan and several men loaded our furniture onto his workboat. He carried our furniture to the harbor and it was all loaded on this big boat with a mast in her. He had to make several trips. I didn't know it then but it was the buyboat *Beryl Marie*. To me, it was my version of an ocean liner and we were heading to Ellis Island. We were all up on deck and as we left Tangier my mother started crying. Her daddy and sister were all standing on the bank watching. I could tell it was hard on her.

"Halfway across the Bay a storm came up and most of our furniture got water spots all over it. Some of the furniture I have now still has those water spots. I sat in the captain's lap with all those small windows around me. We came into Urbanna Creek and we rented a big old house."

Terry is now forty-three years old and his parents have long since died, but he still makes Urbanna his home.

## TANGIER ISLAND GROCERY BOAT

After his father died, Terry and his mother would visit relatives on the island by going to Reedville and catching a ride on the island's grocery boat, a buyboat.

"Mother didn't drive so she and I would catch a ride to Reedville and go over to the island on the gro-

Telephones were introduced to Tangier Island in 1966 and the deck boat *Mary E. Haynie* was used to haul cable and supplies from the mainland. This drawing was used as an advertisement by Western Electric Company, the firm that brought telephones to the island. Courtesy Lewis Parks.

cery boat. They would take Tangiermen for free if you helped load the boat," says Terry. "I've loaded watermelons when I was six years old to get Mother and me a ride to the island.

"Mother had diabetes so she would sit at a little fountain at the dock and I would help load the boat until I paid for our way over there. Every time I'd drop a melon one of the men would curse me. I knew right many curse words at an early age. The Tangier Island store was owned by Terry Daily, and he would send a boat over to pick up food delivered by Richmond Food Company."

Terry does not remember the name of the boats but Steve Pruitt recalls that two of the grocery boats were *Nellie Jane* and *Lorie Robins*. Both boats were built

*Island Star* ran "School Boat Route No. 53" for the State of Maryland from 1959 until the early 1970s. Originally named *Frances*, she was built by Linwood Price of Deltaville, Virginia, in 1925. Here she is in 2002 dredging oysters at the mouth of the Rappahannock River.

in Deltaville and *Lorie Robins* was originally named *C. E. Wright*.

## *ISLAND STAR:* SMITH ISLAND SCHOOL BOAT

Starting in 1959 the State of Maryland created "School Boat Route No. 53" from Smith Island to Crisfield High School, and the school boat was *Island Star*, owned by the Whitelock Brothers of Ewell. The first year the Whitelocks had the contract with the state, the three brothers were paid $2,500.

High school students from Smith Island had been attending Crisfield High School since before World War II, but there was no official means of transportation until 1959. Prior to that, families from the island had to provide their own transportation for the children.

School was eleven miles away across Tangier Sound. It would take *Island Star* about an hour and a half to make the run to Crisfield. Fog and ice have made the trip last as long as four hours. Students boarded at homes in Crisfield for $50 a month paid by the state as an education allotment. Monday morning at 6:30 A.M., *Island Star* would leave from Ewell bound for Crisfield. Their suitcases packed with a week's worth of clothes, students stayed until Friday and the boat would pick them up and take them home to Smith Island for the weekend.

Rose Somers Evans was a teenager on the island when she started at Crisfield High School in the mid-1960s. She graduated in 1969 and part of her weekly agenda was to board the island's school boat *Island Star*.

"We would go over to Crisfield by boat every week and we got used to it," says Rose. "It was an experience I can tell you. Now the boats go every day to school but when we were in school we had to leave Monday morning, board with a family all week, and come back to Smith Island on Friday.

"I graduated in 1969 from Crisfield High School. I was very fortunate. I stayed with a good family. I had never met them until the first day I went to school. We had first through eighth grades on the island and ninth through twelfth grades at Crisfield High School." Rose lived in Ewell but schoolchildren who lived on Tylerton, another island that is part of the Smith Island chain, went to a one-room school in Tylerton for grades 1 to 6. Students in grades 7 and 8 caught a school boat across Tylerton Creek to Rhodes Point, where they boarded a school bus to attend junior high school at Ewell.

"I swore if I ever got out of high school, I'd never go to Crisfield again and now we live there," she says. "I loved school but I hated to leave home. At that time, we really were a lot more secluded on Smith Island than they are now. I never really had left home before and I hated to leave my parents.

*Eleanor White* was the last wooden fuel tanker on Chesapeake Bay. She was used to haul fuel oil to Tylerton and Ewell on Smith Island from Crisfield on Maryland's Eastern Shore.

"We had a hard time participating in extracurricular activities because we went home every weekend and it wasn't the same for us as for those children who lived in Crisfield all the time.

"At that time buyboats or workboats were the only transportation off the island. The trip on *Island Star* really wasn't so bad. The boat had accommodations but now that I think back on it, it was an unusual experience. Tangier Island was as isolated as we were on Smith but they had their own high school.

"I really didn't mind it but I realized when I had children of my own how much my parents had missed," says Rose. "They didn't get to see me dressed for the prom or any of the other school activities."

Rose and her husband Eugene Evans live in Crisfield, Maryland, where they run a fiberglass boatbuilding operation.

## LEE WHITELOCK

"The Whitelock brothers owned *Island Star* and they owned two other boats, *Island Belle* and *Whitelock*," says Lee, whose father was one of the Whitelock brothers. "They used *Island Belle* and *Whitelock* to transport people to and from Crisfield on weekends. The boats were slow too. On a Saturday run to Crisfield, we left at 7:30 A.M. and would come back at 12:30. So by the time we got there, we had to turn around and come home. It seemed like it took all morning, but it would

take about an hour to an hour and a half. We didn't get to stay for the Saturday matinee, I'll tell you that.

"*Island Star* was a regular buyboat but she had been converted into a school boat by my family. My father and uncles took her over to Krentz Railway at Harryhogan, Virginia, and had Herman Krentz make the forepeak and center into a seating area for the children."

*Island Star* was originally named *Frances*. According to the *Merchant Vessels of the United States* listing, she was built in 1925 by Linwood Price in Deltaville, Virginia.

"My family had owned several boats. They had an old boat named *Fish Hawk*. She was a buyboat and was a double-ender. My uncle Ben stayed on *Island Belle* and my uncle Edwin used *Island Star* as a buyboat.

"*Island Belle* was an old boat and had been built at Ewell for my grandfather, John Whitelock. She was built in 1917 and was 46.8 feet by 13.3 feet. She had an old Gray engine in her for years.

"I remember the boats but the thing I remember the most was that my first bicycle came on *Island Belle*. They were using the boat to haul slag for highway construction from Baltimore and one day I was down on the dock when they were coming in and there was this bright new bicycle sitting on top of the slag. It was a Columbia bicycle with big balloon tires. It was for me and it was the greatest bike in the world. It's funny the things you remember."

*Over many years of wandering around the Chesapeake, I've heard many stories of Bay fishermen who volunteered their boats or had the boats conscripted into the armed services during World War II.*

*Several buyboats and their captains roamed the Bay and the ocean as official United States government craft, and stories from that era of the "greatest generation" have been passed down through the years. This chapter deals with some of those boats.*

# 14: BUYBOATS AT WAR

Shortly after the Japanese invasion of Pearl Harbor in December 1941, the United States government began a nationwide conscription of boats that were large enough to help with the war effort. These watercraft became official U. S. government boats, and many of their captains were given rank in the "temporary reserves" of the U. S. Coast Guard.

The vessels were composed of pleasure boats and traditional workboats such as Chesapeake Bay buyboats. One reason for the creation of the fleet was the constant threat of German U-boats coming and going along the Atlantic Coast of the United States. The buyboats were used to patrol the region and report U-boat sightings. Some were also used for government freighting between Cuba and the states, and smaller buyboats were used to haul personnel, ammunition, and goods around the Chesapeake. Many of the boats left the Bay region. Noah C. Carr, Sr., of Glass, Virginia, whose father owned the deck boat *Janice*, said she was used as a fireboat at Charleston, South Carolina. He also said some boats were carried on large freighters across the ocean to be used overseas in the war. One of those boats was *Comanche*, owned by Captain Rob Billups. When she returned to the United States she was purchased by Moody Tillage of Gloucester Point, Virginia, and was a well-known oyster buyboat on the lower Bay for many years.

As the war progressed, advancement in radar and air patrol, as well as the creation of a convoy system for crossing the Atlantic, meant there was less need for this hodgepodge of a navy, and some of the boats and crews were released from service. Some, however, remained in service to the end of the war, carrying supplies and goods to lighthouses and to other isolated areas of the region.

According to Steve Pruitt, whose father and brother were both involved with boats volunteered into the Coast Guard, most of the boats were very well maintained, and they came back from the war with some fancy features. The deck boat *Harold* had a brass clock and brass barometer left from her war days—Morris Snow has both items mounted on the wall at his home in Bavon, Virginia. When Steve's brother Winnie bought *Lora Lee* from the Coast Guard after the war, she had brass desk hardware and drawer handles and steam heat.

## WANDA

Charlie Ward of Gwynn's Island, Virginia, recalls when the Godsey family's 56-foot buyboat *Wanda* stopped buying and hauling oysters and became a "man-of-war."

"In the spring of 1942, *Wanda* was volunteered into the Coast Guard for civil defense by my uncles

*Nellie Crockett* worked as a Bay buyboat from 1926 until 1989 except for three years during World War II when she served in the U.S. Coast Guard. Courtesy Robert W. Jensen.

Bud and Garnett Godsey," says Charlie. "Bud was made a chief petty officer right on the spot." *Wanda* had been built in 1927 for the Godsey family and up until then had been used in the seafood and freighting business.

"*Wanda* was stationed in Norfolk and they would patrol up and down the Bay looking for enemy submarines. Then they put *Wanda* in the ocean and Bud told them she was not built for that. It got real rough out there one day when a storm come up and Bud told them he was coming back inside of Cape Henry or he would surely lose the boat.

"Some officer told him if he came in he would be court-martialed. Well my uncle Bud could throw a real summer-timer, and he told him he didn't give a damn what they did to him, that he was coming inside the Bay before he lost the boat. Later on, he was commended for bringing the boat in when he did, because several got caught out there and nearly didn't make it back.

"As part of being a military vessel, *Wanda* was painted battleship gray, and the Coast Guard painted the name United States Coast Guard on her and gave her a number on her sides," says Charlie. "They put a ship-to-shore radio on her, gave the crew a vintage World War I submachine gun mounted to the top of

the pilothouse, and that was the extent of what they got.

"*Wanda* had a 45-horsepower diesel engine in her. She wasn't very fast, and I don't know what they would have done if they found a U-boat other than call for help.

"Another Gwynn's Island boat that went into service was *Harold*. From the 1920s to the 1940s, the buyboats *Wanda* and *Harold* were like sentinels on Edwards Creek at Gwynn's Island. One was moored to the east of the mouth of the creek and the other to the west.

"*Harold* was Mr. Jim Rowe's boat. She had a 36-horsepower Atlas Imperial engine. *Harold* was smaller than *Wanda*." *Harold* was 49 feet 3 inches long and 13 feet 2 inches wide.

## A. G. PRICE

In 1993, *Coastal Queen* was being serviced at Deagle's railway in Deltaville. At that time her captain, Deacon Nelson, shared this wonderful story of the buyboat *A. G. Price*, later renamed *Coastal Queen*, facing a German U-boat on the high seas.

"The boat was on a mission off the Florida Keys, coming from Guantanamo Bay, Cuba, filled with goods

*Harold* is still carrying her steadying sail in this photo on Edwards Creek at Gywnn's Island, Virginia. The buyboat was built in 1925 by John Wright and used during World War II as a patrol boat by the U. S. Coast Guard. Captain Everett Brown is pictured aboard the boat. Courtesy Robert Lee Brown.

for American officers' clubs. She was loaded with some of the best Cuban cigars, rum, and other supplies," says Nelson.

"About halfway back, a German U-boat captured the boat and her crew. It was common practice for the Germans to take the supplies, set the crew adrift without food and water, and sink the boat. This time, though, the Germans took the supplies but let the boat and crew go in hopes she would come back again with some more of those fine Cuban cigars."

## BURTON LEAF

Burton Leaf of Urbanna, Virginia, started his military career aboard a deck boat. "I enlisted in 1941 into the Coast Guard in Norfolk. My first orders were on a buyboat that was volunteered into service by her owner Delmas Price of Crisfield, Maryland," says Burton, who was eighty-seven years old in 2002. "She was moored at Little Creek. They gave Delmas a warrant officer rank, issued him a uniform, painted the boat gray, and gave her a number. The number was *CGR 599*. I think the original name of the boat was *Greenhill*, but it was not on the boat at the time.

"There were four men on the boat at first and I was the last to come aboard so they made me cook,"

says Burton. "Our job was to go past the naval base to a place called St. Julian Creek [near Portsmouth, Virginia] where there was an ammunition depot, pick up a load of ammunition, and take it back to Little Creek.

"One time we had to go to the York River to the Naval Mine Depot at Yorktown, Virginia, and pick up some depth charges and haul them back to Little Creek," he says. "They weren't supposed to explode unless a timer was installed and they weren't armed. Even though we knew that, we dropped one on the deck and it scared us all nearly to death. They were hoisting it onto the boat when it slipped off a big hook and hit the deck and made a big cut in the wood. We knew it wasn't armed but it still scared us.

"Another job was to transport sailors up the Bay to the old target boats. We took them to a boat that had an old 3-inch gun on it and they were taught to shoot it at the target ships. We would take a bunch up, wait around, and bring them back. The government decided to arm all merchant ships and the sailors had to be taught to shoot the guns. I don't think it went very far because unless a submarine came to the surface, they would have nothing to shoot at. Our gun was an old World War I machine gun that was mounted up on top of the pilothouse," says Burton.

"We'd fool around and shoot it just to be doing something.

"Delmas was tight with some of the navy people and one of them gave him a boat—like a runabout. It had lapstrake planking, maybe 12 or 15 feet long, and it lay on deck in front of the pilothouse. Well, the boys started shooting on the pilothouse and one of the men shot the rope holding the boom and it dropped down on top of our little boat and crushed it.

"Like I said, there were four men on the boat in the beginning, but two more came on later. I thought when they got two more they would put one of them to cooking but they didn't. I guess they liked my cooking. There was a little country store across the railroad tracks. I'd go over there every day and get food. We were allocated a certain amount each day for each person. There were no refrigerators on the boat so I had to purchase food daily. Actually, we had it better than my Mama did at home because we had a lot of rationed food. When I'd hitchhike home to Urbanna, I'd stuff my pockets with sugar and other things to take home to her.

"The galley was in the back part of the pilothouse and there was a small coal stove that I cooked on," he says. "Once it got so rough that I had to catch the stove to keep it from turning over. I was lucky it wasn't hot. It can get real rough around Thimble Shoals.

"I slept in a bunk and there were plenty of bedbugs. They were hard to get rid of too for some reason. They got into the tongue-and-groove wood paneling on the walls. We'd spray them but they were hard to kill. They liked to eat on you in the night and it didn't take but one to ruin a night's sleep.

"I was on the boat for about a year and then I was on other ships for most of the rest of the war. I crossed the Atlantic two times on a troop transport ship and went to Panama. I went to England, France, and Italy and was stationed on the West Coast when the war ended."

## STEWART BROTHERS AND ELSIE VIRGINIA

Linwood Price of Amburg, Virginia, built the 55-foot deck boat *Stewart Brothers* in 1923. By the start of World War II, she was owned by William "Winnie" Pruitt of Tangier Island, who used her to crab dredge and haul grain in fall and winter, run watermelons

Burton Leaf, eighty-seven in 2002, cooked and mated aboard *CGR 599*, a buyboat from Crisfield, Maryland.

from North Carolina to Baltimore in the summer, and buy seed oysters on the James River in the spring.

The vessel, along with several other Tangier Island deck boats, went into service for the United States Coast Guard during the war. Winnie's brother, Steve Pruitt, recalls an incident that occurred aboard *Stewart Brothers* one night in Crisfield harbor, resulting in the death of Winnie's mate and cousin.

"My Dad [Will Pruitt] owned *Stewart Brothers,* but a little bigger boat came along up on Smith Island," he says. "That was *Elsie Virginia.* So my dad sold *Stewart Brothers* to my brother [Winnie] and bought *Elsie Virginia.*

"At the start of World War II, my father had *Elsie Virginia* and my brother had *Stewart Brothers* and both were drafted into service. They took a bunch of boats out of Crisfield, Tangier, and Smith Island. When the

*Callis Brothers,* originally named *Julian,* served as a supply boat for lighthouses at the mouth of Chesapeake Bay during World War II under the auspices of the U. S. Coast Guard. Courtesy Robert W. Jensen.

The United States Coast Guard gave this plaque to Captain Will Pruitt of Tangier Island for the service of his boat *Elsie Virginia* in World War II.

Coast Guard came and took the boat, they would pay you the value of her and if you wanted to go on her they would make you a chief warrant officer. My Dad and my brother went with their boats, and the Coast Guard fixed the boats up into first-class shape—new bottoms and everything. They took my Uncle Homer's [Pruitt] boat *Bessie L.,* and when they went to fix her up they had to prop her up with stakes so she wouldn't lose her sheer. She was in bad shape," Steve laughed.

"My Daddy had just bought *Elsie Virginia* and she had been used to run fish to Washington all of her life. She was rottener than a pear in the bottom. You see, they would keep ice in the cargo hold, to keep the fish fresh and keep it closed off. Nothing will rot a boat quicker than freshwater. Well when the Coast Guard got her, they put a new bottom in her so when she came out of the service she was just about brand-new. That bunch from Crisfield let the Coast Guard take their boats because they were in such bad shape. Later, when the Coast Guard discharged a boat, the man who owned her before the war had first option to buy her back.

"My dad's and Winnie's boats were used to carry supplies to the lighthouses. They went to Smith Point Lighthouse and several other lighthouses. My brother's boat *Stewart Brothers* didn't make it to the end of the war. They had a crew of eight on board, and the Coast Guard had taken her forward cargo hold and built a cabin over it and made quarters. They put bunks down in her. There was a mate on board from New Jersey and his name was Dominic. I remember him because he could take a heavy stick, put it in his mouth, and make a sound like the song 'Yankee Doodle.' I remember that. I was a kid.

"It has always been a real mystery as to why [it happened] but *Stewart Brothers* was blown up at Cape Charles. My cousin James Crockett, who was the engineer on *Stewart Brothers,* was asleep on the boat that night and was killed," he says. "That was 1943 and there was a lot of sabotaging [going on] and a lot of Germans around. They first thought an air tank had caused the explosion but when they brought her up the air tank was still intact. We always thought the Germans did it.

"When they got *Stewart Brothers* up off the bottom, my brother bought her back at the end of the war," he says. "Winnie bought her for $1,000. The side work and bottom was still good. All the top work—pilothouse and top decks—were blown off her. Winnie and James were real tight. They were cousins but they were also best friends. They grew up next door to one another on Tangier. When Winnie got the boat, he couldn't fix her up because he couldn't stop thinking about James, so he decided to sell her. He sold her to Lorne Tull, who was a great boat carpenter at Crisfield and he fixed her up and gave her to his two boys. As far as I know she is still up on the Honga River.

"When the Coast Guard released the boats after the war, if the former owners did not want the boats, they were put up for bid," says Steve. "Winnie bought *Lora Lee*. She was actually a confiscated boat that had been caught during Prohibition running whiskey and had been used by the Coast Guard for twenty years. When she was a rum runner she was *M. V. Chadwick*, and Winnie named her *Lora Lee* after his daughter. Winnie owned *Yamacraw* and worked her for many years around the Bay, and Will Pruitt ran the rebuilt *Elsie Virginia* for many years thereafter."

At the end of the war, the Coast Guard gave a plaque to Captain Will for his boat's service in the war. It hangs on Steve's wall at his home at Sunnybank and it reads, "In Recognition of Valuable Service Performed by *Elsie Virginia* in the United States Coast Guard in World War II."

*In the late 1950s, somewhere on the Ware River, my father purchased a wooden deadrise boat with a Gray flat-head marine engine. The boat had been built in the 1940s for Callis Oyster Company to guard the company's oyster grounds.*

*She was a wonderful boat that even now brings back memories of cool, moonlit summer nights on the Rappahannock; December rockfishing trips that seemed as cold as an Arctic night; and the boat I used to earn my boating skills merit badge in Scouts. My father lovingly named her* Miss Susan, *after my sister Susan (Chowning) Hoar.*

*This chapter is about two other ladies who had buyboats named for them.*

# 15: A LADY'S TOUCH

So many times a boat's name speaks to a man's innermost thoughts and feelings. Maybe a boat is a reminder of home when he is far away, or maybe the name is there out of respect for a loved one. As a tribute, many boats carry the name of a grandmother, mother, wife, daughter, or granddaughter.

## WANDA

*Wanda* was built in 1927 by Deltaville boatbuilder John Wright for James Walter "Captain Jim" Godsey, Sr., of Gwynn's Island. Her documentation says she was built in 1929, but Ella Wanda Godsey Edwards—"Wanda" to family and friends—knows different. "I remember the year quite well because I would go to Deltaville with Papa and he would leave me at Virginia Harrow Ward's house on Jackson Creek while he went to Mr. Wright's boatyard. I was seven years old then. I was his baby and Papa named his new boat *Wanda* after me." [Virginia Harrow Ward was wife to William H. "Captain Will" Ward, captain and owner of *Virginia Belle* and *Lula M. Phillips*. They lived on Lovers Lane in Deltaville just a few houses from Captain John Wright's home and boatyard. The Wards and Godseys were longtime friends.]

"He would go over to Mr. Wright's boatyard and I remember going to the yard once or twice with him and seeing *Wanda* when her sides were just being started," she says. "Papa was real proud of his boat. He never thought that his boys would sell her, but after he died they did, and that made everyone real sad. My brother Bud grieved over selling Papa's boat the rest of his life.

"Mamma was already gone when Papa had *Wanda* built. She died in 1923. Mamma was in her early forties when she went to heaven and I was just three years old. I was the last of thirteen children and Papa really loved me. I guess that's why he named the boat after me.

"If our Papa ever thought of going to see anybody [a girlfriend], we would have a fit," says Wanda. "We were a selfish bunch but we were a close family. There were thirteen children but two died when they were young. The oldest boy, John Elmo, died of the croup when he was a baby. Our sister Catherine was born in 1908 and she died when she was three years old.

"Papa bought oysters and fish for Ballard Fish and Oyster Company and E. R. Clark Seafood, both of Norfolk. He'd come up on the Rappahannock or York Rivers, buy a load of oysters from watermen, and then haul the load to the oyster shucking houses in Norfolk.

"I went with Papa many times on *Wanda* to Norfolk. I've never seen New Point Lighthouse from land

This old faded photo of the deck boat *Wanda* at a mooring in Norfolk, Virginia, is the only photo the Godsey family has of the family buyboat. Captain Jim Godsey is sitting by his niece. Courtesy Mrs. Charles E. Edwards.

in my entire life, and I've lived in Mathews County all my life, but I've seen it many times from the deck of *Wanda* out on the Bay.

"Papa was always working his boat. When *Wanda* wasn't working for the seafood plants buying oysters, Papa would move people around the Bay. He was like a moving company today except he traveled by water. There was a family here on the island named Owens. They would come here and live a few years and then move back to Norfolk, and Papa would move them lock, stock, and barrel.

"Cousin Romie Williams was a Methodist minister and every three or so years he would have to move, and Papa moved him to Hampton and to the Eastern Shore or wherever.

"He also hauled fertilizer from Norfolk for local farmers. He'd go down to Norfolk loaded with oysters and would bring back bagged fertilizer rather than come back empty. Papa also hauled watermelons from over in Deltaville in the summertime and would carry

Captain Jim Godsey had John Wright build *Wanda* in 1927. Here he is with grandchildren near his home on Gwynn's Island, Virginia. Courtesy Mrs. Charles E. Edwards.

The deck boat *Wanda* was named after seven-year-old Ella Wanda Godsey. Today, Mrs. Charles E. (Wanda Godsey) Edwards, eighty-two, still lives on Gwynn's Island, Virginia, where she was born, and she recalls with fondness the boat her father named after her.

them to Baltimore, Washington, D.C., and Norfolk. He would sell the watermelons at the docks in the cities.

"I loved to go to Norfolk with him. He would carry lots of young girls and boys from the island to visit relatives. You see a lot of our people [from Gwynn's Island] went to Norfolk to find work at the shipyards or seafood plants.

"Papa and my brother Garnett were well thought of as captains and parents trusted them," says Wanda. "My brother Garnett ran the buyboat *Beryl Marie*. [*Beryl Marie* was built in 1925 at Laban, Virginia. Laban is in Mathews County near Winter Harbor.]

"She was owned by John Miller of Susan, Virginia, and was used to haul scrap or junk fish to a Reedville

fish meal plant. Garnett would buy menhaden from haul-seine fishermen and haul it to Reedville. It was the smellingest boat I've ever been on. Most everyone wanted to ride with Papa because *Wanda* was kept so clean.

"Papa had a boat years ago named *Old Brat*. She was an old workboat but he also had a buyboat before *Wanda* named *Ruby & Alice*. She was named after my two sisters, but the boat was not as big as *Wanda*. *Ruby & Alice* was sold to Roy King in Guinea Neck [in Gloucester County, Virginia]."

*Ruby & Alice* was built in 1916 by John Wright and was registered in 1929 to Wanda's father Captain J. W. Godsey. She measured 43.2 feet by 12.7 feet by 4 feet.

"Most of the time my brother Bud and Johnny Smith were the crew aboard *Wanda* and sometimes my brother Jack went along as the cook," says Wanda. "When Jack went he would buy everything for the trip at Callis's Wharf Store and he'd always buy a bag of prunes. One trip he got out on the water and he could not find his bag of prunes. Lord, Jack loved prunes. He knew for sure they'd forgotten to put them in his bag at the store, and he was giving the storekeeper a cussing. After a few days on the water Jack noticed Bud had his bag of prunes in his pocket. Bud didn't like prunes. He just did that to make Jack mad.

"I had an older sister living in Norfolk. So, my other sister Sue and I, who were still at home, would go down to Norfolk on *Wanda* and stay with her. We would go down and have a nice time. When it was time to come home, we would meet Papa and *Wanda* at Ballard's dock.

"I never spent a night on the boat but I'd take naps on her when we were going down the Bay," she says. "I remember carved in the forepeak of the boat was 'named for the thirteenth child.' It didn't say my name but it was named for me.

"Also in the forepeak was the nicest little table that could fold back to make standing space. There were benches built into the walls and a little stove. The pilothouse was nice and the wheel was handmade by my brother-in-law Willard Bensten. That's one reason I'd love to find that boat. Bud wanted the wheel but he didn't take it out before he sold it.

"Garnett and Bud inherited the boat from my Papa and we were all real hurt when they sold her," says Wanda. "I think my brother Garnett had more input into it because he had gotten a land job and wanted to get off the water.

"For the rest of his life, Bud was sorry about selling the boat, and it's the thing we remember him most for doing," says Wanda. "I'm sure Papa turned over in his grave the day *Wanda* was sold.

"Bud was a good man though. He was superstitious too. I don't know why but he wouldn't let anyone polish their shoes or whistle while on board *Wanda*. If they did, he would threaten to throw them overboard. I think he got that stuff from some of the old boys who had worked on the boats for years, all the way back to sailing days.

"*Wanda* looked so pretty. She was always moored on the right-hand side of Edwards Creek and *Harold* was on the left-hand side. I've been to Norfolk on *Harold* too. Big Frank Hudgins was the captain of her and he was very particular about his boat. I would fix sandwiches on the way to Norfolk in the galley and he'd be right behind me making sure every crumb was picked up.

"*Harold* was used to bring Mr. Floyd Williams's body back from Tangier Island. His son, Floyd Williams, Jr., and he were bottom fishing in their boat when a storm came up and turned the boat over. Floyd, Floyd, Jr., and their little doggie that was in the cabin were all drowned. Floyd, Sr.'s body washed up near Tangier and the Methodist preacher here on Gwynn's Island was over there as a visiting preacher and he identified Floyd's body. Big Frank went over in *Harold* and brought him home. It was a sad time around here.

"Mr. Jim Rowe and Papa were instrumental in getting 'the Narrows' dug out," she says. "Papa could not come in except through 'Hole in the Wall' because *Wanda* was too big and the water was not deep enough for her to get in. He had to go all the way around the island to get to Edwards Creek before the Narrows was dug out. [The Narrows is a narrow channel on the west side of the island that runs between Narrows Point on Gwynn's Island and the Cricket Hill area of Mathews County. Hole in the Wall is a narrow opening on the east side of the island between Chesapeake Bay and Milford Haven. Both provide entrance into Milford Haven. Edwards Creek is located on the Gwynn's Island side of Milford Haven, much closer to the Narrows than Hole in the Wall.)

"When Papa had *Ruby & Alice*, he would take a boatload of people over to Wharton Grove near Weems from Gwynn's Island Baptist Church," she says. "I heard him talk about going over there to hear

This model of *C. E. Wright* belongs to Lewis Parks of Richmond, Virginia. Captain G. L. "Ladd" Wright built the boat for himself in 1916, and named her for his daughter, Countess Elizabeth Wright. The boat was one of just a few frame-built, stem-to-stern planked-bottom deck boats built in Deltaville. Most Deltaville deck boats were deadrise with cross-planked bottoms. Courtesy Lewis Parks.

Billy Sunday preach. Papa really liked Billy Sunday. He liked him so much that he named his horse after him.

"My Papa must have really loved me to name his boat after me because he loved that boat so," says Wanda. "His life centered around the boat and the business of working the boat. When he died it broke my heart but when they sold *Wanda*, it hurt me so much that I felt like my Papa had died all over again.

"Here I am now, old and tired and most everyone I knew as a child and as a young person is gone now. When I look back over my life, I realize there are only a few days that really stand out—some good and some bad," she says.

"The days I was out on the boat with my Papa were standout days!"

## "C. E. WRIGHT" BY COUNTESS ELIZABETH WRIGHT

*When searching back issues of the* Southside Sentinel, *I came across this 1981 column by Countess Dudley, longtime "Deltaville News" columnist for the* Sentinel. *I had the pleasure of interviewing Countess for our paper in the 1980s, and we talked some about her father and the boat he named for her. I'm sorry to say Countess died long before I started this project but this por-*

*tion of one of her columns is a tribute to her and to her fine work. The column appeared in the paper on August 20, 1981.*

"I have been told many times by my parents that when I was an infant my father built a large gasoline-powered bateau—which he called the *C. E. Wright*—after me. He used the boat to carry freight—melons, grain, lime, shells, oysters, and even lumber—up and down the Chesapeake Bay and its tributaries anywhere from Norfolk to Baltimore, sometimes even as far as Delaware. He sold her for a larger vessel before I was old enough to remember much about her but I have a faint recollection of that sleek white boat anchored off shore from our home in the waters of Jackson Creek.

"A man named Johnny Spillman sailed with him and lived on the boat. I was old enough to remember the sweet sound of music coming from the boat as Mr. Spillman entertained himself at night with his violin. We used to go down on the hill just to listen to him but if he knew we were listening he would stop.

"George L. Wright—that was my father's legal name, but everyone knew him as Captain Ladd—built that boat for himself and if you knew my father, not even the best was quite good enough for him. *C. E. Wright* contained the best materials, the best workmanship, and the best of everything according to his standards. The boat was completed sometime in 1916 and has plied the water of the Bay ever since. I understand that the present owner [in 1981], Mr. Kenneth W. Rhodes, is using her to dredge for shellfish off the Atlantic coastline of the Eastern Shore peninsula. *C. E. Wright* is still a grand old lady.

"Of course there have been some changes made through the years. She has been lengthened and is now approximately 65 feet long. They have even changed her name to *Lorie Robins,* but I have changed my name too and even grown a bit. Just as many of my old friends still call me Countess Wright, *Lorie Robins* is still referred to by those who knew her as *C. E. Wright.* The E is for Elizabeth."

*For most of the year, the family buyboat was used in the course of making a living, but at certain times, the workboat became the platform for recreational purposes.*

# 16: DECK BOATS AT PLAY

The versatile deck boats were used during family reunions, Labor Day boat races, church picnics, camp meetings, and Fourth of July celebrations. Family and friends would gather aboard a boat, bringing lots of cold soda and home-cooked food and taking away lifelong memories.

## SOAKING WET RELIGION

Evangelist Dr. H. M. Wharton established Wharton Grove near Weems, Virginia, in 1893. It was founded as the site of an interdenominational two-week religious "camp" meeting that was held each summer. John Wilson wrote in his book *Northern Neck—A Pictorial History* that instead of the old-fashioned tent revival, Wharton Grove had a three-tiered, 90-foot square tabernacle with huge beams and a bell at the top. Christians from up and down the Bay would congregate there for two weeks of powerful religion. There were numerous cottages on the site for overnight lodgers and a quarter-mile-long wharf extended out into the Rappahannock to accommodate those who came by boat. Many a wayward soul found the Lord at Wharton Grove and it changed forever their lives. It closed down in 1927 when Dr. Wharton passed away.

Edna Deagle Shackelford of Deltaville recalls visiting Wharton Grove as a youngster in the early 1920s by way of a buyboat. She and other members of Philippi Christian Church in Deltaville made the trip on a Saturday out of Jackson Creek around Stingray Point and down the Rappahannock River to Weems in the buyboat *Lagonia*, owned by Captain Johnny Ward.

"Years ago, a crowd of people from Philippi would go to Wharton Grove on *Lagonia*," says Edna. "On one of those trips when I was real small, a storm came up and everyone tried to crowd into the pilothouse but we couldn't all get in there. I got soaking wet along with most everyone else.

"It was one of the worst storms that I had been in out on the water, but we made it there. Once we got to the dock that extended out into the river for a long ways, the sun came out and it was a nice day. It was a full day of eating and preaching. They used to say 'all day dinner and preaching on the grounds.' I was a little girl so I guess I remember more about the eating than I do the preaching. I do remember the food was good.

"The old *Lagonia* got us there and got us back. The boats were used for little things other than just work. They had a little leisure. As a child, it was fun being out on the water in such a big boat. We had her loaded down with people but what fun it all was. I have fond memories of those trips. I miss those old people.

During revivals the dock at Wharton Grove on the Corrotoman River at Weems, Virginia, was loaded with boats. Deck boats from all around brought churchgoers to the annual two-week event. Interdenominational camp meetings were held at Wharton Grove from 1893 to 1927. Courtesy John Wilson.

These young people are crossing the Rappahannock River in the 1920s on their way to Wharton Grove from Urbanna, Virginia, aboard a deck boat. Courtesy Betty Burton.

## WHICH SUNDAY GIRLFRIEND?

Bill Sullivan, fifty-nine, of Hartfield, Virginia, remembers with fondness Sunday afternoon family reunion trips aboard the 65-foot buyboat *Seven Brothers.*

*Seven Brothers* was owned by two of Bill's uncles, Wroten and Stewart Simmons. They used the boat in the deepwater pound-net fishery. There were seven brothers in the Simmons family so the boat was named after Bill's father and his six uncles. There were also four sisters in that family. One of those sisters lived across the Chesapeake Bay on the Eastern Shore of Virginia, and in the summertime the whole family would board the vessel and carry a Sunday picnic lunch to the shore.

It was always a great time for Bill but as he got older it became even more interesting. "When I got older, it was an experience to bring a girlfriend to a Sunday family picnic, which always ended up with a ride on *Seven Brothers,*" says Bill.

"You had to bring your loved one of the future to this family picnic and endure such teasing. We'd be out on *Seven Brothers* in the Bay and Uncle Wroten would walk up to me and say something like, 'Bill, this girl is prettier than the one you had down here last week. I wonder what the one next Sunday will look like.'

The buyboat *Annie P. Parks* was used for summertime rendezvous on Lynnhaven Inlet. Everyone from the small boats would go aboard the bigger buyboat for a Sunday feast. Swimming and fishing were part of the day's activities, and Arlene Matthews recalls using the top of the pilothouse as a diving platform. This photo was taken in 1957. Courtesy Arlene Matthews.

"They'd all start laughing and I would turn beet red and the redder I would get the more they would laugh," says Bill.

## *ANNIE P. PARKS*

Arlene Matthews of Crittenden, Virginia, recalls the summertime fun out at Lynnhaven Inlet as more than a dozen boats would raft up against the buyboat *Annie P. Parks* for a floating party. *Annie P. Parks* had been built as a sailing bugeye in 1888 and had been converted to power.

## Sunday Rendezvous

"Uncle Will Mathews owned *Annie P. Parks.* We called him Uncle Will and he was kin to me through my mother. Sometimes on Sundays in the summertime, Uncle Will would take *Annie P. Parks* out into Lynnhaven Inlet off Norfork, and we'd all take our boats and raft up against her.

"If the weather was good, we would spend the night on the boats and it was like living in a hotel with no walls around you," Arlene says. "We had little boats so the men could go off fishing and the women would all gather on *Annie P. Parks.* There was a nice awning to keep the sun or rain off and there was plenty of room for everyone when mealtime came, and boy was it some good eating. Everybody would bring a dish and some of those older women could really cook."

## Trips to Buckroe and Ocean View

"Sometimes we'd leave from home in Crittenden on a buyboat and go to Newport News, get on a streetcar, and go to Buckroe Beach to the amusement park and a beach," Arlene says. "Sometimes we'd go to Norfolk, get on a streetcar and go to Ocean View to the amusement park.

"When I was a real little girl, every summer we would get on *Annie P. Parks* and take the Mammas and the kids to Norfolk to City Park. Mammas would do some cooking so we'd have some food and we'd spend the day. It was a wonderful time and we'd catch the boat back when we were ready to go home.

"When I was a teenager and after I was married too, I remember the moonlight boat rides on *Annie P. Parks,*" she recalls. "The boat was wonderful because it would hold a lot of people. Those summer nights with a cool breeze and the sounds of the water hitting up against the boat were real romantic times. I'll tell you that."

The Verlander and Parker families of Water View, Virginia, are enjoying the Labor Day boat races aboard *Rema H.* sometime in the 1950s. The families owned seafood packing houses on Parrott Creek on the Rappahannock River, but on Labor Day many friends and relatives journeyed to Urbanna for a day of fun. *Rema H.* was built in 1946 by Harry "Steve" Smith of Horn Harbor, Virginia. Courtesy Carroll Davies.

This Gwynn's Island group took a pleasure ride to Tangier Island on the deck boat *Mary Ann II* in the late 1950s. Courtesy Robert Roland Hudgins.

## POQUOSON WORKBOAT RACES

*On October 13, 2002, Bill Hight and I had the privilege of going aboard the buyboat* East Hampton *to watch the workboats races on Back River near Poquoson, Virginia. Senior Editor Lincoln Bedrosian of* National Fisherman *gave me the assignment to cover the races, and when I called to get on a boat it was suggested that I cover the race on the "line boat" which happened to be* East Hampton. *The owners, David and Trudy Rollins, were the supreme host and hostess.*

*The 63-foot workboat was built in 1925 in Laban in Mathews County, Virginia, by Freeman Hudgins and Boney Diggs as an open boat with a V-stern and was used in the pound-net fishery. She was later converted to a deck boat; the V-stern was taken off and the present round stern installed.*

## A DAY ABOARD *EAST HAMPTON*

*East Hampton* was moored on Bennett Creek. The thirteenth annual Poquoson workboat races were being held on Back River, which, as the crow flies, is not far but by water it was an hour and a half run.

Dave Rollins comes from a long line of Chesapeake Bay boatbuilders and bought *East Hampton* out of love for the boats. The boat was to be stationed at the finish line so Dave could relay the results of each race via radio to the judges on shore.

*East Hampton* is in the Opsail 2000 boat parade at Thimble Shoals near Norfolk, Virginia. Courtesy David and Trudy Rollins.

Workboat races have been a part of Chesapeake Bay watermen's culture as long as there have been watermen and workboats. In the days of sail-driven log canoes, watermen would race to fishing grounds, race to sell their catch to buyboats, and then race home. There was pride in having the fastest boat and the prize was bragging rights that started at the dock, moved throughout the community, and was the main conversation down on the docks or at Saturday night gatherings at the local country store. The race in Poquoson is a throwback to that heritage.

Virginia and Maryland have events that feature Chesapeake Bay buyboats. Norfolk's Harborfest and the Yorktown Watermen's Museum race are held annually and always feature a number of deck boats. When Chestertown, Maryland, launched *Sultana,* buy-

boats were invited as an added attraction. Little *Muriel Eileen* and *P. E. Pruitt* were there in the harbor. People love to see the boats.

Rollins uses *East Hampton* for recreation, and he has made the boat extremely comfortable and bright by finishing the wood in the roomy pilothouse with varnish and installing built-in bunks and tables. The aft portion of the house is a modernized galley with refrigeration and cabinets for food storage and glasses and dishes and a stove for preparation of food on trips just like this one.

*East Hampton* was built either in 1924 or 1925. Her official documentation says 1925, but she has 1924 painted across the pilothouse.

On the way to Bennett Creek, David, at the helm, talked about his boat. "Whoever built her had to have

The 2002 Poquoson workboat races were exciting as these deadrise workboats roared through the water.

been someone who worked for Lennie Smith," says David. "If you look at *Ellen Marie* from the side they are almost identical in looks. [*Ellen Marie* was built by Lennie and Alton Smith in 1926. Many boatbuilders in Mathews County learned the trade from Lennie and his son Alton.] Now *Ellen Marie* is narrower and real narrow on the back end, but the rake of the stem, the shape of the stern, and the sheer line are all alike. Now the pilothouses are different but neither one have original pilothouses on them.

"*East Hampton* was built for Curtis Hudgins from Foxhill [Virginia] as an open trap boat for pound-net fishing," he says. She has always been named *East Hampton* and has the name 'East Hampton' carved in the hull."

With his hands on the wheel, David says running the 60-foot deck boat is "a matter of getting used to. *East Hampton* is all pilothouse-controlled, and it is not so much slow as it is heavy. It's easy to control compared to the early boats with engine-room controls. Engine-room controlled vessels had an engineer below shifting the cam to put her in reverse. Can you imagine coming up on a dock and having to ring a bell to get the engineer to stop her? I've heard them talk about a guy nicknamed Buck Toad down here

who was captain of a deck boat named *Inez*. He had to cut her [the engine] off and restart it in reverse to get her to go in reverse. I've heard them say he could maneuver her just like we do now with our hydraulic clutches." [*Inez* was 60 feet long, built in Wake, Virginia, in 1936.]

As *East Hampton* arrived at the mouth of Bennett Creek from the Poquoson River, David mentioned that the marshes nearby are called the "big salt marshes." They run all the way around to Back River. He and his wife Trudy grew up in the area and gunkholed through the marshes in small boats as children and teenagers.

He almost bought the deck boat *Delvin K*. "Trudy and I love to look at boats and we had just sold a fiberglass boat. So we started looking for a new boat. I was down at Mathews County one day on Davis Creek looking at *Delvin K*. when her owner Lorie Hudgins came down to the dock and started talking. He said he'd sell us the boat and gear for $30,000. I thought he was going to say $60,000 or $70,000.

"Well we were driving home from Mathews and Trudy and I started talking and we both agreed $30,000 was not a lot of money for a boat that big and we could really enjoy playing on it.

"I told her I knew where another one was and they were asking $65,000 for *East Hampton*. I knew we

This 1930s workboat race on Mill Creek on the Rappahannock River had two deck boats acting as line boats. Courtesy Carolyn Revere Henkel.

couldn't come up with that much money but we stopped to look at her anyway.

"Trudy didn't like her as much as *Delvin K.* because she didn't have as much room on the stern deck for chairs or whatever. *Delvin K.* had a great big stern deck but when we went aboard *East Hampton* and started looking around, I fell in love with her. So, we went back again the next weekend to look at *Delvin K.* I got to looking and there must have been fifty boards on deck, 2-inch boards, where the ends were rotting.

"*East Hampton* had very little wood rot and the price had come down to $45,000. It was still more than I could afford. I told the owner I had just sold a boat for a certain amount and that's all I had and all I could afford. He said to me that he had owned his grandfather's boat *Seminole* [a 1923 deck boat built by Alton and Lennie Smith] and he had sold that boat for a lot of money to a guy who took her and trimmed her windows and everything with black paint. He said he was sick for two days after he saw her. The next time he saw her six months later the man had taken the pilothouse off her. She died with no pilothouse

on her and he said he could not stand to see that happen to *East Hampton*. He said he knew I would take care of her. So we came to an agreement and *East Hampton* got a good home."

## The Races

*East Hampton* arrived at the mouth of Bennett Creek and proceeded to the finish line of the race. Through radio communication between the boat and shore, David anchored the vessel in the prescribed location. Friends and family in smaller boats came up and cut their motors off to talk with Trudy and David. Some came aboard to watch the races. There was plenty of room for lawn chairs and coolers. A workboat parade was held as skiffs and deadrise workboats decked out in banners and flags of all kinds paraded in front of the line boat and the judges' stand on shore. There was a large crowd of people around the shore watching the event.

The boats were broken down into classes and runoff heats were held. After each race, David would radio in the results. Around 1 o'clock, Trudy fixed hot chili in the galley and between races lunch was served. As usual, food cooked and served on a boat tastes better than anywhere else.

There were fifteen races with three final competitions determining who would reign as "King of the Bay" in the outboard, gas boat, and diesel classes. Scott West of Gloucester County, Virginia, took the outboard title in a Seahawk skiff powered by a Johnson engine.

Buck Schackelford of Hampton, Virginia, aboard *Miss Dot,* powered by a 454 Chevy engine, won the gas-boat crown. Hampton's C. D. Hancock was the diesel champ in the 6-71 Detroit-powered *Maria Lynn.*

With the conclusion of the final race, everyone who had been watching from *East Hampton* got into their own boats, and the captain and crew made the pleasant journey home.

*Although not commonplace aboard buyboats, tragedy has been a part of their history. Fog, northeast storms, hurricanes, tornadoes, snow, and the dangers of being on the Chesapeake Bay in the middle of the winter working on ice-covered decks sometimes resulted in tragedies.*

# 17: FEAR, INJURY, AND DEATH

The Chesapeake Bay is no different from any other body of water—it has many faces and many moods. On a clear, windless day, a trip across the Bay in a 12-foot skiff is feasible, but when the weather turns foul and storms come, life can be placed in jeopardy even aboard a 70-foot buyboat. Those involved in this chapter can attest to that.

## THE SINKING OF *KLONDIKE*

The community graveyard in Crittenden, Virginia, has many tombstones of captains and mates who worked aboard buyboats. One of the most haunting stories concerns the graves of Bert Hazelwood, Jr., and Gray Adams. The family plots are side by side and the two young men were buried side by side in the corners of the plots.

They died together in the buyboat *Klondike* on March 22, 1968. *Klondike* had been loaded with 1,500 bushels of seed oysters from the James River, and Captain Hazelwood had planned to carry the load to oyster grounds on the York River that night.

Gray Adams was along for the ride and two crewmembers, William Mann and Thomas Crocker of Hobson, Virginia, were along as mates. No one knows exactly what happened that night, but the next day the boat was found off Buckroe Beach, sunk and awash. All four men were killed in the sinking, which is detailed in *Living Memories of Crittenden and Eclipse*, by Minnie Moge Corson.

On Sunday, March 24, the *Newport News Daily Press* reported the tragedy.

Coast Guardsmen were to continue the search today for four crewmen believed aboard an oyster boat that sank off Buckroe Beach late Friday or early Saturday.

Coast Guard spokesmen said wreckage of the boat was spotted Saturday morning a half mile off the beach.

The craft was carrying seed oysters from a point on the James River near Fort Eustis, and [was] on route to Capahosic on the York River. Planes and vessels searched the area Saturday but no bodies were found.

Sidney Burt Hazelwood, Jr., twenty-eight, of Eclipse, captain of the 60-foot diesel-powered boat, *Klondike,* owned by the Battery Park Fish and Oyster Co., left the home port on the south side of the James River on Friday along with a friend and recently returned veteran of Vietnam Charles Gary Adams, twenty-four, on route to the seed oysters.

They took with them two deckhands, Thomas P. Crocker, twenty-eight, and William Henry Mann, in his fifties. They went to a point near Fort Eustis known as Horsehead and picked up a load of seed oysters. Later they paid tax on the oysters at a tax collection facility of the commission at Battery Park.

The commission representative has records showing that the load was 1,500 bushels and they left between 6:30 P.M. and 7 P.M.

Early reports indicated there had been an explosion or a collision with another vessel. Milton Hickman, commissioner of fisheries for the Commonwealth of Virginia, told the *Daily Press,* "Our men have a feeling that the boat capsized. This does not mean that the load was too great for many boats carry heavier loads.

It must be remembered that high winds made the water quite rough. We just don't know what happened at this time. The reason our people believe the boat capsized is that the boat had a high mast and the mast is now missing."

The boat is in 9 feet of water and only the pilothouse is visible. Coast Guard spokesmen said it is very likely that whatever occurred to the boat took place only a short distance from where the wreckage was found since the heavy cargo would have prevented any long-distance drifting by the vessel.

On Tuesday, March 26, the *Daily Press* reported the following:

Rough seas have moved the vessel some distance from where she was first sighted and a door has been found near Cape Charles.

Other wreckage was found Saturday at the Chesapeake Channel north of the Chesapeake Bay Bridge Tunnel.

Searchers were hopeful some of the men aboard had put on life jackets before the ship went down.

"This is why we have been using an airplane in hopes that we could find a body floating on the surface," said a Coast Guard spokesman. He added he believed the water was too cold for anyone to live very long under such exposure.

The bodies of all four men were eventually found.

# TORNADO BRINGS TRAGEDY

Over the years, I've talked to many watermen who have recalled the great storms and accidents in the Chesapeake Bay region. The galley must have been one of the worst places to be in time of danger because it seems that when death occurred it was often a cook or crewmember killed in the galley. A 1939 tornado caused the death of the cook on *Seven Brothers.*

The oral story of the cook drowning was told by Andrew Simmons, who heard the story from his father, Stewart Simmons. The written version of the tornado of August 24, 1939, in the *Rappahannock Record,* a weekly newspaper in Kilmarnock, Virginia, gives the tragedy a little different perspective.

## Andrew Simmons's Account

"Daddy, Wroten, and their cook Raymond Campbell were coming from Baltimore on *Seven Brothers* when they got caught in a bad storm. There used to be a watermelon grower over here [Northern Neck of Virginia] called Lou Baker and he raised enough watermelons to load three boats for the Baltimore market. [There were three buyboats in the family—*Simmons, Seven Brothers,* and *Oriole.*]

"*Seven Brothers* had been to Baltimore to deliver watermelons and was on the way home when an awful storm struck them off Smith Point [near the mouth of Great Wicomico River]. Daddy said it was beating down on them right good so they went into Fleeton [on Cockrell Creek in Virginia], anchored off from shore, and were in their bunks ready to go to sleep when a tornado came and picked them up and turned *Seven Brothers* upside down.

"Lightning showed Daddy where the window was, and Wroten went through the door, but the colored cook, Raymond, got drowned," says Andrew. "He was the only one I know of to drown while working on *Seven Brothers* and a many a man worked aboard her. She was literally flipped upside down and her mast was six feet in the mud, but they got her up," he says.

"People used to joke about how tight Wroten was with his money, and after the boat turned over people joked that he left his pants in the cabin with $100 in his pocket," says Andrew, "and when he found out the $100 was still in his pants he swum back through that terrible storm to get that money—like all he was worried about was the money.

"It is true that he swam back for his pants but it was after they got ashore and discovered Raymond was still on board that they both swam back to the boat looking for him," says Andrew. "They tried but they couldn't find Raymond and then Wroten swam through the cabin window and got his pants and the $100.

"When the boat was hauled, Raymond was found dead in the galley."

## *Rappahannock Record's* Version

The main headline read "Fleeton and Reedville Hard Hit by Tornado." The subheading read "Local Colored Man Loses Life as Boat Turns Over."

The story in part read as follows:

A colored man was drowned and damage to the extent of tens of thousands of dollars was done in the Northern Neck Friday night when a tornado with its terrific force hit the Fleeton-Reedville area and at Mundy Point.

The greatest damage done by the wind storm was at Fleeton where several houses were demolished and others were badly damaged and a powerboat was blown over with the loss of one member of the crew.

Stewart and Wroten Simmons of Kilmarnock in the 65-foot powerboat *Seven Brothers* put into the harbor at Fleeton for protection from the storm less than an hour before the tornado hit. They tied up at the dock and were preparing to retire for the night when they heard the wind approaching.

Suddenly the boat turned over and began to fill with water. One of the Simmons brothers came out through a door, the other through a window. Both swam a few feet to the wharf and climbed to safety. They said the storm lasted only a few seconds. A watch on one of them had stopped at 12:15 A.M.

Raymond Campbell (colored) of Kilmarnock, the only other man on the boat, was in the galley at the time and did not get out. His body was recovered Saturday afternoon when the boat was gotten up. His wife and seven children survive him.

The boat did not appear to be damaged to any great extent. Everything loose on the boat was blown away.

From Reedville the twister jumped to Mundy Point farther up the Potomac where it smashed two warehouses, damaged a canning factory, several homes, and a number of other buildings. No serious injuries were reported there.

From Mundy Point the storm crossed the Potomac to Leonardtown on the Maryland side where Miss Julia Richardson, seventy, was crushed to death when her home collapsed. Other buildings in that section were also damaged.

## DEATH AND *LOUISE TRAVERS*

*For deck boat captains and crew, there is always fear of sinking in the Chesapeake Bay on the worst of nights when the weather is not fit for "fish nor fowl." For Maurice Ward of Crisfield, Maryland, and his mate and the mate's young son, that fear came true on a cold winter night near Herring Bay, just below Annapolis, Maryland, on the converted bugeye* Louise Travers.

Henry Ward of Crisfield owned *Louise Travers,* a converted bugeye that was built by J. T. Marsh of Solomons Island, Maryland, in 1896. Henry worked *Louise Travers* when she was a sail-powered bugeye, and he had her converted over to a powerboat. When Henry got old he turned the boat over to his youngest son, Maurice Ward. "One time in the early 1930s she sank going up the Bay with a load of lumber on her, and two men froze to death," recalls Melvin Ward, Henry's grandson.

"I remember it but I was just a little boy when it happened. They had got up near Annapolis when *Louise Travers* started taking on water. She was loaded with lumber in the hold and on deck. My Uncle Morris was on her and it got real nasty and was cold and snowing and blowing a gale. It was three of them on board—my uncle, a mate, and the mate's young son was along. At first, they all got in a skiff and pushed away from *Louise Travers.*

"However, my uncle left his wallet in the wheelhouse and when he realized it, they paddled and struggled to get back to the boat. You know a Ward is supposed to be tight with his money so he was for certain going back for that wallet.

"While he was in the pilothouse, the lumber shifted and the wind picked up even worse. The man and boy in the skiff got loose from *Louise Travers* and

183

couldn't get back to pick up my uncle so he spent the night in the pilothouse. The boat started to go down, but when it reached the point that the lumber was in the water, the wood provided enough buoyancy to keep the hull afloat.

"My uncle spent the night in the top bunk of the pilothouse. There were three bunks high and the top bunk was not underwater. A fisherman picked him up around Herring Bay the next morning.

"My uncle survived but he was in the hospital for a long time, but the man and boy tied themselves with the bow line to the boat and they were found froze to death floating in the skiff going up the Bay. My uncle, more than likely, would have froze to death too had he stayed in the skiff."

## INJURY ABOARD *P. E. PRUITT*

*One of the most dangerous jobs on the Bay is working in the winter crab-dredge fishery. Untold numbers of men lost their lives and limbs working in this fishery. Jonesey Payne of Urbanna, Virginia, was a lucky one. He lost only a portion of his hand.*

Paul Pruitt of Tangier Island and later Urbanna, Virginia, worked *P. E. Pruitt* in the Bay's winter crab–dredge fishery. Jonesey Payne of Urbanna was a young man, not long out of service in the 1950s, when he came home and worked aboard *P. E. Pruitt* for four or five years.

They were dredging for crabs on a wintry day off the mouth of the Rappahannock River when Jonesey lost a portion of his hand. "That's where I lost my fingers was on *P. E. Pruitt*," says Jonesey. "I think crab dredging is one of the most dangerous [kinds of] work you can do on the water. It's the middle of winter, cold, and if you fall overboard you are dead. That's sort of what happened to me. It was wintertime, rough, and ice all over the boat and gear.

"The spray would come up off the water and form ice on you when it hit you," he says. "I just happened to slip and my instinct was to grab anything I could so I would not go overboard. I grabbed the chain and that was the wrong thing to do. Paul was hauling the dredge in and when he saw me he kicked it out of gear but it was too late. It was real quick and pulled me right up to the block. If he hadn't seen me and kicked it out, it would have killed me. As it was, it grabbed my hand.

"They took me to Norfork Marine Hospital in Norfolk and operated on it but I lost some of my hand," says Jonesey. "It was bad but I went back the next year adredging with Paul. A whole lot of people got hurt a crab dredging. I know men who have lost arms and feet aboard deck boats. It is dangerous work."

## THE NIGHT *MARY E. HAYNIE* SANK

Terry Haydon, then captain of *Mary E. Haynie*, recalls the night she sank and was lost. Lewis A. Callis of Callis Seafood, Haydon's father-in-law, owned *Mary E. Haynie*. Terry and his mate Stanley Lewis had bought a load of seed oysters from tongers on the James River and were headed to the Rappahannock River in the 60-foot buyboat.

"It was October 7, 1981, and it was a warm day and thank goodness for that. I get nervous every time I talk about this. That's one night I don't want to relive again," says Terry at his home in the Millenbeck area of Lancaster County, Virginia.

"We had loaded her with 1,100 bushels of seed oysters and 75 bushels of shucking stock on the James River, and it had been blowing all day long," he says. "We were tied up at Rescue, Virginia, at Billy Carter's dock, and along about 5 o'clock the wind died right down. Usually when the wind dies down in the evening it stays down until the sun comes up the next morning. I asked Stanley what he thought about us heading back and he said, 'well the wind's died down and sun's going down—we ought to have a beautiful night running.'

"We started on out and when we got to Mobjack Bay it started blowing a gale," says Terry. "All of a sudden, it just got so bad and about 9 o'clock I looked down in the engine room and there was plenty of water. I knew we had a major problem so I told Stanley to take the wheel and I went out on deck and started tripping doors [the sides that keep oysters from going overboard] to let the oysters fall overboard and to lighten us up. With the amount of water in the engine room, I knew I had to do something.

"After I tripped the doors, I came back in and looked and there was more water in the engine room than before. All the pumps were running as hard as they could run and still more water. It didn't help at all, so I called the Coast Guard and told them I was in dire need of help.

"While I was calling the Coast Guard, Melvin and Milton [Mit] Ward, two of the Ward brothers in *M. V. Chief,* heard the distress call and turned around and came back towards us. They were at New Point Light when we were at York Spit. When they came back towards us they called me over the radio and told me they were coming, but they couldn't see us. It was dark as I don't know what out there. I turned my spotlight on and turned it several different directions to help them spot us. Finally they saw us and were coming towards us.

"After that, I grabbed two life jackets and told Stanley I was going back out to turn the wash-down pump on and wash more oysters off the deck. By then, all I was thinking was can I save the boat and us. When I walked out on deck that last time I knew then we were going to lose her. I had enough time to tell Stanley to 'come on we are going to lose the boat.' In a split second, I could see a big sea coming and it came right over the deck, washed me overboard and turned the boat over with Stanley inside the wheelhouse.

"I had two life jackets in my hand but when I came up out of the water I only had one. I was 30 or 40 feet from the boat, floating in the water. I had never heard such a horrible sound in my life as when the boat turned over. The sound of shells and stuff coming off and then the motor stopped and there was total stillness.

"When Stanley tried to leave the pilothouse a drawer came out and kept him from getting out before the boat went over. With the boat upside down in the water, he was still in the wheelhouse and he couldn't get the door open because of the pressure. He tried to knock a window out but it would not break. Finally, the house filled with water and released the pressure on the door. The boat was bottom upwards so when he swam out he kept hitting decks so he had to swim down and out away from the railing.

"When he came up out of the water, I could see him but he didn't say a word. He grabbed a pro-

pane tank that was floating from the boat but he couldn't keep it level in the water so I swam over and held the other end to keep it balanced in the water. He still didn't say anything so I asked him what was wrong, and he spit a wad of tobacco and a mouth full of water out of his mouth. The wad had gotten hung in his throat and then he said he was all right.

"Melvin saw our lights go out and he put a compass on us and came over to pick us up," says Terry. "One of the funny things that happened was when we were swimming my foot hit Stanley's leg and he said, 'was that you?'

"I think he thought it was a shark.

"We were extremely lucky. Melvin came within 100 feet of us, took the engine out of gear, and yelled for us to swim to him. I mean the wind was howling and he was afraid if he came too close we might get sucked into the prop.

"Stanley was a little heavy so I told him I'd go up first and I helped him get up. Once we got up on deck, Milton brought us dry clothes and told us to go change. No one at that point had gotten hurt, but when we went in to change clothes Stanley bent over, fell back into the exhaust pipe, and it burned him right bad.

"We went through all that and Stanley ends up hurting himself on the *Chief.*

"When we left, Melvin put the spotlight on *Mary E. Haynie* and she was over on her side and there was more bottom than top showing. To this day I have no idea what made her take on water. Maybe it just got so nasty it knocked a bottom plank loose.

"We came back later and tried to get her up," says Terry. "We tied onto her but the only thing we got was the top of her mast.

"I can honestly say that I was not afraid at the time because everything happened so fast, but I get more nervous talking about it now than I did when it happened."

*When interviewing those associated with buyboats, conversations often move from one thought to another—to a specific day or happening that tells much about how life was for those associated with the boats. Some of these memories show how different life is now from the time when Chesapeake buyboats were an everyday scene on Bay waters.*

# 18: BUYBOAT TALES

The way people think and act during a particular time period in history can often be understood more clearly through stories of everday life rather than records of historical facts. In modern-day terms, life during the buyboat era would be considered hard, but there was some fun and humor in it all, and plenty of good food too. Even in those days, there was proof that boys will be boys.

## YOU BOUGHT ONE YESTERDAY

Thelma Sullivan, ninety-four, of Kilmarnock, Virginia, recalls with fondness the days when her father and brothers worked the water. Her story is about her two brothers who owned the deck boat *Seven Brothers.*

"My brothers, Wroten and Stewart, both had a good sense of humor," she says. "Stewart loved to read. Wroten loved money, and he took care of all the money aspects of the business. He never read much of anything unless it had to do with money. They would haul watermelons to Baltimore in the summer on *Seven Brothers* and Stewart loved to read the *Baltimore Sun.* One day they were in Baltimore and Stewart ask Wroten for some money to buy a copy of the *Sun.*

"Wroten said to Stewart, 'Jesus Christ, man, you just bought one yesterday!'"

## BLACK WINDOWS

Morris Snow of Mathews County, Virginia, recalls that most buyboat captains were practical jokers. "Once Bud Godsey of Gywnn's Island was on *Wanda*, a 60-foot deck boat, and Winnie Pruitt of Tangier Island was on *Yamacraw,* a 55-footer. They were always playing jokes on one another. At that time in Cape Charles, Virginia, crab-dredge boats were tied up eight or ten abreast to the dock, and there were so many deck boats lined up that a man could walk across the boats with a basket of crabs under his arm and never miss a step.

"One night at the dock, Bud was asleep in *Wanda,* and he and Winnie had been playing around all day so as a joke Winnie took some rags and stopped the stovepipe up and Bud woke up with smoke all in his cabin. It was in the winter and Bud had to lower his windows all night long in the cold air to get the smoke and smell of smoke out.

"They went along for two or three nights without anything happening. Then it happened on this one night after a group of the boys had stayed up late chatting and after they had gone to sleep. You see, Bud Godsey had gone to town that day and bought a gallon of black paint and a paint brush. That night he painted every window on *Yamacraw* pitch black. Next morning, Winnie woke up thinking it should be morn-

On both *Simmons* and *Seven Brothers,* the galley was located in the forepeak. Note the stovepipe coming out of the roof of the forepeak. Courtesy Cathy Winegar Davenport.

ing but saw it was still dark and went back to sleep. When he finally did get up, half the day was gone and all the boys had left in their boats to go crabbing. His was the only boat left at the dock. Boy, Bud got Winnie that day!" [The late Winnie Pruitt is the father of William Pruitt, longtime commissioner of the Virginia Marine Resources Commission.]

## A COUNTRY BOY'S FIRST MAJOR LEAGUE BASEBALL GAME

For young men, a trip on the boat to Washington or Baltimore often marked the first trip away from home. The excitement of city life frequently left lifelong memories. In the case of young J. J. Hardy of Hardyville, Virginia, life in the nation's capital was much different than in rural tidewater where he was born

and raised. That first trip aboard a deck boat to Washington left a lasting impression.

One of J. J.'s. first jobs was aboard the freight boat *Harriet* in the 1920s. He made several trips aboard the boat hauling freight and buying seed oysters.

"*Harriet* was owned by Captain Willard Wake and she was used as an oyster buyboat, but she was also used to haul freight. *Harriet* was a horse. I mean she was a big boat.

"We would go to Washington and take a little of everything. We hauled oysters, potatoes—a lot of everything. We were a freight boat. People around the neighborhood wanted things shipped so we would take it to commission merchants up there in Washington for them to sell.

"The first time I ever went to Washington on the boat, we had to wait a while to sell the stuff, so I went

187

*Yamacraw,* shown in the foreground, once had all its windows painted black by another buyboat captain as a practical joke. Other boats in the photo are *Joyce Sterling, Marion Sue Handy,* and *Ruth S.* Courtesy William Pruitt.

on my first racing dip [roller coaster ride] at an amusement park and I went to my first major league baseball game.

"Boy, that was something. I saw the Washington Senators play ball and it was before there were lighted fields. Walter Johnson was pitching and the hitters couldn't hardly see the ball when there was plenty of light, but when it got a little dark nobody could hit Walter Johnson. He had a fast ball as fast as any modern-day pitcher. They called him Big Train. I mean that was something for a young man from the country to see. When I got home and told all the boys that I had seen Walter Johnson pitch, they could hardly believe it."

Walter Perry Johnson pitched for the Washington Senators from 1907 to 1927 and many experts to this day consider him the greatest fast-ball pitcher of all time.

## ONE FOR A DIME OR TWO FOR A QUARTER

Bill Sullivan of Hartfield, Virginia, recalls that his two uncles Wroten and Stewart Simmons would sell watermelons at Long Dock in Baltimore from the 65-foot buyboat *Seven Brothers.* One story that Wroten liked to tell, recalls Bill, was that in the summertime they'd haul watermelons to Baltimore on *Seven Brothers.* They'd go around and buy watermelons from farmers up and down the shore and then go to Baltimore and sell them retail off the boat.

"Uncle Wroten used to say they'd sell them for a dime apiece or two for a quarter. He said those people up there would buy them all day long for two for a quarter. I guess they thought two coins was more than one quarter. Uncle Wroten always had an angle."

*Ruth S.,* a pretty image in this photo on Tangier Island, was built by Linwood Price of Deltaville, Virginia. Price once said she was the ugliest boat he ever built. Courtesy W. C. Hight Collection.

## FIRE IN THE BOAT

Willis Wilson of Deltaville, Virginia, was five years old in the 1920s when he was aboard *Oriole,* a 60-foot buyboat owned by Ray Simmons of Kilmarnock, Virginia.

Willis's father, Obie Wilson, was a crewmember aboard the deck boat that was used in the deepwater pound-net fishery on the Potomac River and Chesapeake Bay.

In those days, there was no day care for a boy of five years old who was too young to start school. It was not unusual for a lad to tag along with his dad to work even if it meant rising early in the morning and being out on the Chesapeake Bay most of the day.

"In those times, kids not old enough to go to school would go with their fathers to work, and I was with him on this particular day when *Oriole* caught fire," says Willis.

"We were coming into Dymer Creek [Lancaster County, Virginia] and I was sitting on the stern when the motor caught fire. They were trying to smother the fire with rags and one of the men attempted to throw a rag that had caught fire overboard. It landed in one of the skiffs we were towing.

"Then, the skiff caught fire and it was spreading," says Willis. "No one saw the fire in the skiff be-cause they were all working to save *Oriole.* I was sitting on the stern watching. So I pulled the rope tied to the skiff close enough that I could jump down into the burning skiff. There was a bailing scoop in the bottom of the skiff so I picked it up and threw water on the fire and was able to put it out. When the men saw what I had done they praised me for saving the skiff and probably the other skiffs that were beside it.

"I thought I was a big boy that day, and the captain told my daddy to bring that boy to work anytime."

## A HOMEMADE PISTON

In the late 1920s and early 1930s, Lee Deagle of Deltaville, Virginia, operated a small machine-shop/railway next to the public dock at the end of Lovers Lane on Jackson Creek.

At his shop, Deagle converted sail-powered log canoes to power boats using only hand tools as there was no electricity. Using these tools he also worked on motors in several of the early buyboats, fabricating parts as they were needed. This story is recalled by his son Ed and shows how improvising was a way of life in those days.

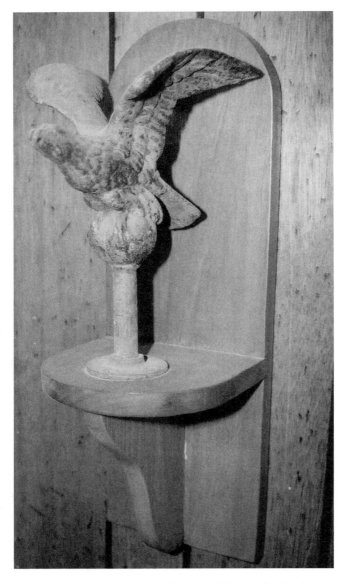

The pilothouse eagle that flew above the Chesapeake Bay deck boat *Ruth S.* is part of W. C. Hight's collection. Many of the boats carried similar good luck charms.

"When the Old Man started out in a machine shop over on Jackson Creek, he didn't have any electricity or steam power. He had hand tools—foot adz, broad axes, crosscut saws, and a lathe that he had to crank by hand.

"Old man Johnny Stiff had a boat called *Ruth S.* [a buyboat] that had been built at Price's Boat Yard in Deltaville and she had an old four-cylinder Caliberry motor in her. He carried watermelons and stuff to Baltimore in the boat.

"On one of the trips, Captain Johnny burned one of the barrels up in the motor and ruined a piston. He couldn't find a piston for her anywhere so the Old Man [Lee] went and got a piece of pipe and made a piston for it.

"Captain Johnny cranked the lathe while my daddy made that piece of pipe into a piston and years later the Old Man would say that was the only piston in *Ruth S.* that only had to be replaced once."

*Ruth S.* was built for Captain Johnny Stiff in 1927 by Linwood Price. James Crittenden says, "Price once said the only 'ugly' boat he ever built was *Ruth S.*, and he blamed Captain Johnny Stiff for changing the lines when he was away from the yard."

## A CLEAN FREAK

Another story about *Ruth S.* is recalled by Addison Cockrell, Jr., of Heathsville, Virginia, on the Northern Neck of Virginia. Over the years, Cockrell's Marine Railway in Northumberland County has serviced many deck boats from the Bay area. Addison remembers a time in the late 1940s when Charlie Pruitt of Tangier Island owned *Ruth S.* and brought her in for some major repairs.

"When the boat was on the railway Mr. Pruitt stayed right here at the yard and lived on the boat while she was on the rails. Every day around lunchtime we would take a break to eat," says Addison. "To see if we were finished working, Mr. Pruitt would poke his head around the corner of the building. We'd go inside to eat and when we'd come back all the sawdust had been swept up and our tools were placed in an orderly fashion.

"When we would quit for the day, you know how workmen are, we'd throw things down and get dirt and sawdust all over the deck. We'd come back the next morning and the deck was so clean that you could eat off it. I'm not kidding, every day he kept every area of that boat as clean as any house I've ever been in. He was a nice man and took a lot of pride in his boat."

## SAWED HALF IN TWO

Ed Deagle also recalls the time his father lengthened a buyboat named *Colony* by 20 feet 2 inches.

*Colony* was built in 1930 by Linwood Price at the yard before Deagle took it over. In the early 1950s, her owner brought her to Deagle's for a spring hauling.

"One day the captain by the name of Howard Ward of Crisfield, Maryland, came to the railway to have some work done on his boat," says Ed. "*Colony* was about 65 feet long, fairly wide, and he had her up on the railway here. Howard and the Old Man [Lee] were in the office one afternoon having a few drinks and Howard, who'd had more drinks than he should have, said, 'You know Lee, I wish that boat was 20 feet longer. She would make me a good boat.'

"The Old Man said, 'We can make her 20 feet longer if you want to,' and Howard said, 'Yeah, we might do that Lee. Yeah, I think we ought to do that.'

"The liquor wore off and Howard went on home to Crisfield for a few days. When he came back, the Old Man had cut the boat half in two. What he did was he backed the railway down; blocked the boat from the ground up; sawed the boat and railway half in two with a two-man crosscut saw; then pulled the front half 20 feet 2 inches ahead; and built on in the center of the boat.

"Howard, who didn't recall his conversation with the Old Man, about cried when he saw his boat cut half in two but he got over it when the Old Man had it finished and he had himself an 85-foot boat."

After being enlarged, *Colony* was registered at 81 feet 5 inches by 23 feet 7 inches by 7 feet 4 inch draft.

## A NAKED DRAWING PAD

Another story about Captain Lee Deagle was when a prospective buyer for a new deck boat came to the Fishing Bay yard to talk to him about building a boat. They went out under the massive oak tree there at the yard and sat on a Model A Ford car seat that Captain Lee had pulled from a car.

He explained to the man the type of boat he could build but when he was finished the man seemed confused. So Lee went inside and pulled a calendar with a picture of Marilyn Monroe in the nude off the wall, flipped it over, and sketched his style of boat on the back of the calendar for the man.

Legend has it he got the job, but when the man asked for that particular copy of the plans, Lee said,

"I'll be damned if I'm going to give you this calendar" and hung it back on the wall.

## WIFE IN THE TRUNK

*(The names in this story have been changed so as not to offend relatives, and the storyteller prefers not to be named.)*

The Cozy Cove Bar in Crisfield, Maryland, is a well-known hangout of many Chesapeake Bay watermen. For generations it has been a place of pleasure for local watermen as well as those who are away from home. For some a few drinks at the Cozy Cove would rank above going home to family.

In the 1940s, Samuel, a buyboat captain, owned one of the better-known boats on the Bay and he was often out buying and transporting seafood all around the Chesapeake.

He and his wife Fannie lived in Crisfield, and for Samuel the Cozy Cove was his first stop after days away from home. His stays at the bar often lasted well into the night. Needless to say, this did not make Fannie very happy, and one hot August day she broke into the bar mad as a hornet, screaming at Samuel to come home, using language unfit for a sailor.

Samuel had already had too much to drink and wasn't about to come home. He grabbed Fannie by her hair, pulled her out of the bar to their car, opened the trunk, and stuffed her inside. Then he closed the trunk, straightened himself up, and went back to his drinking inside the bar.

Meanwhile, several watermen could hear Fannie banging against the inside of the trunk and pleading for her release. They told Samuel that Fannie was going to die from the heat if he didn't let her out. One of the watermen went and found Samuel's brother, and he arrived to try to persuade his brother to open the trunk. When this did not produce the keys, two large watermen grabbed Samuel while another worked the keys from his hand.

Finally Samuel released the keys and Fannie was freed. Nearly dead from the heat, she hugged Samuel, and he felt sorrow for what he had done and he hugged her back. In front of everyone he told her that he would always come home to her first from here on out, and they went home together.

On Monday Samuel was back out on the Bay for a week-long stay. When he got home on Friday, he went straight to the Cozy Cove for a drink.

## A BUMP ON THE HEAD

When Ed Deagle was four years old in 1928, his father Lee was hired to install a four-cylinder Regal engine in *Iva W.*, a newly built Chesapeake Bay deck boat. Captain Johnny Ward had John Wright build the boat and hired Lee to install the engine. John Wright and Deagle lived and worked on Lovers Lane not a half mile from each other in Deltaville at that time. Captain Johnny also lived on Lovers Lane on Jackson Creek.

"My daddy installed the engine when he was at his little railway on Jackson Creek," says Ed. "Every time I see that boat I think about that time. *Iva W.* had a port light [porthole] on the left side. I was on her deck and had my head stuck through that port light watching my daddy install the engine. When he cranked the engine for the first time, she went off like a cannon and I banged my head good. It put a great big bump on the back of my head.

"Every time I see *Iva W.*, I look at that port light and wonder how I got my head through that little porthole.

## MUD IN THE SEAMS

Joe Conboy worked for Milford Price at Price's Boat Yard in Deltaville, Virginia, in the early 1960s. "I remember the day a new owner of an old log buyeye [that had been] converted to power radioed Mr. Price in desperation," says Joe. "He was on his way from Norfolk and was right off Stingray Point. He told Mr. Price to clear the railway because he was full steam ahead, all pumps running and he was sinking fast.

"When he got to the mouth of Broad Creek, the boat was so low in the water we could see water splashing over the waist. Hardly slowing down and with steam coming out of the engine room, he drove her right up to the railway and we all rushed to get her up on the rails.

"When she was up on the rails, two bottom chunk pieces broke and water gushed from the inside of the boat all over the ground," says Joe. "If he had been five minutes later, he would have never made it.

"I talked to the new owner and he said he paid $5,000 in cash for the old boat and said he should have known something was wrong because when he asked the owner if he wanted to count the money the owner said 'no' and left rather hurriedly.

"The new captain said the boat was 'dry as a bone' until he got her underway," says Joe. "What happened was the boat's seams were full of creek mud and she was dry as long as she was at the dock but when he got out on the Bay the Chesapeake Bay chop washed the mud out of the seams and she started sinking. He was damn lucky he made it to the railway.

"We wrapped that boat in a coffin from guard to guard and she left there without a leak," he said.

A "coffin" was the term used to describe a layer of 40-pound felt that was nailed to the hull and then covered with a layer of galvanized metal. The term was used long before motorized buyboats, and a coffin was installed on many of the old sailing vessels on the Chesapeake to keep them afloat a bit longer. A coffin was also added to a deck boat so it could break ice on the creek to get out to the fishing grounds. The boat in a coffin led the way through the ice and the others followed. Ice would cut up a wooden stem line.

## DISTRESS CALL FROM *FLORA KIRWAN*

William E. Wright, longtime foreman at Deagle and Son Marine Railway, recalls the night he got a distress call from a deck boat captain on *Flora Kirwan*. The boat was sinking in the middle of Delaware Bay and the captain phoned William for help.

*Flora Kirwan* was built in 1892 in Baltimore, Maryland, and was a two-masted schooner before she was converted to power at Deagle's in Deltaville. As a sailboat she had been used in the pineapple trade between the West Indies and Baltimore.

"I was sitting in this chair [at his farm home in Syringa, Virginia] one Saturday night at 9 P.M. when the phone rang. It was the United States Coast Guard, and they said that the captain of *Flora Kirwan* wanted to talk with me.

"He got on the phone and said, 'I'm in sinking condition and I've got four feet of water in the engine room. As I speak there are two helicopters lowering pumps down on deck to keep us afloat. What do you think the problem is?'

"I told him, 'Captain, if the water is confined to the engine room you need to get the water down in the engine room and check all the through-hull connections' [hoses that bring cooling water to the motor], and when they did that they found a 3-inch hose connection had burst and was allowing water in.

"I told him what to do and told him to call me in the morning if he needed the railway," says William. "I told him I had *Sarah Conway* on the rails but I could finish her enough to get her in the water in eight hours and I'd have it open for him when he got to Fishing Bay.

"I had called the men in on Sunday and we had *Sarah Conway* ready to go in the water but he called about 2 P.M. and said he had it all fixed. He thanked me several times. I felt pretty good that I had helped him out."

## YOUR PILE OF LUMBER IS OVER THERE

By the 1920s and 1930s, boatbuilding in Deltaville, Virginia, had taken off and there were numerous yards throughout the waterfront community. Master builder John Wright was in his heyday then building deck boats, deadrise commercial fishing boats, and skiffs. Over the years, he had many men working for him and several of them branched off into their own backyard boatbuilding businesses.

Billy Norton of Deltaville recalls this story about Captain John that he heard from his father. "Captain John Wright had taught nearly everybody in town how to build boats," says Billy. "Once they learned enough they went off on their own and built boats in their own backyards.

"Nobody worked on Sunday in those days and after church the builders and hands would congregate in Captain John's boatyard," he says. "John Wright was the master builder, but there was always somebody who thought they could do it better. Many of those Sunday afternoon sessions at the yard were discussions on ways of doing things better.

"One man who Captain John had taught to build boats started giving him boatbuilding advice on one of his boats there on the yard.

"Captain John said, 'You boys come on over here and we'll talk.'

"He walked over to a stack of lumber that was air drying. 'Now you boys can stay right here and talk about how to put that lumber together into a boat all you want, but don't stand next to my boat and tell me how I ought to build it.'"

*Good food is a part of life that always seems to be worth remembering—for some reason food always tastes better cooked and*

This Oriole cookstove was in the galley of *Iva W.,* a 60-foot deck boat.

*served out on the water. Many people are surprised to learn what came out of the galleys of Chesapeake Bay deck boats.*

## CODFISH AND FATBACK

In a 1985 interview at his home in Deltaville, Virginia, the late Captain Johnny Ward, then eighty-three years old, recalled his father's favorite dish that he himself prepared as a thirteen-year-old boy in the galley of the 60-foot bugeye *Louise Travers.* His father was Captain Henry Ward of Crisfield, Maryland.

It was on the bugeye that he first learned to cook and over the years during long days and nights on the water he did a lot of his own cooking on the buyboat *Lagonia,* a 50-foot log boat, and later on the 60-foot *Iva W.*

Scrambled eggs and fried sausage cakes awaited the crew of the deck boat *Seven Brothers* most mornings. Roland George was owner, captain, and cook of the 65-foot deck boat used in the Bay's menhaden snapper-rig fishery. Courtesy Roland George.

"When I first started with my daddy, I was chief cook because he liked my cooking," says Captain Johnny. "His favorite breakfast food was codfish. I'd skin the fish and soak it overnight, and cook it the next morning until it would fall off the bone. I'd pick the bones out and mix the meat with hot mashed potatoes and onions cut up real fine. Then, I'd fry up a piece of fatback and pour the grease from it over the fish, potatoes, and onions. Boy, you got a good feed when it's all done.

"When Daddy would finish eatin' the fish and potatoes, he'd always ask for the fatback [to eat]. He liked it brown after the grease was all out of it."

## TUCKER THE COOK

Thelma Simmons Sullivan was the daughter of Captain William E. Simmons, who owned and worked a deck boat named *Simmons* in Virginia's deepwater pound-net fishery at the turn of the century.

Some of her fondest memories are of the food. "I remember as a child the cook on *Simmons* was a black man named Tucker," she said during an interview in 2001 at Mayfair House, an assisted-living home in Kilmarnock. "When the boat was home, I used to go down and have supper any old time. Tucker fixed lots of navy beans and he would take blow toads, skin 'em and then fry 'em up good in corn meal. It tasted just like fried chicken. He knew I loved those blow toads and he would fix 'em when he knew I was coming down to the boat. He was the best cook in the world."

## THE BEST PART WAS THE FOOD

In the 1960s, Bay Rowe, fifty-three, of White Stone, Virginia, worked aboard *Simmons*. In an interview in 2001, he talked about the food aboard the boat. "The best part of working on *Simmons* was the food. I'd get up at 4:30 A.M. and walk down to the boat, and breakfast was already cooking on a wood cookstove. The galley was in the forepeak," says Rowe. "We had thick cuts of bacon, pancakes, fried eggs, and coffee brewed in one of those old-timey coffee pots.

"Lunch was like having a Sunday dinner every day of the week. There was usually some type of roast beef with mashed potatoes and gravy, or fried chicken with mashed potatoes and gravy, or baked chicken. It was a big lunch and that was part of the gig. I didn't get much pay but the food was great.

"The best part of the entire meals were the pies—apple, cherry, and pineapple—or made from whatever other canned fruit was available. I was just a boy but I looked forward to getting up and going to work to get something to eat," he says.

## THE COOK LOVED TO EAT

Edna Deagle Shackelford is the younger sister of Iva Deagle Ward, the wife of Captain Johnny Ward. Captain Johnny named his 1928 deck boat *Iva W.* in honor of his wife. Captain Johnny and his sons owned several classic buyboats over the years. Edna remembers this story of one of the cooks aboard the boats.

"Graydon Harrow was one of the cooks aboard the boats," recalls Edna, who was born in 1915. "Graydon would always cook because he loved to eat.

"I used to hear them say that when Graydon would make biscuits he would make two pans. One pan he would set underneath the stove so no one could see it and he'd let the crew have the other pan. When everybody was gone and not looking, Graydon would pull that pan out from under the stove and eat the whole pan of biscuits by himself. He loved to eat."

## FLOUR BREAD, MOLASSES, HOMEMADE LARD, AND FRESH FISH

Thomas E. "Tommy" Owens of New Point, Virginia, worked aboard all of his father's and grandfather's pound-net boats. Henry and Everett Owens of Mathews County owned the deck boats *Thomas E., Ellen Marie, L. R. Smith,* and *Lavenia H.*

"My grandfather was friends with a man in Richmond who owned a broom factory. He would come down once a year in the summer and bring a truckload of brooms. He would sell the brooms to stores around and he would come visit and eat on the boat with my grandfather.

"He'd say it was the best food he ever tasted in his life to go down in that galley in that boat and get homemade bread and fresh fish, beans, and stuff cooked right there. He'd say, 'There isn't a restaurant in Richmond or anywhere to have any better food.'

"We had fresh fish caught right out of the net and cooked right there," says Tommy. "I don't know why but fish right out of the water tastes better than anything.

"Granddaddy and Daddy raised and killed their own hogs and dried their own lard from the hog's fat for cooking. When they'd cook the fish in that lard, they were so fresh they would curl right up and melt in your mouth.

"A lot of people went fishing with Granddaddy and they'd say it was the best eating in the world. There was usually an older man who did the cooking. He might be too old to work the nets. Some of those old men would make what we called flour bread and it was unreal. Some people call it 'ho-cakes.' I've tried to make it myself here at home but I can't get it right. They used wheat flour and it was made into thick bread and we would take King Po-T-Rik black molasses—the kind with the big lion on the label—and we would sop it into that bread. Boy, that was something good. There is no taste in the world any better."

Going back to colonial times, bread sopped in black molasses was common fare aboard Chesapeake Bay workboats in tidewater Virginia and Maryland. Working in sail-driven log canoes, Bay watermen kept a can of molasses under the deck for the same type of eating as Tommy and his relatives did on the deck boats.

Years back, the neighborhood country store would have a barrel of molasses, and watermen would bring

A classic water barrel was located right beside the door to the galley on *Iva W.* in easy reach of the cook. The same type of barrel was used on Chesapeake Bay sailing craft.

their own cans into the store and have them filled on a regular basis.

## EATING ABOARD *MURIEL EILEEN* AND *ELSIE LOUISE*

Rufus Earl Mills was the manager of Morattico Packing Company in Urbanna, Virginia. When his son George got old enough for a summertime job, he worked aboard the buyboats *Muriel Eileen* and *Elsie Louise.* George recalls with great fondness those days and some of his best memories relate to the chow.

"*Muriel Eileen* was captained in the mid-1950s by Lee McNamara of Baltimore," says George. "He had two sons, Kenny and Elmo, and he always referred to his wife as 'the madam.' When I got old enough to work in the summertime, twelve to fifteen years old, I

Galley food on *Thomas E.* was as tasty as "Richmond restaurant food." Mealtime featured flour bread dipped in Po-T-Rik molasses and fresh fish right out of the nets, fried up in homemade lard. Courtesy Thomas E. Owens.

worked on the boats. That would have been in the early 1960s. The summertime purpose of *Muriel Eileen* was to bring empty cans down from Baltimore to Morattico Packing Company in Urbanna. It was a canning company that canned English peas in the spring, black-eyed peas in the late summer, and spinach and tomatoes in the fall.

"These empty cans were boxed and stacked up high on the deck and all down in the hold. When *Muriel Eileen* arrived in early summer loaded with cans from Baltimore, Captain McNamara would always blow the horn three times to announce his arrival. *Muriel Eileen* would go over to Lord Mott's dock to be unloaded. There were boxes of cans with twenty-four cans in a box. One of my summer jobs was to help unload. We would unload by a hand bucket-brigade type operation. Someone in the hold would throw boxes up to us on deck, and we would put them on a conveyor that would take it inside the warehouse. It was well over 100 degrees in the warehouse. We just about burned up.

"At noon the whistle would blow to announce the start of the lunch half-hour. It would blow again at 12:30 to end the break. Being the boss's sons, Bobby, Billy, and I got to eat lunch with our father in the galley of *Muriel Eileen*. The galley was on the lower deck and there was a small table, like a hatch table, that would fold up out of the way when not in use. It was small but large enough for us to sit on three stools and eat comfortably.

"Typically we had a nice steak accompanied by potatoes and sliced tomatoes with cucumbers served with lots of vinegar with salt and pepper and a little sugar added, and covered with ice cubes. Captain Lee always had a big pickle jar filled with pickles and we loved to pull big ones out of the jar. Even today I love pickles and I think I got addicted to them eating on *Muriel Eileen.*

"Occasionally, particularly in the cool weather, Captain Lee would make a big five-gallon pot of clam chowder with big pieces of clams, potatoes, celery, onions, and tomatoes. It had an unbelievable taste. I've eaten in restaurants all over the world and none have ever been able to duplicate Captain Lee's clam chowder.

"Anybody who has been aboard these boats has experienced the smell. It's a combination of salt air, probably lead-based paint, marine paint, and diesel fuel. It doesn't sound very appealing but it was and sometimes when I close my eyes I can capture the feeling and smells of being aboard that boat. At 12:30 we'd go back to work after quite a nice lunch.

"I also went out when they bought oysters in the winter from tongers, but more often than not I would be on the boat when they were planting seed oysters," says George. "Sometimes we'd get up real early in the morning and have breakfast and that was a treat. Fried eggs cooked to order, bacon as thick as I've ever had, sausage, toast, and a big glass of milk. I didn't drink coffee then but there was plenty of coffee for the men. We'd work up an appetite by shoveling the seed oysters over the sides. I'd do that on weekends in the fall and I remember Johnny Hodgers and some of those guys on the boat. They could work me to death. I thought I was in good shape from playing [high school] football, but no way could I keep up with them."

## The Captain

"Some of my earliest recollections of Captain Lee was when he would come to our house not in a working mode," says George. "Sometimes when he'd come to town he would stay aboard ship and sometimes he would stay at [Ada] Burton's boardinghouse on Watling Street in Urbanna. He'd rent a room there and he'd come over and eat dinner at our house. He was always dressed in a nice blue pinstripe suit, crisp white shirt, and tie. Captain Lee smoked Lucky Strike nonfilter [cigarettes] and he would often stop before coming over at the Green Front [grocery store] and have Pete [Robins] the butcher cut enough steaks for dinner. My father would grill it up. Mother was a great cook and she would make six or so side dishes—four or five vegetables, celery trays, desserts—and it was wonderful.

"After dinner in the summertime we'd go down on the dock in front of our house [on the Rappahannock River] and Captain Lee always had a pocket full of money, coins," says George. "There were three of us boys and he'd throw the money in the river and we'd dive down and try to find it in the sand. We would find a few but he really enjoyed that. We absolutely enjoyed it.

"After dinner, we'd take him back to the boat but he always wanted to stop at Marshall's Drug Store for what he called a 'blowout.' A blowout consisted of an ice cream cone or a chocolate milk shake and he would always buy us a toy. He was a wonderful man."

Lee McNamara, captain of *Muriel Eileen,* made a mighty fine clam chowder. Courtesy George Mills.

The galley in *Muriel Eileen* was located in the lower house. Courtesy George Mills.

## *Elsie Louise*

"*Elsie Louise* did not have near as extensive a galley as *Muriel Eileen,* says George. "She wasn't a double-decker so there was only the wheelhouse and a little cookstove and a small area for eating behind the wheelhouse, but I do remember eating aboard her going to plant seed oysters.

"Charlie Sayre who lived in Urbanna was the first mate and cook on *Elsie Louise* and on *Muriel Eileen* at times too," says George.

"Charlie would take an egg and put it in a frying pan and swirl it around with a fork. When he finished it was somewhere between fried and scrambled and was very good. He also fried big, big thick slices of bacon, and it was on *Elsie Louise* that I had my first cup of coffee.

"I later bought a little boat that I still have and I named it *Elsie Louise* in honor of that wonderful boat and all those memories."

*In 1993, I wrote a story for* National Fisherman *entitled "Chesapeake Buyboats Go 'Uptown.'" I was aware then that several of the Bay's deck boats were being converted to pleasure boats and when this project came along I knew a chapter on "life after work" would be essential to the story of Chesapeake Bay buyboats.*

# 19: LIFE AFTER WORK

Today, motor-powered buyboats are at the same stage of life as the Bay's sailing schooners were in the 1930s and 1940s. Some schooners at the end of their working careers were converted to pleasure craft. Improved transportation, the decline of the Maryland and Virginia oyster and finfish fisheries, changes in harvesting methods in Virginia's crab-dredge fishery, and other factors have combined to put most of the Chesapeake deck boats out of work.

For some fortunate few, there is life after work, as boats have been converted for recreational and educational use. Projects range from simple, relatively inexpensive changes to high-dollar renovations that easily hit six figures.

## KATHLEEN II

A good example of a top-dollar conversion is *Kathleen II,* a 56-foot deck boat. She was one of the last of the backyard-built buyboats to come out of Deltaville, Virginia. Boatbuilders George Clark, his father-in-law Ernest Bryant, and Alvin Sibley completed her in 1961 and she was used until 1983 in the Virginia crab-dredge fishery. She was called *Midland* before becoming *Kathleen II,* and Clark worked the boat himself in the winter crab-dredge fishery.

She was converted to a pleasure boat in the mid-1980s by builder Bill Jeter of Gywnn's Island, Virginia. Naval architect Alan F. Bowles and Jeter came up with the design to transform the commercial dredge boat into an elegant pleasure boat.

"We gutted her completely," says Jeter. "We took a chain saw and took everything out. When we finished gutting her she looked like a giant skiff. Then we put her back together.

"We put on a new trunk cabin and had to pull the pilothouse off and build another one, because there was not enough room to put the captain's quarters aft of the pilothouse," says Jeter. "It was a thrill to work on that boat.

"The owner wanted to use the boat for charter," he says. "The original plan was to take it to Washington, D.C., and charter it out for private meetings and parties."

The boat is elegantly laid out with skylights where the cargo hatches were once located. The saloon is 18 feet by 14 feet; it seats eight for formal dinners and has a settee that pulls out to sleep two. The vessel will sleep eight.

A forward stateroom sleeps two, and there is a large hanging locker, nine storage compartments, and a vanity. The forward head has a full-sized shower, lavatory, and vanity.

*Kathleen II,* built by Ernest H. Bryant of Deltaville, Virginia, in 1961 as *Midland,* found new life in the 1980s as a well-polished pleasure boat. Boatbuilder Bill Jeter gutted *Kathleen II* and built a stem-to-stern trunk cabin to provide plenty of living quarters below. Note the pilothouse is built atop the trunk cabin. Many conversions leave the cabin/pilothouse configuration alone and install a trunk cabin in the hold for living quarters. Jeter and naval architect Alan F. Bowles came up with the design to transform the commercial dredge boat into an elegant pleasure boat.

The after stateroom has a double bed, dressing table, and two hanging lockers. Nearby is a head with a full-size shower, lavatory, and large vanity; it is fitted with Victorian fixtures. The pilothouse head and laundry is equipped with a pedestal sink, washer, and dryer. A third shower is located on the after deck.

## MILDRED BELLE

*Mildred Belle* was built in 1948 in Odd, Virginia, by boatbuilder Odell Carmines. She was built for Captain Garland Evans who named the boat after his two daughters, Mildred Lee and Hattie Belle Evans.

Carmines used yellow pine, known in that area as Bull Island mahogany, for her framing and planking. (Bull Island is a name used by many for the area around Poquoson, Virginia. Perhaps this is where the wood was cut.) He handpicked the wood in 1947, cut it, and dragged it by mule team to a salt marsh to season properly. One year later, the logs were hauled out of the marsh to dry out and then sawed into planks.

Evans worked *Mildred Belle* in the oyster and crab-dredge fisheries and the offshore trawl fishery. In later years he used the vessel as a charter boat for offshore hook-and-line recreational fishing.

Tom Howell is one of the most experienced craftsmen on the Bay when it comes to converting buyboats into pleasure boats. He converted the buyboat *Mildred Belle* into an excursion boat to carry cruises down the Wye River on Maryland's Eastern Shore. (In the 1980s, Howell built one of the last buyboats built on the Bay, *Mister Jim*.)

As part of *Mildred Belle's* conversion, the trunk cabin was raised 2 feet above the deck to give more than 6 foot of headroom. Several structural bulkheads had to be moved to create space belowdeck.

Howell and his partner spent $40,000 on *Mildred Belle's* conversion, excluding labor. "We worked hard to keep the hull looking original," says Howell. They had it Coast Guard–approved for forty-seven passengers. Since 1988, the Living Classroom Foundation, a Baltimore education group, has owned the vessel and has used *Mildred Belle* as a classroom to teach students through a hands-on experience.

Even though a few buyboats are being converted to pleasure boats for fun, charter, and educational uses, Howell says most of the boats have not been so fortunate. "The upkeep, maintenance, and insurance just eats you up," he says.

"The expense of maintaining these boats makes them unattractive to many pleasure boat owners," says Quentin Snediker, formerly with the Chesapeake Bay Maritime Museum. "Also, you've got to have an appreciation of the old workboats. Most people, when they want to buy a pleasure boat, they want a boat that looks like a yacht."

According to Snediker, "For someone to convert these boats, the person has to have a great deal of love for old boats and more money than they know what to do with."

## MUNDY POINT

David and Sheila Carr of Reedville, Virginia, prove that Snediker is at least half right. The couple have a great deal of love for old wooden boats, but for them it took more hard work and elbow grease than money to transform *Mundy Point* into a comfortable pleasure craft.

The couple bought *Mundy Point* in 1992 from waterman Elwood Turner of Harryhogan, Virginia, and they worked meticulously to make her into a wonderful home on the water. David was not a boatwright in the sense that he had a great deal of woodworking

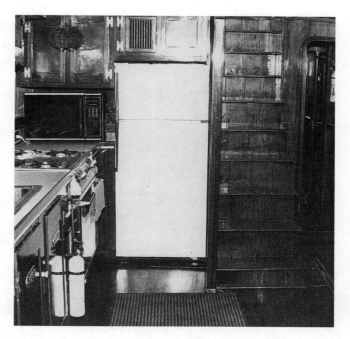

Below, a fully equipped galley provides meals for up to eight at formal dinners in the 18-foot by 14-foot saloon of *Kathleen II*.

experience, but he grew up working in a family construction business in Nags Head, North Carolina, and obviously has developed a sense for boat construction.

For a number of years, the couple moored the boat in the tributaries of the Yeocomico River, including Kinsale, Virginia, but they moved to Fairport on Cockrell Creek between the Great Wicomico and Potomac Rivers. The main reason for the move was to be at Jennings Boat Yard, where they moor *Mundy Point* today. The yard has a traditional railway with a long history of working on wooden boats.

David and Sheila owned a 1937 Alden yawl, a 48-foot wooden sailboat, before buying *Mundy Point*. "We wanted more comfort, more room, and for the wind to not be blowing in my face," says David.

"He also needed a new project," says Sheila. "He had gotten the Alden to the point he couldn't make it any more beautiful so he needed something new. He gets like that."

The couple looked for five years before deciding on *Mundy Point*. "I liked Chesapeake Bay deck boats," says David. "I liked the shape of them and the size capacity. They are from the Chesapeake and you don't see them anywhere else. Maine sardine carriers are close but the bow is different and they are from up north and probably wouldn't last down here."

201

Owners David and Sheila Carr recently converted *Mundy Point,* built in 1928 by Gilbert White, Sr., of Lancaster County, Virginia, into their home on the water. Courtesy David and Sheila Carr.

David and Sheila looked at several decks boats before buying *Mundy Point.* "We looked at *L. R. Smith* but I didn't like the shape of her and she wasn't in as bad shape as she is now." (In 2003, *L. R. Smith* is moored right next to *Mundy Point* at Jennings Boat Yard.) "We also looked at *Yeocomico.* She was an old trawler. We looked at *O. A. Bloxom.* She was an old lumber schooner and still had the mast steps in her, but she was too big. She was a monster. We saw her down in the Bahamas several years ago running cargo."

"When we found *Mundy Point,* she was just what we were looking for. She was structurally sound and the right size for us to live on," says Sheila.

## A Little History

*Mundy Point* was originally called *Lawson,* named for the Lawson family of Whitestone, Virginia, who had asked boatbuilder Gilbert White to build the vessel in 1928. "They used her to fish deepwater pound nets in

Sheila and David Carr are standing on the bow of *Mundy Point* on Cockrell Creek at Fairport, Virginia.

the lower portion of the Bay for herring," he says. "They worked nets on 90-foot poles and in 60 feet of water."

The boat was renamed when Reedville Oil and Guano Company purchased her. The company owned a herring and herring roe canning business at Mundy Point on the Yeocomico River, a Potomac tributary.

The saloon on *Mundy Point* is spacious and comfortable. "Right where we are sitting, they would load 100,000 herring in the hold," says Sheila. "Cleave Hinson, who often stopped by to chat while we were hauled out on Jennings' railway, recalls being down in the hold when he was fifteen years old shoveling herring into a bucket and using the gaff to haul the fish up on deck.

"He also worked aboard her when Captain Shelton worked her. The story goes Cleave got tossed overboard in a storm, and his slicker got hooked in the fluke of the anchor that was out of the water but over the side of the boat.

"Captain Shelton had hands like [baseball] mitts. He reached down, grabbed him up and hauled him right back on the boat. All he said after that was, 'Get to work, Boy.' "

## The Builder

"Gilbert White, Sr., built this boat mostly with hand tools," says Sheila. "You can see the adz marks all through the keel."

"We've been told that he had gas engines to run his saws and things like that, but he did a lot by hand," says David.

"There is a story that Gilbert White, Sr., was originally from Mathews County and owed taxes on some land over there so he rowed a skiff from Lancaster County to Gywnn's Island, walked five miles inland to pay his taxes, walked back, and rowed home," says Sheila. "Back then, it was shorter to go across the water than overland.

"Gilbert White's daughter, Ella Joe, told me that she, her mom, and her father would go by steamboat to Baltimore and he would shop for lumber. Then he would have it barged down to his yard," says Sheila.

"His son Gilbert White, Jr., had told us that he would go out into the woods with his father and they would pick out white oak [trees for] hanging

The dining room table on *Mundy Point* pulls out from the starboard wall to accommodate four people. The wood in the table is made from thick coaming that was cut out to make the trunk cabin.

knees. Mr. White, Sr., used these pieces of natural white oak for structural support on *Mundy Point*," says Sheila.

"He built good boats and the fact they are still around is a testimony to that," says David. "There are three right here on the creek that he built. *Mundy Point*, *Elva C.*, and *Dudley* are all right here. *Elva C.* was built before this boat [1922] and *Dudley* about ten years after [1938]." *Elva C.* is owned by the Reedville Fishermen's Museum in Reedville, and Fred Biddlecomb of Reedville owns *Dudley*. Mr. Biddlecomb worked *Dudley* in the pound-net fishery for years but several years ago converted her to a charter vessel.

"They all look a little different," says David.

The saloon is neatly arranged and is built into the hold, which at one time would carry 100,000 herring on a good fishing day. Note the official hull number of *Mundy Point,* 228217, chiseled into the forward beam.

## David and Sheila Did All the Work

"In 1979, I bought the Alden and I was living in Nags Head. The closest yard then was Elizabeth City Shipyard and they did all the work on it. But I started working on other people's boats and got so I understood boat construction," says David.

"People would come down and ask us, 'Who did all the work on *Mundy Point?*' " Sheila said.

"David would say, 'I did it.'

" 'Yeah, but who did all the trim?'

" 'I did it.'

"Then they asked, 'Who did all the [close] work?'

"And then after a while David would say, 'The yard did it.' "

David and Sheila have done the work on the boat with the help of Larry Jennings from Jennings Boat Yard and Roy Headley, owner of Fairport Marina and Restaurant right next door to the boatyard.

"A boat is an ongoing project. When we first got the boat, we sat in the hold on five-gallon buckets turned upside down and decided together what was going where," says Sheila.

"We would say the woodstove would go over here. A stained glass window would go over there, but it mostly just evolved over time. David had an overall vi-sion of it and never drew a thing down. He dreamed and envisioned it and I can't do that. It drives me crazy.

"We put the plastic tent to cover it in November of 1992 and had the work done so we could take it off by March 1993. We were living on board her by July 4, 1993, and it has been ongoing. The interior is still not finished," says Sheila.

"The first thing I actually redid was the wheel in the pilothouse," says David. "The boat was still at Elwood's dock at Harryhogan. I called it a dock but he called it a wharf. I told him I was going to take the wheel off and he said what would we do if a storm came up?

"I asked him what he meant?

"If a storm comes up we'll have to take her out and tie her off to trees on shore and put down bow and stern anchors in a protected cove. Then you stay up all night, bailing out the dinghy and hoping the storm takes another path far away from where you are. We've been fortunate so far." [It is common practice for Chesapeake Bay watermen to move boats out away from shore, usually in a protected area of a river or cove, when a bad storm comes through. The middle of a protected harbor might be safer than near shore; if the boat were to break loose, there are fewer docks and obstructions to damage her and there is also no dock for her to beat against during the storm.]

"I said if a storm comes up I'd bring the wheel back. Well, I finished the wheel in about a week and no storm came up.

"When I brought the wheel back he said, 'You went out and bought a new wheel, didn't ya?'

"No, I just repinned and refinished her," says David.

"Elwood said, 'Pshaw! That wheel looks better than the first day it was put in her.'"

Since they started, the couple has replaced forty-three planks on the bottom with juniper. In 2001, they replaced a portion of the rail and decking on the port side. "*Mundy Point* was worked harder on her port side, so it needed more repair than the starboard side," Sheila says.

"The repair really tightened up the wood in the boat," she says. "She still leaks though but David says that anybody who has a wooden boat and says it doesn't leak is a liar. He is right because wood seams open and close up with the weather."

Thirty years of paint over paint over paint had to be stripped off the hull and decks with a propane torch and scrapers. "The whole boat has been stripped three times," says David. "The entire inside of the pilothouse was covered with [shipyard] green paint." The two original 7-foot-long wainscoted bunks are still in the back room of the pilothouse and still painted green.

The setting of the traditional Bay railway at Jennings Boat Yard has been ideal for David and Sheila. "We like the atmosphere of working yards. There is just something about the character of old places," says Sheila.

"They have a nice ship saw too," says David. "When you are doing construction on an old wooden boat you don't want to be in a fancy marina. When a guy has a $300,000 yacht sitting next to you, he doesn't want to hear it and I don't blame him. He doesn't want sawdust all over his boat."

## Galley and Living Quarters

Inside the living quarters of the boat, David built in some of his own special touches. The main table in the boat slides out from the starboard wall. When they have a number of people for dinner, the table is pulled out. The wood in the table is made from the

There is a place for everything aboard *Mundy Point*. David and Sheila made room for their greater Patagonian conure who talks loudly and a lot.

wide, thick hold coaming that was cut out to install the trunk cabin. The paint was burned off and refinished to the point the wood sparkles.

The galley is very comfortable. "David does all the cooking but we knew we wanted it so two people could comfortably stand in there," says Sheila. There is a 12-gallon hot-water heater and a refrigerator is installed under the kitchen counter, accessed from a lid cut into the counter. Galley cabinet doors are slatted so air can move and reach the interior walls of the boat. "A boat needs air to breath or she will rot," says Sheila. The cabinet under the sink in the head matches the cabinets in the kitchen. The boat is finished with a lot of brightwork and has all the modern conveniences of home.

The main living area is neatly arranged in the old fish hold. Two large, comfortable leather chairs are

A double bed is in the forward compartment. David and Sheila have utilized overhead space for bookshelves.

the main furnishings of the room. Everything has a place and is neatly arranged. The television is tucked away between the outer and inner walls of the boat and a sound system is arranged with speakers behind the walls and throughout the living area. Fred, a greater Patagonian conure, has his own cage in a corner with bookshelves, drawers, and a music compartment for tapes and compact disks.

Headroom is fine for those under 6 feet. David says he built it to his own height, which is 5 feet 10 inches. "We have a friend who is 6 feet 4 inches and he says when he comes here, 'I don't see how you can live here.' He always goes to the lowest point in the cabin when he says it. It works out fine for Sheila and me."

David and Sheila used a portion of the hold and forepeak for their stateroom. The large bunk takes up most of the room but shelves and ledges run along the sides for storage and a large chest of drawers for storage of clothes is built into the aft wall.

David says, "There is nothing extraordinary about the joinery work down here. It's not yacht finished but it's not meant to be that way."

## Memorabilia and Stories

David and Sheila have collected old photos and memorabilia that are part of the boat's history. Pictures on the walls include one of Gilbert White and his wife standing at his yard near Foxwells, Virginia, and photos of the day David and Sheila won first place in the Kinsale Boat Parade.

They also have ration documents from the World War II era, dated February 8, 1944, when the boat was owned by Lawson and Lawson of White Stone, Virginia, and named *Lawson*. The crew was allowed only a certain amount of sugar, coffee, cheese, butter, canned milk, fruit, and other provisions. The document came from the Office of Temporary Controls, Office of Price Administration, in Richmond, Virginia, and was given to David and Sheila by the great-grandson of one of the Lawsons who initially owned the boat.

Former owner Elwood Turner also shared stories of *Mundy Point*. He owned her for thirty-seven years. Turner told them the story of how his father died eating lunch aboard the boat. "They were in a Maryland port buying oysters. Elwood's father was sitting on the front edge of the fish hold eating a raw oyster sandwich on white bread for lunch," says David. "That's what he had every day for lunch. He would go out and pick a couple big oysters from on deck, open them, and put them on white bread. At first, they thought he was asleep but he had died. Elwood came over in a smaller boat to bring him home but the State of Maryland would not let him carry him by boat so he had to hire a funeral home to carry him to Virginia.

"Elwood said, 'It took me a lot longer to bring Daddy home when I could have brought him right on across in the boat.'

"When we bought the boat and I told Elwood I was going to do the work myself, he asked if we had done anything like this before, and when I said no, he said, 'Oh pshaw! You best get somebody who knows what they are doing!' " David says.

"We heard later he was real proud of the job we had done and that means a lot to us," says Sheila.

*Driving up Route 13 on the Eastern Shore of Virginia near Exmore, I have often noticed along the side of the road a wreck of a deck boat named* Cleo. *She may have been a draketail, but time and weather have pulled her apart so that it cannot be clearly determined.*

*At times I thought it a shame she ended up high and dry next to a highway. However, even in a state of deterioration, many who pass by admire her, and she makes a great advertisement for the Trawler Restaurant next door. Many of the old boats were not so fortunate.*

# 20: WHERE THE BOATS WENT

As the seafood industry began to decline in the Chesapeake and trucks took over the freighting business, many deck boats were sold off the Bay.

Many of the larger boats went north and were used in the mid-Atlantic clam fishery or in the Delaware Bay oyster business. Others went south to North and South Carolina or Georgia to haul freight and supplies offshore to developing islands; still others went farther south to run freight between Florida and the West Indies. Some are being worked today in those regions.

Most made honest livings for their owners but as in the days of Prohibition, when Chesapeake Bay buyboats were used as rum and bootleg whiskey runners, the boats have also been used to haul illegal drugs.

The history of the boats has not yet ended as there are still a few deck boats throughout the Bay area, but their days as commercial vessels may soon come to an end. Already, museums put the boats on display to show a bygone era of the Bay's maritime history.

Those boats that are left in the private sector are struggling for survival, as deck boats can hardly generate enough income to offset the high cost of upkeep and maintenance. Also, there is a decline in boatyards that cater to wooden boats, as fiberglass, steel, and aluminum have become the materials of choice for so many boatowners. The small neighborhood boatyard where just about anything could be fixed for local watermen is all but gone.

Many of the boats have foundered at the very docks where they once off-loaded thousands of bushels of oysters, barrels of crabs, and baskets of fish. Others have been left to die at the headwaters of isolated guts, coves, and marshes.

Their fate is the same as that of all the wooden hulled vessels that evolved throughout the Bay region and outlived their usefulness. The log canoe, coasting canoe, pungies, brogans, skipjacks, schooners, rams, bateaux, sloops, and bugeyes have all faced or are facing the same fate. And now, the Chesapeake Bay buyboat joins the list.

Here are a few accounts of where the boats went.

## DRUG-RUNNING *THOMAS E.*

For many years, the deck boat *Thomas E.* was owned by Everett Owens of New Point, Virginia, in Mathews County. She was built by boatbuilder Alton Smith, who ran his boatyard on Horn Harbor just up the creek from Owens's home. Everett and his father Henry and son Tommy were pound-net fishermen and during the peak of the family's career, they owned four deck boats—*Thomas E., L. R. Smith, Lavena H.,* and *Ellen Marie.*

Many Bay buyboats ended up like *Cleo* but not in such a public way. The vessel is in total disrepair and is located right on Route 13 near Exmore, Virginia, next to the Trawler Restaurant. Many of the boats died at the headwaters of creeks and coves far away from the public eye.

*Thomas E.* was built by Smith for the Owens family and was named after Thomas E. "Tommy" Owens, Everett's son. Today Tommy lives at New Point on Horn Harbor just up the way from where *Thomas E.* was built. He remembers the boats and the times. On February 4, 2003, we talked about those times at his home at New Point.

"I worked with Daddy for a lot of years when I was young," says Tommy. "When my grandfather Henry Owens and my uncle died, my daddy told me I needed to find another way of making a living. 'We are going to try and get out of this because all the older heads who work the nets are dying and no young people want to work in it,' he said to me.

"The pound-net fishery is labor-intensive and requires a number of fishermen to work and install nets.

"The last year we fished was 1978 and in 1979 I went to Louisiana on a [menhaden] fish steamer. In May of 1979, Daddy sold *Thomas E.* to a Gloucester County man.

"It was about a year later, the United States Coast Guard called Daddy in the middle of the night, trying to locate the man he sold the boat to," says Tommy. "They said they had tried to find him but couldn't. They also told him that *Thomas E.* had been confiscated in Miami, Florida, with a boatload of marijuana.

"When the men who bought *Thomas E.* from Daddy came by for a sea trial I was home and took them out on the boat to show her off," he says. "They were young men about my age then, but they didn't purchase her right out. The next day, I went back to Louisiana and a couple weeks later they came back and told my Daddy they wanted the boat.

"So Daddy and the men agreed to meet up at Mathews Courthouse to make the final deal and do the final paperwork. Daddy said they came with a big black suitcase and they opened it up and it was loaded with cash money.

"The price was $50,000 for *Thomas E.* so they knocked a little bit [of money] off one corner of the suitcase and counted out $50,000," he says.

"The next thing we knew about her the phone was ringing in the middle of the night for Daddy," says Tommy. "First it was the Coast Guard and then the *Daily Press* called." The *Daily Press* is the Newport News daily newspaper that covers the Middle Peninsula, of which Mathews County is a part.

The headline in the October 10, 1980, *Daily Press* read, "Coast Guard Fires On And Seizes Area Boat."

The article read:

The Coast Guard cutter *Point Francis* opened fire with a .50-caliber machine gun Thursday to disable a buyboat registered in Gloucester Point, Virginia, believed smuggling drugs off Miami.

The gunfire was not returned and there were no injuries. The cutter was towing the vessel to Miami and was expected to arrive at 3 A.M.

It was the first time a U. S. Coast Guard vessel has fired directly at another ship in peacetime in recent years, authorities said. During the Prohibition era, cutters sometimes exchanged gunfire with rumrunners along the Atlantic Coast.

The vessel had about 12½ tons of marijuana on board, a Seventh District Coast Guard spokesman said.

A Drug Enforcement Administration agent in Miami said the vessel is registered to a Gloucester Point [Va.] man and was purchased from local waterman Everett Owens of New Point. He sold the boat, named *Thomas E.*, about May 1, 1979.

He said he was told the boat was going to be used for bass fishing off the Georgia coast.

Three people aboard *Thomas E.* were arrested after the vessel halted with smoke billow-

*Thomas E.* was built by Alton Smith for the Owens family in 1948. She was used in the Bay's pound-net fishery until sold in 1979 to a buyer who used her for running illegal drugs in Florida waters. In 1980, with $13 million worth of marijuana aboard, she was captured, but not without a fight. The United States Coast Guard shot fifty-five rounds of ammunition into the stern and bow of *Thomas E.* to get the crew of the vessel to stop. She survived the attack and is reportedly still alive in New Jersey waters. Courtesy Thomas E. Owens.

ing from its stern. All of the men claimed to be Cuban nationals, but were said to have Florida driver's licenses with Miami addresses, the Coast Guard said.

The burst of 55 rounds from the machine gun was meant only to disable the vessel, Coast Guard officials said.

"It's the first time anybody around here can remember a ship being fired on," Chief Paul Scotti said. "Warning shots have been fired before when suspected drug boats tried to elude the Coast Guard, but it's never been necessary to fire at the boats before," he said.

Scotti said the crew of *Point Francis* hailed the boat for a routine boarding near the Dog Rocks area early Thursday.

*Thomas E.* cut its lights and sped toward Bahamian waters, Scotti said, and continued even after the cutter fired a series of warning shots.

"The ship continued to evade despite the warning shots and the decision was made to use disabling machine-gun fire," Scotti said.

The first rounds were fired into the ship's bow and when *Thomas E.* continued, the cutter began firing into the stern.

The ship came to a halt as smoke began pouring out, Scotti said. It wasn't immediately known how much damage the boat suffered. The crewmembers didn't resist arrest after a boarding party discovered bales of marijuana aboard.

Owens says it was reported that the street value of the marijuana was $13 million. "I talked to some guys who had seen her and they said they took the mast out of her and put what we called wings on her. From the edge of the pilothouse the decks were tapered all the way back to the stern. They say that thing would fly. There was a V-12 Detroit Diesel in her and she would fly and she had power too."

*Thomas E.* survived its role as a drug runner and it has been reported that she is still alive in New Jersey waters.

## LAST RUN OF BIG *MURIEL EILEEN*

The life history of the double-deck buyboat *Muriel Eileen* is well documented in the chapter on double-deck buyboats. The tragic events of her last day

This photo of big *Muriel Eileen* and the converted-to-power bugeye *John Branford* was taken when the vessels were moored on Urbanna Creek in the 1950s. Both these vessels left the Chesapeake Bay to work in the mid-Atlantic sea clam fishery. Big *Muriel Eileen* sank in 1969 off Chincoteague, Virginia, in the Atlantic Ocean, while *John Branford,* at 103 years old, still works out of Cape May, New Jersey. Courtesy Carroll Chowning.

tell a story how several of the boats ended their days after a long life of working the Chesapeake Bay.

By 1967, the oyster industry was beginning to decline and the big *Muriel Eileen* was getting old. So, Lord Mott Company sold her for $20,000 to two men who converted her to a surf clam trawler for the mid-Atlantic sea clam fishery. Her home port was Cape May, New Jersey.

On October 21, 1969, she was 20 miles offshore from Chincoteague, Virginia, in the Atlantic Ocean when she sank in 61 feet of water at latitude 37°48'N and longitude 75°14.8'W.

An Associated Press report that ran in a newspaper the following day tells the story. The headline read, "Four Crewmen Are Rescued From Boat".

The 85-foot trawler *Muriel Eileen,* taking water under pounding by heavy seas, sank 20 miles off Chincoteague yesterday shortly after her four-man crew was taken aboard a Coast Guard patrol vessel.

"I thought the Lord had me; it was rough as bricks out there," said Robert L. McVey, forty-one, of Cape May, New Jersey, part owner of the trawler. The vessel was loaded with 40,000 pounds of sea clams.

Rescued with McVey were three other New Jersey men—James Norton, forty-three, of Bivalve; Robert Fishler, thirty-one, of Morristown; and Jack Wobensmith of Millville.

"The trawler was heading for Chincoteague to unload the clams when she began to sink Monday night," McVey said.

"We had water waist-deep in the hold of the boat," he said. "It was an awful feeling."

McVey said a minor problem was caused by a fire. It resulted from a short circuit caused by seawater in the wiring.

A Coast Guard airplane that responded to the trawler's distress call dropped a portable pump at 12:40 A.M. The trawler men could not reach the pump, so a Coast Guard helicopter swooped down, recovered the pump from the ocean and placed it on the trawler's deck.

"That 'copter did a helluva job," McVey said. "It picked the pump out of the water and brought it to us. It was remarkable in that strong wind."

A 44-foot patrol vessel, sent by the Coast Guard, arrived at the scene at 2:40 A.M. The trawler's pumps began to fail at 4 A.M. and her crew prepared to abandon her. At 4:40 A.M., the

Little *Muriel Eileen* is more fortunate than big *Muriel Eileen.* The vessel is alive and has been well kept by her present owner, David M. Cantera of New Castle, Delaware. This photo was taken in the late 1980s when the vessel's home port was on the Piankatank River and she was owned by John C. and Ellen Willis of Hartfield, Virginia. The Willises used *Muriel Eileen* for charter. Courtesy Robert Ramsay.

four trawler men were safe aboard the Coast Guard vessel.

*Muriel Eileen* went down at 6:30 A.M. McVey estimated she was worth $70,800 and would cost $120,800 to replace.

Interestingly her sister vessel, the little *Muriel Eileen,* is still alive and in great condition. David M. Cantera of New Castle, Delaware, owns her. Cantera has refurbished the boat to her original beauty. He uses the boat for pleasure.

## LEAVING THE BAY

During the late 1960s and 1970s, the boats began to leave the Bay in relatively large numbers. The vessels' sturdy construction and large, stable hull configuration were part of the reason so many of these vessels were sold out of the Bay region. Many of the boats found new life in strange waters.

About 1968, the late Guy Ireland of Great Bridge, Virginia, began to buy Bay deck boats, fix them up, and sell them to southern buyers. His son Jimmy owns Ireland Barge Incorporated, the firm Guy started in 1974. Prior to 1974, Guy went around the Bay, found the boats, negotiated price, made the purchase, and

then moored the vessels at Ballard Fish and Oyster Company docks in Norfolk, Virginia. There Guy and his family fixed the boats up on weekends and holidays for resale. This continued for a while after Guy purchased waterfront property in Great Bridge, says his son Jimmy during an interview at the firm's yard on March 25, 2003.

"My father was in the car business most of his life but he grew up in North Carolina and his father and uncles were all commercial watermen," says Jimmy. "He loved the water and boats but he couldn't make a living on the water so after he got out of the Coast Guard he sold cars.

"Before he got into buying buyboats he would buy a pleasure boat, clean it up, paint it, and sell it," he says. "My father would get several newspapers throughout the Bay area that he would use to find boats. He got weekly papers from Exmore and Kilmarnock. He just kept buying and selling boats and the boats got bigger and bigger.

"When he saw a buyboat or a box-stern boat he would contact the people that owned it and try to buy it. What hurt us was that people began to realize the value of them. The owners started asking more for them. You can't buy a boat for $25,000 and sell it for $30,000. You've got to buy it for $10,000 or $15,000,

*Eva W.*, built in 1935 at Dare, Virginia, is being used in 2003 as a commercial fishing boat out of Miami, Florida. When this photo was taken in Hampton, Virginia, in the 1960s, the vessel was in the Atlantic Ocean finfish trawl fishery. Note the smaller mast just aft of the pilothouse, which was a standard rig for buyboats used as ocean trawlers. Courtesy Thomas E. Owens.

put $5,000 in it and maybe sell it for $30,000. You might make $10,000 but you've had it for six months and put a lot of labor in it so you didn't exactly make $10,000.

"Like John Ward's boat [*Ward Bros.*]. He put that thing in *Boats and Harbors* for $65,000. You can't buy it and resell because it's so high to start with.

"A lot of our boats went down to Florida during that time when [President Jimmy] Carter opened the gates and allowed Cubans to come into the country. We had several Cubans come up here looking for boats. Some were really nice people and we sold two or three of the boats to them. They were trying to get their parents out of Cuba and I don't know whether they were able to get them out or not.

"Every one we sold went south. We never resold a boat here on the Bay or to New York or Philadelphia. All of our boats went below North Carolina. I guess my father bought and sold fifteen or twenty Chesapeake Bay buyboats.

"I found it's true of all boats that are built for a particular type of water in a general area, they don't do well in other types of water," says Jimmy. "The bateaux of Louisiana don't do well on Chesapeake Bay and similarly these Bay boats don't do well in the ocean with real long swells. They are ideal for the

short, choppy waves of the Bay. These boats evolved over time out of specific needs of Chesapeake Bay watermen. They figured it out over time what would work best for this region and it is not something that boatbuilders in the [Florida] Keys would have built.

"My father bought a lot of boats. He bought *Oysterman* from Captain Jimmy Belvin from Bena, Virginia. She was a big boat, over 90 feet. Years ago people would kid my father because he had all these old boats and they would call it the electric navy because there were so many bilge pumps running.

"I went with my father to look at a lot of boats. We always carried a gas pump and five or ten gallons of gas. We bought them from all over the Bay. We went to Onancock to get *Regenia*. She was a fast boat. She had a big 6-71 Detroit and she would get up and plane. We went and looked at *Chesapeake*. Lord, she was a big one. She had already been laid up for a few years. She had big Georgia heart-pine timbers. It was just like walking through a big schooner and it had these big hand carved knees, where the deck meets the sides. We had the old *Harry W. Adams* here. She was an old Nova Scotia schooner. She was a bluenose schooner, 137 feet long. It was in the early 1970s. Somebody hauled her out at Norfolk Shipyard and couldn't pay the bill so we bought her. The reason

*Winnie Estelle,* built in 1920 in Crisfield, Maryland, is one of the lucky Chesapeake Bay buyboats. She was sold out of the Chesapeake Bay region in the 1960s and ended up nearly dead in the late 1980s on a shoal off Belize in the Caribbean. She was salvaged by Robert Smith, and it took several years to restore her. She is being used as a tour, dive, and charter boat out of San Pedro, Belize, in 2003. Courtesy Kim Granberry.

I'm making that parallel is because about the same time we had several of the big frame-built buyboats like *Nateague* and *Oysterman.* I found that the blue-nose schooner and the big Bay boats were built a lot alike.

"*Nateague* was a big boat," says Jimmy. "My father bought big and small ones. He bought *Lucy R. Ruark* and she was a small, narrow boat. She must have been no more than 10 feet wide." *Lucy R. Ruark* was built in 1913 in Fishing Creek, Maryland.

"We bought *Inez* and she leaked bad in the stern. We got several people to look at her and no one could stop her from leaking. So we talked to a previous owner and he said the only person that could fix her is the man who built her and he was dead. We sold her though and she went to Marathon, Florida. Some of the boats went to be freight boats and hauled goods to Haiti. Some were used as commercial fishing boats. They put longline reels out over the sides, put refrigerated fish holds in them, and stayed out in the ocean and just fished.

"We bought *Ruth Ann* [originally named *Mitchell*] after she went under down near Norfolk and killed the captain," says Jimmy. "She had a load of oysters on her and when she flipped over she struck the bottom and knocked the house off. We sold her without a house."

"When I think back on it, it was a wonderful time and we met some of the greatest people in the world," he says. "I remember one old captain, tough and crusty looking, standing on the dock as we were leaving, crying like a baby. These boats were like part of the family to many of these people."

"One time my father went to Tangier [Island] to buy a boat and he and the owner were down on the dock dickering over price. They finally came to an agreement, but it was not the price this fellow's wife wanted.

"Well something happened that my father had to spend the night on the island and he was invited to supper by the boatowner. He was at the table and the wife was mad over that price and she never said a word to him. She gave him the cold shoulder the entire meal."

## *WINNIE ESTELLE*—SAVED FROM RUIN

*Winnie Estelle* was built in 1920 in Crisfield, Maryland, and used to buy seafood and dredge for crabs and oysters on Chesapeake Bay. She is an example of a Bay boat that went south and survived.

Guy Ireland bought the vessel in the 1960s, fixed her up, and sold her to a buyer in the West Indies who used the boat to freight between the islands.

*Winnie Estelle* is alive and well today but was almost lost in the late 1980s. Robert Smith, owner and captain of the boat, says, "We first encountered *Winnie Estelle* through her owner, Captain Dave, a resident of Bermuda who spent much of his time with *Winnie* in the Caribbean waters of Belize.

"The story goes that Captain Dave originally purchased *Winnie Estelle* in Virginia and sailed her to Belize to haul pine lumber from Honduras to Belize," he says.

Sometime in the late 1970s, Captain Dave was killed in an airplane crash and *Winnie Estelle* went from owner to owner until she ended up bent and broken on a shoal near Belize.

Smith learned of her fate from another captain and with the help of several friends went about the task of salvaging the boat. She was pulled off the shoal and taken to a local boatyard. "We felt it important to save her because it would be a tribute to the memory of Dave and the incredible history of this old Chesapeake Bay buyboat," he says.

The message from the boatyard was less than optimistic. "The word came. We will need money and we will need courage. Not much left of her. She's all there, but she's also decayed. New wood, we need lots of new wood," says Smith.

What was conceived as a six-month restoration turned into five years. Every plank was replaced and the lumber used was hauled out of the local forest, milled and dried. The Caribbean heart-pine planks came from Honduras, the very same lumber that *Winnie Estelle* had hauled for years. Local hardwood from Belize was used for the framing.

When completed, *Winnie Estelle* went right to work and has been used as a tour/charter boat. She is rated in Belize to carry forty passengers either as a party boat, day charter, or dive boat. She has been working as a tour boat in San Pedro, Belize, for the past eleven years and she makes off-season charter cruises to the Rio Dulce in Guatemala as well as to more remote cays.

Unfortunately, *Winnie Estelle* is an exception rather than the rule. The majority of the Chesapeake Bay buyboats that were built from 1900 through the early 1970s have experienced a much harsher fate and are no longer around.

Throughout those years, Bay buyboats were as commonplace as tractor-trailer trucks are today. The boats played an enormous role in the economic development of the Chesapeake Bay region. Ironically, the expansion of highways and the growth that came out of that economic development is what eventually silenced the jingle and gong of Chesapeake Bay buyboats.

# APPENDIX 1: VESSEL LISTING

William C. "Bill" Hight, who has a love and passion for the buyboat era, researched many of the vessels in this list by using the *Merchant Vessels of the United States,* published by the Treasury Department, Bureau of Navigation, Washington, D.C., in various volumes between 1914 and 1994. Bill has made a concerted effort to locate as many names of deck boats as possible. This listing would not have been possible without his never-ending drive and wonderful enthusiasm throughout the project to document and list the boats.

One of the most valuable sources was the United States Coast Guard National Vessel Documentation Center in Falling Waters, West Virginia, and the research work of Lorrie Tallent, Records and Research Assistant of the Data Management and Administration Division. Once Bill and I had established a list of boats and hull numbers, the numbers of over 100 boats were sent to Lorrie and she found them in the records. The information found on the index card registrations solved many mysteries and corrected many mistakes. Some of the most exciting moments of the entire project occurred when Bill would call when the listing arrived, and he would say, "You won't believe who built what and where."

Another valuable source was the deck boat listing of Chris Judy, who documented 120 boats in the 1980s. The registrar of the Calvert Marine Museum of Solomons Island, Robert J. Hurry, made this list available. It is a tremendous source and Judy should be commended for his work and his love for the boats.

Other sources used were *Chesapeake Bay Schooners* by Quentin Snediker and Ann Jensen; *Working the Water: The Commercial Fisheries of Maryland's Patuxent River* by Paula J. Johnson; *Living Memories of Crittenden and Eclipse* by Minnie Moger Corson; *Chesapeake Bay Bugeyes* by M. V. Brewington; and the various works of Robert H. Burgess and information from many oral interviews.

Some of the people who contributed to this list are Fred M. Biddlecomb, George Butler, Noah C. Carr Jr., Tom Chillemi, Henry S. Chowning, Joe Conway, Fred Crittenden, James Crittenden, Cathy Davenport, Stewart Edwards, John England, Vera England, Kim Granberry, J. J. Hardy, Frances Haynie, Ted Haynie, Sonny Hines, Jimmy Hogge, Robert Roland Hudgins, Swainson Hudgins, Walter Boyd Hurley, Jimmy Ireland, Paula Johnson, Marcia Jones, Billy LeCompte, Mrs. A. G. Mathews, Willard Norris, Ted Parish, Lewis Parks, Charles E. Payne, Ed Payne, Jonesey Payne, Lynn Perry, Paul Pruitt, Steve Pruitt, Edwin W. Rice, Sam Richardson, Don Richwine, Talmadge Ruark, Alvin Sibley, Andrew Simmons, Francis Smith, Morris Snow, Dr. A. L. Van Name, Jr., Paul Vrooman, Melvin Ward, Herman Weston, Lee Whitelock, Kenneth W. Williams, A. Bennett Wilson, Jr., Willis Wilson, Lewis Wright, and William E. Wright.

This vessel listing is a partial listing of Chesapeake Bay deck boats and converted-to-power sailing craft. I'm certain there are several hundred more boats that we were unable to locate. The list does attempt to show as much information as possible on each boat without doing a full search of each vessel. There are not enough pages to cover the paper trail of a full-fledged search of each vessel from start to finish. Also, much of the information in this listing is from the recollections of information told to the individuals. I'm certain that not everything is correct. All I can say is we did the best we could over a two-year period to make this list as accurate as possible.

As an example of the magnitude of an effort to document the life of all these boats, here is the complete paperwork of one vessel, the planked bugeye *Louise Travers,* followed from the day she went down the rails in 1896 at James T. Marsh Shipyard at Solomons, Maryland, to the day she went to the burn pile in 1986, not far from where she started life.

*Louise Travers,* James T. Marsh, Mill Creek, Solomons, Md., 1896, 70' × 19.5' × 5.7'; gross tonnage, 32.43; net tonnage, 25.54; hull no. 141457. Originally listed at 58' × 18' 6" × 4' 4". A change in the size of a converted sailing vessel was not unusual, because many were lengthened and enlarged when converted to powerboats. Some show as many as three different lengths because the boat was enlarged again after the initial conversion. Some powered deck boats were also enlarged years after being launched.

*Louise Travers* was the last sailing bugeye built by Marsh, who was an innovative bugeye builder credited with developing the first plank-on-frame bugeyes as well as the stern ducktail or box which enclosed a bugeye's rudderstock, thus protecting it from collision with other vessels in crowded harbors. *Louise Travers* had a ducktail stern.

She was delivered on October 14, 1896, to Captain B. F. Travis. The *Merchant Vessels of the United States* followed her throughout her life. From 1896 to 1911, she was listed as an oyster-dredge boat requiring a crew of six; her home port was Crisfield, Maryland. She was not listed in the 1912 MVUS book; home port was listed from 1913 to 1918 at Baltimore; not listed in 1920 and 1921; home port listed at Crisfield from 1929 to 1939 and owned by Henry W. Ward of Somerset Avenue, Crisfield, Maryland.

*Louise Travers* gave up her sailing mast and rig in 1930 when Ward converted her to a gas-powered deck boat. Her first engine was 36 horsepower. Thereafter she was operated by a crew of two. She was not listed in the 1940 MVUS and was listed from 1941 to 1945 as owned by Nora Ward, the wife of Henry Ward. The Wards' son, Maurice E. Ward of Crisfield, owned her in 1946. After seventeen years in the Ward family, Mallory S. Stant of Crisfield owned her in 1947 and enlarged her to 68' 6". In 1948, a 140-horsepower gas engine was installed.

She was not listed in 1949–54. From 1955 to 1962, William H. Bailey of Newport News owned *Louise Travers,* and her home port was Newport News. In 1966 and 1967 she was missing from the list. Gladys G. McCready of Cape Charles owned her from 1968 to 1971, and her home port was Cape Charles. From 1972 to 1978, Raymond Chelton Evans of Crisfield owned her and home port was moved back to Crisfield.

From 1978 to 1984, *Louise Travers* was owned by James Byus and was used as a floating vegetable stand at the Maine Avenue fish market in Washington, D.C. Byus donated the vessel to Calvert Marine Museum in 1984. She was towed to Solomons by the Maryland Department of Natural Resources tug, arriving at the museum on October 4, 1984. The museum said the condition of *Louise Travers* was "deemed too deteriorated to restore."

The museum had naval architects from the *Historic American Engineering Record* take lines off the boat and drawings were made of her. On October 21, 1986, she was set afire on the shoreline not far from where she was launched in 1896. Thus ended the ninety-year life of *Lousie Travers.*

Most of the information on the Louise Travers came from the *Historic American Buildings Survey/Historic American Engineering Record* Web site. Richard K. Anderson, Jr., and Paul L. Berry were listed as doing the research.

The vessel listing is divided into two sections: those boats originally built as powerboats and those that were converted from sail to power. Most listings show the vessel's original name, the builder and/or location of builder, year built, and dimensions (length/beam/draft). Additional information may include the name of the owner who first registered the boat, the year and location of registration, hull number, and engine horsepower. The listings for vessels converted to power show weight (net/gross), the type of fishery involved, and the year of conversion to power. Miscellaneous facts may also be added.

If a vessel includes a date with the term, "deleted," it means the vessel was removed from Coast Guard registration and was no longer listed in *Merchant Vessels of the United States*. A boat might be deleted if she was no longer being used for whatever reason, including sinking. However, even if a boat was removed from registration because she sank, it is possible that she was later salvaged and registered again.

An asterisk indicates those vessels that have been thoroughly researched with the assistance of the United States Coast Guard National Vessel Documentation Center in Falling Waters, West Virginia.

# BOATS ORIGINALLY BUILT FOR ENGINE POWER

*A. G. Price,* A G. Price, Mount Vernon, Md., listed as being built at Hudson, Md., 1928, 58.4' × 21' × 6.3', gross 64, net 48, hull no. 228138. (Owned by Frank M. Hardy, passenger, 70 hp, registered at Cambridge, Md., later named *Coastal Queen.*)

*A. R. Myers,* Chincoteague, Va., 1928, 52.9' × 15.2' × 5.6', gross 32, net 21, hull no. 227773. (Owned by Arthur R. Myers, passenger, 1929, registered at Philadelphia, Pa.)

*Adele,* Norfolk, Va., 1926, 48.8' × 13.5' × 6.1', gross 28, net 10, hull no. 225287. (Owned by Edward O. Brex, fishing, 1929, Cape May, N.J., registered Philadelphia, Pa.)

*Adriana,* Deltaville, Va., 1928, 42.1' × 13.2' × 4.1', gross 15, net 9, hull no. 227900. (Owned by K. Everts, freight, 1929, registered Norfolk, Va.)

*Agnes Sterling,* Linwood P. Price and Co., Amburg, Va., 1925, 58.9' × 18.3' × 5.4', gross 40, net 27, hull no. 225026. (Built for and owned by Captain Johnny Sterling of Crisfield, Md., later by Carl Bradshaw, Tangier Island.)

*\*Alert,* Pocomoke City, Md., 1901, 50.9' × 11' × 3.4', gross 14, net 9, hull no. 107651. (Registered Cape Charles, Va., 1901; Tappahannock, Va., 1903; Reedville, Va., 1913; Crisfield, Md., 1924; Charleston, S. C., 1927; abandoned June 4, 1934.)

*Alfred J. Lewis,* Hopkins, Va., 1905, 41.5' × 13.5' × 2.5', gross 7, net 5, hull no. 202518. (Owned by Preston D. Fields, oystering, 1929, registered Reedville, Va.)

*\*Alice & Annie,* D. L. Belvin, Perrin, Va., 1922, 53.5' × 14.4' × 5.4', gross 27, net 11, hull no. 221908. (Prior to October 19, 1922, gross 23, net 10, original 24 hp, owned by Fish Processing Corp. of Virginia, freight, 1946. Robert Burgess's, *Chesapeake Circle* states the boat began on August 10, 1925, hauling freight as a packet boat from the steamboat wharves on the North, Ware and Severn Rivers and connected with the Norfolk steamer at an East River wharf. North, Ware, and Severn wharfs did not have sufficient freight or passenger traffic to warrant the use of a steamboat.)

*Amanda C.,* F. C. Haislip, Harryhogan, Va., 1941, 71.6' × 23.5' × 7.4', gross 73, net 49, hull no. 241194. (Built by Haislip to haul freight and lumber, 60 hp, registered at Reedville, Va.; bought by Captain Johnny Ward of Deltaville and renamed *Nora W.* for Nora Ward of Crisfield, Md., his mother. Owned by Floyd Gene Ward, fishing, 290 hp, Norfolk, Va.)

*\*Amos,* Mitchell Hubbard, Hudson, Md., 1930, 59.5' × 19.6' × 5.4', gross 40, net 27, hull no. 229946. (Owned by W. F. Morgan and Son, freight, early 75 hp, later 165 hp, Reedville, Va.; renamed *Nancy K. Batemen* December 22, 1975; registered Cambridge, Md., 1930; Philadelphia, Pa., 1982; New Orleans, La., 1985.)

*Amy Carol,* see *Geraldine*

*Amy S. Daugherty,* Susan, Va., 1936, 41.7' × 11.6' × 3.4', gross 10, net 6, hull no. 235012. (Owned by Vernon Bozman, oystering, 24 hp, Crisfield, Md.)

*Analbern,* Irvington, Va., 1912, 64.7' × 16.3' × 6.2', gross 40, net 27, hull no. 209693. (Owned by John Ekstrom, freight, 1929, registered Baltimore, Md.)

*Andrew J. Lewis,* E. C. Rice & Son, Fairport, Va., 1929, 69.6' × 21.2' × 6.9', gross 73, net 45, hull no. 229135; original engine 75 hp. (Originally owned by the Lewis family and used to haul canned goods out of Coles Point on Potomac River; later renamed *Ward Bros.* in 1952 and owned by Captain Johnny Ward of Deltaville; and today named *Crow Brothers* and located at Tilghman Island, Md. She was converted to a single-house deck boat at Deagle and Son Marine Railway at Ruark, Va.) "I can remember her laying on the railway at Uncle Lee's [Deagle] railway with nothing on her and he put the house and mast on her," says Melvin Ward.

*\*Andy,* Cambridge, Md., 1930, 71.5' × 23' × 6.3', gross 75, net 51, hull no. 230132. (One of four deck boats owned by Phillips Packing Co. of Cambridge, Md., that were named for cartoon characters. The official registration card listed the boat as being built by Phillips Packing Co., at Cambridge, 1946. Sold May 1, 1952, and alien to Cuban flag. Surrendered registration June 18, 1952, Miami, Fla.)

*Angler,* Pocomoke City, Md., 1923, 49.3' × 15.4' × 4.1', gross 13, net 9, hull no. 222944. (Owned by James A. Boyd, Jr., passenger, 1929, registered Philadelphia, Pa.)

*Annie,* Chuckatuck, Va., 1911, 45.6' × 14.4' × 3.3', gross 11, net 6, hull no. 209420. (Registered 1915, fishing, 30 hp, Newport News, Va.; Savannah, Ga., 1942; vessel lost, abandoned, July 12, 1944.)

*Annie & Elsie,* Gwynn, Va., 1913, 45.2' × 12.5' × 3.3', gross 10, net 6, hull no. 211155. (Owned by J. H. Gwynn, Crickett Hill, Va., freight, 1929 and 1946, registered Norfolk, Va.)

*Annie D.,* Johnny C. Weston, Deltaville, Va., 1957, 44.4' × 14.4' × 3.9', gross 16, net 13, hull no. 275702. (Owned by Thomas Asbury Pruitt, fishing, 90 hp, Reedville, Va.; Echo Hill Outdoor School, 1994, registered Norfolk, Va.)

*Annie M.,* Messongo, Va., 1903, 46' × 15' × 3.7', gross 10, net 7, hull no. 200080. (Owned by C. E. Ridgeway, Portsmouth, Va., 1929, registered Norfolk, Va.)

*\*Annie Marie,* William T. Forrest, Grimstead, Va., 1914, 51.2' × 14.1' × 4.5', gross 18, net 8, 25 hp, hull no. 212087. (Owned by E. S. Pruitt, Tangier, Va., freight, 1915; fishing, 1929; registered Newport News, Va., 1914, 1926, 1960; Cape Charles, 1929; Crisfield, Md., 1934.)

*Annie May,* Poquoson, 1903, 44' × 12.3' × 3.5', gross 10, net 8, hull no. 200297 (Registered 1915 and 1929, freight, Norfolk, Va.)

*\*Anthony Klein,* see *Joyce Sterling*

*Aries,* see *Edith Mae*

*Arlington,* Hopkins, Va., 1901, 45.6' × 14.7' × 2.8', gross 9, net 6, hull no. 107674. (Owned by William Gale, oystering, 1929, registered Cape Charles, Va.)

*Audrey,* Fairport, Va., 1904, 45' × 13.9' × 4', gross 14, net 8, hull no. 201738. (Oystering, 1915, registered Reedville, Va.)

*Audrey,* Laban, Va., 1924, 48.3' × 12.6' × 4.1', gross 13, net 9, hull no. 234752. (Owned by Ira F. Swift, 1946, fishing, Reedville, Va., and later by Larry Lewis of Ophelia.)

*Augusta,* see *Mutt*

*Augusta C. Quinn,* Amburg, Va., 1922, 53.1' × 14.6' × 5.2', gross 25, net 17, hull no. 222584. (Owned by Wallace M. Quinn, freight, 1929, registered Crisfield, Md.)

*Aurora,* Hooper Island, Md., 59.7' × 16.9' × 4.5', gross 35, net 26, hull no. 206022. (Owned by Garland F. Horseman, Broomes Island, Md., freight, 1929, registered Crisfield, Md.)

*Automatic,* J. W. Smith, Bena, Va., 1926, 49.5' × 14.2' × 4.2', gross 18, net 8, hull no. 226157. (Early engine, 50 hp, named *Miss Maggie* in 1981).

*Avalynne,* Crisfield, Md., 1903, 46.8' × 13.2' × 4.8', gross 14, net 14, hull no. 200306. (Owned by George W. Sherman, freight, 1929, New Haven, Conn.; 1915, 25 hp, registered New Haven Conn.)

*Avery Gorman,* Hopkins, Va., 1900, 49' × 16' × 3.9', gross 17, net 9, hull no. 107616. (Registered 1915, Newport News, Va.)

*Avis G. Abel,* Norfolk, Va., 1917, 49' × 13' × 5.1', gross 30, net 24, hull no. 230431. (Owned by Alex Brun, fishing, 1946, Key West, Fla.)

*B. F. Travers,* Linwood P. Price, Amburg, Va., 1924, 76' × 21.4' × 7.1', gross 76, net 44, hull no. 223644. (Early motor, 60 hp.)

*Barb,* Alvin Sibley, Deltaville, Va. (Built by Alvin Sibley for himself. He used the vessel in the winter oyster-dredge fishery.)

*Belvidere,* Harris Lot, Md., 1912, 37.8' × 12' × 3.1', gross 9, net 6, hull no. 212441. (Owned by W. A. Heine, freight, 1929, registered Washington, D.C.; 1915, freight, registered Reedville, Va.)

*Bernice Queen,* Parksley, Va., 1923, 49.7' × 12.7' × 4', gross 19, net 15, hull no. 222931. (Owned by Will Parks, Tangier Island, Va., freight, 1929, registered Crisfield, Md.)

*\*Beryl Marie,* Ned Hudgins, Laban, Va., 1925, 52.6' × 14.9' × 5.4', gross 25, net 13, hull no. 226262. (Registered in Norfolk, 1927; and Reedville, 1965; owned by J. C. Miller, 1946; burned on Tangier Island, Va., April 13, 1966.)

*Bessie,* Baltimore, Md., 1912, 44.6' × 11.5' × 4.9', gross 15, net 10, hull no. 210322. (Registered 1915, freight, Baltimore, Md.)

*Bessie,* Benedict, Md., 1933, 45.3' × 11.4' × 3.8', gross 18, net 12, hull no. 245973. (Owned by J. A. Boehm, fishing, 1946, Alexandria, Va.)

*Bessie Ann,* Solomons, Md., 1944, 44.8' × 15.2' × 7.7', gross 33, net 22, 246929. (Owned by Lewis Crab Factory, fishing, 1946, Brunswick, Ga.)

*Bessie H.,* L. R. and Alton Smith, Susan, Va., 1925, 53.6' × 13.9' × 4.4', gross 19, net 13, hull no. 229123. (Owned by C. R. Hudgins, registered 1946, fishing, Newport News, Va.)

*Bessie L.,* Linwood P. Price, Amburg, Va., 1923, 57.2' × 15.2' × 5.1', gross 28, net 19, hull no. 222836. (Owned by Homer Glenwood Pruitt, Tangier Island, 36 hp engines, later 165 hp. Used to bring the Robert's Brothers Circus feature elephant named Pasha from Tangier to Crisfield after a circus that was part of the island homecoming in 1977; also went into the United States Coast Guard during World War II and was painted black. Used to patrol and haul war supplies.)

*\*Bessie Virginia,* Linwood P. Price Co., Ruark, Va., 1931, 61.8' × 18.7' × 6.4', gross 49, net 35, hull no. 230521. (Owned by A. A. Crockett, 1946, freight, Crisfield, Md., engine room controlled; later owned by Mary L. Smith, Philadelphia, Pa., registered Newport News, 1931; Philadelphia, Pa., 1982; deleted 1988.)

*Betty Page,* L. R. and Alton Smith, Susan, Va., 1931, 58.2' × 13.7' × 4.8', gross 22, net 9, hull no. 231256. (Owned by Henry B. Owens, freight, 1946, Newport News, Va.)

*Bivalve,* Rescue, Va., 1925, 53' × 16.3' × 4.1', gross 23, net 12, hull no. 224873. (Owned by O. A. Bloxom, freight, 36 hp, 1946, registered Newport News, Va.; later transferred to United States government.)

*Black Bird,* Irvington, Va., 1908, 40' × 12' × 5', gross 15, net 10, hull no. 205973. (Registered 1915, freight, Reedville, Va.)

*Blanche,* Irvington, Va., 1905, 58.5' × 11.9' × 3.8', gross 12, net 7, hull no. 202388. (Registered 1915, oystering, Reedville, Va.)

*\*Blanche,* John E. Wright, Enoch, Va., 1912, 40' × 9.8' × 3.4', gross 9, net 6, hull no. 210687. (Early engine 10 hp; destroyed by hurricane September 18, 1936, at Belford, N.J.)

*\*Blue Ribbon,* N. B. Diggs, Laban, Va., 1924, 45.5' × 11.3' × 3.9', gross 10, net 7, hull no. 234318. (Original 25 hp, owned by W. Burroughs, fishing, 1946, Newport News, Va.; abandoned 1972.)

*Bobby.* (Owned 2002 by Gaskins' Seafood of Ophelia, Va., house rebuilt by Francis Haynie of Northumberland County, Va., used in pound-net fishery.)

*Bogue Sound,* Williston, N.C., 1955, 67.6' × 19.5' × 4.7', gross 54, net 36, hull no. 269183. (Owned by Jennings C. Burton, 1994, still alive in Chesapeake region, 2003.)

*Boots,* L. R. and Alton Smith, Susan, Va., 1931, 54' × 13.5' × 4.2', gross 17, net 7, hull no. 230467. (Owned by C. G. Hudgins.)

*Bounty,* Solomons, Md., 1929, 50' × 16' × 6', gross 27, net 18, hull no. 228792. (Owned by George D. Olds, 1946, freight, Baltimore, Md.)

*Bucajiga,* L. R. and Alton Smith, Susan, Va., 1924, 46.9' × 11.5' × 3.7', gross 10, net 7, hull no. 231398. (Owned by W. H. Powell, registered 1946, fishing, Newport News, Va.)

*Buccaneer,* Salisbury, Md., 1924, 52.3' × 14' × 7.8', gross 26, net 17, hull no. 223923. (Owned by Edwin E. Witham, registered 1946, freight, Rockland, Maine.)

*C. A. Loocherman,* Compton, Md., 1923, 58.7' × 17.8' × 5.5', gross 35, net 23, hull no. 223223. (Owned by C. A. Loocherman, freight, 48 hp, registered Crisfield, Md.)

*C. E. Wright,* T. W. "Captain Ladd" Wright, Deltaville, Va., 1918, 59.5' × 16.6' × 5.7', gross 34, net 24, hull no. 216722. (Owned by Ladd Wright, named for his daughter Countess E. Wright. One of the few frame-built deck boats ever built in Deltaville, Va.; later owned by Homer Pruitt, freighting, 165 hp, registered Reedville, Va.)

*\*C. W. Drannek,* Deltaville, Va., 1910, 52.5' × 9.5' × 3.4', gross 11, net 8, hull no. 207669. (Used to haul ice for Kennard Ice Co. in Urbanna, Va.)

*C. W. Fedderman,* Dreka, Va., 1900, 45' × 14' × 3.2', gross 13, net 8, hull no. 127462. (Registered 1915, freight, Norfolk, Va. In 1946 the name was the same but she was cut down to 42.1' × 14.6' × 3.4'; owned by Earl A. Smoot, 1946, passenger.)

*Callis Brothers,* see *Julian*

*Camanche.* (Owned by Rob Phillips, frame built.)

*Canary Bird,* Linwood P. Price, Amburg, Va., 1924, 52.8' × 16' × 4.5', gross 24, net 14, hull no. 224165. (Used for oystering, 36 hp.)

*Captain Latane,* see *Georgie E.*

*Carlisle,* Fairmount, Md., 1903, 55' × 20.6' × 5.3', gross 20, net 9, hull no. 200387. (Owned by J. E. Hubbard, fishing, 90 hp, registered Newport News, Va.)

*Carol Dryden,* James E. Daugherty, Crisfield, Md., 1938, 43.5' × 9.5' × 3.3', gross 9, net 8, hull no. 237532. (Owned by Carol Dryden, freight, 1946, registered Crisfield, Md., powered by 671 Detroit Diesel.)

*\*Carol Sue II,* see *Olive Virginia*

*\*Carrie M.,* Lepron Johnson, Crittenden, Va., 1916, 41' × 11.6' × 3.3', gross 12, net 6, 24 hp, hull no. 214299. (Owned by Mrs. Mary Mahoney Fergus, fishing, Wilmington, N.C., registered Newport News, Va., 1916, 1920; Wilmington N.C. 1943; whereabouts of owner and vessel unknown, 1964.)

*Catherine,* Alexander Gaines, Dare, Va., 1923, 45.1' × 11.2' × 4', gross 11, net 5, hull no. 223436. (Log boat.)

*Cecil W.,* West Norfolk, Va., 1938, 57.7' × 18.5' × 9.8', gross 61, net 27, 237966. (Owned by Ralph Carminer, fishing, 1946, registered Norfolk, Va.)

*Chadwick/Coast Guard No. 1207/Lora Lee.* (Confiscated by Coast Guard for hauling bootleg liquor during Prohibition. Owned by the Coast Guard for twenty years and used as a buoy tender, then sold to Winnie Pruitt and renamed *Lora Lee.*)

*Charlotte,* L. R. and Alton Smith, Susan, Va., 1928, 46.4' × 11.5', gross 10, net 8, hull no. 231886. (Owned by J. Sam Hudgins, Sr., 1946, Northern Neck, Va. Also owned by John Lewis.)

*Charlotte,* Lepron Johnson, Crittenden, Va., 1917, 54' × 15.7' × 5.1', gross 23, net 16, hull no. 214707. (Owned by W. B. Carney Estate of Portsmouth, freight, 1929, registered Norfolk, Va.)

*Charlotte,* Salisbury, Md., 1920, 59.1' × 21' × 6.9', gross 53, net 36, hull no. 220876. (Waterboat, 1929, registered Baltimore, Md.)

*Chesapeake,* Lepron Johnson, Crittenden, Va., 1936, 92.9' × 24.9' × 7', 113 gross, 47 net, hull no. 234599. (Built for Rufus Miles of J. H. Miles & Co. of Norfolk; caught fire and sank off Atlantic City, N.J., while clamming.)

*Chesapeake,* Linwood P. Price, Ruark, Va., 1932, 60.8' × 20.4' × 7.1', gross 58, net 41, hull no. 231395.

*\*City of Crisfield,* T. W. "Captain Ladd" Wright and John E. Wright, Deltaville, Va., 1923, 59.4' × 16.6' × 5.2', gross 31, net 21, draft changed to 6.2', June 30, 1931, hull no. 223437. (Name changed

to *Etta Marie* September 12, 1931, registered Reedville, Va., 1923–29; Baltimore, Md., 1930; Cambridge, Md., 1931–34; Crisfield, Md., 1936; and Reedville, Va., 1968; out of documentation June 3, 1971, owner deceased.)

*Clayton,* Crittenden, Va., 1907, 48' × 11.8' × 4', gross 11, net 10; rebuilt 1930, 47' × 11' × 3.3', gross 9, net 6, hull no. 204043. (Originally built to haul passengers for Johnnie Adams for the 1907 Jamestown Exposition, registered Norfolk, 1907–45; owned by D. A. Winstead, passenger, 1946, Norfolk, Va.; registered Newport News, 1958; abandoned 1962.)

*Cleopatra's Barge,* see *Lillian Ruth*

*Coastal Queen,* see *A. G. Price.*

*Colony,* Linwood P. Price, Amburg, Va., 1930, 81.5', 23.7' × 7.4', gross 92, net 70, hull no. 229504. (Enlarged from 61' to 81.5 ' by Lee Deagle at Deagle and Son Marine Railway in Deltaville in 1950s. Owned by Howard Ward of Crisfield, Md., freight, 150 hp, and later by Standard Boat Co. Inc., New York, N.Y.)

*Congress,* Gwynn, Va., 1914, 50.8' × 13.8' × 3.7', gross 15, net 7, hull no. 212373. (Registered 1915, freight, Newport News, Va.)

*Coral,* Poquoson, Va., 1914, 48.2' × 13.4' × 3.7', gross 17, net 7, hull no. 212373. (Registered 1915, freight, Newport News, Va.)

*Courtney Thomas,* Alton Smith, Susan, Va., 1944, 55.5' × 14.5' × 4.8', gross 24, net 9, hull no. 246784. (Owned by Rudy Thomas, Jr., fishing, Tangier Island, Va., 1994, Norfolk, Va.)

*Croaker,* L. R. and Alton Smith, Susan, Va., 1931, 55.6' × 14' × 4.7', gross 23, net 15, hull no. 230522. (Owned by Morris Snow. Snow changed name from *Croaker* to *Linda Carol* after his daughter, fishing, 225 hp, Norfolk, Va.)

*Crow Brothers,* see *Andrew J. Lewis*

*D. B. Jackson,* Deltaville, Va., 1922, 43.5' × 11.2' × 3.7', gross 11, net 7, hull no. 222538. (Owned by Alexander A. Jackson, registered 1946, freight, Reedville, Va.)

*Daisy May,* Winter Harbor, Va., 1912, 46.6' × 11.3' × 3.6', gross 11, net 5, hull no. 212034. (Registered 1915, fishing, Cape Charles, Va.)

*Daphine,* T. W. "Captain Ladd" Wright, Deltaville, Va., 1926, 52.5' × 14' × 4.1', gross 20, net 13, hull no. 225975. (Registered out of Cape Charles, lost October 2, 1959, stranded on Occohonock Bar, Accomack County, Va.)

*Della Reed,* T. W. "Captain Ladd" Wright, Deltaville, Va., 1924, 46.2' × 12.1' × 3.8', gross 14, net 10, hull no. 223866. (Owned by Delmas S. Tyler, freight, 1946, 14 hp, Crisfield, Md., and Charlie Williams of Tangier Island.)

*Del-Mar-Va,* Linwood P. Price, Ruark, Va., 1926, 74.4' × 22' × 7.8', gross 106, net 72, hull no. 225932. (Owned by W. E. Valiant Co., Delaware.)

*Delphine,* Lepron Johnson, Crittenden, Va., 1915, 47.3' × 15.7' × 3.8', gross 17, net 10, hull no. 213505. (Owned by George Dean, 50 hp engines).

*Delvin K.,* Sidney Smith, Bena, Va., 1949, 57.8' × 18.3' × 5.4', gross 38, net 29, hull no. 258826. (Built for Willie E. King, Newport News, Va., later owned by Lowery K. Hudgins, 1994, 225 hp.)

*Dewey,* Lyman Ewell, Elliott, Md., 1912, 50.2' × 13.6' × 5.2', gross 18, net 12, hull no. 210595. (Log bottom with planked sides, early engine 30 hp, owned by Herman H. Evans, freight, 1946; later owned by Hugh Haynie of Tangier Island and used as grocery delivery boat between Tangier Island and Reedville; by Weldon Ray Crockett, fishing, 160 hp, Reedville, Va.; also Carl Bradshaw of Tangier Island and Herman Evans of Smith Island owned her at different times.

*Dillard,* Whealton, Va., 1905, 42' × 13.7' × 3.5', gross 12, net 6, hull no. 201849. (Registered 1915, oystering, Reedville, Va.; owned by Morratico, Inc., oystering, 1929; registered Tappahannock, Va., 1906–10; Reedville, Va., 1913–49; abandoned, Reedville, 1950.)

*DJIV,* see *Mildred*

*Dolphin,* Johnny C. Weston and Earl Weston, Deltaville, Va., 1950, 44.4' × 13.1' × 4.3', gross 17, net 11, hull no. 261007. (Built for Willis L. Wilson, Lennie Callis, and Charles Montgomery of Deltaville, Va., crab dredging, registered Reedville, Va.)

*Dora Estelle,* Noah T. Evans, Ewell, Md. (Smith Island), 1923, 62.6' × 17.5' × 5.7', gross 42, net 32, hull no. 223337. (Owned by Charles Irving Henderson, freight, 225 hp, Crisfield, Md.; also owned by Dewey Evans, Tangier Island, early engine 50 hp.)

*Dorothy,* Amburg, Va., 1924, 59' × 17.3' × 5.6', gross 39, net 26, hull no. 224016. (Owned by Thomas J. Kellum of Weems, freight, 60 hp, registered Reedville, 1940.)

*Dorothy Foster,* Deltaville, Va., 1917, 41.4 × 11.6' × 4.4', gross 15, net 10, hull no. 215534. (Owned by Orie Lee Smith, freight, registered Reedville, Va.; Carter Giles Stanton, Baltimore, Md.)

*Dorothy Francis,* W. F. Dunn, West Norfolk, Va., 1924, 59.8' × 17.2' × 5.7', gross 25, net 19; rebuilt 1937, 61.2' × 18.9' × 5.7', gross 48, net 34, hull no. 224273. (Early engine, 20 hp, owned by J. C. Burton, Jr., fishing, 165 hp, Newport News, Va.)

*Doswell S. Edwards,* Herman M. Krentz, Kayan, Va., 1926, 77.3' × 23.6' × 7.3', gross 93, net 39, hull no. 226167. (Owned by Beaufort Fisheries, N.C., 1946, 126 hp and crew of twenty, used for menhaden fishing, registered Reedville, Va., 1927–28; New York, N.Y., 1930; Beaufort, N.C. 1947; foundered at Beaufort Inlet December 8, 1952.)

*Dudley,* Gilbert White, Foxwells, Va., 1938, 59.7' × 15.1' × 4.3', gross 27, net 16, hull no. 237670. (Still on the Bay and owned by Fred M. Biddlecomb of Reedville, Va., used as a charter fishing boat. Early engine was 40 hp.)

*E. Arrowsmith,* L. R. and Alton Smith, Susan, Va., 1923, 50.7' × 12.4' × 4.5', gross 14, net 6, hull no. 231280, 35 hp. (Owned by Dolson L. Owens, fishing, five-man crew. Owens was later killed aboard the deck boat *Ruth Ann* while working for Ferguson Seafood of Remlik, Va.)

*E. F. Travers,* Walter B. Cannon, Fishing Creek, Md., 1913, 53' × 14.8' × 4.4', gross 26, net 17, enlarged to 71' × 15.3' × 4.1', gross 32, net 20, July 9, 1915, hull no. 211355. (Owned by Wm. F. Cox, freight, registered Crisfield, Md.; abandoned at Crisfield, March 29, 1966.)

*E. J. Parks,* Patterson Moran, Rappahannock River, 1902, 47.8' × 11' × 3.2', gross 7, net 6, hull no. 209136. (Owned by Harold R. Bassett, freight, Crisfield, Md.)

*East Hampton,* Freeman Hudgins and Boney Diggs, Laban, Va., 1925, 56.4' × 15.7' × 4.4 feet, gross 24, net 16, hull no. 225288. (Original engine 50 hp, registered Newport News, Va., built at Eldridge Diggs's landing at Laban, Mathews County, Va.; originally an open boat with a V-stern, built originally for Curtis Hudgins; converted to a deck boat with a round stern by boatbuilder Frank Smith of Gloucester County, Va.; owned 2003 by David and Trudy Rollins of Poquoson, Va., and being used for pleasure. The name *East Hampton* is her original name and the name is carved in her hull.)

*Edith Mae,* Linwood P. Price, Amburg, Va., 1944, 41.2' × 11' × 3.5', gross 13, net 8, hull no. 245684. (Later named *Aries,* owned by Richard Steven Erdt, fishing, 170 hp, registered Norfolk, Va.)

*Edith S. Wilkins,* Crittenden, Va., 1919, 49.6' × 13.3' × 5.5', gross 21, net 14, hull no. 218898. (Owned by City of Boston, passenger, 1929, registered Boston, Mass.)

*Edna,* Irvington, Va., 1929, 49.7' × 9.6' × 3.3', gross 9, net 5, hull no. 228221. (Owned by R. E. Sisson, 1946, Reedville, Va.)

*Edna L.,* Lepron Johnson, Crittenden, Va., 1922, 47.1' × 14.1' × 4.1', gross 18, net 10, hull no. 222572. (Owned by Wm. J. Bradshaw, fishing, 36 hp, Newport News, Va., 1926–72; Norfolk, 1975; deleted 1984.)

*Edna McLain,* Sidney and Jim Smith, Perrin, Va., 1932, 42.7' × 11.8' × 4.3', gross 10, net 7, hull no 235738.

*Edvina,* Lepron Johnson, Crittenden, Va., 1905, 52' × 17.8' × 3.1', gross 18, net 12, hull no. 202694. (Owned by C. R. Bagnell, freight, registered Norfolk, Va.)

*Edward M.,* Alexander Gaines, Dare, Va., 1920, 46.5', 13.3' × 4.2', gross 18, net 9, hull no. 220905. (Log boat, 35 hp, owned by Ollie P. Montgomery, freight, registered Newport News, two-man crew, 1946; later owned by Wallace Pruitt of Onancock, Va.)

*Edwin W. Rice,* Edwin C. Rice, Fleeton, Va., 1929, 53.7' × 16.9' × 6.2', gross 37, net 25, hull no. 228369. (Built for James Lewis of Walnut Oyster Packing Co.; later owned by Augustus Forbush, freight, registered Crisfield, Md.; and later owned by Floyd S. Thompson, freight, 1946, registered Norfolk, Va.)

*\*Effie Bernice,* Jack Smith, Perrin, Va., 1927, 52.3' × 15.6' × 4.5', gross 22, net 10, hull no. 227033. (Owned by T. E. Thompson, freight, 45 hp, registered Newport News, Va., 1927; Crisfield, Md., 1966; abandoned 1972.)

*Effie Cox,* Fairmount, Md, 1909, 41.6' × 11.5' × 3.2', gross 9, net 8, hull no. 206879. (Registered 1915, freight, Crisfield, Md.)

*Effie R.,* Bridgetown, Va., 1901, 44' × 15' × 3', gross 9, net 8, hull no. 136897. (Registered 1915, oystering, Cape Charles, Va.)

*Eleanor White,* Manteo, N.C., 1928, 42.1' × 13.2' × 3.8', gross 14, net 9, hull no. 228105. (The last wooden-hulled oil tanker on Chesapeake Bay, owned by Ballard Fish & Oyster Co., 1946, Norfolk, Va.; later owned by Allen Tyler of Smith Island, Md.)

*\*Elise,* R. D. Taylor, Deep Creek, Va., 1913, 46' × 12.1' × 3.4', gross 13, net 10, 20 hp, hull no. 211112. (Registered 1915, freight, Cape Charles, Va.; abandoned May 27, 1939.)

*\*Elizabeth,* J. Wood Tull, Irvington, Va., 1913, 75' × 15' × 5.1', gross 35, net 23, 75 hp, hull no. 211414. Registered Tappahannock, Va., 1913; (registered 1915, fishing, Reedville, Va.; Beaufort, N.C., 1918–32; New Bern, N.C., 1933; lost near Beaufort August 16, 1934.)

*Elizabeth Alice,* Bagwells Creek, Va., 1912, 44' × 14.4' × 3.7', gross 14, net 6, hull no. 210691. (Registered 1915, oystering, Cape Charles, Va.)

*Elizabeth D.,* L. R. and Alton Smith, Susan,Va., 1927, 50.7' × 12.8' × 4.3', gross 15, net 6, hull no. 231257. (Owned by Stanley C. Pritchett, fishing, 1946, Northern Neck, Va., six-man crew, V-stern, also called diamond stern deck boat.)

*\*Elizabeth Farrar,* Gilbert White, Mobjack, Va., 1902, 48.3' × 12' × 3.3', gross 8, net 5, hull no. 235473. (Owned by E. H. Machen, 1946, fishing, 25 hp, registered Newport News, Va.)

*Elizabeth Wilson,* Hunting Creek, Va., 1912, 57.7' × 14.9' × 3.6', gross 24, net 11, hull no. 210689. (Registered 1915, oystering, Cape Charles, Va.)

*\*Ella K.,* James Smith, Perrin, Va., 1918, 49.3' × 14.1' × 4.1', gross 20, net 6, hull no. 217505. (Owned by John Henry King, 1946, fishing, registered Newport News, Va.; still dredging crabs in 2003 and one of the last deck boats on the Bay to dredge crabs.)

*Ellen Marie,* L. R. and Alton Smith, Susan, Va., 1926, 55.7' × 13.6' × 4.6', gross 21, net 14, hull no. 225302. (Owned by Henry Owens, 1946; Paul Vrooman, 1999; early engine, 100 hp.)

*Ellen W.* (Owned by Howard Ward, Crisfield, Md.)

*Ellis May,* L. R. and Alton Smith, 1928, Susan, Va., 50.2' × 12.9' × 4.1', gross 15, net 10, hull no. 232104. (Owned by Ballard Fish & Oyster Co., 1946.)

*Elsa Mae,* Wetipquin, Md., 1940, 43.4' × 10.7' × 3.4', gross 9, net 8, hull no. 240899. (Owned by Reed Mister, 1946, freight, registered Crisfield, Md.)

*Elsie K.,* L. R. and Alton Smith, Susan, Va., 1927, 61.2' × 15.9' × 4.4', gross 26, net 11, hull no. 227097. (Owned by Adrian F. Rowe, fishing, 1946, registered Newport News, Va.)

*\*Elsie Louise,* J. Wood Tull, Irvington, Va., 1914, 50' × 14.6' × 3.6', gross 17, net 11, hull no. 213839. (Owned by Lord Mott Co., of Baltimore, Md., and Urbanna, Va., oyster fishery. Now named *Georgeanna* and owned by Eric Headberg and Alfred C. Fisher, Jr., Wicomico Church, Va. The topside was converted to a snapper menhaden rig with a house forward and a fish-spotting tower placed at the top of the mast in 1960s. It is now used for salvage work. Freight, registered Reedville, Va., first engine was 35 hp.)

*Elsie Virginia,* Linwood P. Price, Amburg, Va., 1922, 55.7' × 15.3' × 5.3', gross 28, net 19, hull no. 222566. (Owned by William T. Pruitt, fishing, 36 hp, registered Reedville, Va.)

*Elva,* Perrin, Va., 1924, 50.6' × 12.4' × 4.1', gross 13, net 9, hull no. 235394. (Owned by N. F. Sterling, Sr., fishing, 1946, registered Newport News, Va.)

*Elva C.,* Gilbert White, Westland, Va., 1922, 48.8' × 13.5' × 3.7', gross 16, net 9, hull no. 222481. (Early engine 30 hp, owned by the Reedville Fishermen's Museum in Reedville, Va., 2003.)

*Emily Margarette,* Coinjock, N.C., 1917, 59.6' × 21.3' × 7.4', gross 66, net 42, hull no. 215514. (Owned by Walter Russell Fish, fishing, 60 hp, registered Cape Charles, Va.)

*Emma,* Federalsburg, Md., 1941, 56.3' × 12.7' × 2.8', gross 13, net 9, hull no. 240769. (Owned by Arthur B. Rosser, fishing, 1946, registered Cambridge, Md.)

*Emma Virginia,* Pocomoke City, Md., 1912, 58.2' × 15.5' × 5.3', gross 28, net 10, hull no. 209520. (Registered, 1915, fishing, Reedville, Va.)

*\*Estelle Leonard,* Jabez Tyler, Cambridge, Md., 1927, 59.9' × 22.3', × 7.1', gross 63, net 42, 75 hp, hull no. 226639. (Owned by Wayne W. Evans, freight, 310 hp, Crisfield, Md., registered Cambridge, Md., 1927; Newport News, Va., 1970; Crisfield, Md., 1973.)

*Ethel,* Laban, Va., 1908, 43.7' × 10.7' × 2.9', gross 7, net 5, hull no. 217505.

*Ethel Aices,* Carters Creek, Va., 1912, 45' × 10' × 3', gross 18, net 9, hull no. 210688. (Registered 1915, oystering, Reedville, Va.)

*Ethel H.,* Perrin, Va., 1921, 43.3' × 11.3' × 4.1', gross 10, net 7, hull no. 235559. (Owned by Vivian Forbes, freight, 1946, registered Newport News, Va.)

*Ethel L.,* John and Kirby Smith, Dare, Va., 1927, 47.2' × 14.5' × 4.3', gross 17, net 8, hull no. 227084. (Round-stern log boat, owned by M. D. Shields, fishing, 1946, registered Newport News, Va.)

*Ethel Lewis,* Chesconnessex, Va., 1906, 42.5' × 14' × 3.2', gross 8, net 6, hull no. 203592. (Registered 1915, freight, Crisfield, Md.)

*Ethel Virginia,* L. R. and Alton Smith, Susan, Va., 1921, 46.3' × 11.4' × 4', gross 11, net 7, hull no. 234294. (Owned by A. Lance Fulcher, fishing, 1946, Cape Charles, Va.)

*Etta Marie,* see *City of Crisfield*

*Eulalia,* Crisfield, Md., 1925, 52.5' × 14.6' × 3.7', gross 20, net 10, hull no. 225057.

*Eva Lillian,* Pocomoke City, Md., 1906, 42' × 10' × 2.7', gross 10, net 5, hull no. 203311. (Registered 1915, oystering, Reedville, Va.)

*\*Eva W.,* J. F. Smith, Dare, Va., 1935, 53.6' × 14.8' × 5.9', gross 25, net 6, hull no. 234027. (Owned by H. F. Wainwright, fishing, 1946, registered Newport News, Va.; Herman R. Liddell, fishing, 1994, registered Miami, Fl.)

*Eva W.,* Lepron Johnson, Crittenden, Va., 1907, 46' × 14.5' × 3', gross 11, net 10, hull no. 203873. (Registered 1915, freight, Norfolk, Va.)

*Evelyn,* Deltaville, Va., Grover Lee Owens and Ed Norton, 1971, 41.5' × 14' × 5.4', gross 20, net 13, hull no. 531291. (Built for launch service in Hampton Roads. Owned by Rodney Hugate, Mathews County, Va., crab dredging; one of the last buyboats built in Deltaville, Va.)

*Evelyn G.,* L. R. and Lennie Smith, Susan, Va., 1922, 52.9' × 11.8' × 4', gross 14, net 9, hull no. 234394.

*Evelyn K.,* Sidney Smith, Bena, Va., 1945, 53.4' × 17' × 6', gross 30, net 18, 125 hp, hull no. 249037. (Built for Willie E. King.)

*Excellent,* Bridgetown, Va., 1905, 52' × 18.9' × 4.2', gross 14, net 10, hull no. 202468. (Registered 1915, oystering, Cape Charles, Va.)

*\*F. D. Crockett,* Alexander Gaines, Seaford, Va., 1924, 55.8' × 15.7' × 4.6', gross 28, net 16, hull no. 223533. (A log deck boat built specifically for power for Ferdinand Desota Crockett of Seaford, Virginia; later owned by Edward M. Lindsay, freight, 1946, registered Newport News, Va.; David C. Wescott, fishing, 1994, Norfolk, Va.; still alive in 2003 and owned by Ron Turner of Poquoson, Va.)

*\*Fisherman,* E. J. Moore & Son, Crittenden, Va., 1921, 72.9', 22.2' × 5.5', gross 57, net 28; enlarged 1926, 96.2' × 23' × 5.6', gross 81, net 41, hull no. 221615. (Owned by J. H. Miles & Co., early engine 100 hp Fairbanks-Morse, registered Norfolk, Va., 1921, 1980, later named *Grey Cat.* Noah C. Carr, Jr., said *Fisherman* was moored in Deep Creek on the James River for many years before she was taken out in the Atlantic Ocean and sunk.)

*\*Fish Hawk,* Linwood P. Price, Amburg, Va., 1922, 55.4' × 15.3' × 4.8', gross 25, net 16, 36 hp, hull no. 222651. (Named *Pauline Parks,* 1963, and *Flora Jackie II,* 1978; registered Reedville, Va., 1923, 1929; Crisfield, Md., 1934.)

*Fish Hawk,* Saxis, Va., 1911, 49' × 12.6' × 3.1', gross 13, net 9, hull no. 208368. (Double-ender, registered 1915, freight, Cape Charles, Va.)

*\*Five Sisters,* Sandy Bottom, Va. (later called Deltaville), 1904, 55' × 16.6' × 4.5', gross 14, net 5, hull no. 200842. (Registered 1915, oystering, owned by Irvington Packing Co., 1946.)

*Flora Ellen,* Pocomoke, City, Md., 1899, 42.5' × 15' × 3.8', gross 10, net 6, hull no. 121106. (Registered 1915, freight, Norfolk, Va.)

*Flora Jackie II,* see *Fish Hawk*

*Florence,* Crittenden, Va., 1904, 46.1' × 16.9' × 3.9', gross 18, net 6, hull no. 201512. (Registered 1915, Petersburg, Pa.)

*Florence and Annie,* Galloway, Md., 1898, 45' × 12' × 3.6', gross 9, net 6, hull no. 121083. (Registered 1915, freight, Baltimore, Md.)

*Florence Marie,* Laban, Va., 1922, 56.6' × 15.1' × 5.2', gross 25, net 17, hull no. 221942. (Owned by Burley Hudgins, fishing, 1946.)

*Four Sisters,* Mattapex, Va., 1905, 45' × 13.5' × 3.8', gross 11, net 9, hull no. 202444. (Registered 1915, freight, Baltimore, Md.)

*Frances,* L. R. and Alton Smith, Susan, Va., 1913, 43.6' × 10.7' × 3.3', gross 8, net 5, hull no. 232043. (Owned by Joseph A. New, 1946, fishing, registered Newport News, Va.)

*Frances,* Linwood P. Price, Amburg, Va., 1925, 53.2' × 14.9' × 4.8', gross 26, net 15, hull no. 225253. (Owned by Mearl Crockett, 1946, freight, registered Crisfield, Md.; later owned by Whitelock Brothers of Smith Island, Md., renamed by them *Island Star.* Also owned by Alan Wade Tyler, freight, 225 hp, Crisfield, Md. When owned by Whitelock Brothers she was used for several years as the school boat for Smith Island children to travel from Ewell and Tylerton to Crisfield High School in Crisfield, Md. She was rebuilt to be used as a school boat by Herman Krentz of Harryhogan, Va. The boat was sold from Smith Island in the late 1990s to Jerry Pruitt, Tangier Island, 2002, oyster dredging.)

*Frances,* Shelltown, Md., 1914, 44.3' × 13.6' × 2.5', gross 12, net 8, hull no. 211922. (Registered 1915, freight, Crisfield, Md.)

*Frances T.,* Oxford, Md., 1926, 62.7' × 19.1' × 5.8', gross 52, net 35, hull no. 226044. (Owned by Stanley R. Harrison, 1946, freight, registered Cambridge, Md.)

*Freddie B.,* see *J. A. Wiley*

*Frederick H. Ayers,* Pocomoke City, Md., 1906, 52' × 15.4' × 3', gross 14, net 10, hull no. 203721. (Registered 1915, oystering, Cape Charles, Va.; 1929, J. M. Hudgins, Newport News, Va.; and 1946, R. A. Billups, Newport News, Va.)

*G. S. White,* Gilbert White, Westland, Va., 1923, 55.5' × 14.8' × 5.2', gross 28, net 13, hull no. 222904. (Named for the builder, originally built for Capt. Otis M. Crowther; later owned by Stephen N. Norris, Jr., 1994, 180 hp, Washington, D.C.; and W. G. Taylor, 1946, fishing, registered Reedville, Va.)

*G. T. Forbush,* C. H. Rice, Reedville, Va., 1951, 81.1' × 24.7' × 7.9', gross 125, net 108, hull no. 261822.

*Gaitor,* Gilbert White, Foxwells, Va., 1918, 42.5' × 11.2' × 3.9', gross 12, net 8, hull no. 235287. (Owned by F. Francis Yerby, 1946, fishing, registered Reedville, Va.)

*Gannet,* see *William Somers*

*Gentry,* Greenback, Va., 1901, 40.5' × 12.3' × 3.1', gross 10, net 7, hull no. 86588. (Owned by Hermon W. Birch, 1946, oystering, registered Cape Charles, Va.)

*\*Georgeanna,* see *Elsie Louise*

*Georgie E.,* Alton Smith, Susan, Va., 1944, 55.5' × 14.5' × 4.8', gross 24, net 16, hull no. 246784. (Later named *Captain Latane.*)

*\*Geraldine,* W. T. Smith, Achilles, Va., 1928, 44.4' × 12.7' × 4.5', gross 16, net 11, hull no. 227264. (Owned by W. H. Rowe, 1946, freight, registered Newport News, Va., named *Amy Carol,* 1975.)

*Gertrude,* Baltimore, Md., 1915, 48.9' × 16.6' × 5', gross 27, net 18, hull no. 213238. (Owned by Marine Laund Co., Md., 1946, Baltimore; Chester Rakowski, freight, 95 hp, registered Baltimore, Md.)

*\*Gilbert H.,* L. R. and Alton Smith, Susan, Va., 1938, 47.8' × 12.8' × 4.5', gross 15, net 10, hull no. 238108. (Owned by Boyd Hall, 1946, fishing; registered Newport News, Va., 1931–69; Norfolk, Va., 1973–76; scrapped, 1977; name changed to *Icylene III,* 1975.)

*\*Gilbert S.,* Ned Hudgins, Sarah, Va., 1914, 46.8' × 11.2' × 3.3', gross 9, net 6, hull no. 230504. (Owned by Guy Morgan, 1946, fishing, registered Newport News, Va.)

*Gloria R.,* Laban, Va., 1924, 48.1' × 12' × 4', gross 12, net 8, hull no. 231396. (Owned by Elwood E. Callis, Jr., in 1946, converted from open fish trap boat. Kenneth W. Williams said *Gloria R.* would "roll the soda out of a biscuit in a choppy sea.")

*Gloucester Beauty,* building location and date unknown, 45.5' × 12.7' × 4.1', gross 16, net 8, hull no. 228106. (Owned by L. M. Marshall, Glass, Va., 1929, and W. C. Allen, fishing; registered at Cape Charles, Va.)

*Grace,* Lepron Johnson, Crittenden, Va., 1906, 45' × 12.8' × 3.1', gross 15, net 12, hull no. 203662. (Owned by Clyde Green, Remlik, Va., early engine 24 hp.)

*Grace,* Urbanna, Va., 1903, 39' × 14' × 3.5', gross 14, net 9, hull no. 200318. (Registered 1915, freight, Baltimore Md.)

*Gracie Lee,* Lee Deagle, Deltaville, Va., staved stern. (Built for Alvin Daniels, Urbanna Va., haul-seine fishing.)

*Grey Cat,* see *Fisherman*

*Grover G.,* Linwood P. Price, Amburg, Va., 1923, 43.9' × 13.3' × 4.4', gross 16, net 10, hull no. 222905. (Owned by Richard Monroe Crockett, 1946, oystering, registered Crisfield, Md.)

*H. C. Drewer,* Linwood P. Price, Amburg, Va., 1926, 59.8' × 20' × 6.6', gross 54, net 37, hull no. 225597. (Owned by Duncan Brothers, 1946, freight, registered Crisfield, Md.)

*Hamilton,* Tappahannock, Va., 1906, 51' × 11' × 4.1', gross 10, net 5, hull no. 203164. (Registered 1915, oystering, Reedville, Va.)

*\*Harold,* John E. Wright, Deltaville, Va., 1925, 49.3' × 13.2' × 4.9', gross 20, net 9, hull no. 224548. (Owned by J. A. Rowe, and later by Morris Snow and Alton Smith.)

*Harriett,* (J. J. Hardy of Hardyville, Va., worked aboard her in 1920s. Converted to yacht, owned by Willard Wake, 36 hp, two cylinder Lathrop Engine.)

*\*Harvey A. Drewer,* Percy H. Linton, Pocomoke City, Md. 1949, 60.5' × 18.3' × 5.1', gross 33, net 28, hull no. 258790. (Owned by H. V.

Drewer and Son, official number card states that the vessel was built for Vernon Drewer, Crisfield, Md., oystering, 140 hp, registered Crisfield, Md.)

*Hasel C.,* Enoch, Va., 1910, 43' × 14' × 3.6', gross 9, net 7, hull no. 207945.

*Hattie B.,* Cowart, Va., 1911, 58.5' × 13.5' × 4', gross 19, net 13, hull no. 208383. (Owned by H. P. McNeal, freight, 1929, Fairport, Va., registered Reedville, Va.; George U. Lewis, from Cape Charles, fishing, 1946, registered Reedville, Va.; frame built and planked lengthwise.)

*Hawsie B.,* Linwood P. Price, Ruark, Va., 1932, 60.8' × 20.4' × 7.1', gross 58, net 41, hull no. 231395. (Owned by Richard W. Christy, freight, 1946, Crisfield, Md., later Rudy Thomas; owned by Zapata Haynie Corp., fishing, 275 hp, registered Reedville, Va.; engine room controlled/reversible diesel. "It was the only boat I knew that had a safe aboard to hold stock money for buying oysters," said Steve Pruitt.)

*\*Henrietta Frances,* E. James Tull, Pocomoke City, Md., 1923, 90.3' × 22' × 7.9', gross 102, net 69, hull no. 223003. (Owned by Dan Dize, Smith Island, Md., early engine 100 hp; registered Crisfield, Md. 1923–29; Wilmington Del., 1933; Cambridge, Md., 1973; sold to a Honduran citizen, 1977.) "She was an ugly damn boat with a real high bow," said Jonesey Payne. "He ran a lot of grain on her."

*Henrietta Hearn,* Wingate, Md., 1925, 51.4' × 11.8' × 3.4', gross 12, net 8, hull no. 225011. (Owned by Howard Gambrill, fishing, 1946, registered Annapolis, Md.)

*Herman M. Krentz,* Herman M. Krentz, Kayan, Va., 1928, 52.9' × 15' × 5.5', gross 28, net 12, hull no. 228173. (Owned by Grover C. Lewis, fishing, 1946, registered Reedville, Va.; later owned by Ryland Gaskins, named after the builder; pilothouse is at Reedville Fisherman's Museum in Reedville, Va.)

*\*Hilda,* O. W. Payne, Palmer, Va., 1917, 46.8' × 13' × 3.5', gross 15, net 6, 16 hp, hull no. 221399. (Owned by D. A. Cockrell, fishing, 1946, Reedville, Va.)

*Howard James,* Linwood P. Price, Amburg, Va., 1912, 47' × 12' × 3.9', gross 13, net 8, hull no. 209917. (Early engine, 20 hp.)

*Icylene III,* see *Gilbert S.*

*\*Inez,* Russell Carroll Parker, Wake, Va., 1936, 59.9' × 20.2' × 6.3', gross 48, net 29, 50 hp, hull no. 235551. (Owned by Ballard Fish & Oyster Co. in 1946 and Impeca De Puerto Rico Inc., in 1994; registered Newport News, Va., 1936; Norfolk, Va., 1970; Baltimore, Md., 1974; Key West, Fl., 1982; Miami, 1984; Miami, deleted and redocumented, 1986.)

*Irene,* Palmer, Va., 1916, 58.6' × 13.2' × 4', gross 23, net 13, hull no. 213894. (Owned by L. E. Robertson, 1929, fishing.)

*Irene & Pearl,* Patchogue, N.Y., 1898, 55' × 16' × 4', gross 26, net 12, hull no. 155331. (Listed as a "steam screw oysterman," owned by Isaac Fass, 1929, freight, registered Portsmouth, Va.; later owned by Chesapeake Corp. of Virginia, West Point, Va., 1945.)

*\*Irene & Pearl II,* John E. Wright, Deltaville, Va., 1931, 54.6' × 16.5' × 5.7', gross 31, net 17, 60 hp, hull no. 231036. (Owned by J. A. Templeman, fishing, 1946, registered Norfolk, Va.; and Milton Parks of Tangier Island, fishing, 400 hp, GM diesel, registered Norfolk, Va., 1931.)

*Irma Virginia,* L. R. and Alton Smith, Susan, Va., 1934, 52.3' × 15.5' × 4.8', gross 33, net 24, hull no. 233551.

*Isaetta,* Gilbert White, Foxwells, Va., 1921, 51.7' × 15.5' × 5.2', gross 25, net 13, hull no. 221420. (Owned by T. V. Fitchett, Palmer, Va., registered Reedville, Va.)

*\*Island Belle,* Noah T. Evans, Ewell, Md., 1917, 46.8' × 13.3' × 3.3', gross 20, net 13, 24 hp, registered Crisfield, Md., 1917–71, hull no.

215843. (Owned by John E. Whitelock, 1929, passenger, and later Benjamin E. Whitelock, 1946, passenger.)

*Island Star,* see *Frances,* hull no. 225253.

*Island Town.* (Draketail stern, owned by Henry Hawkins of Tangier Island, freighted oysters and fish to Washington and Baltimore.)

*Isle of Surry,* Lepron Johnson, Crittenden, Va., 1911, 60.1' × 17.5' × 6.3', gross 38, net 16, hull no. 209257. (Owned by Preston Mooney, freight, 1929, registered Elizabeth City, N.C.)

*Isle of Wright,* Crittenden, Va., 1926, 59.8' × 24.2' × 7.7', gross 62, net 42, hull no. 225572. (Owned by J. Q. Adams, ferry, 1929, Eclipse, Va.)

*Isle of York,* John and Kirby Smith, Dare, Va., 1925, 49.2' × 14.4' × 4.5', gross 19, net 7, hull no. 224616. (Log boat, owned by L. V. Forrest, Messick, Va., fishing, 1929, registered Newport News, Va.)

*Iva W.,* John E. Wright, Deltaville, Va., 1929, 55.4' × 16.5' × 4.9', gross 30, net 20, hull no. 229217. (Owned by Captain Johnny Ward of Deltaville, converted to a double-decker in 2001, powered by 60 hp four-cylinder Atlas engine.) "When daddy first got her from John Wright, she moved a little bit when she had a load on her, so daddy got Ladd and William Wright to put sister keelsons into her and that stopped her from moving. She needed a little more backbone down there. They put 6-inch planks one on each side of the main keelson [that ran from just below the stem to just below the stern]. They used foot adz and plane and put her in an oval board to fit it and when they hauled it up they spiked the bottom from the underside to the two 6-inch planks," said Melvin Ward, eldest son of Johnny Ward.

*J. A. Wiley,* Solomons, Md., 1912, 68.4' × 15.3' × 5', gross 40, net 34, hull no. 209620. (Registered 1915, Reedville, Va., owned by G. E. Bowen, Fairport, Va., freight, 1929; and Snow Shipyards Inc., Rockland, Maine, freight, 1946. She was cut in half and enlarged to make *Freddie B.*)

*J. C. Drewer,* Linwood P. Price, Ruark, Va., 1929, 60.5' × 19' × 6.2', gross 44, net 30, hull no. 228850. (Owned by R. D. Ailsworth, early engine 45 hp.)

*\*J. D. Marsh,* B. F. Tull, Tylerton, Md., 1921, 51.5' × 11.1' × 4.1', gross 15, net 10, hull no. 221733. (Owned by Benjamen F. Evans, freight, 30 hp, registered Crisfield, Md., abandoned November 4, 1946.)

*J. E. Sterling,* Linwood P. Price, Amburg, Va., 1923, 56.8' × 15.7' × 5.3', gross 33, net 24, hull no. 223339. (Owned by E. F. Wise, freight, 25 hp, Elizabeth City, N.C.)

*J. E. Stevens,* building location unknown and date unknown, 51.3' × 11.6' × 3.5', gross 13, net 8, hull no. 225922. (Owned by John W. Thomas, freight, 1929, Tangier Island, registered Cape Charles, Va.)

*J. H. Steele,* Solomons, Md., 1916, 84.7' × 22.5' × 6.7', gross 106, net 59, hull no. 214081. (Owned by Reinauer Fuel Transportation Corp. of New York, registered Newark, N.J.)

*\*J. M. Tolley,* Mitchell Hubbard, Hudson, Md., 1926, 58' × 18.8' × 6', gross 41, net 28, 45 hp, hull no. 225884. (Owned by J. M. Tolley, freight, 1929, registered Cambridge, Md.; burned at pier at Hooper Island, Md., 1941.)

*\*J. Q. Adams,* Jos. Edmonds, Eclipse, Va., 1915, 45' × 14.3' × 3.4', gross 13, net 6, 37 hp, hull no. 213584. (Owned by J. Q. Adams, Jr., Eclipse, Va., freight, registered Norfolk, Va., 1915–31; Savannah, Ga., 1942; lost by fire at Vernon View Cut, Ga., May 25, 1943.)

*\*J. S. Taylor,* Linwood P. Price, Moore Creek, Va., 1919, 52.2' × 13.1' × 4', gross 19, net 12, hull no. 219266. (Owned by William H. Smith, freight, 1929, Ottoman, Va.; registered Norfolk Va., 1919–20; Reedville, Va., 1924–31; abandoned November 23, 1937. Moore

Creek is a small creek on the Piankatank River near Amburg, Va., where Price built boats.)

*J. T. Moore*, Poquoson, Va., 1913, 48.5' × 15.8' × 5', gross 20, net 9, hull no. 211797. (Owned by M. G. Brown, towing, 1929, Edenton, N.C., registered Elizabeth City, N.C.; lost February 8, 1939.)

*\*J. V. Davenport*, Herman M. Krentz, Kayan, Va., 1929, 61.6' × 20.5' × 6.9', gross 56, net 26, 50 hp, hull no. 228460. (Owned by J. W. Davenport, freight, 1929, registered Reedville, Va.)

*J. V. Shipley*, Linwood Price, Amburg, Va., 1921, 57.6' × 16.7' × 5.5', gross 36, net 20, hull no. 221690. (Owned by B. G. Willis, freight, 1929, Edenton, N.C., registered Elizabeth City, N.C.)

*J. W. Vane*, Cambridge, Md., 1929, 49.1' × 12' × 3.4', gross 10, net 7, hull no. 224898. (Owned by John W. Vane, 1929, registered Cambridge, Md.)

*James*, Crittenden, Va., 1922, 58.7' × 16.2' × 4', gross 21, net 13, hull no. 221898. (Owned by Pennsylvania-Dixie Cement Corp., freight, 1929, Delaware, registered Washington, D.C.)

*James Aubry*, Solomons, Md., 1925, 44.2' × 10.3' × 2.9' gross 11, net 8, hull no. 225103. (Passenger, Isaac H. Hill, registered Annapolis, Md.)

*James J.*, Linwood P. Price, Ruark, Va., 1926, 46.6' × 12.2' × 4.6', gross 17, net 10, hull no. 226099. (Owned by L. P. Price & Co., freight, 1929, Ruark, Va., registered Norfolk, Va.; later H. F. Dryden, freight, 1946, registered Norfolk, Va.)

*James J. Minot*, see *Edith S. Wilkins*

*\*James J. Murray*, E. James Tull, Pocomoke City, Md., 1921, 61.3' × 20.9' × 7.5', gross 53, net 36, 110 hp, hull no. 221594. (Owned by Anna R. Murray, freight, 1929; registered New York, N.Y., 1921–77; abandoned 1939, redocumented, 1939; deleted 1986.)

*James Thomas*, Messick, Va., 1923, 45.3' × 12.1' × 3.4', gross 10, net 6, hull no. 223201. (Owned by J. C. Diggs, fishing, 1929, Messick, Va., registered Newport News, Va.)

*Jamie*, West Norfolk, Va., 1920, 52.5' × 16' × 5.5', gross 31, net 20, hull no. 219788. (Owned by Evelyn M. Gibbs, freight, 1929, Elizabeth City, N.C.)

*Janet*, Pocomoke City, Md., 1921, 49.1' × 14.6' × 6.7', gross 24, net 16, hull no. 221236. (Owned by Ten STD Dredging Co., New Jersey, registered New York, N.Y.)

*Janice*, John F. Smith, Dare, Va., 1930, 57.3' × 18.2' × 5', gross 31, net 14, hull no. 230064. (Owned by Moody L. Tillage, freight, Gloucester Point, Va., and later Noah C. Carr, Jr., of Glass, Va., named for Janice Anderton. The boat was conscripted during World War II and used as a fireboat at Charleston, S.C. It is believed to have been rebuilt from *Sunflower*, which was originally *Thomas J. Jackson*, built in 1877 in Middlesex County, Va. *Janice* was rebuilt at Smith Marine Railway in Dare, Va., in 1930.)

*Jas. Roper*, Norfolk, Va., 1924, 52.2' × 14.2' × 4.8', gross 23, net 11, hull no. 223946. (Owned by Noah G. Evans, freight, 1929, registered Crisfield, Md.)

*\*Jeff*, Wilfred Tyler, Honga, Md., 1923, 64.7' × 20.5' × 6.5', gross 59, net 40, 65 hp, hull no. 223148. (Owned by Phillips Packing Co., freight, 1929, Cambridge, Md.; registered Baltimore, Md., 1923; Cambridge, Md., 1924–31; abandoned New Orleans, La., November 20, 1950.)

*Jennie & James*, Severn, Va., 1913, 50.6' × 13.4' × 4.2', gross 14, net 7, hull no. 210898. (Owned by S. Shackelford, fishing, 1929, Severn, Va., registered Newport News, Va.)

*\*Jennie and Josie*, B. A. Croasdale, Whitestone, Va., 1906, 47.2' × 13.8' × 4', gross 14, net 6, hull no. 221366. (Owned by B. A. Croasdale, fishing, 1929, Palmer, Va., original 12 hp, registered Reedville, Va.)

*Jennie Dare*, Gilbert White, Foxwells, Va., 1926, 65.8' × 16' × 4.8', gross 36, net 23, hull no. 225439. (Owned by E. Odell Fitchett on Potomac, deepwater pound-net fishing; enlarged to 75' by Gilbert White; used as a breakwater at Fitchett's Landing at the mouth of Antipoison Creek). "I'd like to have had the money she has made," said Steve Pruitt.

*\*Jennie May*, Carters Creek Railway Co., Irvington, Va., 1928, 59.7' × 17' × 6.2', gross 41, net 28, hull no. 227855. (Owned by R. E. Dobyne, freight, 1929, Monaskon, Va., registered Reedville, Va.; later by B. C. Burton, fishing, original 50 hp, Reedville, Va.; abandoned near Washington, N.C., in 1981.)

*\*Jessie*, Jack Smith, Perrin, Va., 1928, 49.9' × 15.7' × 5.7', gross 26, net 16, hull no. 227955. (Owned by N.C. Carr, hauled watermelons and oystering, 1929, Glass, Va., four-cylinder Atlas engine.)

*Jessie Lewis*, Quinsy, Va., 1901, 57' × 16' × 4.5', gross 18, net 13, hull no. 77497. (Owned by W. J. Bradshaw, fishing, towing, crab dredging, 1946, registered Newport News, Va. "Ugly bow with an old raked stem," said Steve Pruitt.)

*Jessie Taylor*, Dighton Taylor, Deep Creek, Va., 1915, 57.5' × 14.7' × 4.6', gross 22, net 19, hull no. 213081. (Owned by L. Chelton Evans, freight, 170 hp, Crisfield, Md., 1946. Named after Dighton Taylor's son Jessie, who owned and crab dredged in the boat.)

*\*John Hardy Jr.*, Allen E. Witman, Crisfield, Md., 1925, originally 35.4' × 12.5' × 3.8', gross 10, net 7, enlarged in 1932 to 47.8' × 13.2' × 3.8', gross 16, net 10, hull no. 224498. (Owned by Nelson B. Coulbourn, Crisfield, Md.)

*\*John Howard*, Herman M. Krentz, Crisfield, Md., 1928, 52.7' × 12.7' × 3.5', gross 14, net 8, hull no. 228461. (Owned by John West Charnock, 1946, freight, draketail stern, Superia diesel. Registered Reedville,Va., 1929–49.) "She was a pretty draketail and she had pretty lines, but she was built thin. She leaked terrible. Over her lifetime she had the Chesapeake Bay pumped out of her thirty times," said Steve Pruitt. "You know how a draketail is—they have a four-foot tail on 'em, great for a swimming platform. As a kid I would swim off her stern. The captain would let us swim off her draketail if we pumped the hand pump 100 times. When there were five of us we'd pump 500 times. She had pretty lines."

*John T. Powell*, Wachapreague, Va., 1901, 61.9' × 17.3' × 4.3', gross 20, net 13, hull no. 77509. (Owned by J. K. Coats, 1946, freight, Cape Charles, Va.)

*Josephine*, Solomons, Md., 1922, 70' × 21' × 7.5', gross 84, net 45, hull no. 222490. (Owned by Edwin N. Cooling, freight, 1929, Chesapeake City, Md., registered Baltimore, Md.)

*Josephine and Margaret*, Ironsides, Md., 1922, 50.7' × 15.6' × 5', gross 25, net 17, hull no. 221955. (Owned by Robert Hope Raleigh, Jr., oystering, 25 hp, registered Baltimore, Md.)

*Josie*, Crab Neck, Va., 1907, 48' × 13' × 4.3', gross 12, net 7, hull no. 204603. (Registered Newport News, Va., 1915.)

*\*Joyce Sterling*, Linwood P. Price, Ruark, Va., 1930, 59.2' × 17.8' × 5.8', gross 43, net 29, hull no. 230274. (Owned by Freddie K. Pruitt of Tangier Island and had an uppercase P on the smokestack for Pruitt; early engine 36 hp, later 85 hp, registered Reedville, Va. Pruitt renamed her *Anthony Klein*, 1963.)

*Juanita*, Pocomoke City, Md., 1906, 57' × 16' × 3.7', gross 15, net 11, hull no. 203446. (Registered Newport News, Va., 1915.)

*Juanita*, Russell Carroll Parker, Wake, Va., 1926, 60.8' × 17.7' × 5.2', gross 39, net 23, hull no. 226094. (Built near Mill Creek Steamboat Dock on Rappahannock River and used by Parker for freighting watermelons. Owned by Marguerite Phillips, 1946, freight, Crisfield, Md.; Charles W. Marsh, freight, 165 hp, registered Crisfield, Md. Named for Juanita Parker, the builder's daughter.)

*Jude and Neva*, see *Alice & Annie*

*Julia G.*, Crittenden, Va., 1910, 47' × 16.9' × 4', gross 18, net 12, hull no. 207591. (Registered Norfolk, Va., 1915.)

*\*Julian*, O. W. Payne, Palmer, Va., 1938, 61.7' × 17.1' × 5.7', gross 43, net 31, hull no. 237830. (Later named *Callis Brothers* and owned by Lewis A. Callis; owned by Emory Kellum of Weems and captained by Morris Snow, 200 hp.)

*Karibou*, Salisbury, Md., 1911, 61' × 12.4' × 7.3', gross 28, net 15, hull no. 209293. (Owned by R. H. Mooring, freight, 1929, registered Newport News, Va., formerly a yacht from Georgia named *Lebanon*.)

*Kathleen II*, see *Midland*

*Katie S.*, Linwood P. Price, Amburg, Va., 1922, 51' × 14.1' × 4.7', gross 20, net 13, hull no. 222311. (Owned by William G. Parks, freight, 24 hp, registered Cambridge, Md.)

*L. R. Smith*, L. R. and Alton Smith, Susan, Va., 1926, 56.4' × 13.2' × 5.1', gross 20, net 11, hull no. 225302. (Owned by Everett Owens, fishing, 115 hp, registered Newport News, Va., named after boatbuilder Lennie R. Smith of Mathews County. "She was originally built for Henry Armstead by Lennie Smith. When Smith asked Armstead what he wanted to name the boat, Armstead said 'I don't give a damn what you name her.' So, Smith named the boat after himself. She was an open pound boat and owned by Eugene Armstead of Mathews County, but when Captain Henry Owens bought the boat he decked her over to make a crab-dredge boat," said Robert Roland Hudgins. "She was a small boat but they cut her off and enlarged her to make her deeper. She had a real sharp bow. She was a fast boat." *L. R. Smith* also spent time in Georgia waters where she was used to transport building materials from the mainland to islands being developed. She came back to the Chesapeake and was used to haul bait and supplies on Tangier Island. Today, she is moored at Jennings Boatyard in Fairport, Va., in need of work and repair.

*L. T. Boggs*, Onancock, Va., 1903, 44' × 13.5' × 3', gross 8, net 6, hull no. 141846. (Owned by J. R. Callis, Deltaville, Va., fishing, 1929, registered Reedville, Va.)

*Lady May*, Keeler, Va., 1901, 48' × 11.7' × 4.3', gross 19, net 11, hull no. 141755. (Owned by George E. Coghill, freight, 1929, registered Norfolk, Va.)

*Lady Sarah*, see *Wanda*

*\*Lagonia*, Jas. H. Moore, Poquoson, Va., 1913, 44.3' × 11.7' × 4.4', gross 11, net 7, 25 hp, hull no. 211586. (Log boat, owned by Captain Johnny Ward in Deltaville early 1920s and W. E. Parker, 1946, Crisfield, Md. Registered Newport News, Va., 1913; Crisfield, Md., 1921–23; Reedville, Va., 1923; Crisfield, Md., 1934; Norfolk, Va., 1974.)

*\*Lagrange*, Urbanna, Va., 1906, 47.6' × 11.7' × 4.4', gross 9, net 6, hull no. 203397. (Used for oystering, 1915, registered Reedville; owned by John Franklin Green, freight, 1929, registered Reedville. Named after Lagrange Creek on south side of Rappahannock River. Green lived in Remlik, Va., which is on Lagrange Creek.)

*\*Lancaster*, O. W. Payne, Palmer, Va., 1920, 45.6' × 15.3' × 4.1', gross 18, net 9, hull no. 219727. (Owned by Warren Denton Co., fishing, 36 hp, registered Annapolis, Md.; registered Norfolk, Va., 1920–28; Newport News, Va., 1934; Washington, D.C., 1980; deleted 1983.)

*Lavenia Anne*, Crittenden, Va., 1928, 47.4' × 13.4' × 3.7', gross 17, net 6, hull no. 228073. (Owned by F. W. Moore, fishing, 1929, registered Newport News, Va.; W. W. Joyner, fishing, 1946, registered Newport News, Va.)

*Lavenia H.*, Alton Smith, Susan, Va., 1946, 52.3' × 13.5' × 4.6', gross 19, net 9, hull no. 251598. (Owned by Alton Wyatt, freight, 1946, registered Philadelphia, Pa.)

*\*Lavinia D.*, Lorenzo Dow Moger, Eclipse, Va., 1913, 49.1' × 15' × 3.6', gross 17, net 9, hull no. 211504. (Owned by Thomas M. Campbell, 1929, registered New York, N.Y.; Spearin, Preston & Burrows, towing, 1946, registered New York, N.Y.; registered Newport News, 1913–20; Baltimore, Md., 1921; Boston, Mass., 1922–25; New York, N.Y., 1925–49.)

*\*Lawson*, Gilbert S. White, Westland, Va., 1929, 61.1' × 15.7' × 4.2', gross 25, net 16, hull no. 228217. (Converted to a pleasure boat and moored in Reedville, Va., 2003. Early engine was 40 hp owned by Elwood K. Turner, fishing, registered Reedville, Va., 1929, renamed *Mundy Point*, 1966.)

*Lebanon*, see *Karibou*

*\*Lelia James*, Palmer, Va., 1922, 60.1' × 15.5' × 4.4', gross 25, net 18, hull no. 221956. (Owned by Jim Robertson, fishing, 1946, Reedville, Va.)

*Lena May*, Peary, Va., 1926, 47.7' × 12.7' × 4.5', gross 16, net 7, hull no. 225464. (Owned by N. F. Deal, 1946.)

*Lester*, Poquoson, Va., 1912, 45.6' × 11.3' × 4.2', gross 10, net 9, hull no. 211190. (Log boat, owned by Elisha "Captain Lish" Pruitt, freight, 20 hp, registered Cape Charles, Va.)

*Lidia B.*, L. R. and Alton Smith, Susan, Va., 1924, 52.6' × 12.6' × 3.9', gross 14, net 9, hull no. 232105. (Owned by John T. White, fishing, 1946, registered Newport News, Va.)

*\*Lillian Ruth*, Charles A. Dana, Crisfield, Md., 1923, 63.5' × 17.6' × 5.9', gross 46, net 24; enlarged August 28, 1937, 63.6' × 18.2' × 6.9', gross 50, net 40, 60 hp, hull no. 223343. (Owned by Ben Nash, Kinsale, Va., registered Crisfield, Md., 1923; Reedville, Va., 1927–37; West Palm Beach, Fla., 1965; transferred to British flag, 1966.)

*Lillian T.*, Linwood P. Price, Ruark Va., 1928, 55.5' × 16.9' × 4.6', gross 28, net 14, hull no. 227769. (Owned by R. D. Ailsworth, 1946, and later owned by Richard Burton Parks, Jr., freight, 125 hp, Tangier Island.)

*Lillie May*, Gilbert White, Foxwells, Va., 1920, 43.6' × 11.7' × 3.4', gross 10, net 7, hull no. 233724. (Owned by Otis Crowther, fishing, 1946, Reedville, Va.)

*Lina*, Deep Creek, Va., 1910, 43.6' × 14.8' × 3.6', gross 15, net 10, hull no. 208093. (Owned by C. Taylor Slaughter, passenger, 1946, registered Reedville, Va.)

*Linda Carol*, see *Croaker*

*Lindberg*, Seaford, Va., 1928, 47.4' × 14.5' × 3.4', gross 16, net 8, hull no. 228010. (Owned by M. D. White, fishing, 1929, Seaford, registered Newport News, Va.; John T. Crockett, fishing, 1946, registered Newport News, Va.)

*Little Kent.* (Owned by Homer Pruitt, frame built, worked day and night; used at night for towing and crab dredging by day out of Tangier Island.)

*Little River*, see *Mildred*

*Lois*, Eclipse, Va., 1927, 43.7' × 12.5' × 3.5', gross 11, net 7, hull no. 235193. (B. B. Winall, 1946, oystering, registered Norfolk, Va.)

*Lois*, Laban, Va., 1924, 48' × 12.5' × 4.1', gross 14, net 9, hull no. 231299. (Owned by W. H. Brownley, fishing, 1946, Newport News, Va.)

*Lola Mae*, Crab Neck, Va., 1907, 48.8' × 13.4' × 4.4', gross 13, net 5, hull no. 204545. (Owned by Wm. Huggett, oystering, 1946, registered Newport News, Va.)

*Lona B.*, Laban, Va., 1929, 48.4' × 12.9' × 4.3', gross 14, net 9, hull no. 231384. (Owned by M. H. Lumpkin, fishing, 1946, Reedville, Va.)

*Lora Lee.* (Built in Elizabeth City, N.C., and was the first deck boat in Crisfield harbor to have a head installed. She had an old Winston engine and belonged to William "Winnie" Pruitt. Named for Winnie's daughter who incidentally spelled her name Laura Lee but the boat is named *Lora Lee*. Engine room controls but later got pilothouse controls. She was confiscated by the U. S. Coast Guard in a rum-running incident and used by U.S.C.G. for many years. Winnie purchased the boat from the Coast Guard and Bill Pruitt, Winnie's son, recalls when she first arrived at Tangier Island she was painted completely black and had no mast.

*Lorena,* (unknown builder and location), 37.1' × 10.3' × 3.6', gross 7, net 5, hull no. 235596. (Owned by Andrew Crockett, oystering, 18 hp, registered Reedville, Va.)

*Lorie Robins,* see *C. E. Wright*

*Louise J.,* Linwood P. Price, Ruark, Va., 1926, 59.3' × 19.9' × 6.6', gross 56, net 33, hull no. 226187. (Owned by Thomas "Captain Tom" Yates Johnston, Amburg, Va., freight; later by Harold W. Holcomb, 1946, freight, Miami, Fl.)

*\*Lucy R. Ruark,* H. W. Ruark, Fishing Creek, Md., 1913, 42.4' × 12.7' × 3.7', gross 15, net 8, 20 hp, hull no. 311783. (Round stern, decked over with a tiny house. Registered Crisfield, Md., 1913; Cape Charles, 1920; Reedville, Va., 1921; Baltimore, Md., 1934; Reedville, Va., 1971; dismantled Beaufort-Morehead City, N.C., 1976.)

*Lucy V.,* Fisherman, Va., 1912, 51.4' × 13' × 4.4', gross 17, net 11, hull no. 218359.

*\*Lydia,* Alonzo P. Conley, Oxford, Md., 1927, 62.3' × 20.9' × 6.8', gross 61, net 42, hull no. 226314. (Owned by Gordon A. Pope, freight, 60 hp; later Hodges Crouch, 1946, freight; registered Baltimore, Md., 1927–37, named *Narcissus,* 1971.)

*M. B. Wright,* John Wright, Sandy Bottom, Va., 1905, 52.4' × 12.2' × 3.7', gross 16, net 11, hull no. 201875. (Owned by John Wright, named after his wife Mabel Blanche Wright, powered by 15 hp White-Middleton gasoline engine, lumber and freight; later owned by Edwin C. Smith, freight, 1946, 25 hp, registered Crisfield, Md.)

*M. S. Watson.* (Photographed by Audrey Bodine at Crisfield drawbridge.) No other information found.

*Mabel,* Hopkins, Va., 1904, 54' × 11.6' × 4', gross 15, net 10, hull no. 201172. (Owned by R. M. Watkins, Jr., fishing, 1946, registered Newport News, Va., registered 1915, freighter.)

*Maleta,* North Beach, Md., 53.4' × 16.7' × 3.8', gross 24, net 16, hull no. 209823. (Registered 1915, freight, Annapolis, Md.)

*Mamie J.,* Linwood P. Price, Ruark, Va., 1925, 50.4' × 13.4' × 4.7', gross 23, net 16, hull no. 225136. (Owned by James L. Jordon, passenger, 1929, original 24 hp, registered Annapolis, Md.)

*Manfield L.,* Denbigh, Va., 1922, 38.9' × 11.1' × 3.3', gross 10, net 5, hull no. 234642. (Owned by B. O. Brock, 1946, freight, registered Newport News, Va. Used in Potomac River pound-net fishery in 2002 and owned by Gaskin's Seafood of Ophelia, Va.)

*\*Margaret,* Crisfield, Md., 1909, 36' × 11' × 3.2', gross 8, net 6; enlarged for freight, 1915, to 45' × 11.3' × 3', gross 10, net 6, hull no. 207115. (Registered Crisfield, Md., 1910–16; Newport News, Va., 1918; abandoned, 1920; reissued Newport News, Va., 1921; Norfolk, Va. 1922; Crisfield, 1923–43; abandoned, 1947.)

*Margaret,* L. E. and Alton Smith, Susan, Va., 1925, 53.5' × 13.4' × 4.3', gross 15, net 10, hull no. 226232. (Owned by F. M. Hudgins, 1946).

*Margaret,* Norfolk, Va., 1911, 59.3' × 10.5' × 3.9', hull no. 209421. (Registered 1915, fishing, Norfolk, Va.; owned by L. W. Insley, freight, 1929, Salisbury, Md., registered Crisfield, Md.; and Harry W. Smith, 1946, registered Crisfield, Md.)

*Margaret,* White Stone, Va., 1912, 50.1' × 13.9' × 4.6', gross 9, net 6, hull no. 209610. (Owned by Hale & Harris Seafood, Inc., Md., freight, 200 hp, registered Baltimore Md.; later owned by J. S. Barnett, 1946).

*Margarett Bell,* Lepron Johnson, Crittenden, Va., 1924, 59.9' × 18' × 4.4', gross 29, net 12, hull no. 223743. (Owned by Floyd Thompson, 1946.)

*Margarette,* Pocomoke City, Md., 52' × 14.6' × 3.5', gross 13, net 10, hull no. 202114. (Registered 1915, oystering, Cape Charles, Va.)

*Marion H.,* see *Evelyn*

*Marion J.,* Bena, Va., 1925, 50.6' × 15.2' × 4.1', gross 20, net 7, hull no. 225262. (Early 50 hp engine. Owned by Joseph A. Mazacco, towing, 225 hp, New York, N.Y.) "Gannie Crockett owned her on Tangier Island and she sank off Watts Island in Chesapeake Bay," said Steve Pruitt.

*\*Marion Sue Handy,* James E. Daugherty, Crisfield, Md., 1924, originally 41.3' × 14' × 4.1', gross 14, net 10, hull no. 223650. (Enlarged in 1927, 51.6' × 14.2' × 4.7', gross 21, net 14, owned by Charlie Pruitt, Tangier Island, 1946, 25 hp engine, deleted from registration book in 1983 in Miami, Fla.)

*Martha Virginia,* Deltaville, Va., 1940, 39' × 11.9' × 3.6', gross 9, net 6, hull no. 240190. (Owned by Vernon W. Crockett, 1946, fishing, Reedville, Va.; later owned by Eddie Gaskins of Ophelia, Va., pound-net fishing; burn pile 2001.)

*Martha W.,* Battery Park, Va., 1905, 44.6' × 16' × 4.3', gross 18, net 5, hull no. 202104. (Registered 1915, freight, Norfolk, Va.)

*Mary,* Gilbert White, Foxwells, Va., 1921, 42.8' × 11.9' × 3.6', gross 11, net 7, hull no. 233698. (Owned by Ray R. Rose, 1946, fishing. Converted from an open boat to a deck boat around 1966 by Walter Boyd Hurley, Urbanna, Va. Still alive 2002 around Cobb Island, Md., registered to Henry Klein.)

*Mary Ann II,* Alton Smith, Susan, Va., 1945, 57.6' × 14.7' × 5.4', gross 26, net 12, hull no. 249048. (Owned by J. L. Hutson, 1946.) "Built as an open pound-net boat but later decked over and made into a deck boat." said Willis Wilson.

*\*Mary A. Sharp,* Sharps, Va., 1908, 65' × 14' × 5.3', gross 24, net 14, hull no. 208097. (Named after Mary Ann Sharp, wife of DeWitt Clinton Sharp, of Sharps, Va., registered Tappahannock, Va., 1910; Reedville, Va., 1914–17; Norfolk, Va., 1925; Savannah, Ga., 1925–32; Tampa, Fla., 1933–34; abandoned 1944.)

*Mary Carlisle,* Chuckatuck, Va., 1906, 51' × 14.8' × 4.5', gross 16, net 14, hull no. 203588. (Registered 1915, freight, Norfolk, Va.)

*Mary Colmon,* Perrin, Va., 1924, 54.5' × 19.3' × 4.5', gross 31, net 18, hull no. 224131. (Early engine, 45 hp.)

*\*Marydel,* Linwood P. Price, Ruark, Va., 1927, 97.6' × 28.2' × 7.7', gross 171, net 116, hull no. 227063. (The largest deck boat built on Chesapeake Bay, owned by W. E. Valliant & Co. Delaware, 1946, early power 120 hp, freight, sank near York Spit Channel, 37°15'N lat., 76°09'W long., on January 3, 1970, registered Baltimore, Md., 1927; Wilmington, Del., 1937–70.)

*Mary E. Haynie,* Linwood P. Price, Amburg, Va., 1924, 56.3' × 16.4' × 5.6', gross 35, net 20, hull no. 224375. (Owned by Capt. Charles Crockett, Lance Fisher, and later owned by Lewis A. Callis, fishing, 165 hp, registered Reedville, Va. When telephones arrived on Tangier Island in September 1966, the vessel was used by Western Electric Co. and Chesapeake and Potomac Telephone Co. of Virginia to bring over cable and supplies. She was lost on October 7, 1981, off York Spit in Chesapeake Bay with a load of seed oysters.)

*\*Mary F.,* T. G. Julian, Palmer, Va., 1920, 54.4' × 14.7' × 4.4', gross 21, net 8, hull no. 221187. (Owned by B. C. Julian, 1946, fishing, registered Reedville, 1921–71, abandoned, April 5, 1972.)

*\*Mary Fletcher,* Eclipse, Va., 1912, 51.6' × 15.2' × 3.3', gross 14, net 10, hull no. 209769. (Registered 1915, freight, Norfolk, Va.)

*Mary Jane,* Parksley, Va., 1942, 40.3' × 11.3' × 3.8', gross 11, net 6, hull no. 242097. (John T. Handy Co., fishing, 1946, Crisfield, Md.)

*Mary Jane,* Salisbury, Md., 1909, 47.3' × 11.5' × 3.8', gross 11, net 8, hull no. 206143. (Benson Phillips Co. Inc., towing, 1946, registered Newport News, Va.)

*Mary M.*, Linwood P. Price, Amburg, Va., 1924, 60' × 17.7' × 6', gross 42, net 29, hull no. 224256. (Owned by R. D. Taylor, 1946, freight, registered Crisfield, Md.)

*Mary Mildred*, Perrin, Va., 1923, 42.1' × 12' × 3.7', gross 12, net 6, hull no. 223276. (Owned by J. T. Messick, freight, 1946, registered Newport News, Va.)

*Mary Stine*, Madison, Md., 1910, 57.2' × 16.3' × 4.7', gross 22, net 15, hull no. 207746. (Registered 1915, freight, Baltimore, Md.)

*Mary Sue*, Crab Neck, Va., 1908, 63' × 15' × 4', gross 20, net 12, hull no. 206010. (Registered 1915, freight, Norfolk, Va.)

*\*Maud*, Urbanna, Va., 1906, 46' × 10.4' × 3.5', gross 10, net 6, hull no. 203613. (Registered Tappahannock, Va., 1906–10; Reedville, 1913–22; abandoned, Sept. 30, 1924.)

*Mava Kathryn*, Linwood P. Price, Ruark, Va., 1928, 51.1' × 14.5' × 4.4', gross 20, net 11, hull no. 228077. (Owned by Wm. H. Matthews, Newport News, Va., 1946, freight, early engine, 45 hp.)

*Metunga*, Hampton, Va., 1916, 52.6' × 17.4' × 4.8', gross 25, net 13, hull no. 214434. (Owned by J. S. Darling, Newport News, Va., oystering.)

*\*Midland*, Ernest H. Bryant, Deltaville, Va., 1961, 49.4' × 15.9' × 5.6', gross 28, net 19, hull no. 287119. (Owned by Hazel Clark, fishing, 200 hp, Newport New, Va.; owned by Ward Brothers of Deltaville, Va., and renamed *Thomas W.*, 1977; later renamed *Kathleen II* and remodeled into a pleasure craft.)

*Midland*, Herman Krentz, Kayan, Va., 1922, 42' × 10.9' × 4', gross 11, net 7, hull no. 222301. (Owned by Donald Lowe Trafton, Washington, D.C., freight.)

*\*Mildred*, Gilbert S. White, Foxwells, Va., 1927, 52.3' × 14.6' × 4.1', gross 19, net 12, enlarged 1941 to gross 22, net 16, hull no. 227312. (Owned by W. H. Hinson, 1946; registered Reedville, Va., 1928–77; Baltimore, Md., 1979–83; fishing, named *DJIV*, 1971, and *Little River*, 1976, and owned by George Gaskins, fishing, 225 hp; deleted Norfolk, 1986.)

*Mildred*, Lepron Johnson, Crittenden, Va., 1915, 42.9' × 14' × 3.6', gross 17, net 9, hull no. 213653. (Owned by G. G. Raynor, registered Newport News, Va., 1946, freight.)

*Mildred Belle*, Odell Carmines, Odd, Va., 1948, 46.7' × 15' × 4.9', gross 22, net 13, hull no. 256515. (Named for Mildred Lee and Hattie Belle Evans, daughters of Captain Garland Evans who had the boat built. Owned by The Living Classrooms Foundation of Baltimore in 2003 and used as a floating classroom.)

*Milford*, Laban, Va., 1921, 43.8' × 10.8' × 4', gross 9, net 6, hull no. 231399. (Owned by Arthur Gay, Newport News, Va., 1946, fishing.)

*\*Millicent*, Herman M. Krentz, Harryhogan, Va., 1936, 43.7' × 12.6' × 5.3', gross 22, net 18, hull no. 235256. (Owned by Otis W. Douglas, Jr., 1946, passenger, registered Reedville, Va., 1936–57; abandoned April 27, 1967.)

*Milton E.*, Poquoson, Va., 1915, 45.4' × 11.2' × 3.1', gross 10, net 7, hull no. 234965. (Owned by Allen Pruitt, fishing, 165 hp, registered Cape Charles, Va.)

*\*Mina Crockett*, O. W. Payne, Palmer, Va., 1923, 65' × 18' × 5.3', gross 40, net 22, hull no. 223480. (Built for Andrew A. Crockett, Tangier Island, Va.; later owned by Guy L. Evans, Norfolk, Va., 1946, freight; foundered in Chesapeake Bay, April 4, 1973.)

*Miown*, Crisfield, Md., 1927, 42.6' × 14.8' × 4.5', gross 17, net 11, hull no. 226977. (Owned by A. O. Lynch, 1946, Crisfield, Md.)

*\*Miss Allentown*, Sterling & Somers, Crisfield, Md., 1927, 46' × 10.7' × 3.7', gross 10, net 7, hull no. 226852. (Owned by Markel Thomas, 1946, Crisfield, Md., small draketail deck boat used on Tangier Island to run oysters and fish to Washington and Baltimore and also used as the mail boat for a while. Henry Hoskins later owned her and ran oysters to Washington, D.C.; registered

Crisfield, Md., 1927–34; deleted May 7, 1982; named *Nettie Irene*, 1969.)

*Miss Carrie*, Lepron Johnson, Crittenden, Va., 1929, 74.4' × 16.7' × 6', gross 45, net 18, hull no. 228346. (Enlarged by 15' added to her middle before 1946.)

*Miss JoAnn*, see *Nellie Jane*

*Miss Joanne*, Amburg, Va., 1939, 44.8' × 13.6' × 5.1', gross 20, net 12, hull no. 239152. (Owned by Daley & Sons Grocery Inc., fishing, 1994.)

*Miss Maggie*, see *Automatic*

*Miss Mary*, see *Audrey*

*Miss Tangier*, Crisfield, Md., 1929, 43.8' × 9' × 3.5', gross 7, net 5, hull no. 235351. (Owned by A. A. Crockett, 1946, freight, registered Reedville, Va.)

*Miss Terry*, see *Old Point*

*Miss Tylerton*, Crisfield, Md., 1929, 46.4' × 11.1' × 3.9', gross 12, net 8. hull no. 229126. (Owned by H. Coulbourne Brandshaw, 1946, fishing, registered Crisfield, Md.)

*\*Miss Virginia*, Ernest H. Bryant, Deltaville, 1957, 45.9' × 14.1' × 4.5', gross 18, net 12, hull no. 275507. (Built for Everett Miles, Cape Charles, Va.; later, owned by Angellia A. Hall, fishing, 1994, Norfolk, Va.)

*Miss York*, Tilghman, Md., 1936, 44.4' × 11.5' × 5', gross 14, net 9, hull no. 235352. (Owned by Charles A. McGuise, 1946, passenger, Philadelphia, Pa.)

*\*Mitchell*, Mitchell Hubbard, Hudson, Md., 1934, 60.6' × 18.7' × 6', gross 44, net 30, hull no. 233604. (Original 45 hp, owned by J. W. Ferguson Oyster Co. Captain Dolson Owens was killed on her when she turned over with a load of seed oysters in Norfolk, Va.)

*Mitzie Ann*, Nevitt, Md., 1927, 46.3' × 9.1' × 4', gross 12, net 8, hull no. 235026. (Owned by Ernest P. Niewig, 1946, passenger, Wilmington, Del.)

*Mobjack*, Linwood and Milford Price, Amburg, Va., 1946, 72.2' × 24.6' × 5.5', gross 69, net 17, hull no. 249397. (Owner J. H. Miles Co., 1946. Owned 2003 by Jim and Bonnie Vautrot of Urbanna, Va.)

*Monitor*, Salisbury, Md., 1917, 60.1' × 20.6' × 5.4', gross 20, net 13, hull no. 234561. (Owned by Ballard Brothers Fish Co., 1946, fishing, registered Cape Charles, Va.)

*Morning Star*, Havre de Grace, Md., 1911, 49.4' × 12.4' × 3.5', gross 19, net 16, hull no. 232165. (Owned by Webster Boyd Bines, 1946, fishing, registered Baltimore, Md.)

*\*Mundy Point*, see *Lawson*

*\*Muriel Eileen* (Big) J. W. Smith, Perrin, Va., 1928, 59.1' × 19.1' × 6.3', gross 48, net 20, enlarged in Irvington, Va., 1935, to 78.8', × 20' × 6.3', gross 67, net 45, hull no. 228078. Sank 1969 in Atlantic Ocean clam dredging. (Owned by Lord Mott Co., Baltimore, Md., registered Newport News, 1929; Baltimore, Md., 1935; Philadelphia Pa, 1967; lost at 37°38'N lat. and 75°14'W long. October 21, 1969.)

*\*Muriel Eileen* (Little), J. W. Smith, Bena, Va., 1926, 58.3' × 18.1' × 5.2', gross 36, net 22, hull no. 226086. (Once owned by Willie Brown of Bena, Va., Lord Mott Co. of Baltimore, Md., and Captain Johnny Ward of Deltaville. The boat is now owned by David M. Cantera of New Castle, Del., and is used for recreation, registered Newport News, Va., 1926, 1928, and 1937; Reedville, Va., 1927.)

*\*Mutt*, Jabez Tyler, Cambridge, Md., 1923, 67' × 20.4' × 6.8', gross 68, net 46, hull no. 223149. (Name changed to *Augusta*, November 1, 1956; owned by Phillips Packing Co., Cambridge, 1930s; by J. M. Tolley, Cambridge, 1946; registered Baltimore, Md., 1923; Cambridge, Md., 1924–31; Miami, Fla, 1956; transferred to Liberian registry and flag, March 18, 1957.)

*Myrtle,* Gilbert White, Foxwells, Va., 1922, 44.7' × 10.1' × 3.5', gross 11, net 7, hull no. 234553. (Owned by E. Dewey Raines, 1946, fishing, registered Reedville, Va.)

*Myrtle and Thelma,* Linwood P. Price, Ruark, Va., 1910, 47.2' × 10.8' × 4.4', gross 14, net 8, hull no. 210528. (Registered 1915, oystering, Cape Charles, Va.)

*\*Myrtle Virginia,* Lepron Johnson, Crittenden, Va., 1923, 62.3' × 19.1' × 6.2', gross 49, net 23, hull no. 223296. (Owned by Dighton Taylor and later by Jesse R. Taylor, Crisfield, Md., 1946, freight, registered Cape Charles, 1923.)

*N. E. Wright,* Deltaville, 1911, 48' × 11.2' × 4.5', gross 17, net 9, hull no. 208985. (Registered 1915, oystering, Norfolk.)

*\*Nancy K. Bateman,* see *Amos*

*Nanikote,* Nanikote, Md., 1908, 45.5' × 12' × 2.8', gross 15, net 7, hull no. 205475. (Registered 1915, freight, Crisfield, Md.)

*Naoman,* Port Haywood, Va., 1905, 44' × 13.8' × 2.8', gross 7, net 6, hull no. 203277. (Registered 1915, oystering, Cape Charles, Va.)

*Naomi,* Perrin, Va., 1915, 47.7' × 13' × 4.4', gross 14, net 10, hull no. 213728. (Owned by Simpkins Fish Co., Georgetown, S.C., 1946.)

*\*Naomi Todd,* Irving F. Cannon, Fishing Creek, Md., 1934, 52.4' × 12.3' × 5.3', gross 19, net 13, 35 hp, hull no. 233034. (Registered Crisfield, Md., 1934; Annapolis, Md., 1966; dismantled, 1971. Draketail stern, owned by Freddie Pruitt, Tangier Island, Va. "She came from Crisfield and my cousin from Tangier Island bought her for crab dredging. She wasn't a very pretty one because she was so high sided," said Steve Pruitt.)

*\*Narcissus,* see *Lydia*

*Nasemond,* Lepron Johnson, Crittenden, Va., 1922, 58.3' × 18.1' × 4', gross 31, net 20, hull no. 222222. (Owned by J. H. Miles Co., Hampton, Va., 1946.)

*Nellie Bly,* Marsh Market, Va, 1900, 43.5' × 15' × 3.4', gross 9, net 6, hull no. 130883. (Registered 1915, freight, Norfolk, Va.)

*Nellie Crockett,* Charles A. Dana, Crisfield, Md., 1925, 61.7' × 20.4' × 6.5', gross 52, net 35, hull no. 225369. (Built for Andrew A. "Shad" Crockett of Tangier Island, Va.; later owned by James Ward, Deltaville, Va., and used as a buyboat; later owned by Ted Parish of Georgetown, Md., 2002. Used in World War II by the War Shipping Administration. Listed in the National Historic Landmarks Program, April 19, 1994.)

*Nellie Jane,* Buddy Sable, Amburg, Va., actually built on Fishing Bay near Ruark, 1939, 44.8' × 13.6' × 5.1', gross 20, net 12, hull no. 239152. (Owned by George Pruitt, Tangier Island, and ran groceries between Crisfield and Tangier. Early engine, 24 hp Lathrop. Also owned by Clyde A. Pruitt, oystering, 225 hp, registered Reedville, Va.) For a short while she was used as the centerpiece of a putt-putt golf course in Crisfield, Md., on dry land.

*Nellie R.,* Glass, Va., 1922, 47.6', 13.4', 4.4', gross 17, net 7, hull no. 221699. (Owned by G. T. Elliott Inc., registered Newport News, Va., 1946, freight. "Never had much care taken of her, but if she had been painted up she would have been beautiful," said Steve Pruitt.

*Nettie Irene,* see *Miss Allentown*

*Nettie May,* Whitestone, Va., 1902, 52' × 13.8' × 3', gross 10, net 8, hull no. 130989. (Registered 1915, freight, Reedville, Va.)

*Nivin,* Hampton, Va., 1904, 46' × 16.6' × 3.3', gross 17, net 10, hull no. 200650. (Registered 1915, oystering, Newport News, Va., later owned by Chatam Oyster Co., Ga, 1946, registered Charleston, S.C.)

*Nomad,* Deal Island, Md., 1934, 44.3' × 10.1' × 4', gross 10, net 9, hull no. 233427. (Owned by Fred C. Rodenhausen, 1946, registered Baltimore, Md.)

*Nonie,* Lepron Johnson, Crittenden, Va., 1908, 42.6' × 16.6' × 3.3', gross 11, net 5, hull no. 205758. (Registered 1915, freight, Newport News, Va., owned by Garland L. Spencer, fishing, 1946, Cape Charles,Va.)

*Nora Lee,* see *Norma Lee*

*Nora V.,* St. Michaels, Md., 1939, 43.2' × 12.1' × 4', gross 13, net 11, hull no. 238841. (Owned by Henry M. Swanhaus, fishing, 1946, registered Baltimore, Md.)

*Nora W.,* see *Amanda C.*

*\*Nordreco,* David Lowe, Battery Park, Va., 1935, 47.7' × 10.7' × 3.9', gross 10, net 7, hull no. 234989. (Owned by Norfolk Dredging Co., towing, 1946, registered Norfolk, Va., 1936–47; abandoned Norfolk, Va., June 16, 1953.)

*\*Norma Lee,* C. Lyman Ewell, Elliott, Md., 1932, 47.6' × 11.3' × 4.8', gross 14, net 9, hull no. 231554. (Owned by Lennie W. Foxwell, fishing, 1946, 21 hp, Cambridge, Md.; abandoned, Cambridge, Md., February 3, 1950.)

*Norman,* Beckley, Va., 1915, 46.3' × 17.4' × 3.8', gross 27, net 17, hull no. 212930. (Registered 1915, freight, Norfolk, Va.)

*Norman T.,* Perrin, Va., 1928, 50' × 16' × 5', gross 26, net 13, hull no. 227193.

*O. S. Lloyd,* Salisbury, Md., 1909, 46' × 11.4' × 4.2', gross 11, net 9, hull no. 206143. (Registered 1915, freight, Crisfield, Md.)

*\*O. W. Payne,* O. W. Payne, Palmer, Va., 1911, 64' × 15.2' × 3.7', gross 23, net 16, hull no. 209442. (Original 25 hp, built for Ralph Sterling, Crisfield, Md., named after the builder; registered Tappahannock, Va.; Reedville, Va.; Crisfield, Md.; Port Arthur, Texas; and finally Perth Amoy, N.J.; burned on Compton's Creek near Port Monmouth, N.J., 1965.)

*Ocean Pearl,* L. R. Smith, Susan, Va., 1912, 43.7' × 10.9' × 3.2', gross 7, net 5, hull no. 230523.

*Ocean View,* Linwood and Milford P. Price, Deltaville, 1949, 71.9' × 24.3' × 5.6', gross 69, net 19, hull no. 257685. (Originally built for J. H. Miles & Co. of Norfolk, Va.; owned 2003, Robinson's Oyster Farm, Port Norris, N.J., registered Philadelphia, Pa.)

*Old Fox,* Winter Harbor, Va., 1910, 42.9' × 11.1' × 3.2', gross 11, net 8, hull no. 230523.

*Old Point,* J. G. Wornom, Poquoson, Va., 1909, 51.9' × 12.10' × 4', gross 14, net 9, hull no. 206349. (Seven-log boat, owned by Ernest Thomas Brandshaw, 1946, freight, registered Newport News, Va.; also, Norman Crockett, freight, 35 hp, Newport News, Va.; now owned by the Chesapeake Bay Maritime Museum, St. Michaels, Md.)

*Old Squaw,* see *Agnes Sterling*

*Olive T.,* Linwood P. Price, Ruark, Va., 1930, 60.7' × 17' × 5.9', gross 41, net 30, hull no. 230346. (Owned by T. E. Thompson, registered Newport News, Va., freight, 1946. Early engine 75 hp.)

*\*Olive Virginia,* T. W. Wright, Deltaville, Va., 1926, 54.3' × 14.5' × 4.6', gross 24, net 16, hull no. 225327. (Alton Smith installed a new, deeper bottom on *Olive Virginia* in the 1940s; owned by Lorie Q. Pruitt, fishing, 150 hp, registered Reedville, Va.)

*\*Oriole,* Palmer, Va., 1911, 58' × 15.2' × 4.1', gross 20, net 15, hull no. 209454. (Owned by G. Ray Simmons, 1946).

*Oysterman,* Lepron Johnson, Crittenden, Va., 1913, 56.2' × 17.6' × 5.1', gross 30, net 16, hull no. 211635. (Once owned by J. H. Miles & Co., still alive in 1994 in Miami, Fl.)

*Oyston,* Pocomoke City, Md., 50' × 13' × 4.2', gross 15, net 10, hull no. 200534. (Registered 1915, oystering, Newport News, Va.)

*\*P. E. Pruitt,* Howard & Smith, Crisfield, Md., 1935, 51' × 15.5' × 5.1', gross 24, net 16, hull no. 233637. (Registered, freight, 1946, Crisfield, Md. Paul Pruitt of Tangier Island and later of Urbanna, Va., had the boat built in Crisfield but did not like the stern so shortly after the boat was completed he had Linwood Price of Deltaville put on another one; original engine 36 hp Lathrop.)

*Panama,* West Norfolk, Va., 1915, 55.7' × 20.4' × 5.5', gross 41, net 29, hull no. 213276. (Registered 1915, freight, Norfolk, Va., owned by George A. Philpotts, freight, 1929, Mobjack, Va., registered Norfolk, Va.)

*\*Papoose,* Chuckatuck, Va., 1913, 43' × 14.5' × 3.2', gross 12, net 5, hull no. 210921. (Registered 1915, fishing, Newport News, Va.)

*\*Pappoose,* Crisfield, Md., 1903, 47' × 10' × 3.3', gross 7, net 6, hull no. 201207. (Registered 1915, freight, Crisfield, Md., 1904–23; abandoned June 29, 1929.)

*Pat,* John F. Smith, Dare, Va., 1934, 58.2' × 21.3' × 6.2', gross 48, net 14, hull, 60 hp, no. 233539. (Owned by J. H. Miles Co., fishing, registered Newport News, 1934.)

*Pattie May,* Lepron Johnson, Crittenden, Va., 1919, 58.6' × 16.8' × 6', gross 37, net 16, hull no. 217823. (Owned by Ballard Fish & Oyster, 1946, bought and dredged seed oysters on James River.)

*Pauline Parks,* see *Fish Hawk*

*Paul Jones,* Poquoson, 1911, 45' × 11' × 4.6', gross 10, net 8, hull no. 209927. (Owned by C. A. Loockerman estate, Crisfield, Md., 1946.)

*Pearl D. Evans,* Weems, Va., 1908, 56.1' × 16' × 4.5', gross 23, net 9, hull no. 205615. (Registered 1915, freight, Newport News, Va.; later owned by Benjamin D. Rooks, Providence, R.I., 1946, oystering.)

*Pearl Faye,* see *Lillian T.*

*\*Peggy,* Harry A. Hudgins, Peary, Va., 1925, 49.9' (55' on deck) × 12.2' × 4.3', gross 13, net 9; changed to gross 16, net 6, 1994, hull no. 234333. (Originally an open trap or pound-net boat, built for Walter Burroughs, New Point, Va., named for his daughter Peggy; other owners Edward O. Grinnell, 1994, and Kim Granberry, 2003; early engine 35 hp.)

*Pilot,* Crittenden, Va., 1913, 62.7' × 17.4' × 5.8', gross 41, net 21, hull no. 210930. (Registered 1915, freight, Newport News, Va.)

*Pompano,* Pocomoke City, Md., 1906, 55.7' × 13.6' × 4', gross 15, net 10, hull no. 202926. (Registered 1915, freight, Elizabeth City, N.C.)

*Poquoson,* Poquoson, Va., 1902, 47.4' × 12.7' × 3.5', gross 10, net 8, hull no. 150977. (Registered 1915, freight, Newport News, Va.)

*Princess Virginia,* Lewisetta, Va., 1911, 49.7' × 14.5' × 4.8', gross 20, net 13, hull no. (Registered 1915, fishing, Baltimore, Md.)

*Queen Mary,* Chincoteague, 1940, 45.7' × 13.6' × 3.9', gross 15, net 12, hull no. 240274. (Owned by A. J. Wimbrow, oystering, 1946, registered Cape Charles, Va.)

*Quick Step.* Laban, Va., 1930, 55.3' × 13.7' × 4.7', gross 22, net 9, hull no. 230417. (Owned by Russell Callis, Deltaville, Va.)

*R. C. Brown,* Linwood P. Price, Ruark Va., 1928, 60.4' × 19.5' × 6.8', gross 53, net 30, hull no. 227995. (Owned by Barge Towing Co. of Va., tanker, 1946, registered Newport News, Va.)

*R. C. Gaskins,* Herman Krentz, Kayan, Va., 1928, 52.9' × 15' × 5.5', gross 28, net 12, hull no. 228173. (Owned by Ryland C. Gaskins, fishing, 600 hp, registered Reedville, Va.)

*\*R. L. Brown,* Gilbert S. White, Palmer, Va., 1912, 49.6' × 12.6' × 4.4', gross 11, net 7, enlarged in 1935 to 51.2' × 12.6' × 4.3', gross 16, net 11, hull no. 210335. (Owned by E. E. Lawson, Jr., fishing, 160 hp, 1946; registered Reedville, Va., 1914–20; Norfolk, Va., 1921; Reedville, Va., 1922–35; Washington, D.C., 1977; Wilmington, Del., 1980.)

*Ready,* Palmer, Va., 1911, 62.4' × 19.5' × 6.8', gross 22, net 14, hull no. 209443. (Owned by B. T. Chilton, Jr., fishing, 1946, registered Reedville, Va.)

*\*Rebecca,* W. F. Dunn, West Norfolk, Va, 1931, 58.5' × 15.4' × 7.9', gross 49, net 24, 240 hp, hull no. 241670. (Owned by M. Lee Hudgins, towing, 1946; registered Norfolk, Va., 1942–69.)

*Rebecca Ann,* Moody, Alvin, and Raymond Walden (Walden brothers), Deltaville, Va., 1949. (Owned by Walden brothers, named after Alvin's wife, Rebecca Ann Walden. Later named *Miss Mathews;* owned 2003 by the Deltaville Maritime Museum.)

*Rebecca Forbush,* C. H. Rice, Reedville, Va., 1954, 77.1' × 25.7' × 6.3', gross 89, net 69, hull no. 267332. (Orginally built for Gus Forbush of Crisfield, Md., later owned by Charles C. Marsh, passenger, Norfolk, 1994, also C. E. Hartman, passenger, 260 hp, registered Annapolis, Md.)

*Regenia,* Onancock, Va., 1933, 52.2' × 11' × 3.8', gross 16, net 11, hull no. 232833. (Owned by W. Spencer Smith, 1946, registered Crisfield, Md.)

*Rema H.,* Harry Steve Smith, New Point, Va., 1936, 42.9' × 13' × 4.3', gross 14, net 9, hull no. 235449. (Owned by Kibler Parker, Water View, Va., oyster planter, early engine, 24 hp.)

*Richardson Brothers,* Lepron Johnson, Crittenden, Va., 1918, 43.7' × 9.3' × 4.1', gross 12, net 18, hull no. 217366. (Owned by Richardson Brothers, freight, 1946, registered Charleston, S.C.

*\*Robert Leo,* Ned Hudgins, Laban, Va., 1923, 46.1' × 12.6' × 4.3', gross 13, net 8, 27 hp, hull no. 222906. (Built for L. N. Powell, Reedville, Va.; later owned by Leonard Balderson, fishing, 1946, Reedville, Va.; in 2002, owned by Frederick Rogers, pound-net fishing, Reedville, Va.)

*Rowena,* Severn River, Va., 1919, 46.5' × 12.9' × 4.1', gross 11, net 5, hull no. 219099. (Owned by W. A. Mitchell, fishing, 1929, Seaford, Va., registered Newport News, Va.)

*\*Rowley,* E. H. Rowley & Son, Chincoteague, Va., 1922, 58' × 21.3' × 4.9', gross 47, net 28; enlarged August 11, 1928, to 71.9', gross 54, net 38, hull no. 222388. (Owned by J. W. Burnell, freight, 1929; registered Cape Charles, Va., 1922; Norfolk, Va., 1924–28, Tampa Fla., 1951; abandoned, 1956.)

*Ruby & Alice,* John Wright, Deltaville, Va., 1916, 43.2' × 12.7' × 4', gross 14, net 6, hull no. 214633. (Named for Ruby and Alice Godsey of Gwynn's Island, Va., by their father James Walter Godsey, Sr., who owned the boat until 1929.)

*Ruby Chrystal,* Lepron Johnson, Crittenden, Va., 1924, 54.8' × 16.1' × 5.2', gross 26, net 8, hull no. 224285. (Owned by Rob Phillips of Newport News, Va., frame boat, also, Ruby Chrystal Corp., fishing, 115 hp, Norfolk, Va., used as an oyster-dredge boat and later crab-dredge boat.)

*Ruby L. Davis,* Battery Park, Va., 1906, 51.5' × 17.6' × 4.7', gross 23, net 14, hull no. 203119. (Owned by P. M. Mathews, freight, 1929, South Mills, N.C., registered Norfolk, Va.)

*Russell,* L. R. and Alton Smith, Susan, Va., 1936, 37.2' × 10.9' × 3.6', gross 8, net 5, hull no. 235732. (Owned by Russell Mason Pugh, fishing, 115 hp, Newport News, Va.; later owned by Ulas Thomas, Tangier Island.)

*Russell,* Laban, Va., 1915, 49.6' × 11.9' × 4.2', gross 13, net 9, hull no. 224657. (Owned by Henry G. Edwards, fishing, 1929, Gwynn's Island, Va., registered Newport News, Va.)

*Ruth,* Baltimore, Md., 1921, 61.1' × 22' × 7.3', gross 60, net 50, hull no. 221591. (Owned by R. J. Taylor, 1929, registered Baltimore, Md.)

*\*Ruth,* Broomes Island, Md., 1910, 58.7' × 16.1' × 3.8', gross 24, net 20, hull no. 208341. (Rebuilt in 1921, 58.6' × 16.4' × 3.9', gross 24, net 20, owned by Ernest G. Lee, freight, 1929, registered Baltimore, Md., abandoned in 1931.)

*Ruth,* Deltaville, Va., 1913, 53.7' × 13.6' × 4.9', gross 24, net 12, hull no. 211814. (Owned by Carlos Tyler, freight, 1929 and 1946, registered Crisfield, Md., early engine, 125 hp.)

*\*Ruth,* J. Wood Tull, Irvington, Va., 1913, 59.2' × 13.2' × 4.3', gross 18, net 12, hull no. 235289. (Original engine 25 hp; foundered at Norfolk Tallow Company dock, Chesapeake, Va., in 1963.)

*Ruth,* West Norfolk, Va., 1920, 58.5' × 12.3' × 5', gross 19, net 13, hull no. 221081. (Owned by E. S. Phillips, towing, 1929, registered

Newport News, Va.; and J. L. Morewitz, 1946, registered Newport News, Va.)

*Ruth and Annie,* Linwood P. Price, Amburg, Va., 1923, 58.2' × 16.1' × 5.4', gross 35, net 21, hull no. 223510. (Owned by Raymond L. Haynie, freight, 1929, registered Reedville, Va.; Willard Evans, 1946, registered Crisfield, Md.; and Victor Ray Pruitt, fishing, 100 hp, registered Cape Charles, Va.)

*\*Ruth & Helen,* L. R. Parker, Syringa, Va., 1925, 44.1' × 12.6' × 4.4', gross 16, net 8, hull no. 224847. (Original engine 24 hp, owned by B. L. Wood, freight, 1929, Lot, Va., registered Newport News, Va. Brothers Bernard and Wallace Wood were in the lumber business and used the boat to haul lumber.)

*Ruth Ann,* see *Mitchell*

*Ruth Ellen,* Fishing Creek, Md., 1927, 47.7' × 10.8' × 4.3', gross 13, net 11, hull no. 226329. (Owned by Charlie Crockett, 1946, freight, registered Crisfield, Md., George W. Ellis, freight, 18 hp, Crisfield, Md.)

*Ruth S.,* Linwood P. Price, Ruark, Va., 1927, 60.3' × 17.7' × 5.7', gross 42, net 19, hull no. 226698. (Built for Captain Johnny Stiff; later owned by Harry W. Smith, 1946, Ward Brothers of Deltaville and Charlie W. Pruitt, Tangier Island, registered Reedville, Va.).

*S. C. Kirk,* Dreka, Va., 1901, 45' × 14.2' × 3.5', gross 10, net 8, hull no. 117084. (Owned by Wesley L. Green, freight, 1929, registered, Washington, D.C.)

*S. L. Wood,* Fairbank, Md., 1925, 43.5' × 10.8' × 3.3', gross 8, net 5, hull no. 224446. (Owned by James T. Fluhart, freight, 1929, registered Cambridge, Md.)

*Sachem,* Pocomoke City, Md., 1904, 50' × 15' × 3.5', gross 14, net 11, hull no. 200746. (Owned by Matthew E. Walter, freight, 1929, registered Crisfield, Md.)

*Sada,* Pocomoke City, Md., 1908, 78.5' × 24' × 5.6', gross 55, net 29, hull no. 204996. (Owned by William Sneed, freight, 1929, Hampton, Va., registered Newport News, Va.)

*Sadie,* Achilles, Va., 1913, 45.3' × 11.8' × 3.7', gross 12, net 7, hull no. 216017. (Owned by Thomas J. King, 1946, fishing, registered Newport News, Va.)

*Samuel H. Hermon,* Dare, Va., 1925, 43.9' × 14.7' × 4.7', gross 20, net 12, hull no. 225294. (Owned by Joseph H. Jordan, 1946, oystering, registered Newport News, Va.)

*Samuel M. Bailey,* Avenue, Md., 1957, 43.3' × 15.3' × 3.4', gross 14, net 12, hull no. 274607. (Owned by Capt. Sam's Seafood Inc., 225 hp, 1994, Norfolk, Va.)

*Samuel Thomas,* Elliott, Md., 1913, 48.5' × 15' × 4.4', gross 18, net 13, hull no. 211780. (Owned by Ulman White, freight, 1929, registered Crisfield, Md.)

*Sarah E.,* Laban, Va., 1924, 48.2' × 12.2' × 4.5', gross 13, net 9, hull no. 234334. (Owned by George E. Hutson, 1946, fishing, registered Newport News, Va.)

*Sea Gull,* Deltaville, Va., 1931, 42.9' × 11.6' × 3.4', gross 9, net 6, hull no. 230665. (Owned by Ira Mitchem, 1946, fishing, registered Newport News, Va.)

*Sea Pal,* Alton Smith, Susan, Va., 1943, 69.7' × 17.5' × 7.3', gross 52, net 26, hull no. 245034. (Owned by H. Milton Forrest, 1946 and built for Atlantic Ocean fish trawling fishery.)

*Secret,* Portsmouth, Va., 1916, 48' × 10.4' × 5.4', gross 19, net 13, hull no. 221904. (Owned by Arthor T. Cox, towing, registered Crisfield, Md.)

*Seminole,* L. R. and Alton Smith, Susan, Va., 1923, 46.3' × 12.5' × 4.5', gross 58, net 42, hull no. 217516. (Owned by William Columbus Brown, 1946, freight.)

*Seven Brothers,* Gilbert White, Foxwells, Va., 1928, 59.8' × 16.4' × 4.1', gross 28, net 17, hull no. 227314. (Sank off Stingray Point, 2001.

Owned by Stewart and Wroten Simmons of Kilmarnock, Va., and Roland George of Ocran, Va. A mate was killed aboard her in a 1939 tornado.)

*\*Shamrock,* R. H. Hudson, Irvington, Va., 1925, 47' × 12.6' × 4.5', gross 16, net 8, 25 hp, hull no. 224514. (Owned by Travis Thomas, 1946, registered Reedville, Va., 1925, Crisfield, Md., 1963, abandoned Crisfield, Md., 1967.)

*Shannon,* Laban, Va., 1913, 50.1' × 14.1' × 3.9', gross 19, net 8, hull no. 211148. (Registered 1915, freight, Norfolk, Va.)

*Silas T. Webster,* Solomons, Md., 1925, 72.9' × 23.6' × 5.5', gross 63, net 43, hull no. 225141. (Owned by Nonie Holland, 1946, fishing, registered Washington, D.C.)

*Simmons,* Gilbert White, Foxwells, Va., 1925, 52' × 14.1' × 4.4', gross 19, net 12, hull no. 224436. (Owned by Capt. William E. "Billy" Simmons and Carlye Simmons of Kilmarnock, Va.)

*Squirrel,* Pocomoke City, Md., 1901, 56' × 15.5' × 4', gross 14, net 10, hull no. 117094. (Frame built, owned by W. B. Forrest, 1946, fishing, registered Newport News, Va.)

*Static,* Deltaville, 1929, 44.8' × 10.9' × 3.5', gross 9, net 6, hull no. 231397. (Owned by James Brown, 1946, registered Newport News, Va.)

*\*Stella,* H. E. Robertson, Palmer, Va., 1900, 49.4' × 12' × 3.9', gross 13, net 9, 18 hp, hull no. 235290. (Owned by Earnest J. Lawson, 1946, fishing, registered Reedville, Va., 1936 and 1972; abandoned Reedville, Va., 1976.)

*Sterling,* Linwood P. Price, Ruark, Va., 1928, 55.2' × 17.1' × 5.1', gross 32, net 22, hull no. 228004. (Early power 35 hp.)

*Sterling,* Peary, Va., 1926, 54.7' × 13.9' × 4.7', gross 20, net 11, hull no. 225333. (Owned by L. D. Amory & Co., 1946, fishing, registered Newport News, Va.)

*Sterling Brothers,* Crisfield, Md., 1914, 42' × 10.8' × 3.9', gross 9, net 6, hull no. 212802. (Owned by W. L. Tull, freight, 25 hp, registered Crisfield, Md.)

*Sterling Sisters,* Selden, Va, 1904, 61' × 16.2' × 4.6', gross 23, net 15, hull no. 201469. (Owned by C. E. Foreman, freight, 14 hp, and Major C. Todd, Jr., 1946, freight, registered Crisfield, Md.)

*Stewart Brothers,* Linwood P. Price, 1923, Amburg, Va., 54.2' × 14' × 5', gross 24, net 16, hull no. 222783. (Powered by three-cylinder 30 hp Atlas, one of first diesel-powered deck boats on Tangier Island. Blew up at Crisfield as a World War II patrol boat. Rebuilt by Lorne Tull of Crisfield, Md.; owned by William Pruitt of Tangier Island prior to World War II; and Elva Tull, 1946, and Leon Lewis of Hooper Island, Md., freight, 36 hp; registered Crisfield, Md.)

*Sue Constance,* Reedville, Va., 1923, 44.9' × 12.9' × 5.3', gross 18, net 9, hull no. 222907. (Owned by Ralph Biddlecomb, 1946, fishing, registered Reedville, Va.)

*Sunflower,* may have been *Janice*

*Thelma,* Fairbanks, Md., 1905, 47.8' × 17' × 4.5', gross 20, net 17, hull no. 202598. (Owned by Arthur Windfohr, oystering, 1946, registered Philadelphia, Pa.)

*Thelma,* Linwood P. Price, Amburg, Va., 1935, 51.4' × 12.7' × 4.8', gross 20, net 12, hull no. 234223. (Owned by W. H. Wake, freight, 1946, registered Newport News, Va.)

*Thelma Earl,* Tom and Lewis Wright, Deltaville, Va., 1924, 47.1' × 12.3' × 4.3', gross 15, net 5, hull no. 223835. (Owned by Robert V. Taylor, Deltaville, and later Randolph Ashburn, Urbanna, Va., 60 hp engine.)

*Thelma H.* (Photo caption in a 1999 *Southside Sentinel* "Vintage Years" supplement states boat was owned by Willard H. Wake and lost in 1950 when a spark from the battery ignited gasoline fumes, causing an explosion. The vessel burned; Capt. Wake escaped with his life but spent many weeks recovering in the hospital. No other information found.)

*The Russell,* Linwood P. Price, Amburg, Va., 1924, 56.8' × 16' × 5.5', gross 33, net 19, hull no. 224208. (Owned by Charles H. Bradshaw, freight, 1946, registered Crisfield, Md.)

*Thomas E.,* Alton Smith, Susan, Va., 1948, 65' (Owned by Henry Owens, crab dredging.)

*Thomas F. Jubb,* Weems, Va., 1909, 65.8' × 20.9' × 6.8', gross 63, net 43, hull no. 206307. (Owned by Thomas B. Hallock, freight, 1946, registered Annapolis, Md.)

*\*Thomas J.,* J. S. Jenkins, Severn, Va., 1948, 51' × 16.8' × 4.2', gross 24, net 16, 225 hp, hull no. 256561. (Built for Thomas J. Tillage, Newport News, Va.; also owned by Marion A. Tillage, freight, 1994, registered Norfolk, Va.)

*Thomas Jason,* Deltaville, Va., 1976, 47' × 12.9' × 4.3', gross 15, net 11, hull no. 578913. (Owned by William T. Walston, Jr., passenger and freight, registered Norfolk, Va.)

*Thomas W.,* see *Midland* (There were two boats named *Thomas W.* after Thomas Ward of Deltaville by his father Floyd Ward; one was *Midland* and the other was *P. E. Pruitt.*)

*Thomas W.,* see *P. E. Pruitt*

*\*Thomas W. Carroll,* New Point, Va., 1920, 58.7' 14.5' × 5.8', gross 29, net 16, hull no. 220146. (Owned by F. H. Ayers, 1929, freight, registered Norfolk, Va.; W. D. Bonniville, registered Newport News, Va., 1946, freight; and Thomas W. Carrol Inc., fishing, 1994, registered Norfolk, Va.)

*Three Brothers,* Crisfield, Md., 1922, 48.3' × 14.1' × 4.1', gross 15, net 10, hull no. 222496. (Owned by C. W. Pruitt, fishing, registered Crisfield, Md.)

*Three Brothers,* Poquoson, Va., 55'. (Seven-log canoe built for Edward "Captain Ed" Pruitt of Tangier Island and named after his three sons, Paul, Charlie, and Stanley Pruitt. No other information found.)

*\*Three Sisters,* P. C. Ingram, Palmer, Va., 55.1' × 14.8' × 4.9', gross 25, net 15, hull no. 225719. (Owned by Edward P. Blake, early engine 36 hp, registered Reedville, Va., 1926; Newport News, Va., 1926–68.)

*Time,* Palmer, Va., 1921, 46.6' × 11.2' × 3.5', gross 13, net 7, hull no. 228116. (Owned by C. W. South, passenger, 1946, registered Reedville, Va.)

*Verna R.,* C. H. Rice, Reedville, 1948, 52' × 14.9 × 4.5', gross 26, net 14, hull no. 256793. (Built by C. H. Rice for himself, crab dredge, named after C. H. Rice's second wife.)

*Vernon Drewer,* see *Annie D.*

*Vernon Jr.,* Saxis, Va., 1932, 43.1' × 11.6' × 3.3', gross 10 net 7, hull no. 236974. (Owned by Vernon Drewer, 1946, fishing, registered Crisfield, Md.)

*Verona,* Linwood P. Price, Ruark, Va., 1933, 60.9' × 20' × 7.3', gross 60, net 44, hull no. 232422. (Owned by Delmas Price, Crisfield, Md., hauled watermelons and small grain and crab dredged; early engine 60 hp, engine room controlled/reversible diesel. Later went to Morehead City, N.C., and used as a snapper rig for menhaden.)

*Virgie Garrison,* Coros Creek, Va., 1911, 58.3' × 13.2' × 3.7', gross 23, net 15, hull no. 209287. (Owned by Otis P. Evans, freight, 25 hp, registered Crisfield, Va.)

*Virginia,* Linwood P. Price, Ruark, Va., 1928, 52.4' × 13.9' × 4.6', gross 19, net 13, hull no. 234399. (Early engine 54 hp.)

*Virginia,* Ruark, Va., 1912, 47.2' × 11.2' × 4.1', gross 14, net 7, hull no. 210289. (Registered 1914, Crisfield, Md.)

*Virginia,* Willis Wharf, Va., 1938, 43.6' × 13.6' × 4.3', gross 14, net 9, hull no. 237417. (Owned by W. W. Matthews, fishing, 1946, registered Cape Charles, Va.)

*Virginia Belle,* Linwood P. Price, Amburg, Va., 1923, 57.7' × 16' × 5.2', gross 33, net 20, hull no. 223512. (Originally built for William H.

"Captain Will" Ward of Crisfield, Md. While Ward was in Deltaville having his boat built, he met Miss Virginia Harrow and he later married her. He named the boat *Virginia Belle* in honor of his fiancée; later owned by Beaufort Fisheries, N.C., 1946, menhaden fishery.)

*Virginia Estelle,* Linwood P. Price, Ruark, Va., 1931, 60.7' × 19' × 6.2', gross 49, net 33, hull no. 230996. (Built for Cliff Evans of Salisbury, Md., early engine 140 hp.)

*Virginia Lee,* see *O. W. Payne*

*Virginia Mae,* Burgess Store, Va., 1944, 52.5' × 15.9' × 5.2', gross 34, net 21, hull no. 246871. (Owned by Earl Crockett, 1946, fishing, Reedville, Va.)

*Virginia Mae,* Shady Side, Md., 1927, 45.5' × 12' × 3.7', gross 12, net 9, hull no. 242204. (Owned by Lee Rohner, 1946, fishing, registered Baltimore, Md.)

*\*Virginian,* Gilbert S. White, Mosquito Creek, Va., 1919, 55' × 15.2' × 5.3', gross 28, net 16, enlarged in 1933, gross 34, net 23, hull no. 219297. (Owned by Thomas J. Kane, miscellaneous use, registered Baltimore, Md., 1919–36; Houston, Tex, 1958; abandoned August 24, 1960, at Houston, Tex.)

*Voyager,* Lepron Johnson, Crittenden, Va., 1931, 63.6' × 17.7' × 7.8', gross 50, net 19, hull no. 231214.

*W. A. Ballard,* Pocomoke, City, Md., 1916, 80.1' × 19.1' × 6.8', gross 66, net 27, hull no. 214041. (Owned by Ballard Fish & Oyster Co., Norfolk, Va.)

*\*W. B. Carter,* Irvington, Va., 1911, 56' × 15.4' × 5.5', gross 20, net 11, hull no. 208907. (Owned by Garner Brothers, 1929, Lewisetta, Va., registered Reedville, Va. 1913–36.)

*Walter Bailey,* River Springs, Md., 1926, 54.2' × 17.3' × 6.2', gross 35, net 24. (Owned by G. C. Davis, Kilmarnock, Va., freight, 1929, registered Reedville, Va.; Howard W. Ward, Crisfield, Md., 1946, Reedville, Va.)

*Walter Boyd,* Linwood P. Price, Amburg, Va., 1925, 47.6' × 15.5' × 4.3', gross 19, net 8, hull no. 225222. (Owned by Boyd Hurley of Urbanna, Va., 45 hp, named for his son Walter Boyd Hurley.)

*Wanda,* John E. Wright, Deltaville, Va., 1929, 56.1' × 15.7' × 4.9', gross 28, net 13, hull no. 228650. (Named after Wanda Godsey, the youngest daughter of James Walter "Captain Jim" Godsey.)

*Ward Bros.,* see *Andrew J. Lewis*

*White Wing,* Chincoteague, Va., 1904, 64.3' × 17.5' × 4.4', gross 21, net 15, hull no. 201667. (Owned by I. P. Rowe, 1929, Claybank, Va., oystering, registered Newport News, Va.)

*White Wing,* Whitehaven, Md., 71.6' × 16.5' × 4.3', gross 37, net 31, hull no. 206927. (Owned by J. W. Marshall, West Point, Va., freight, registered in Newport News, Va., and later Crisfield, Md.)

*Wicomico,* Shadpoint, Md., 1905, 52' × 12.3' × 3.3', gross 19, net 12, hull no. 202725. (Owned by Whitehaven Packing Co., Maryland, 1915 and 1928, passenger, registered in Crisfield, Md.)

*William H. Rawley,* Cambridge, Md., 1907, 65.3' × 21' × 5.5', gross 51, net 31, hull no. 203962. (Owned by Wilbert Rawley, 1929, freight, registered Philadelphia, Pa.)

*William M. Upshar,* Oyster, Va., 1902, 56' × 15' × 3', gross 12, net 9, hull no. 81841. (Owned by E. W. Brown, 1929, freight, registered Norfolk, Va.)

*\*William Somers,* Linwood P. Price, Amburg, Va., 1923, 58.7' × 16' × 5.8', gross 36, net 25, hull no. 223256. (Owned by Ballard Fish & Oyster Co., 1946, and Ryland Gaskins; registered Baltimore, Md., 1923; Crisfield, Md., 1924–32; Newport News, Va., 1934; renamed *Gannet,* 1973.) "She was a heavy built boat," said Steve Pruitt.

*Winnie Estelle,* Crisfield, Md., 1920, 61.2' × 16' × 4.8', gross 32, net 19, hull no. 220507. (Still alive 2003; completely rebuilt and used as a dive/charter boat in Belize.)

*Wm. G. Dryden*, Linwood P. Price, Ruark, Va., 1927, 60.3' × 18.6' × 5.7', gross 46, net 27, hull no. 226948. (Early engine 45 hp.)

*Yamacraw*, Pocomoke City, Md., 1922, 50' × 12.5' × 5', gross 19, net 13, hull no. 221900. (Owned by William "Winnie" Pruitt, Tangier Island, later owned by Michael V. Goodwin, yacht, 160 hp, Miami, Fla. "She was a sea boat. Now she wasn't big or nothing but put her head into a sea—her and the *Lucy R. Ruark*—[they] were the prettiest sea boats in a sea because they were just like a butcher knife. But any other way she was a bitch to stay aboard because she would roll the yeast out of a biscuit," said Steve Pruitt.

*Yeocomico*, Linwood P. Price, Ruark, Va., 1931, 60.2' × 19.3' × 6.7', gross 51, net 37, hull no. 231382. (She was built for two brothers with the last name of Parks, early engine 50 hp; later owned by Arthur Richardson Eubank of Lewisetta, Va., and Robert C. Basman, freight, 165 hp, Reedville, Va.) The contract to build *Yeocomico* was drawn up by bookkeeper James Crittenden at Price's Boat Yard in 1931. "My wife Mizpah and I took a vacation on a cruise ship about twenty-five years ago to Nassau, Bahamas," said James Crittenden in an interview on December 16, 2002. "While we were there, we walked down on a beach and walked up on a fuel dock. I told Mizpah, 'I don't believe it, there's the *Yeocomico*.' She still carried the same name. She was named after the Yeocomico River on the Potomac. She was being used to haul building supplies from Florida to the islands."

*Yeocomico Planter*, Crisfield, Md., 1929, 42.8' × 11.7' × 3.2', gross 10, net 8, hull no. 229191. (Owned by Bevans Oyster Co., 1994, fishing, registered Norfolk, Va.)

*Yeomac*, see *Zella M. Hurley*

*York Spit*, Alton Smith, Susan, Va., 1949, 45.6' × 13' × 4.5', gross 16, net 11, hull no. 258871. (Owned by Richard D. Miles of J. H. Miles & Co., 1994, registered Norfolk, Va.)

*York Spit*, Deltaville, 1947, 44.1' × 11.6' × 5.4', gross 17, net 12, hull no. 253815.

*\*Zella M. Hurley*, T. W. Wright, Deltaville, Va., 1924, 60.5' × 17.2' × 5.5', gross 34, net 28, hull no. 224277. (Owned by Joseph L. Smith, 1946; later owned by Kelley Seafood of Kilmarnock, Va., and used as a snapper purse rig; later owned by Jim Lee Co., 1994, fishing, registered Norfolk, Va.)

# CONVERTED FROM SAIL TO MOTOR POWER

It has been assumed that boats built in the late 1800s and before were sailboats that were later converted to power. Brewington's bugeye listing in *Chesapeake Bay Bugeyes*, Snediker and Jensen's *Chesapeake Bay Schooners* listings, and Burgess's writings have all confirmed that many of the boats were sail-powered bugeyes and schooners before they became powerboats. However, there may have been a few boats built just before 1900 that carried only the standard auxiliary sail of the buyboats and may be listed here as conversions.

It is obvious from this listing the enormous role Maryland boatbuilders played in building sail-powered bugeyes and schooners for the Chesapeake region. Most sailboats in fairly good shape were converted from sailing vessels to motor-powered deck boats. I am sure many more were converted, though we could not find documentation.

*A. Booth*, T. Kirby, Talbot County, Md., 1880. (Converted to power schooner in 1947, used in Miami, Fla., later sold to Costa Rica.)

*A. E. Parks*, Fairmount, Md., 1893, 60' × 16.7' × 4.6', gross 20, net 13, hull no. 107054. (Owned by A. P. Dawson, freight, 1929, Mayo, Md., registered Annapolis, Md.)

*A. Gillis*, Somerset County, Md., 1888, 53.6' × 14.4' × 3.5', gross 11, net 7, hull no. 106584. (Owned by J. M. Kellum, Weems, Va., freight, 1929, registered Reedville, Va.)

*A. H. Schulz*, Woodall, Baltimore, Md., 1872, 77.4' × 23.5' × 7.4', gross 77, net 61, hull no. 105403. (Two-masted schooner converted to power. Owned by Harvey Conway who changed name of the boat in honor of his wife Sarah C. Conway; lost off Atlantic City, New Jersey, March 6, 1986.)

*A. J. Tubman*, Somerset Co., Md., 1875, 56.8' × 19.9' × 5.9', gross 35, net 32, hull no. 105572. (Owned by Claude Messick, oystering, 1929, registered Philadelphia Pa.)

*A. Rasmussen*, J. B. Harrison, Tilghman Island, Md., 1890, 58' × 16.4' × 4', gross 20, net 9, hull no. 106784. (Converted bugeye, owned by Theodore M. Phillips, oystering, 1929, freight, Hampton, Va., registered Newport News, Va.)

*A. Victor Neal*, Kirkwood, Oxford, Md., 1924, 74.8' × 24.8' × 7.2', gross 81, net 62, hull no. 224253. (Two-masted schooner, rebuilt from *John C. Kelso*.)

*A. W. Ruark*, Madison, Md., 1885, 56.3' × 14.5' × 3.7', gross 15, net 7, hull no. 106377. (Converted bugeye, owned by George K. Carlton, 1929, West Point, Va., registered Newport News, Va.)

*Ada Ballenger*, Alexandria, Va., 1898, 49.2' × 15.9' × 6.4', gross 17, net 13, hull no. 107410. (Owned by Wm. A. Faunce, 1929, Brook, Va., registered Reedville, Va.)

*Ada C. Schull*, Solomons, Md., 67' × 21' × 5.8', gross 34, net 21, hull no. 106596. (Owned by Island Sue Co., freight, 1929, Nantucket, registered Martha's Vineyard, Mass.)

*Agnes*, John Branford, Fairmount, Md., 1892, 50.5' × 13.7' × 3.4', gross 10, net 9, hull no. 106965. (Converted bugeye, owned by Horace H. Cox, freight, 1929, Nanticoke, Md., registered Crisfield, Md.)

*Agnes C. Leonard*, see *Willie H. White*

*Alexander Bond*, Kirby & Son, St. Michaels, Md., 1893, 65.5' × 19' × 5.4', gross 32, net 30, hull no. 107046. (Square-rigged bugeye, burned off Old Point Comfort on Sept. 14, 1933, and was abandoned.)

*Alice E. Walker*, Oriole, Md., 1888, 58' × 15.7' × 3.3', gross 14, net 9, hull no. 106585. (Registered 1915, oystering, Newport News, Va.)

*Alva and Hettie*, J. E. Jewell, St. Michaels, Md., 1885, 52.6' × 14.5' × 3.2', gross 10, net 9, hull no. 106396. (Converted bugeye, freight, 1915, registered Baltimore, Md.)

*Alvin C. Somers*, St. Peters Creek, Md., 1889, 50.2' × 12.3' × 3.4', gross 10, net 5, hull no. 106670. (Converted bugeye, owned by W. B. Hopson, freight, 1929, Odd, Va., registered Newport News, Va.)

*Ambition*, T. L. Dawson, St. Michaels, Md., 1883, 53.2' × 15.1' × 4.3', gross 17, net 11, hull no. 106205. (Oystering, 1915, registered Newport News, Va.)

*Anna E.*, C. Harper, St. Michaels, Md., 1900, 60' × 17.5' × 3.8', gross 17, net 17, hull no. 107603. (Converted bugeye, owned by Clarence Patterson, freight, 1929, Philadelphia, Pa.; abandoned, January 12, 1943)

*Anna Florence*, J. A. Thompson, Chester, Md., 1918, 57.6' × 15.8' × 4', gross 20, net 16, hull no. 216764. (Converted bugeye, owned by Marion Sherbert, Deal, Md., freight, 1929 and 1946, registered Annapolis, Md.)

*Annie Cleveland,* Somerset Co., Md., 1885, 47.5' × 10.1' × 3.2', gross 7, net 7, hull no. 106375. (Converted bugeye, owned by John H. Anderson, freight, 1929, registered Baltimore, Md.)

*Annie E. Ellsworth,* Baltimore, Md., 1869, 50' × 13' × 3.8', gross 14, net 7, hull no. 106722. (Registered 1915, oystering, Cape Charles, Va.)

*Annie M. Leonard,* William Benson, Oxford, Md., 1877, 77.5' × 22' × 5.6', gross 61, net 53, hull no. 210862. (Rebuilt in 1913, Bethal, Del., as *Lula M. Phillips,* for captain Matt Moore, and later converted to power and owned by Will Ward of Deltaville, Va.)

*Annie May,* Accomac Co., Va., 1870, 63.2' × 22.3' × 4.7', gross 29, net 14, hull no. 1943. (Owned by Thomas E. Morris, oystering, 1929, Bowen, Del.)

*Annie P. Parks,* J. A. Smith, Saint Peters, Md., 1888, 59.1' × 16.4' × 4.4', gross 29, net 12, hull no. 106583. (Owned by Samuel C. Mathews, passenger vessel, 1946, Norfolk, Va. Also, W. E. Kellum Seafood owned her and named her *Debbie Mae.*)

*Annie T. Haley,* Wachapreague, Va., 1898, 45.3' × 14' × 3', gross 8, net 5, hull no. 107797. (Owned by L. H. Hamblin, oystering, 1929, Oyster, Va.)

*Ariel,* Oriole, Md., 1901, 60' × 18.1' × 4.7', gross 29, net 18, hull no. 107688. (Converted bugeye, owned by P. D. Gwaltney, Smithfield, Va., freight, 1929.)

*Arthur Stewart,* J. B. Harrison, Tilghman, Island, Md., 1892, 61.1' × 17.7' × 4.5', gross 23, net 10, hull no. 106969. (Converted bugeye, owned by Harry F. Blades, oystering, 1929, registered Seaford, Del.)

*Avalon,* Pocomoke City, Md., 1891, 59' × 18.1' × 4.8', gross 22, net 15, hull no. 106861. (Converted bugeye, owned by George S. White, freight, 1946, registered Baltimore, Md.)

*Avalon,* Stockton, Md., 39' × 13.8' × 3.8', gross 9, net 9, hull no. 106791. (Registered 1915, freight, Norfolk, Va.)

*B. W. Leigh,* Oriole, Md., 1903, 75.4' × 23.5' × 6.4', gross 33, net 33, hull no. 200148. (Converted bugeye, owned by D. A. Winslow, freight, 1929, registered Norfolk, Va.)

*Benny W. Baker,* Somerset Co., Md., 1872, 62.6' × 22.2' × 5.6', gross 34, net 33, hull no. 2822. (Registered 1915, freight, Annapolis, Md.)

*Bernadette,* Oriole, Md., R. L. & B. P. Miles, 1902, 63.5' × 17.6' × 4.8', gross 18, net 18, hull no. 3941. (Converted bugeye, 1915, oystering, registered Cape Charles, Va.)

*Bernadine Williams,* Oriole, Md., 1893, 61' × 17.2' × 4.7', gross 21, net 16, hull no. 3600. (Owned by Clarence Hannock, Exmore, Va., oystering, 1929, registered Cape Charles,Va.)

*Bertie.* (Converted schooner.)

*Bertie E. Tull,* Pocomoke City, Md., 1895, 125.4' × 21.8' × 6.1', gross 236, net 165, hull no. 3648. (Owned by G. F. Horsmon, freight, 1929, registered Baltimore, Md.; 1915, freight.

*Bessie Hamblen,* Fairmount, Md., 1892, 61' × 16' × 4.1', gross 19, net 10, hull no. 3564. (Registered 1915, oystering, Newport News, Va.)

*Betty I. Conway,* see *George A. Allison*

*Beulah C. Phoebus,* Tangier, 1884, 52' × 16.4' × 4.4', gross 12, net 5, hull no. 3294. (Converted bugeye, owned by Walter Drako, oystering, 1929, registered Wilmington, Del.)

*Beulah M. Holland,* St. Peters, Md., 1890, 51' × 13.6' × 3.5', gross 10, net 9, hull no. 3483. (Registered 1915, freight, Cape Charles, Va.)

*Black Hawk,* Crisfield, Md., 1893, 45' × 12.8' × 3.7', gross 8, net 8, hull no. 3607. (Registered 1915, freight, Norfolk, Va.)

*Bye,* Elmer E. Leary, Rock Hall, Md., 1901, 45' × 13.3' × 3.9', gross 12, net 10, hull no. 3887. (Converted sloop, used as a freight boat 1915; owned by Thomas J. Kane, 1946, registered out of Baltimore from 1901 until "scrapped" September 29, 1970.)

*C. F. Miles,* R. F. Miles, Oriole, Md., 1909, 75' × 22' × 5.5', gross 50, net 32, hull no. 206789. (Converted thirteen-log bugeye, owned by J. H. Miles & Co. of Norfolk, Va.)

*Callie M. Pruitt,* Cape Charles, Va., 1899, 44.9' × 13.8' × 2.6', gross 11, net 9, hull no. 77352. (Roland Collins, oystering, 1946, registered Cape Charles, Va.)

*Carlisle,* see *Gussie C.*

*Carol Ann,* see *William Layton*

*Carrie L. Whiting,* B. P. Miles, Crab Island, Md., 1890, 57.6' × 15.4' × 4', gross 14, net 14, hull no. 126674. (Owned by T. A. Reakle, fishing, 1946, registered Reedville, Va.)

*Catherine E. Shores,* Oriole, Md., 1892, 52.5' × 14.2' × 3.2', gross 10, net 9, hull no. 126926. (Converted schooner, owned by J. E. Barnes, freight, 1946, registered Reedville, Va.)

*Cathy C.,* Somerset. Co., Md., 1885, 56.5' × 14.6' × 3.9', gross 15, net 10, hull no. 100386. (Owned by Berlie T. Custis, fishing, 150 hp, registered Cape Charles, Va.)

*Charles M. Kelly,* Severn River, Va., 1892, 74.2' × 19.3' × 5.8', gross 51, net 27, hull no. 126928. (Registered 1915, Baltimore, Md.)

*Clara J.,* Hungars Creek, Va., 1898, 44.4' × 17' × 3.5', gross 12, net 7, hull no. 127250. (Registered 1915, Cape Charles, Va.)

*Cyclone,* Mappsburg, Va., 1901, 48' × 13.3' × 3.7', gross 19, net 8, hull no. 127551. (Registered 1915, freight, Cape Charles, Va.)

*D. G. Callis,* Poquoson, Va., 1893, 47' × 13.8' × 3.6', gross 13, net 6, hull no. 157391. (Registered 1915, Newport News, Va.)

*Dan,* T. Kirby, St. Michaels, Md., 1891, 58.5' × 17' × 4.7', gross 22, net 21, hull no. 157323. (Converted bugeye 1936, owned by Roland W. Seward, freight, 1946, Cambridge, Md. She originally had a draketail stern and a patent stern was added later.)

*David Goldstrom,* Oriole, Md., 1901, 62.2' × 17.9' × 5.1', gross 21, net 20, hull no. 157627. (Converted bugeye with patent stern; owned by E. Thomas Somers, oystering, 1929, registered Cape Charles, Va.; Alfred Pruitt of Tangier Island, fishing, 1946, three-man crew, crab dredging and seed oysters; also owned by Albert D. Talbot, freight, 150 hp, registered Reedville, Va.)

*Debbie Mae,* see *Annie P. Parks*

*Dola Lawson,* Oriole, Md., 1888, 56' × 16.9' × 6.2', gross 24, net 15, hull no. 157231. (Owned by Captain Johnny Ward, Deltaville, Va., and later by George A. Philpotts, freight, 1946, registered Newport News, Va.)

*Dola May,* Monie, Md., 1896, 46.8' × 13.6' × 3.9', gross 8, net 6, hull no. 157403. (Registered 1915, freight, Baltimore, Md.)

*Dorchester,* J. W. Brooks, Madison, Md., 1882, 80' × 24' × 5.6', gross 56, net 40, hull no. 157059. (Later named *W. J. Matthews,* abandoned 1969.)

*E. E. Moore,* Oriole, Md., 1901, 64.4' × 17' × 5.1', gross 22, net 15, hull no. 136918. (Converted bugeye, owned by N. E. Miles, freight, 1946, registered Cape Charles, Va.)

*E. Goldstrom,* Monie, Md., 1883, 48' × 12.8' × 3.5', gross 9, net 8, hull no. 136012. (Registered freight, 1915, Crisfield, Md.)

*E. P. Evans,* Pungoteague, Va., 1881, 62.5' × 20.2' × 5.6', gross 35, net 31, hull no. 135539. (Owned by Sylvester Edward Meinert, fishing, 50 hp, registered Philadelphia, Pa.)

*Eben,* William A. Noble, Oriole, Md., 1911, 54.3' × 18.7' × 5.2', gross 27, net 21, hull no. 209231. (Originally sloop-rigged; abandoned, Crisfield, Md., September 5, 1951.)

*Edith F. Todd,* Oriole, Md., 1901, 63.4' × 18.2' × 4.6', gross 20, net 19, hull no. 136922. (Converted bugeye, registered Crisfield, Md.)

*Edith M. Dryden,* Oriole, Md., 1892, 52.5' × 14.2' × 3.5', gross 9, net 7, hull no. 136318. (Owned by John N. Collison, freight, 1915, 15 hp, registered Annapolis, Md.)

*Edith Marcy*, M. M. Davis, Solomons Island, 1895, 67.5' × 20.4' × 6.8', gross 55, net 44, hull no. 136497. (Converted round-stern bugeye, owned by F. C. Haislip, freight, Reedville, Va.; later owned by Maurice Ward, nicknamed Lonnie Ward, hauled watermelons out of North Carolina.)

*\*Edward and Lesta*, J. Davis, Port Haywood, Va., 1896, 50.2' × 13.6' × 3.9', gross 11, net 5, hull no. 13674. (Converted bugeye, oystering, 1915, registered Newport News, Va.)

*Edward L. Martin*, Sussex Co., Del., 1882, 87.2' × 23.6' × 6.8', gross 84, net 80, hull no. 135629. (Two-masted schooner, converted to power 1943 and renamed *Honey B.,* lost by fire off Oxford, Md., 1956.)

*Elisha*, Tilghman Island, Md., 1887, 58.3' × 16' × 2.9', gross 10, net 5, hull no. 135945. (Registered 1915, oystering, Annapolis, Md.)

*Eliza J. Thompson*, St. Michaels, Md., 1874, 46.5' × 11.4' × 3.2', hull no. 135056. (Registered 1915, Norfolk, Va.)

*Ella and Ora*, Piankatank, Va., 1885, 51' × 14.5' × 4', gross 17, net 9, hull no. 135859. (Registered 1915, oystering, Newport News, Va.)

*Ella Covington*, Currioman, Va., 1891, 57.9' × 16.6' × 4.4', gross 22, net 21, hull no. 136184. (Converted bugeye, owned by Dora Madkins, 1946, freight, registered Baltimore, Md.)

*Ella Dail*, Dorchester Co., Md., 1880, 47' × 11.9' × 3.4', gross 9, net 6, hull no. 135457. (Registered 1915, freight, Annapolis, Md.)

*Ella E. Robbins*, Solomons, Md. 1884, 67.3' × 18.5' × 5.3', gross 32, net 22, hull no. 135786. (Registered 1915, Annapolis, Md.)

*Ella Noble*, Somerset Co., Md., 1888, 51' × 14.5' × 4', gross 12, net 6, hull no. 136015. (Registered 1915, Newport News, Va.)

*Ellarainia*, Sharptown, Md., 1886, 51.6' × 14.8' × 4.2', gross 14, net 8, hull no. 135914. (Registered 1915, fishing, Norfolk, Va.)

*Emma*, Solomons, Md., 1889, 56.2' × 15.3' × 3.5', gross 9, net 9, hull no. 136089. (Converted bugeye, registered 1915, freight, Baltimore, Md.)

*Emma W.*, Beckley, Va., 1895, 44' × 15' × 4', gross 19, net 18, hull no. 136515. (Registered 1915, freight, Norfolk, Va.)

*Ethel H.*, John Branford, Fairmount, Md, 1893, 57' × 14.8' × 4.3', gross 18, net 9, hull no. 136394. (Converted bugeye, registered 1915, Newport News, Va.)

*Etta V. Phillips*, Taylors Island, Md. 1894, 48.7' × 13.6' × 3.2', gross 8, net 8, hull no. 136480. (Converted bugeye, registered 1915, freight, Crisfield, Md.)

*Eugene H. Brown*, B. P. Miles, Oriole, Md., 1892, 58' × 15.4' × 4', gross 14, net 10, hull no. 136327. (Converted bugeye; registered 1915, Cape Charles, Va.)

*Eugenia*, Baltimore, Md., 1864, 66.9', 23.7', 5.2', gross 43, net 40.85, hull no. 8365. (Converted two-masted schooner, owned by Authur Eubank of Lewisetta, Va.; lost off Windmill Point when a fish steamer collided with her.)

*Eva Blanche*, Pocomoke City, Md., 1883, 61.8' × 18.3' × 6', gross 41, net 19, hull no. 135725. (Converted bugeye, owned by Warrinton L. Hollinger, oystering, 330 hp, registered Philadelphia, Pa.)

*Eva Booze*, 1885, Cambridge, Md., 53.3' × 15.3' × 3', gross 10, net 9, hull no. 135863. (Registered 1915, freight, Baltimore, Md.)

*Eva Bramble*, Dorchester Co., Md., 1881, 61.5' × 16.3' × 4.8', gross 23, net 16, hull no. 135529. (Registered 1915, oystering, Reedville, Va.)

*F. H. Lake*, Crittenden, Va., 1897, 47.8' × 14.2' × 3.5', gross 15, net 11, hull no. 121062. (Freight, 1915.)

*F. L. Godman*, Crisfield, Md., 1899, 43.5' × 14' × 3.8', gross 10, net 9, hull no. 121103. (Registered 1915, fishing, Charleston, S.C.)

*F. P. Coleman*, Madison, Md., 1892, 57.6' × 15.9' × 4', gross 19, net 14, hull no. 120919. (Registered 1915, oystering, Norfolk, Va.)

*Fannie E. Hayward*, M. M. Davis, Solomons Island, Md., 1883, 60' × 16.8' × 4.7', gross 21, net 17, hull no. 120603. (Converted bugeye, registered 1915, freight, Baltimore, Md.)

*Fannie T. Harrington*, Taylors Island, Md., 1896, 47.8' × 13.4' × 3.4', gross 10, net 7, hull no. 121030. (Registered 1915, freight, Baltimore, Md.)

*Fay*, Jones Creek, Md., 1891, 43.3' × 11' × 3', gross 6, net 5, hull no. 209396. (Registered 1915, freight, Crisfield, Md.)

*Flora Bell*, John Branford, Fairmount, Md., 1893, 57' × 14.8' × 4.3', gross 16, net 8, hull no. 120950. (Converted bugeye, registered 1915, oystering, Newport News, Va., owned by Thomas J. Kellum, Weems, Va.)

*Flora Kirwan*, McCosker, Baltimore, Md., 1892, 81.2' × 23.8' × 6.6', gross 73, net 49, hull no. 120918. (Converted two-masted schooner; lost 1983 as clam dredge rig; originally built for Kirwan-Schall Fruit Company of Baltimore, Md.; once owned by Roland Dean and Rick E. Savage, 100 hp, Crisfield, Md.)

*Flora W. Willing*, St. Peters, Md., 1891, 50' × 14' × 3.6', gross 10, net 7, hull no. 120866. (Converted bugeye, owned by Mary Linton, Annapolis, Md., 1929, 9 hp.)

*Florence & Julia*, Churchtown, Md., 1899, 41.7' × 14.4' × 3.5', gross 10, net 6, hull no. 121112. (Registered 1915, freight, Annapolis, Md.)

*Florence Northam*, M. M. Davis, Solomons, Md., 1890, 65' × 17' × 5', gross 26, net 24, hull no. 120803. (Owned by Captain T. W. Wright, Deltaville, Va.)

*Florence Rosenbaum*, Oriole, Md., 1893, 63.5' × 18.2' × 5.1', gross 33, net 17, hull no. 120954. (Converted schooner; 1915, sailing schooner registered Newport News, Va.; powerboat owned by W. T. Fronmonger, freight, 1946, registered Newport News, Va.)

*Flossy M. Muir*, Oriole, Md., 1892, 57.5' × 15.4' × 4.1', gross 13, net 12, hull no. 120911. (Registered 1915, passenger vessel, Elizabeth City, N.C.)

*Francis J. Ruth*, Dorchester Co., Md., 1871, 73' × 23.2' × 6.7', gross 60, net 57, hull no. 20011. (Registered Baltimore, Md.)

*Fred Jones*, Pocomoke City, Md., 1893, 46' × 14.4' × 3.8', gross 10, net 9, hull no. 120928. (Registered 1915, freight, Crisfield, Md.)

*G. Frank Miles*, Oriole, Md., 1893, 52' × 13.5' × 3.2', gross 10, net 6, hull no. 86268. (Converted bugeye, owned by Orville Stevens, 1946, fishing, registered Newport News, Va.)

*G. W. Robinson*, Whitehaven, Md., 1882, 75.7' × 23.7' × 6.7', gross 56, net 53, hull no. 85752. (Two-masted schooner. Name changed to *Minnie May Kirwan*, 1907, owned by T. Preston Webster; sold in 1935 at a U. S. Marshal's sale for $550 to Captain Robert Shores of Chance, Md.; converted to power in 1941 at A. Smith and Sons Shipyard, Curtis Bay; renamed *W. C. Witt;* owned by Luke Parker, 1956, and name changed to *L. R. Parker;* sold to Florida owner 1968 and listed as abandoned in 1970 on a coral shoal at Marathon, Fla.)

*George A. Albaugh*, Oriole, Md., 1896, 63.8' × 18' × 5', gross 34, net 28, hull no. 86366. (Converted bugeye, W. Y. Stevens, 1946, fishing, registered Charleston, S.C.)

*George R. Marshall*, Monie, Md., 1885, 50.9' × 14.6' × 3.9', gross 16, net 10, hull no. 85905. (Owned by Struvan Evans, 1946, freight, registered Crisfield, Md.)

*George S. Allison*, Stoney Point, N.Y., 1866, 90' × 27.5' × 6.3', gross 123, net 84, hull no. 10420. (Converted two-masted schooner, burned in 1964 but rebuilt. Owned by Samuel J. E. Todd, freight, 140 hp, Cambridge Md.)

*George Todd*, T. Byrd, Crisfield, Md., 1883, 52.6' × 14.1' × 3.5', gross 10, net 9, hull no. 85818. (Converted bugeye, owned by Clarence T. Todd, 1946, oystering, registered Crisfield, Md. Before being converted to power the sail-driven vessel won the bugeye event in the Chesapeake Bay Workboat Regatta four times between 1921 and 1931. The annual race was sponsored by the *Baltimore Sun* newspaper.)

*Gladys L.,* see *Miriam*

*Grace,* Fairmount, Md., 1892, 50.5' × 13.7' × 3.4', gross 13, net 7, hull no. 86218. (Registered 1915, oystering, Newport News, Va.)

*Gracie C. Wallace,* Crisfield, Md., 1883, 59' × 16.3' × 4.6', gross 20, net 13, hull no. 86270. (Converted bugeye, 1915, freight, registered Reedville, Va.)

*Grape Shot,* Tappahannock, Va., 1870, 38' × 14' × 4.1', gross 12, net 11, hull no. 85096. (Converted schooner, registered 1915, Norfolk, Va.; died in Lower Machodoc Creek, Va.)

*Greyhound,* Mathews Co., Va., 1872, 44' × 15' × 4.4', gross 13, net 8, hull no. 85226.

*Gussie C.,* Fairmount, Md., 1903, 55' × 20.6' × 5.3', gross 21, net 21, hull no. 200387. (Pungy with a centerboard, referred to as a she pungy, converted to power in the 1920s.)

*H. H. Conway,* see *William Sommers*

*Hallie K.,* J. T. Marsh, Solomons, Md., 1889, 62.7' × 17.8' × 4.8', gross 23, net 20, hull no. 96131. (Converted bugeye, owned by Victor G. Malone, fishing, 40 hp, Miami, Fla.)

*Harry C. Brown,* Crisfield, Md., 1882, 58.6' × 15.8' × 4.4', gross 18, net 11, hull no. 95721. (Converted bugeye, registered 1915, oystering, Cape Charles, Va.)

*Harvey H. Conway,* see *Richard Cromwell*

*Helen Windsor,* B. P. Miles, Oriole, Md., 1900, 61.2' × 16.9' × 4.5', gross 24, net 16, hull no. 96520. (Converted bugeye, owned by A. T. "Stinky" Davis of Christchurch, Va., freight, 1946, registered, Reedville, Va.; listed as abandoned in 1968.)

*Honey B.,* see *Edward L. Martin*

*Ida B. Conway,* see *William Layton*

*Ida and Lula,* Somerset Co., Md., 1885, 48' × 12.5' × 3.5', gross 10, net 9, hull no. 100389. (Converted bugeye, 1915, freighting out of Reedville, Va.; 1929, freighting, George L. Smith and Brothers of Sharps, Va.; 1946, oystering, G. L. Smith; and 2003 died in Farnham Creek near Sharps, Va.)

*Isaac H. Keeler,* Somerset Co., Md., 1885, 56.5' × 14.6' × 3.9', gross 15, net 10, hull no. 100386. (Converted bugeye, owned by George W. Todd, freight, Crisfield, Md.)

*JDC Hanna,* Somerset Co., Md., 1884, 53' × 13.9' × 3.6', gross 10, net 6, hull no. 76546. (Owned by Joseph R. Langley, freight, 1929, Solomons, Md., registered Annapolis, Md.)

*J. D. Patterson,* Bordentown, N.J., 1894, 50' × 11.2' × 4.9', gross 16, net 11, hull no. 77157. (Owned by Charles E. Ehrman, 1919, registered Baltimore, Md.)

*J. F. White,* W. Moore, Grafton, Va., 1896, 43' × 13' × 3.8', gross 10, net 5, hull no. 77222. (Converted bugeye, owned by J. T. Bradshaw, fishing, 1929, Dare, Va., registered Newport News, Va.)

*J. Hammitt Lake,* see *Leroy Woodburn*

*J. J. Saunders,* J. J. Saunders, Solomons, Md., 1901, 66' × 18.9' × 5.3', gross 30, net 19, hull no. 214081. (Converted bugeye, owned by Maurice R. Lee, Philadelphia, Pa., oystering, registered Port Norris, N.J.)

*J. J. Underhill,* Madison, Md., 1892, 68' × 20.3' × 4.8', gross 35, net 33, hull no. 77052. (Owned by Asa C. Ketchum, Solomons, Md., registered Annapolis, Md.)

*J. P. Moore,* Poquoson, Va., 1888, 48.3' × 13.5' × 4', gross 14, net 8, hull no. 76744. (Converted bugeye, owned by J. W. Smith, fishing, 1929, Lady, Va., registered Newport News, Va.; Marion L. Smith, 1946, Newport News, Va. The 1946 *Merchant Vessel* book showed her measurements at 50.9' × 15.4' × 4.4'. She was later owned by William Pruitt of Tangier Island.)

*J. T. Parks,* Oriole, Md., 1892, 51' × 13.5' × 3.6', gross 10, net 6, hull no. 77059. (Owned by Henderson Robinson, Dandy, Va., oystering, 1929, registered Newport News, Va.)

*J. W. Wilson,* Salisbury, Md., 1907, 53.3' × 17.5' × 4.2', gross 16, net 11, hull no. 204073. (Converted bugeye, owned by W. A. Barnes, freight, 1929, registered Crisfield, Md.)

*James C. Tawes,* Monie, Md., 1899, 53.5' × 14' × 3', gross 14, net 8, hull no. 77383. (Converted bugeye, owned by M. L. Marshall, freight, 1929, registered Norfolk, Va.)

*James E. Kirwan,* Kent Island, Md., 1895, 64' × 17.7' × 4.3', gross 22, net 14, hull no. 77169. (Converted bugeye, owned by James R. Elliott, freight, 1929, Broomes Island, Md., registered Annapolis, Md.)

*James G. Blaine,* Somerset Co., Md., 1892, 62.8' × 17' × 4.2', gross 20, net 12, hull no. 76363. (Owned by G. M. Neldham, freight, 1929, registered Elizabeth City, N.C.)

*James P. Thurston,* Berkley, Va., 1884, 45.7' × 15.7' × 4.6', gross 16, net 8, hull no. 76502. (Owned by A. T. Donnell, freight, 1929, West Point, Va., registered Newport News, Va.)

*James T. Dennis,* Oriole, Md., 1899, 54' × 15.3' × 4', gross 14, net 9, hull no. 76837. (Converted bugeye, owned by W. W. Henley, oystering, 1929, Cobbs Creek, registered Cape Charles, Va.)

*J & P Bradford,* Solomons Island, Md., 1885, 54' × 13.9' × 3.6', gross 10, net 6, hull no. 76627. (Owned by T. F. Anderton, freight, 1929, Gloucester Point, Va., registered Newport News, Va.)

*Jeff,* see *Richard Cromwell*

*Joe Wheeler,* Cape Charles, 1899, 49' × 14' × 3', gross 10, net 8, hull no. 77352. (Owned by Joseph S. Pruitt, oystering, 1929, Chincoteague, Va., registered Cape Charles, Va.)

*\*John Branford,* John Branford, Fairmount, Md., 1900, 67.5' × 19.2' × 6.5', gross 43, net 33, hull no. 77436. (Converted bugeye, early engine 60 hp before conversion, later 67' × 18.6' × 5.5', gross 24, net 24.)

*\*John B. Robins,* Oriole, Md., 1905, 64' × 18' × 4.3', gross 19, net 15, hull no. 202510. (Owned by Eugene Richardson, Charleston, S.C., originally schooner-rigged, registered Crisfield, Md., 1905; Cape Charles, 1906–08; Norfolk, 1910–11; Cape Charles, 1912–16; Charleston, S.C., 1920 until abandoned 1960; first engine installed 1920.)

*John J. Crouch,* see *Ida B. Conway*

*John Martin,* Baltimore, Md., 1884, 69.8' × 20.4' × 6.2', gross 48, net 33, hull no. 76507. (Owned by B. C. Burton, freight, 1946, Newport News, Va.; schooner converted to power around 1933; listed as abandoned in 1968.)

*Joseph I. Dawson,* Rhode River, Md., 1889, 50' × 12.7' × 4', gross 10, net 6, hull no. 76850. (Registered 1915, freight, Charleston, S.C.)

*Josephine,* R. Lambdin, St. Michaels, Md., 1897, 48.5' × 15.7' × 4', gross 17, net 11, hull no. 77267. (Converted bugeye, registered Wilmington, Del., 1915.)

*Julia Adeline,* Monie, Md., 1892, 53.5' × 14.8' × 4', gross 13, net 7, hull no. 77057. (Converted bugeye, registered 1915, freight, Newport News, Va.)

*\*Julian T. Bradshaw,* Oriole, Md., 1901, 72' × 21.5' × 6.2', gross 34, net 17, hull no. 77491. (Owned by Elmer L. Anderson, freight, 1929, registered Cape Charles, Va.)

*Julia W. Garrison,* Pocomoke City, Md., 1882, 55.6' × 16.8' × 3.9', gross 18, net 11, hull no. 76287. (Registered 1915, Annapolis, Md.)

*\*Kent,* Chestertown, Md., 1905, originally 46' × 17.6', 4.4', gross 18, net 18; enlarged 1909 to 64.4' × 18.5' × 5.3', gross 29, net 20, hull no. 202253. (Originally schooner-rigged, owned by James Thomas Blane, freight, registered Baltimore, 1905–47, burned and lost near Love Point Lighthouse, Md., Dec. 29, 1953.)

*L. R. Parker,* see *G. W. Robertson*

*\*LaForrest L. Simmons,* Milford, Del., 1909, 88.9' × 27.8' × 7.5', gross 154, net 127, hull no. 206347. (Converted two-masted schooner; as a schooner, gross 132, net 104. Brought down from Taunton, Massachusetts in 1936 for Bay lumber trade. Converted to power by A. Smith & Sons Shipyard, Curtis Bay, Baltimore, Md. Lost Aug. 12, 1955, in a hurricane one mile north of Sharps Island, Md.)

*Lavenia Pearl*, Alexander Gaines, Poquoson, Va., 1910, 60.7' × 14.1' × 4.4', gross 19, net 12, hull no. 207516. (Converted bugeye, owned by A. O. Inckham, oystering, 1929, Weems, Va., registered Reedville, Va.)

*Leroy Woodburn*, M. M. Davis, Solomons, Md., 1913, 68.5' × 22.2' × 5.3', gross 49, net 43, hull no. 211624. (Converted bugeye, owned by State of New Jersey, 1929, Trenton, N.J., registered Philadelphia, Pa.; later named *J. Hammitt Lake*)

*Lillian*, John Branford, Fairmount, Md., 1885, 50.5' × 13.7' × 3.4', gross 10, net 6, hull no. 141233. (Converted bugeye, registered Annapolis, Md., freight, 1915.)

*Lillian C. Cooper*, Oriole, Md., 1902, 64' × 18' × 4.5', gross 22, net 16, hull no. 141821. (Planked bugeye, early engine 50 hp, owned by M. F. Ashburn of Carters Creek, laid to rest and used as a breakwater at Fitchett's Landing at the mouth of Antipoison Creek.)

*Lina Cox*, Somerset Co., Md., 1883, 61' × 17.5' × 5.3', gross 24, net 18, hull no. 140654. (Converted bugeye, registered Reedville, Va., 1915.)

*Little Bay*, Portsmouth, Va., 1883, 47' × 14.4' × 3.2', gross 14, net 13, hull no. 140606. (Registered 1915, freight, Norfolk, Va.)

*Little George*, Baltimore, Md., 1891, 48' × 14.5' × 4.3', gross 14, net 8, hull no. 141172. (Registered 1915, freight, Norfolk, Va.)

*Little Jennie*, Calvert Co., Md., 1884, 57.9' × 16.3' × 4.6', gross 22, net 20, hull no. 140825. (Charles A Bigelow, 1946, registered Cambridge, Md.)

*Lottie L. Thomas*, J. W. Brooks, Madison, Md., 1883, 65.6' × 17.3' × 4.9', gross 27, net 16, hull no. 140621. (Owned by Vincent F. Hancock, freight, 28 hp, Fall River, Mass.)

*Louise*, E. J. Tull, Pocomoke City, Md., 1884, 58.6' × 17.4' × 5', gross 22, net 16, hull no. 140707. (Converted bugeye, registered 1915, Annapolis, Md.)

*Louise Travers*, complete life in introduction to this appendix.

*Lula M. Phillips*, see *Annie M. Leonard*

*M. L. Warfield*, Madison, Md., 1893, 65.8' × 20.6' × 5.4', gross 46, net 42, hull no. 217567. (Owned by Charles Tozour, 1946, oystering, registered Philadelphia, Pa.)

*M. T. Tucker*, Solomons, Md., 1900, 48.9' × 14' × 3.8', gross 11, net 7, hull no. 93035. (Registered 1915, oystering, Annapolis, Md.)

*M. V. Bennett*, Oriole, Md., 1893, 51.3' × 13.3' × 3.5', gross 10, net 9, hull no. 92545. (Registered 1915, freight, Annapolis, Md.)

*Maggie C.*, Drawbridge, Md., 1895, 63' × 18' × 4.9', gross 32, net 27, hull no. 92635. (Converted bugeye, owned by James E. Butchelor, freight, 1929, registered Baltimore, Md.; and R. J. McAllister Co., 1946, freight, registered Baltimore, Md.)

*Maguire*, Northumberland Co., Va., 1892, 49' × 16.3' × 3.3', gross 10, net 6, hull no. 92481. (Owned by S. W. Robbins, freight, 1929, registered Newport News, Va.)

*Major Todd*, Somerset Co., Md., 1883, 50.3' × 13.7' × 2.9', gross 10, net 9, hull no. 91808. (Registered 1915, freight, Annapolis, Md.; later owned by H. K. Wilson, freight, 1929, registered Newport News, Va.)

*Mannie T. Venable*, Fairmount, Md., 1893, 53' × 14.1' × 3', gross 10, net 9, hull no. 92547. (Registered 1915, freight, Crisfield, Md.; owned by Raymond Knopp, freight, 1929, Deale, Md., registered Annapolis; and G. I. Rupert Lore, fishing, 1946, Solomons, Md., registered Annapolis, Md.)

*Marcus Fass*, see *Mattie Bliss*

*Margaret Atkinson*, Lankford, Md., 1904, 71.5' × 21.6' × 5.9', gross 50, net 50, hull no. 162316. (Converted bugeye; 1909, registered Norfolk, Va.; owned by William R. Lewis, freight, 1929, registered Cambridge, Md.; 1946 Lewis still owned the boat but the tonnage had changed to gross 60, net 41.)

*Margaret A. Travers*, Otis S. Lloyd, Salisbury, Md., 1901, 71.3' × 21.3' × 6', hull no. 93162. (Round-stern bugeye, converted to power 1935. On December 16, 1952, the vessel left old West Urbanna Wharf from Lord Mott Canning Factory with 4,400 cases of canned beans bound for Baltimore. On the way, she struck a group of target pilings at the mouth of Patuxent River. The impact knocked the pilothouse off and jammed the vessel's rudder. The vessel circled the pilothouse four times before sinking. Inside the pilothouse was Captain Jennings Burton and a mate who clung for safety. They survived.)

*Marietta*, Pocomoke City, Md., 1896, 43.6' × 15.5' × 3.9', gross 15, net 8, hull no. 92695. (Registered 1915, freight, Norfolk, Va.)

*Marion Lee*, Mathews County, Va., 1883, 46.5' × 15.5' × 3.8', gross 17, net 16, hull no. 91578. (Registered 1915, fishing, Norfolk, Va.)

*Martha A. Shores*, St. Peters Creek, Md., 1889, 58' × 16' × 4.1', gross 19, net 12, hull no. 92133. (Converted bugeye, registered 1915, freight, Norfolk, Va.)

*Mary*, Norfolk County, Va., 1889, 44.6' × 14.6' × 3.9', gross 15, net 14, hull no. 92095. (Registered 1915, freight, Norfolk, Va.)

*Mary A. Bradshaw*, Smith Island, Md., 1883, 49.3' × 14.5' × 3.6', gross 14, net 13, hull no. 91616. (Registered 1915, freight, Norfolk.)

*Mary and Virginia*, W. R. Jones, Pocomoke City, Md., 1885, 54.1' × 16.1' × 4.1', gross 16, net 9, hull no. 91812. (Converted bugeye, registered 1915, freight, Norfolk, Va.)

*Mary E.* Solomons, Md., 1900, 45' × 15' × 4', gross 14, net 7, hull no. 93090. (Registered 1915, oystering, Newport News, Va.)

*Mary Etta*, Somerset Co., Md., 1885, 49.7' × 12.9' × 3.4', gross 10, net 7, hull no. 91804. (Registered 1915, oystering, Annapolis, Md.)

*Mary Frances*, Dorchester, Co., Md., 1876, 49.5' × 13.1' × 3.6', gross 10, net 9, hull no. 90867. (Registered 1915, freight, Baltimore, Md.)

*Mary Priscilla*, Oriole, Md., 1890, 53' × 14.2' × 3.6', gross 14, net 6, hull no. 92229. (Converted bugeye, 1915, oystering, registered Newport News, Va.)

*Mattie Bliss*, Somerset Co., Md., 1892, 60.8' × 15.9' × 4.4', gross 18, net 12, hull no. 92467. (Converted bugeye, registered 1915, oystering, Norfolk, Va., owned by J. L. Wilson, freight, 1929, registered Elizabeth City, N.C., later named *Marcus Fass*.)

*Mattie F. Culver*, Otis Lloyd, Tyaskin, Md., 1891, 61' × 17' × 5', gross 26, net 16, hull no. 92317. (Converted bugeye, 1915, fishing, registered Newport News, Va.)

*Mattie May*, Isle of Wight Co., Va., 1882, 62' × 16' × 3.4', gross 20, net 19, hull no. 91515. (Registered 1915, freight, Norfolk, Va.)

*May Seline*, Madison, Md., 1890, 52' × 14' × 3', gross 9, net 9, hull no. 92266. (Registered 1915, oystering, Reedville, Va.)

*Mildred*, Solomons, Island, Md., 1911, 82' × 22' × 5.5', gross 81, net 67, hull no. 208729. (Two-masted schooner, used to haul railroad ties from Tappahannock to Portsmouth, Va., before being converted to power; owned by Herbert Bryant, Alexandria, Va., 1946; burned about five miles north of Hooper Island Lighthouse in 1970.)

*Minnie Mae Kirwan*, see *G. W. Robertson*

*Miriam*, Joseph W. Brooks, Madison, Md., 1903, 81' × 22.7' × 6', hull no. 93398. (Converted bugeye, owned by Andrew J. Lewis of Walnut Point, Va., 1920. When the Baltimore and Virginia Steamboat Company closed in 1932, the vessel under the name of *Gladys L.* was used by Lewis to take over the steamer business; later owned by M. L. Tillage, oystering, 225 hp, Newport News, Va.; listed as abandoned in 1959.)

*Mizpah*, Salisbury, Md., 1897, 46' × 14.6' × 4', gross 13, net 9, hull no. 92763. (Owned by Nathan Peltz, 1946, freight, registered Newport News, Va.)

*Mollie V. Leonard*, F. Cantwell, Cambridge, Md., 1904, 82.5' × 22.8' × 6.1', hull no. 200794. (Converted bugeye, second longest bugeye built and the largest in terms of tonnage. First bugeye to carry a patent stern. She had an engine long before her mast and sailing rigs were dismantled, and she became an outright powered deck boat after World War II. She would carry 3,700 bushels of wheat.)

*Nannie,* Amburg, Va., 1919, 45.2' × 12.7' × 3.9', gross 16, net 9, hull no. 218737. (Owned by Captain Dave Taylor, Deltaville, Va., and later by J. W. Ferguson, Remlik, Va., 1946; named after Nannie Elizabeth Saunders Taylor, wife of Captain Dave. She was converted to power by Linwood Price.)

*Nannie May,* John Branford, Somerset Co., Md., 1887, 55' × 14.3' × 3.7', gross 15, net 8, hull no. 130382. (Converted bugeye, 1915, oystering, registered Newport News, Va.)

*Nannie P. White,* John Branford, Somerset Co., Md., 1891, 50.5' × 13.6' × 3.4', gross 13, net 7, hull no. 130567. (Converted bugeye, 1915, oystering, registered Newport News, Va.)

*Nettie B. Greenwell,* J. W. Brooks, Madison, Md., 1897, 72' × 19.3' × 5.3', hull no. 130754. (Converted bugeye; under sail won the 1930 bugeye class of the Chesapeake Bay Workboat Regatta; converted to power in 1936. On March 11, 1947, was rammed by Chesapeake and Ohio ferry steamer *Virginia* off Newport News, Va., and sank.)

*Nettie May,* J. T. Marsh, Madison, Md., 1884, 63.8' × 17.1' × 4.5', gross 23, net 22, hull no. 130301. (Converted bugeye, 1915, freight, registered Norfolk, Va.)

*Nicholas,* Marion, Md., 1899, 50.5' × 13.9' × 3.8', gross 9, net 9, hull no. 130842. (Registered 1915, freight, Reedville, Va.)

*Nora Phillips,* J. T. Marsh, Solomons, Md., 1901, 75.5' × 20.7' × 5.4', gross 32, net 31, hull no. 130945. (Owned by Rufus M. Lewis, freight, 1929, Exmore, Va., registered Cape Charles, Va.; Elmer L. Anderson, 1946, registered Crisfield, Md.; rebuilt in 1949 at Deagle and Son Marine Railway in Ruark, Va., and named *O. A. Bloxom.* She was later owned by Ballard Fish and Oyster Co. and by Noah C. Carr, Jr., of Glass, Va. She is still alive in 2003 and is hauling freight in Florida waters. Named for a former owner who ran an oyster house on Pagan Creek. "It took thirteen gallons of white paint and ten gallons of bottom paint to cover *O. A. Bloxom* at a cost of $500," says Noah C. Carr, Jr., owner and captain for many years.

*Norma,* O. Lloyd, Salisbury, Md., 1901, 72.3' × 22.1' × 6.9', gross 69, net 45, hull no. 130536. (Converted to power in 1922 and was a round-stern bugeye. She was engaged in running whiskey and Scotch malt valued at $100,000 when she was caught by the Coast Guard near Salisbury and taken to Baltimore where the contraband was removed.)

*North Star,* see *Willie H. White*

*O. A. Bloxom,* see *Nora Phillips*

*O. P. Roberts,* St. Peters Creek, Md., 1889, 61' × 17.1' × 3.8', gross 16, net 15, hull no. 155172. (Registered 1915, freight, Annapolis, Md.)

*Oriental,* Messongo, Va., 1887, 51.7' × 18.4' × 5.3', gross 28, net 16, hull no. 155044. (Registered 1915, fishing, Somers Point, N.J.)

*P. Jay Elbourn,* Madison, Md., 1897, 70.8' × 19.4' × 5.2', gross 37, net 25, hull no. 116787. (Owned by Purnell Elbourn, freight, registered Baltimore, Md.)

*Peerless,* Baltimore, Md., 1874, 44.8' × 15.4' × 4.8', gross 15, net 6, hull no. 150030. (Registered 1915, freight, Newport News, Va.)

*Rena A. Callow,* Oriole, Md., 1897, 67.2' × 18.6' × 5.7', gross 30, net 22, hull no. 111161. (Converted bugeye, patent stern, owned by B. P. and R. L. Miles and later by Major C. Todd, Jr., of Crisfield, Md.; freight, 1946, registered Crisfield, Md.; also Charles W. Marsh, freight, 50 hp, Crisfield, Md.)

*Richard Cromwell,* Joseph W. Brooks, Madison, Md., 1888, 99.5' × 26.5' × 6.6', gross 127, net 86, hull no. 110808. (Converted two-masted

schooner, owned by Harvey H. Conway of Cambridge, Md., and later by Phillips Packing Company of Cambridge. Later named *Harvey H. Conway.*)

*Richard J. Vetra,* G. N. Vetra, Deal Island, Md., 1888, 50' × 15.5' × 3.2', gross 10, net 9, hull no. 110790. (Owned by G. James Livingston, fishing, 1946, registered Annapolis, Md.)

*Russell A. Wingate,* J. W. Brooks, Madison, Md., 66.8' × 19.4' × 5.4', gross 30, net 20, hull no. 111365. (Converted bugeye, owned by Down Jersey Marine Historical Society, 80 hp, Philadelphia, Pa.)

*Russell De Hughlett,* J. W. Brooks, Madison, Md., 1902, 66.8' × 17.6' × 4.6', gross 35, net 34, hull no. 111416. (Converted bugeye, owned by Oscar F. Pope, freight, 1929, registered Cambridge, Md.)

*Russell L.,* J. B. Harrison, Dorchester Co., Md., 1892, 63.5' × 17.6' × 4.6', gross 20, net 16, hull no. 110996. (Converted bugeye, owned by J. F. O'Neal, freight, 1929, Ocracoke, N.C., registered Washington, N.C.)

*Ruth Richardson,* Madison, Md., 1896, 62.5' × 19' × 5.5', gross 28, net 20, hull no. 111122. (Owned by Luke Parker, freight, 1929, registered Cambridge, Md.)

*S. J. Todd,* Oriole, Md., 1902, 55' × 16' × 3.8', gross 14, net 6, hull no. 117175. (Owned by Frank McCobe, freight, 1929, registered Charleston, S. C.)

*S. T. Howard,* Dames Quarter, Md., 1889, 50.6' × 12.4' × 3.8', gross 13, net 8, hull no. 116287. (Owned by H. H. Mitchell, freight, 1929, registered Wilmington, N.C.)

*S. W. Darby Jr.,* Milford, Del., 1879, 70' × 23' × 4.5', gross 48, net 46, hull no. 115672. (Owned by Lewis Holzer, freight, 1929, registered Wilmington, Del.)

*Sadie E. Culver,* O. Lloyd, Whitehaven, Md., 1896, 69.4' × 19.9' × 5.5', gross 36, net 16, hull no. 116743. (Owned by J. W. Thompson, fishing, 1929, Southport, N.C., registered Wilmington, N.C.)

*Sadie M. Parks,* St. Peters, Md., 1891, 54' × 14' × 3.8', gross 13, net 7, hull no. 116448. (Converted bugeye, owned by American Welding Co., freight, 1946, registered Baltimore, Md.)

*Sallie L. Bramble,* Otis Lloyd, Whitehaven, Md., 1890, 50' × 17.7' × 12.7', gross 21, net 18, hull no. 116383. (Converted round-stern bugeye, owned by Walter S. Wingate, oystering, 1929, Hudson, Md., registered Cambridge, Md.; Wilson Todd, oystering, 1946, registered Cambridge, Md.)

*Sand Snipe,* St. Michaels, Md., 1882, 67' × 23.8' × 5.5', gross 69, net 47, hull no. 115888. (Owned by Bert A. Keiser, 1946, freight, registered Wilmington, Del.)

*Sarah C. Conway,* see *A. H. Schulz*

*Sidney R. Riggin,* Oriole, Md., 1896, 55.5' × 14.1' × 3.8', gross 10, net 10, hull no. 116740. (Converted bugeye, owned by Wm. Preston Lore, freight, 110 hp, registered Annapolis, Md.; registered as a sailing schooner 1915 issue of *Merchant Vessels,* but listed as a bugeye in Brewington's book.)

*Sophie A. Durm,* Baltimore, Md., 1902, 66' × 19' × 5.3', gross 33, net 24, hull no. 117193. (Converted bugeye owned by George "Captain Ladd" Wright of Deltaville, Va., 1920s; blown aground around 1927 on Potomac River; salvaged and rebuilt by Capt. Johnny Ward of Deltaville, registered to Iva J. Ward, 1946, freight, Reedville, Va. Iva was Captain Johnny's wife.)

*Sunflower,* see *Thomas J. Jackson*

*Thomas J. Jackson,* Middlesex Co., Va., 1877, 53' × 17.6' × 4.6', gross 28, net 22, hull no. 145157. (Her name was changed to *Sunflower* and she was converted to power under that name. Interestingly, it is believed that *Sunflower* was rebuilt in 1930 and renamed *Janice.* It should be noted that *Janice* is shown in the list of vessels built for engine power. Her rebuilding effort must have been so extensive that she received a new hull number and was considered a new boat.)

*Vixen,* Selden, Va., 1887, 49.4' × 12' × 3.8', gross 14, net 7, hull no. 161797. (Owned by W. F. Leigh, Claybank, Va., registered Newport News, Va.)

*W. C. Witt,* see *G. W. Robertson*

*W. J. Matthews,* see *Dorchester*

*W. P. Ward,* P. Spencer, Cambridge, Md., 1882, 85' × 23.9' × 6.3', gross 84.77, net 80.53, hull no. 145311. (Two-masted schooner, sold to Honduras as a powerboat in 1947.)

*Water Lily,* J. T. Marsh, Solomons, Md., 1884, 58.7' × 17.2' × 4.2', gross 19, net 18, hull no. 81032. (Converted bugeye, owned by Roy E. Roberts, freight, 1929, registered Baltimore, Md.)

*White Wing,* Peter W. Smith, New Point, Va., 1896, 50.1' × 14.3' × 3.6', gross 17, net 11, hull no. 81556. (First owned by the builder, later home port Elizabeth City, N.C., freight, two-man crew.)

*William Layton,* Zac Layton, Nanticoke, Md., 1873, 79.8' × 24' × 6.3', gross 73, net 69, hull no. 80340. (Also named *Ida B. Conway, John J. Crouch,* and *Carol Ann.* Converted two-masted schooner. Owned by the Conways of Cambridge, Md., and later Authur Eubank of Lewisetta, Va.)

*William Sommers,* Baltimore, Md., 1883. (She was also named *H. H. Conway* by Harvey Conway about 1921. She was also owned by Captain Johnny Ward of Deltaville, Va.)

*William T. Stallings,* Oriole, Md., 1892, 59.7' × 15.8' × 4.1', gross 17, net 10, hull no. 81393. (Converted bugeye, owned by Washington Bean, 1929, freight, registered Baltimore, Md.)

*William C. Lore,* Bridgetown, N.J., 1876, 56' × 18' × 5', gross 35, net 17, hull no. 80566. (Owned by Horatio B. Sockwell, 1929, Port Norris N.J., registered Philadelphia, Pa.)

*William H. Killman,* Pocomoke City, Md., 1898, 59' × 18' × 4.4', gross 19, net 13, hull no. 81625. (Owned by H. D. Hall, 1929, fishing, Ditchley, Va., registered Reedville, Va.)

*Willie H. White,* M. M. Davis, Solomons Island, Md., 1883, 65.5' × 18.5' × 5.3', gross 34, net 23, hull no. 81015. (Converted two-masted schooner, owned by Clarence A. Christy, 1946, freight, registered Crisfield, Md.; also named *Agnes C. Leonard* and *North Star.*)

*Wm. B. Tennison,* Frank Laird, Crabb Island, Md., 1899, 60.5' × 17.5' × 4.5', gross 18, net 11, hull no. 81674. (Originally built as a nine-log sailing bugeye for Benjamin P. and Rufus L. Miles of Norfolk, Va.; 1910–30 owned by Alphonse Lafayette Hazelwood, converted her to a powerboat in 1911; 1930–41 Barney Winnal; 1941–78 J. C. Lore & Sons, Solomons Island, Md.; finally by the Calvert County, Md., Board of Commissioners, 1996; used as a passenger vessel by Calvert Marine Museum and designated a National Historic Landmark on April 19, 1994.)

*Wm. E. James,* Madison, Md., 1889, 63.3' × 20.5' × 5.7', gross 42, net 25, hull no. 81231. (Owned by Emerson Tarburton, 1929, oystering, registered Philadelphia, Pa.)

*Wm. H. Bunting,* Oriole, Md., 1889, 56.3' × 15.6' × 4.4', gross 15, net 15, hull no. 81237. (Owned by Smithfield, Northern Neck, and Norfolk Steamship Co. of Virginia, 1929, freight, registered Norfolk, Va., located Smithfield, Va.)

*Wm. McGee,* Somerset Co., Md., 1881, 63.3' × 18.2' × 4.5', gross 25, net 23, hull no. 80860. (Owned by John A. Lowery, 1929, freight, registered Cambridge, Md., located Tilghman Island.)

*Zeph S. Conover,* Atlantic City, N.J., 1886, 46.9' × 16.1' × 4.5', gross 18, net 12, hull no. 28109. (Owned by Ballard Fish & Oyster Co., freight, 1946.)

# APPENDIX 2: BUYBOAT BUILDERS

Since actual boatbuilders' names are not listed in the volumes of the *Merchant Vessels of the United States,* the names of buyboat builders below were collected through conversations, telephone calls, interviews, and writings. Many buyboats were built at small, isolated railways and backyards up and down the Chesapeake region. Bill Hight and I have attempted to collect as many names of builders as possible, but it is a good bet that some have been left out of this listing and for any omissions we apologize.

Approximately one hundred vessels were researched through the United States Coast Guard Vessel Documentation Center in Falling Waters, West Virginia, and many of the builders' names were located there.

The *Merchant Vessels* books provide the location where a boat was built, and we discovered that builders often built in several different locations over a career. This explains why a listing may show several locations for one builder.

D. L. Belvin. Perrin, Va.
John Branford (bugeye builder). Fairmount, Md.
Ernest H. Bryant (apprenticed under Johnny "Crab" Weston). Deltaville, Va.

Irving F. Cannon. Fishing Creek, Md.
Walter B. Cannon. Fishing Creek, Md.
Odell Carmines. Odd, Va.
P. H. Carter. Rescue, Va.
George Clark (apprenticed under his father-in-law Ernest H. Bryant). Deltaville, Va.
Alonzo P. Conley. Oxford, Md.
Carters Creek Railway Co. Irvington, Va.
B. A. Croasdale. White Stone, Va.

Charles A. Dana. Crisfield, Md.
James E. Daugherty. Crisfield, Md.
Larry Daugherty. Crisfield, Md.
J. Davis (bugeye builder). Port Haywood, Va.
Lee Deagle. Deltaville, Va.
Edgar Diggs. Peary, Va.
Edward Diggs (son of Edgar Diggs). Redart, Va.
N. B. "Boney" Diggs. Laban, Va.
W. F. Dunn. West Norfolk, Va.

Jos. Edmonds. Eclipse, Va.
Noah T. Evans. Ewell, Md.
C. Lyman Ewell (built side-planked log-hulled buyboats). Elliott, Md.

Gus Forbush. Crisfield, Md.
William T. Forrest. Grimstead, Va.

Alexander Gaines (built log chunk boats and is listed by Brewington as a bugeye builder). Poquoson, Va.; and Seaford, Va.
Paul Green, Jr. Deltaville, Va.
Paul Green, Sr. Deltaville, Va.

Oscar Howard (built under the name Howard and Smith). Crisfield, Md.
Howard and Smith. Crisfield, Md.
Mitchell Hubbard. Hudson, Md.
Alfred "Alf" Hudgins. Laban, Va.
Freeman Hudgins (built under the name Diggs and Hudgins). Laban, Va.
Harry A. Hudgins (cousin of L. E. and Alton Smith). Peary, Va.
Ned Hudgins (son of Alfred "Alf" Hudgins). Laban, Va.; and Sarah, Va.
R. H. Hudson. Irvington, Va.

P. C. Ingram. Palmer, Va

J. S. Jenkins. Severn, Va.
Lepron Johnson. Crittenden, Va.
T. Johnson (bugeye builder). Cambridge, Md.
T. G. Julian. Palmer, Va.

Herman M. Krentz. Crisfield, Md.; Harryhogan, Va.; and Kayan, Va.

Frank Laird (bugeye builder). Crab Island, Md.
R. Lamdbin (bugeye builder). St. Michaels, Md.
Elmer E. Leary. Rock Hall, Md.
Percy H. Linton. Pocomoke City, Md.
David Lowe. Battery Park, Va.

V. Machen (bugeye builder). Mathews County, Va.
B. F. Miles, (bugeye builder). Crab Island, Md.
Virgil Miller. Deltaville, Va.
Lorenzo Dow Moger. Eclipse, Va.
E. J. Moore and Son. Crittenden, Va.

William A. Noble. Oriole, Md.
Ed Norton. Deltaville, Va.

Grover Lee Owens. Deltaville, Va.

L. F. Parker. Syringa, Va.
Russell Carroll Parker. Wake, Va.
O. W. Payne. Palmer, Va.

A. G. Price, Mount Vernon, Md.

Linwood P. Price. Amburg, Va.; Deltaville, Va.; Moore Creek, Va.; and Ruark, Va.

Milford Price. Amburg, Va.; and Deltaville, Va.

C. H. Rice. Reedville, Va.

Edwin C. Rice. Fairport, Va.

Emory Rice. Fairport, Va.

H. E. Robertson. Palmer, Va.

E. H. Rowley and Son. Chincoteague, Va.

H. W. Ruark. Fishing Creek, Md.

Buddy Sable. Ruark, Va.

Alvin Sibley (apprenticed under Johnny "Crab" Weston). Deltaville, Va.

Alton Smith (apprenticed under his father Lennie Smith). Susan, Va.

Frank Smith. Bena, Va.

Harry Steve Smith. New Point, Va.

Jack Smith. Bena, Va.; and Perrin, Va.

James "Little Jim" Smith (son of J. W. Smith). Bena, Va.

John F. Smith (built log chunk boats). Dare, Va.

J. W. "Big Jim" Smith. Bena, Va.; and Perrin, Va.

Kirby Smith (built log chunk boats). Dare, Va.

L. E. "Lennie" Smith. Pepper Creek and Horn Harbor, Mathews County, Va.

Sidney Smith. Bena, Va.; and Perrin, Va.

W. T. Smith. Achilles, Va.

Sterling and Somers. Crisfield, Md.

R. D. Taylor. Deep Creek, Va.

B. F. Tull. Tylerton, Md.

E. James Tull (built standard deck boats and is listed by Brewington as a bugeye builder). Pocomoke City, Md.

J. Wood Tull. Irvington, Va.

Lorne Tull. Crisfield, Md.

Jabez Tyler. Cambridge, Md.

Wilfred Tyler. Honga, Md.

Alvin Walden. Deltaville, Va.

Moody Walden. Deltaville, Va.

Raymond Walden. Deltaville, Va.

Stanley W. Walden. Deltaville, Va.

Earl Weston (son of Johnny C. Weston). Deltaville, Va.

Herman Weston. Deltaville, Va.

Johnny C. Weston (apprenticed under John Wright). Deltaville, Va.

Johnny W. "Crab" Weston. Deltaville, Va.

Gilbert S. White. Foxwells, Va.; Mobjack, Va.; Mosquito Creek, Va.; Palmer, Va.; and Westland, Va.

Allen E. Whitman. Crisfield, Md.

J. G. Wornom. Poquoson, Va.

G. L. "Ladd" Wright. Deltatville, Va.

John E. Wright. All same location: Deltaville, Va.; Enoch, Va.; and Sandy Bottom, Va.

Lewis Wright. Deltaville, Va.

T. W. Wright. Deltaville, Va.

# BUYBOAT GLOSSARY

*adz.* A hand tool used by deck boat builders for shaping wood. One of the oldest boatbuilding tools, it has an arching blade connected to a wooden handle.

*amidships or midships.* Used in a general sense to indicate the approximate center of a boat.

*bateau.* A planked hard-chine skiff with a shallow deadrise bottom. Used in the pound-net fishery to haul the pound pocket full of fish to the surface.

*Bay boat.* A term used to describe a deck boat that hauls freight up and down the Bay.

*Bay freighter. See* Bay boat.

*beam.* The width of a boat measured at the widest point.

*bell boat.* A deck boat powered by an engine that required an engineer to start, stop, and change fore and aft directions from the engine room. To direct the engineer, the captain used bells that signaled commands.

*boat Bible.* A Bible used by the captain and crew. It stayed aboard the boat.

*booby hatch.* On a deck boat, a hatch that leads to the forepeak.

*boom.* A spar attached to the base of the mast. It holds the bottom portion of a sail on a deck boat, and it may be used for hoisting.

*bow.* The forward end of a boat.

*bowsprit.* A large spar extending from the bow of a sailboat to support the headsail. Early sailing vessels that were converted to power continued to carry a bowsprit and were referred to as hybrids by some Bay historians.

*box boat.* A traditional, hard-chine, deadrise hull with a cross-planked bottom. Most Bay buyboats were built in this style.

*brakes.* Two large beams that extend over both sides of a deck boat to hold and haul pound-net poles.

*brogan.* A large variation of a sail-powered log canoe. Characteristics that distinguished the brogan from the canoe were size and interior arrangement. The hull was longer, washboards were real pieces of deck, and the open body of the canoe was divided by bulkheads and covered with hatches.

*bugeye.* A log or planked round-bilge boat designed for the Chesapeake Bay oyster-dredge fishery. Originally built for sail, many were converted to power.

*Bull Island mahogany.* The name used by boatbuilders in the Poquoson, Virginia, area for yellow pine. Bull Island describes the area around Poquoson.

*bunker.* A term used by Chesapeake Bay watermen and others for menhaden.

*buyboat.* Vessel engaged in buying and hauling oysters, crabs, fish, clams, and other seafood. When a captain uses his own vessel to buy seafood from watermen, it is referred to as a buyboat. (When a boat is owned by a dealer or oyster planter who is working his own grounds, the vessel carrying oysters back to the processing plant is referred to as a run boat or runner.)

*carvel planking.* A type of side planking that uses overlapping boards thinner than those used in single-planked boats. This construction makes the boat lighter in weight.

*ceiling.* The floorboard on the inside of a boat.

*chine.* The fore-and-aft timber that connects and supports the bottom and side planking on a deadrise hull.

*chunk canoe.* A Virginia-built log canoe. Virginia builders used chunks of wood in the sides and in the bow and stern.

*chunk stern.* A round stern on a deck boat and a smaller deadrise workboat. Made from chunks of wood that are layered so the seams on a layer are covered by the chunk of wood above it.

*cleaned culled oysters.* Oysters that have been separated according to size and are legally ready for market.

*coasting canoe.* The second generation of sail-powered log canoe on the Chesapeake. Instead of being completely open like early log canoes, the vessel was larger and had a cabin between the washboards beginning just abaft the foremast and extending aft some six feet.

*cribbing oysters.* Placing oysters in a tub in such a way that the tub would appear to be full when it was not. Many oystermen learned the art of placing a shovelful of oysters in a tub so they would stand straight up, thus taking more room than oysters lying flat.

*crosscut saw.* A handsaw used to cut large logs. Usually had a handle on each end so two men could work the saw.

*cross-planked.* Bottom planking that is fastened athwartships from keel to chine.

*culling board.* A platform extending across an oyster boat that holds oysters as oystermen cull their catch, checking for legal-size oysters.

*culling boy.* A young boy whose job was to cull oysters on a Chesapeake Bay workboat.

*culling oysters.* Inspecting each oyster as it's brought aboard an oyster boat to determine if it is legal size to keep for market.

*cutting house.* A processing house where roe is extracted and herring is filleted and cured into salted and pickled herring.

*deadrise.* A straight rise from the keel rabbet to the chine.

*deck boat.* A generic term for wooden Chesapeake Bay vessels with decks fore and aft, and a mast and boom forward of a house and pilothouse.

*diamond stern.* Several deck boats, mostly in the pound-net fishery, were built with diamond-shaped or V-sterns. The V-shape of the stern allowed the boat to work well in strong following seas and also provided pound-net fishermen the same angle of approach to install pound poles from either the bow or stern.

*double-deck buyboat.* A buyboat that has a pilothouse on top of a house.

*double-ender.* A deck boat, usually a converted sailboat or a log boat that has a V-shape at both bow and stern.

*down-run herring.* Watermen's term for herring that are caught in rivers as they come back out toward the Bay after spawning in the rivers' headwaters.

*"down the Bay" boats.* A term used by some to describe buyboats from the lower part of the Chesapeake Bay region.

*draft.* The depth of a boat from its waterline to the deepest point of its keel.

*draketail stern.* Several deck boats had draketail sterns. Maryland boatbuilders came up with the Hooper Island draketail by modeling the stern after early twentieth-century racing launches and torpedo boats. The draketail stern has a reverse rake, as well as a chine that follows the waterline throughout the length of the boat.

*dredge catch bag.* The top portion of an oyster or crab dredge where oysters and crabs are caught. Made from cotton.

*dredge chain bag.* The bottom portion of an oyster or crab dredge that helps keep the dredge on the bottom. Made from chain.

*dredge post.* A large post installed aft of the mast on an oyster or crab deck boat to hold the blocks and tackles and chain used to lower and hoist the dredge.

*dredge roller.* Metal rollers mounted near amidships on the starboard and port sides of an oyster- or crab-dredge boat to help bring the dredge up on deck in order to empty it.

*dredge turning stick.* A 2 × 4 used to straighten a dredge as it surfaces from the water.

*driver.* A fisherman in the menhaden fishery whose job was to spot and direct fishermen in purse boats to schools of menhaden. He worked alone in a small boat out in front of the purse boat. He was also called a striker. (Airplanes spotting fish from the air eliminated the need for a driver.)

*drudging.* Watermen's term for dredging.

*ducktail stern.* Primarily found on Chesapeake Bay bugeyes. A large piece of timber (or fastened timbers) extending from the stern deck aft over the rudder to protect the rudder. It has the appearance of a ducktail.

*dugout canoe.* A vessel made from one or more logs. It is sharp at both ends and is powered by sail or oar.

*engine-room controlled boat.* A boat that has an engineer who controls boat speed, forward and reverse, and the starting and stopping of the engine from the engine room.

*fish carton.* A cardboard container used to hold fifty pounds of fish ready for market.

*fish meal.* A feed supplement made from fish. It is high in protein and is used in hog and chicken feed.

*fish meal plant.* A plant where menhaden and fish scraps are processed into fish meal.

*fish oil.* Oil extracted from menhaden was used for fuel in lamps before electricity. It was also used for tanning, soap and rope making, and as an ingredient in paints and lipsticks. In foreign countries today fish oil is used as an ingredient in margarine and other foods.

*fish scrap.* Fish cuttings left over from a fish-processing house. Also menhaden, small trout, and pinhead croakers that are unsalable at a fish market. Fish scrap is used to bait crab and eel pots and is ground and processed into fish meal.

*fish trap.* A pound net. George Snediker of Gravesend, Long Island, introduced the pound net to the Chesapeake region about 1870. It is a stationary fish net consisting of poles and nets.

*frame-built boats.* Frames are used to shape and support the hull and sides of a boat. Usually a frame-built boat has stem-to-stern bottom planking and a deeper draft than a boat with traditional cross-planked deadrise construction. Several Bay builders built framed deck boats.

*freeboard.* The distance between the sheer line on a boat and the waterline.

*freight boat.* A throwback to the days when large sail-driven vessels hauled freight on the Chesapeake. When motor-powered vessels started hauling freight, the term continued to be used.

*galley.* The kitchen on a boat.

*gang crabs.* A term used by crab dredgers to describe a large pocket of crabs which they find buried in the bottom of the Bay.

*gong.* One of two types of bells used by the captain on a deck boat to signal the engineer.

*grubbed up.* A term used on deck boats when the cook goes to the store and purchases "grub" or food for a trip.

*half model.* A block or layers of wood shaped into a half-hull form. Used by Chesapeake Bay deck boat builders to pull lines and get measurements to loft a boat.

*hand winders.* Early gear used to haul oyster dredges to the surface by hand.

*hard driver.* A captain of a boat who works his boat and crew hard.

*hold.* Area belowdeck where payload is carried.

*hull.* The main body of a boat, not including the cabin and pilothouse.

*hunting cabin.* A cabin containing two built-in wooden bunks and a small woodstove at the forward end. The cabin occupied all the space between the washboards beginning just abaft the foremast and extending aft some six feet. These cabins were on log canoes and some Chesapeake Bay deck boats.

*hybrid.* A sailing vessel that has been converted to power but still carries its bowsprit and other characteristics of a sailboat.

*jewfish.* A large grouper, usually dusky green or blackish, thickheaded and rough-scaled. Usually found in warmer waters than the Chesapeake.

*jimmies.* Mature male hard crabs.

*jingle.* A type of bell used on Chesapeake Bay deck boats to give instructions to the engineer from the wheelhouse.

*keel.* The main structural beam that runs from stem to stern in the bottom of the boat.

*Labrador herring.* Sea herring, sardine, sperling, and brit are other names for Labrador herring, the typical herring *(Clupea harengus)*.

*leadline.* A weighted line used to sound the bottom to determine depth of water.

*lick.* One haul of an oyster or crab dredge onto a boat.

*longhead.* The head of a bugeye that supports the bowsprit. It extends from the bow and the trailboard is attached to it.

*lumber luggers.* Converted-to-power schooners and bugeyes used to haul lumber.

*market boat.* Another name used by Chesapeake Bay watermen for buyboats.

*mast.* Wood or metal pole that supports booms, gaffs, and gear for carrying sails. Used on deck boats to hoist seafood up onto deck and to off-load it to shore. In the early years of motor-powered deck boats it was used to carry an auxiliary sail.

*mast boat.* When Virginia watermen began using 42- to 50-foot deadrise workboats for the crab-dredge fishery, watermen, mostly from Tangier Island, started calling Chesapeake Bay deck boats mast boats, obviously because these larger vessels carried a mast while the smaller boats did not.

*mast step.* The base of a mast that has been cut off and left inside a converted-to-power sailing vessel. It also refers to the base of a crab-dredge post.

*measure.* A term used on an oyster buyboat for the bushel tub used to haul oysters from tong boats up onto the deck of the buyboat.

*natural oyster rock.* The bottom of a river or creek where oysters grow naturally.

*oilskins.* A term used by Chesapeake Bay watermen for foul weather gear.

*oyster bed.* The bottom of a river or creek where oysters are planted and grown.

*oyster ground. See* oyster bed.

*oyster rock. See* oyster bed.

*oyster tongers.* Men involved in harvesting oysters by hand using wooden-handled scissorlike shaft tongs.

*packet boat.* A deck boat used to haul freight and passengers.

*"paid with a boom."* Upon arrival in this country, Irish and other early immigrants often found work aboard sail-powered oyster-dredge boats only to be paid at the end of the trip by being knocked overboard as the boom swung around.

*patent-dip trotline.* A variation of a trotline used to harvest hard crabs. A trotline is a long line, baited with meat at regular intervals, used to attract hard crabs. A patent dip is a metal frame funnel structure made of iron rods with a large net and a roller. As a crab surfaces on the trotline and crosses the roller, two vertical rods welded to the frame knock it down into a metal catch. On a regular trotline, watermen must use a dip net to catch the crab.

*pickled herring.* Herring that has been salt-cured and then preserved by a pickling process.

*pilothouse controlled boats.* A deck boat that has engine controls inside the pilothouse for start and stop, reverse and forward, and reduce or increase speed.

*pound boat.* A large deck boat or open boat used to carry payload or to tow skiffs in the pound-net fishery. In many cases the hull of an open boat was identical to the hull of a deck boat and was easily converted to a deck boat later on.

*pound net.* A stationary arrangement of netting used to harvest fish. It was introduced to the Chesapeake region in 1858 and became widely used in the area.

*pound poles.* Poles used to hold the net and lines of a pound net.

*power block.* A hydraulic-powered gear used to haul a purse net to the surface.

*purse boat.* A boat used to haul and work a purse seine in the menhaden fishery.

*rack of eye.* Instead of working from plans, boatbuilders determined the shape and lines on a vessel by eye.

*railway.* A marine railway hauls boats out of the water. It consists of two parallel tracks similar to railroad tracks. A cradle runs along the tracks and the boat sits on the cradle.

*rake.* The angle of the stem line, stem post, or mast in relation to the keel.

*ripped sawed planks.* Planks sawed in the direction of the grain.

*round-stern boat.* A Chesapeake Bay deck boat that has a round stern.

*run boat. See* buyboat.

*runner. See* buyboat.

*scrap shed.* A shed used to store fish meal after it has been cooked, pressed, and dried.

*sculling.* Using a single paddle from the stern of a skiff. A side-to-side twisting motion moves the boat through the water.

*sculling paddle.* A paddle used to scull a skiff.

*shaft tongers. See* oyster tongers.

*sheer line.* The profile of the top edge of a boat hull.

*shuck stock oysters.* Legal market-size oysters.

*six-pack.* A term used for a charter boat that can legally carry up to six recreational fishermen on a fishing trip.

*snapper.* An independently owned boat used to harvest menhaden. The origin of the word snapper as it relates to small menhaden fishing boats has been lost to time. Some watermen, however, think it may have come from a size comparison. Snapper blues are smaller than fully mature bluefish, and snapper menhaden boats are smaller than the large company-owned menhaden fish steamers.

*snapper blues.* A bluefish that is not fully mature.

*sooks.* Mature female hard crabs.

*sou'wester.* A name for a foul-weather hat used by Chesapeake Bay watermen.

*staved stern.* Some round-stern and draketail boats have narrow wooden staves fastened to shape the stern. The planks are fitted vertically from the bottom of the boat to just under the gunnels.

*staving.* Narrow wooden planks fitted in the vicinity of the stem to create a deep V in the bow.

*steering becket.* A string tied to the side of the pilothouse to hold the wheel so the captain can leave the wheelhouse and go out on deck.

*stem.* The upright beam at the bow.

*stock money.* Money kept in the pilothouse to pay for seafood on a buyboat.

*striker. See* driver.

*striker boat.* In the early years of the menhaden fishery, a striker was used to direct fishermen in purse boats to a school of fish. The small boat used by the striker is called a striker boat.

*striker house.* A herring or shad cutting house. When fish are placed in a tank full of a brine solution, the procedure is called striking the fish. Thus, many in the Chesapeake region used the term striker house to identify a fish house where herring and shad were gutted and cured.

*tally board.* A board used by buyboat captains to keep a tally on the number of bushels of oysters purchased from tongers.

*tom.* A thousand-pound weight used to anchor the ends of lines on a purse net and also to anchor the net.

*tow-bat.* A term used for a pound-net bateau in the Mathews County area of Virginia. *See* bateau.

*trap boat.* *See* pound boat.

*trotline.* See patent dip trotline.

*up the beach.* A term used when a sail-driven or power-driven freight boat went out into the ocean and up the coast to get to northern states.

*V-stern.* *See* diamond stern.

*yawl boat.* A small motor-powered boat used to push a sailboat when there is no wind or when the sailboat is in tight quarters. It is carried on stern davits and lowered into the water when needed to push or pull.

# BIBLIOGRAPHY

Bailey, Anthony. *The Inside Passage.* New York: The Macmillan Company, 1965.

Birdsong, Ray S., John A. Musick, and Edward O. Murdy. *Fishes of Chesapeake Bay.* Washington, D.C.,: Smithsonian Institution Press, 1977.

Blackistone, Mick. *Sunup to Sundown: Watermen of the Chesapeake.* Acropolis Books Ltd., 1988.

Bodine, A. Aubrey. *Chesapeake Bay and Tidewater.* Baltimore, Md.: Bodine and Associates, Inc., 1967.

Brewington, M. V. *Chesapeake Bay Bugeyes.* Newport News, Va.: The Mariners' Museum, 1941.

Burgess, Robert H. *Chesapeake Circle.* Cambridge, Md.: Cornell Maritime Press, 1965.

———. *Chesapeake Sailing Craft, Part I.* Cambridge, Md.: Tidewater Publishers, 1975.

———. *This Was Chesapeake Bay.* Cambridge, Md.: Cornell Maritime Press, 1963.

Chapelle, Howard I. *Boatbuilding—A Complete Handbook of Wooden Boat Construction.* New York: W. W. Norton and Company, Inc., 1941.

———. *The National Watercraft Collection.* Washington, D.C.: Smithsonian Institution, 1960.

Chowning, Larry S. *Barcat Skipper: Tales of a Tangier Island Waterman.* Centreville, Md.: Tidewater Publishers, 1983.

———. *Chesapeake Legacy.* Centreville, Md.: Tidewater Publishers, 1995.

———. *Harvesting the Chesapeake: Tools and Traditions.* Centreville, Md.: Tidewater Publishers, 1990.

Corson, Minnie Moger. *Living Memories of Crittenden and Eclipse,* 1983.

DeBusk, Jessie M., Charles L. Price, Jr., Louise E. Gray, and Dorothy M. Price. *Family Histories of Middlesex County.* Sponsored by The Ralph Wormeley Branch, Association of the Preservation of Virginia Antiquities, 1982.

Dill, Thomas Alonzo. *York River Yesterdays: A Pictorial History.* Norfolk, Va.: The Donning Company, 1984.

Frye, John. *The Men All Singing: The Story of Menhaden Fishing.* Norfolk, Va.: The Donning Company, 1978.

Goode, George Brown. *History and Methods of the Fisheries: The Fisheries and Fishery Industries of the United States.* Washington, D.C.: Government Printing Office, 1887.

Gregory, Joseph F. *Deadrise Is From Here . . . To Yonder.* Grafton, Va.: First American Printing Co., Inc., 1987.

Hollingsworth, Michael A. R. K., *Five Boatbuilders From Virginia's Northern Neck and Middle Peninsula.* Senior Research Project. Fredericksburg, Va.: Mary Washington College, Department of Historic Preservation, 1998.

Johnson, Paula J. *The Workboats of Smith Island.* Baltimore, Md.: Johns Hopkins University Press, 1997.

Johnson, Paula J., editor, *Working the Water: The Commercial Fisheries of Maryland's Patuxent River.* Charlottesville, Va.: Calvert Marine Museum and The University Press of Virginia, 1988.

Lang, Varley. *Follow the Water,* Winston-Salem, N.C.: John F. Blair, 1961.

Marvil, James E. *Sailing Rams: A History of Sailing Ships Built in and Near Sussex County, Delaware.* Lewes, Del.: The Sussex Press, 1974.

Reader's Digest Association. *Family Encyclopedia of American History.* Pleasantville, N.Y.: The Reader's Digest Association, Inc., 1975.

Rolfs, Donald H. *Under Sail: The Dredgeboats of Delaware Bay, A Pictorial and Maritime History.* Millsville, N.J.: Wheaton Historical Association, 1971.

Shomette, Donald G. *Shipwrecks on the Chesapeake: Maritime Disasters on Chesapeake Bay and its Tributaries, 1608–1978.* Centreville, Md.: Tidewater Publishers, 1982.

Shores, David L. *Tangier Island, Place, People, and Talk.* Newark, N.J.: University of Delaware Press, 2000.

Snediker, Quentin, and Ann Jensen. *Chesapeake Bay Schooners.* Centreville, Md.: Tidewater Publishers, 1992.

Tyer, David Budlong. *The Bay and River Delaware: A Pictorial History.* Cambridge, Md.: Cornell Maritime Press, 1955.

Warren, Marion E., and Mame Warren. *Bringing Back the Bay.* Baltimore and London: Johns Hopkins University Press, 1994.

Whitehead, John Hurt III. *The Watermen of the Chesapeake Bay.* Centreville, Md.: Tidewater Publishers, 1979.

Wharton, James *The Bounty of the Chesapeake: Fishing in Colonial Virginia.* Charlottesville, Va.: The University Press of Virginia (second printing), 1973.

Williams, John Page, Jr. *Chesapeake Almanac:, Following the Bay through the Seasons.* Centreville, Md.: Tidewater Publishers, 1993.

———. *Exploring The Chesapeake in Small Boats.* Centreville, Md.: Tidewater Publishers, 1992.

Wilson, John. *Virginia's Northern Neck: A Pictorial History.* Norfolk, Va.: The Donning Company Publishers, 1984.

## ARTICLES

Black, Ira. "Couple aims to preserve classic Bay buyboat. *The Mariner,* Vol. 10, No. 15 (October 4, 1991).

Chowning, Larry S. "Chesapeake buyboats go 'up town.'" *National Fisherman*, Vol. 74, No. 5 (September 1993).

————. "Exodus of *O. A. Bloxom* reflects changing status of Bay fisheries. *Southside Sentinel*, Vol. 96, No. 48 (November 27, 1991): 1.

————. "Historic buyboat gets overhaul at Deltaville boatyard." *Southside Sentinel*, Vol. 101, No. 33 (August 15, 1996): 1.

————. "Time and Tinkering Converted 36' Bateau to a 53' Buyboat." *National Fisherman*, Vol. 62, No. 7 (November 1981): 80.

————. "The Venerable Buyboat: Tractor Trailer of the Chesapeake," *National Fisherman*, Vol. 66, No. 13 (Yearbook), 1986.

Corddry, Mary. "Six O'clock Scholars, 'Bus' It By Boat." *Baltimore Sun Magazine*, 1972.

Dudley, Countess W. "Deltaville News." *Southside Sentinel*, Vol. 86, No. 33 (August 20, 1981): 11.

Flesber, Harry. "Oyster Boat Sinks: Four Believed Missing." *Newport News Daily Press* (March 24, 1968).

Makovich Lee, "Diesels Then and Now." *National Fishermen* Vol. 83, No. 10 (February 2003): 36.

*Newport News Daily Press,* wire and staff reports. "CG Fires On and Seizes Area Boat." (October 10, 1980).

*Newport News Daily Press.* "Search Continues for Boat's Crew." (March 26, 1968).

*Rappahannock Record.* "Fleeton and Reedville Hard Hit By Tornado." Kilmarnock, Va., (August 24, 1939).

*Richmond News Leader.* "The Great Elephant Float." (July 15, 1977).

## UNPUBLISHED WORKS

Letter from Mrs. Charles E. Edwards, information on deck boat named *Harold*, February 12, 2003.

Letter from Morattico Packing Company, Inc., to Clarke Langrall, Baltimore insurance adjuster, June 29, 1959.

*Nellie Crockett* logbook, 1962–1986.

*Nellie Crockett* ledger book, 1959–1988.

*Nellie Crockett* boat Bible.

L. R. (Lennie) and Alton Smith's boatbuilding records, 1926–1967.

## WEB SITES

Chesapeake Bay Maritime Museum, *Old Point*, St. Michaels, Md.

Friendly Forest Products, "The MV *Winnie Estelle:* A Chesapeake Bay Buyboat Working as a Dive Charter Boat in Belize."

Historic American Buildings Survey/Historic American Engineering Record, "Bugeye *Louise Travers*," Solomons, Md.

Living Classroom Foundation, *Mildred Belle*, Baltimore, Md.

National Historic Landmarks Program, *Nellie Crockett*.

# INDEX